Los Angeles Documentary and the
Production of Public History,
1958–1977

The publisher and the University of California Press Foundation gratefully acknowledge the generous support of the Lisa See Endowment Fund in Southern California History and Culture.

Los Angeles Documentary and the Production of Public History, 1958–1977

Joshua Glick

UNIVERSITY OF CALIFORNIA PRESS

University of California Press, one of the most distinguished university presses in the United States, enriches lives around the world by advancing scholarship in the humanities, social sciences, and natural sciences. Its activities are supported by the UC Press Foundation and by philanthropic contributions from individuals and institutions. For more information, visit www.ucpress.edu.

University of California Press
Oakland, California

Library of Congress Cataloging-in-Publication Data

Names: Glick, Joshua, 1983- author.
Title: Los Angeles documentary and the production of public history, 1958–1977 / Joshua Glick.
Description: Oakland, California : University of California Press, [2018] | Includes bibliographical references and index. | Identifiers: LCCN 2017022264 (print) | LCCN 2017025048 (ebook) | ISBN 9780520966918 (ebook) | ISBN 9780520293700 (cloth : alk. paper) | ISBN 9780520293717 (pbk. : alk. paper)
Subjects: LCSH: Documentary films—United States—History and criticism. | Motion pictures—Political aspects—United States.
Classification: LCC PN1995.9.D6 (ebook) | LCC PN1995.9.D6 G54 2018 (print) | DDC 070.1/8—dc23
LC record available at https://lccn.loc.gov/2017022264

Manufactured in the United States of America

27 26 25 24 23 22 21 20 19 18
10 9 8 7 6 5 4 3 2 1

For my parents, Marilyn and Jeffrey Glick, my first teachers.
And for Masha, who shows me how to see the world.

CONTENTS

ILLUSTRATIONS

ACKNOWLEDGMENTS

This book is the result of countless conversations with friends, colleagues, students, and family members. Our freewheeling discussions in Bethesda, Little Rock, Los Angeles, New Haven, and New York have propelled this book forward over the past six years.

The Film and Media Studies and American Studies programs at Yale provided the ideal home for the incubation period of this interdisciplinary project. It was through numerous seminars on documentary and film historiography with Charles Musser that I arrived at a dissertation topic on Los Angeles as a nonfiction capital. Charlie's rigorous historical methodology and genuine love of a good archival dig encouraged me to return time and time again to primary documents and to seek out under-examined and even previously unknown films. I am also grateful to J. D. Connor, whose careful attention to chapter structure and flow helped to shape the book in a very literal sense. His shrewd advice to "always be synthesizing" helped me make crucial connections between disparate films and filmmaking practices in Los Angeles. My profound gratitude goes out as well to Matthew Jacobson and Jean-Christophe Agnew. Their vast understanding of American social history and cultural studies theory has taught me to speak the language of cinema studies with an American studies accent. Finally, sincere appreciation goes to Ryan Brasseaux, Ronald Gregg, Dolores Hayden, and John MacKay, who made valuable comments on individual chapters during the initial drafts of the project.

As the dissertation transformed into a book manuscript, most of my summers and holidays were spent in East and West Coast archives. This project would have been impossible without the generosity of the many archivists and librarians who provided me with access to the films and primary documents and shared their insights about the material. I am deeply grateful to Richard Holbrook (Paley Center for Media); Josie Walters-Johnston, Zoran Sinobad, and Brian Taves (Library of Congress, Motion Picture, Broadcasting & Recorded Sound Division); Michael Desmond and Emily Watlington (John F. Kennedy Presidential Library); Wendy Horowitz and Glen Creason (Los Angeles Public Library); Dino Everett (Hugh M. Hefner Moving Image Archive); Abraham Ferrer and Helen Kim (Visual Communications); Jeff Kollath and Jennifer Campbell (Stax Museum of American Soul Music); and May Haduong and Cassie Blake (Academy Film Archive).

Sona Basmadjian at the David L. Wolper Center enthusiastically supported this project from the beginning. I benefited from her passion and expertise concerning all things related to David Wolper. Sona's meticulous attention to chronology proved essential as I pieced together the complex history of Wolper Productions. Auriel Sanderson and Janette Webb also provided me with important details as to the professional biography of David Wolper. Mark Quigley at the UCLA Film & Television Archive led me toward a storehouse of KCET films and was always up for a conversation about public broadcasting and the 1960s. He kindly invited me to participate in the archive's inspiring symposium "This Is the City: Preserving Moving Images of Los Angeles" back in 2015.

Patrick Reagan and Samantha Bates are two of my closest friends and fellow lovers of music, documentary, and Los Angeles. They provided a home away from home during my research trips. The Roland family were also welcoming guides to the city. Their hospitality made traveling out West a pure delight.

Dennis Doros and Amy Heller of Milestone Film & Video went above and beyond to make stills from *The Exiles* (1961) and *Killer of Sheep* (1977) available for this book. The cover looks fabulous! I appreciate their patience and persistence to render the best-quality images.

One of the pleasures of researching this topic was spending time with filmmakers involved with the postwar documentary scene in Los Angeles. Our eclectic conversations led me down new avenues of exploration and made the history come alive. As a result of our discussions, I was better able to comprehend the media climate of the period and the social impact of their documentaries. I am indebted to Charles Burnett, Linda Buzzell, William Cartwright, Erik Daarstad, Dan Gingold, Gary Goldsmith, Dennis Hicks, Tom Horton, Duane Kubo, Lynne Littman, John Morrill, Robert Nakamura, Vaughn Obern, Joe Saltzman, Terry Sanders, John Soh, Mel Stuart, Thandeka (Sue Booker), Jesús Salvador Treviño, and Eddie Wong. Diane Mackenzie, Kiki Mackenzie, and Jillynn Molina kindly shared personal insights about their parents' lives in front of and behind the camera.

Hendrix College provided me with a nurturing environment to bring this book over the finish line. I could not ask for more compassionate, devoted, and brilliant students and colleagues. Much gratitude goes to Hope Coulter, James Dow, Alice

Hines, Tyrone Jaeger, Toni Wall Jaudon, Giffen Maupin, Kristi McKim, Michael Miyawaki, Elizabeth Rogers, Debapriya Sarkar, Dorian Stuber, Marjorie Swann, Alex Vernon, and Carol West. Our stimulating conversations about pedagogy and the public humanities spilled over into this project. John Shutt and Matthew Windsor were tenacious in tracking down images, articles, and secondary texts that I needed for specific chapters. The Faculty Project Grant I received from Hendrix allowed me to clear image rights as well as embark on an important research trip to Los Angeles.

Much of the day-to-day grind of writing and editing was achieved through the sustained support of friends, colleagues in the field, and my vibrant graduate school cohort. I'm thankful for the advice, humor, and words of encouragement from Annie Abrams, Mal Ahern, Josh Alvizu, Brian Bates, Caetlin Benson-Allott, Annie Berke, Claudia Calhoun, Vicki Callahan, Michael Cramer, Kirsty Sinclair Dootson, Victor Fan, Nick Forster, Alex Gardner, Katherine Germano, Michael Gillespie, Erica Ginsberg, Wills Glasspiegel, Jane Kennedy, Jeremy Kessler, Michelle Komie, Brandon Kramer, Lance Kramer, Cecile Lagesse, Nick Lyon, Elizabeth Manekin, Nathan Marsak, Seth Niedermayer, Suzy Newbury, Vika Paranyuk, Luca Peretti, Miriam Posner, Mike Radow, Marie Roberts, Zelda Roland, Raisa Sidenova, Eli Jelly-Schapiro, Colin Snow, Josh Sperling, Richard Suchenski, Lauren Tilton, Andrey Tolstoy, Takuya Tsunoda, Andrew Vielkind, and Grant Wiedenfeld. These people kept me grounded throughout what felt like a whirlwind of a project.

I received invaluable feedback from events associated with Visible Evidence, the Society for Cinema and Media Studies, and the American Studies Association. My interactions with members of the Urbanism/Geography/Architecture Scholarly Interest Group at the Society for Cinema and Media Studies led to many panels and workshops. Stan Corkin, Josh Gleich, Noelle Griffis, David James, Brendan Kredell, Merrill Schleier, Mark Shiel, and Erica Stein have remained engaged interlocutors. And it has been a thrill to stay connected with Sabine Haenni and Mary Woods through my involvement with these organizations. Sabine and Mary were generous mentors during my undergraduate years at Cornell and set me on a trajectory toward film and media studies.

I sincerely appreciate the time and attention of those kind souls who read chapters or even the entire manuscript during the late stages of the book. Kim Cooper joined the project to offer her expert knowledge of Los Angeles. Having her on board helped me to see the social geography of the city in a new way. Seth Fein assisted in pivotal ways with the introduction and conclusion, encouraging me to tell the story I wanted to tell. Jordan Brower gave the language of the project critical polish and pointed me toward what I was unable to see on the page. Jeff Menne offered razor-sharp observations about the mechanics of my chapters and how everything fit together into a conceptual framework. Sally Shafto's careful and thorough edits greatly strengthened my prose and helped me to foreground my own claims.

At the University of California Press, Mary Francis and Raina Polivka were strong advocates of the project and I'm honored to have worked with both of them. Mary gave me keen suggestions at the proposal stage, and Raina was deeply involved at every step of the way during the revising, editing, and layout phases. Zuha Khan assisted with the design and overall organization of the project as it moved through production. My official readers at the University of California Press wrote detailed comments that clarified the stakes of my project and served as a springboard for revision. My copy editor at University of California Press, Lindsey Westbrook, provided crucial guidance on the formatting of the manuscript and offered valuable corrections to make the writing accurate and concise.

Finally, deep appreciation goes to my family—Mom, Dad, Irena, Melissa, and Grandma Eleanor. Each has been a source of inspiration and has passionately encouraged my humanities pursuits from the very beginning. They have provided unflagging support and helped me to see the joys and rewards of public service. Masha Shpolberg has enriched every page of this book beyond measure. I'm grateful for her intelligence, wit, understanding, and grace.

Joshua Glick
Little Rock, 2017

Introduction

Beyond Fiction

Institutions of the Real Los Angeles

In the late 1950s Erik Daarstad was just beginning his career as a cinematographer in Los Angeles. His passion for film had brought him from his native Norway, where he grew up in the small industrial town of Sandnes, to the University of Southern California (USC) to pursue an undergraduate degree in the cinema department. He found lifelong friends and collaborators in the school's film fraternity, Delta Kappa Alpha, learned his craft in courses led by Warner Bros. cinematographer Ralph Woolsey, and developed a keen interest in documentary from the seminars of the Dutch émigré film theorist Andries Deinum. Daarstad wrote in his memoir that Deinum "was one of those very special kinds of teachers who influences your life to such a degree that you always remember them. . . . [He] considered film very important in its ability to present and influence social issues and spoke eloquently in defense of film as art."[1] Daarstad's thesis documentary, *A Light for John* (1957), focused on the tender relationship between a mentally disabled US Air Force veteran and his elderly mother. The two lived in a small apartment three blocks north of USC and struggled to make ends meet. After graduation, Daarstad worked as a cameraman and shared an apartment with his USC friends in Hollywood. He served as a gaffer, grip, and cinematographer on commissioned short films for Pat Dowling Pictures in the Pico-Robertson district near Beverly Hills. In addition, he shot low-budget features that targeted the youth audience, including the World War II action film *Hell Squad* (1958) for director Burt Topper, and *Teenage Caveman* (1958), *A Bucket of Blood* (1959), and *The Raven* (1963) for producer Roger Corman.

Daarstad would find more appealing opportunities with David Wolper's newly formed documentary studio, Wolper Productions, located on the Sunset Strip. The

Hollywood production company had emerged onto the national broadcasting scene with its acclaimed *The Race for Space* (1958), a film about the US–Soviet Union competition for space supremacy. The studio was swiftly expanding due to the increasing popularity of television, as well as government pressure on network executives and studio heads to educate viewers about the virtues of American democracy and the perils of Soviet Communism. Wolper would soon become the most prolific documentary producer in the country.

One of Daarstad's early achievements at Wolper Productions was *The Rafer Johnson Story* (1961). The film followed the early career of the African American Olympian turned Peace Corps recruiter Rafer Johnson. The director of the United States Information Agency, Edward R. Murrow, saw the documentary and eagerly arranged for its exhibition overseas. Crewing on films for the studio offered Daarstad a steady paycheck and the chance to hone his craft. Employment at Wolper Productions also afforded him opportunities to travel to "real places" and interact with "real people" instead of working with actors playing roles in fictional stories.[2] In his off hours Daarstad pursued independent films that defied the commercial market.

He answered the call of his old USC classmate Kent Mackenzie to help shoot his passion project, *The Exiles* (1961), an experimental documentary about working-class American Indians living in the downtown neighborhood of Bunker Hill. Daarstad filmed members of the close-knit community in their clapboard apartments, in the bars they frequented along Main Street, and at their favorite late-night meeting spot on a plot of land known as Hill X overlooking Chavez Ravine (soon to be Dodger Stadium). By means of observational cinematography and voice-over narration, *The Exiles* evocatively captured the anxieties and aspirations of a people marginalized within the municipal politics of Los Angeles. The film also criticized Hollywood's derogatory treatment of the "red man" at a time of renewed popular interest in Westerns. Daarstad enjoyed dedicating sustained attention to filming individuals whose experiences did not fit neatly within mainstream storytelling conventions or the federal government's rosy vision of an equitable and integrated American polity. He also took pleasure in the creative challenge of shooting in crowded interiors and wide-open streets at night, which involved coordinating a combination of natural and artificial light sources.[3] *The Exiles* took more than three hard years to complete. It played to enthusiastic journalists at festivals in California, New York, and Europe, but failed to attract distributors.

Examining Daarstad's back-and-forth trajectory from Hollywood to Hill X reveals much about his personal investments and practical needs as a professional cinematographer. It also reveals three significant aspects of film and television production in Los Angeles at the dawn of the 1960s. First, political forces along with shifts in the city's media landscape made Los Angeles a vibrant center for a variety of documentary practices. In the era of Cold War liberalism and its discontents, filmmakers not only experimented formally, but also imagined documentary as a popular commercial product, a powerful form of mass persuasion, an artful medium of personal expression, and a tool of grassroots organizing. Second, documentaries made by individuals, collectives, and studios fashioned conflicting representations of social reality. As President John F. Kennedy's "New Frontier" stressed a strong welfare state with active citizen participation at home and an aggressive military abroad, documentaries affirmed the administration's official platform or interrogated its weaknesses, inadequacies, and faults. And third, the high potential for intersection among documentaries made under different circumstances and with clashing motivations was characteristic of local production. Documentaries could be ideologically opposed, yet connected by way of sharing overlapping labor pools, facilities, or subject matter. Documentaries would continue to exist in tension with one another as Kennedy's administration gave way to Lyndon B. Johnson's "Great Society" vision of an expanded welfare state, the minority liberation movements of the late 1960s, and the time of fragile unification around the US bicentennial in 1976. *Los Angeles Documentary and the Production of Public History, 1958–1977* explores these tensions through key filmmakers active during this period, the institutions in which they worked, and the social impact of their films.

DOCUMENTARY IN THE CAPITAL OF MOVING IMAGES

At the moment that Daarstad was finishing his studies at USC, Los Angeles was in a state of rapid transformation. The automotive, shipping, aerospace, and military defense industries brought massive economic growth that was accompanied by an unprecedented population boom. *US News and World Report* ran a cover story on the topic, proclaiming, "Los Angeles is growing faster than any other place in America. . . . [The] result is that 'L.A.,' the urban mass that attracts most sun, fun and job seekers, has been exploding into mountain valley, farmland, desert and seacoast."[4] Manufacturing sectors geared to World War II were retooled for Cold War military defense as well as the domestic initiative of suburbanization. Government-backed freeway construction accelerated the horizontal expansion of the city, turning Los Angeles into a sprawling metropolis. Over the course of the 1940s and 1950s, the lure of jobs and the Southern California climate attracted black, white, and American Indian laborers from the South, Southwest, and Midwest. Immigrants from Latin America and Asia also came in rising numbers, especially following the 1965 Hart-Celler Act's changes to the government's immigration quota system and exemptions for close relatives of US citizens. But Los Angeles was far more fragmented and segregated than media-made images of a sunlit paradise suggested. For many, upward mobility remained chimerical. Minorities regularly confronted residential segregation, police brutality, and workplace prejudice. By the mid-1960s, the Watts Uprising and rousing claims of Black Power fueled how Chicanos, Asian Americans, and American Indians saw self-definition and representation as essential to the broader struggle toward self-determination. Their interrelated movements continued well into the next decade, even as infighting, government repression, cultural cooptation, and the selective deindustrialization of the city would diminish their strength.[5]

Contemporaneous with uneven growth and social unrest in Los Angeles, the film and television industries were undergoing seismic changes. A number of factors radically altered their systems of production, including the increasingly dispersed American audience; the 1948 Supreme Court verdict in United States v. Paramount Pictures Inc., which broke up the monopoly of the big studios; the mass proliferation of television into American homes; and the increasing use of 16mm film in classrooms, offices, and community centers. Gone were the days when a small number of large, vertically integrated studios used their respective stables of talent to generate a high volume of features. USC professor Richard Dyer MacCann explained in his 1962 book *Hollywood in Transition* how the "television revolution" resulted in a new platform and, with it, big changes in media production.[6] The old majors did not shut down; rather, they reinvented themselves in the 1950s, 1960s, and 1970s by making fewer, bigger productions and reconfiguring their back lots and soundstages for telefilm and sponsored assignments. There was a reduction in long-term contract labor, and it became increasingly common for people to crew on a greater variety of films on a project-by-project basis. Also, smaller studios and television stations, along with independent directors and organizations, began making films.

While scholars have devoted considerable attention to this period of film and television in Los Angeles, the relationship between documentary and the city has been doubly obscured. First, nonfiction theorists and historians have concentrated on New York and Boston, positioning these traditional East Coast intellectual centers and the documentaries created within them against Hollywood and the entertainment generated by the culture industries. Such studies are largely devoted to the pioneering American cinema verité efforts of D. A. Pennebaker, Richard Leacock, the Maysles brothers, and Robert Drew, who sought to transform social observation into an aesthetic experience by using sync-sound and mobile camera rigs.[7] Another body of scholarship within this first group has sought to investigate filmmakers who closely aligned their practices with a specific minority community or political cause.[8] Second, cinema scholars have typically explored Los Angeles in terms of theatrically released fiction films and television programs created by major studios. Recent Hollywood historiography has resulted in more nuanced understandings of corporate authorship as well as of the entangled relationship between the economics and the art of industrial modes of production. The studios Paramount and Warner Bros., the television operations of Desilu and Disney, and the countercultural insurgent American International Pictures are at the heart of these accounts.[9]

Los Angeles Documentary recalibrates the geography of documentary production during this period from New York and Boston to Southern California. David James's *The Most Typical Avant-Garde: History and Geography of Minor Cinemas in Los Angeles* (2005) has laid important groundwork for understanding multiple kinds of film in the metropolis and has been instrumental in dislodging New York as the often-presumed heart of avant-garde media. James surveys a vast swath of filmmakers throughout the twentieth century who were motivated by artistic and political interests rather than fame and profit. He begins with proletarian labor films in the 1910s and concludes with structural meditations on landscape at the turn of the century. These "minor cinemas" point to a range of distinct but related kinds of film: "experimental, poetic, underground, ethnic, amateur, counter, noncommodity, working-class, critical, artists', orphan, and so on."[10] Importantly, as James has argued, the minor cinemas of Los Angeles are not a world away from Hollywood. The former have in fact always been constantly responding to and deviating from the latter:

> Unstably and obliquely positioned, these local cultural formations are caught between the centrifugal pull of the indigenous practices of local communities and the centripetal pull of the hegemonic entertainment industries. The reciprocal core-periphery relations between the industrial mode of production and alternatives to it reflect the spatial situation of both. The structural tensions that shape the city geographically have recurred in the potentials that shape its arts, and Hollywood exists not only as a spatial center around which other cultural practices construct themselves but also as a formal or thematic point of reference for them.[11]

In James's account, minor cinemas form a "periphery" around the "core" that is the commercial film and television sector. This relationship is expressed through the ideological conflicts between each kind of cinema, as well as through the geographic location in which each is created. Minor cinemas have frequently existed in constrained and ephemeral fashion beyond Hollywood studios, celebrity homes, and affluent entertainment destinations.

However, commercial Hollywood and alternative documentary did not necessarily conform to a core-periphery relationship. Documentary entailed geographic variation contingent on the material represented; on-location shooting, sound recording, the consulting of experts, and archival digs for footage happened all over the city and well outside of the metropolis. Additionally, the overt social aspirations of documentaries involved wide-ranging audiences. Small, independent films could potentially have a significant impact, while robustly funded Hollywood films could fail to resonate. James's core-periphery model is helpful for clarifying characteristics of the mainstream-alternative dynamic that I navigate, but ultimately does not carry over to the field of documentary. Investigating documentary production and reception culture reveals the traffic of personnel, ideas, and resources circulating to and from Los Angeles. Furthermore, this approach emphasizes the importance of Los Angeles on the national stage and its influence on the political culture of the country.

Los Angeles Documentary concentrates on how the city's production facilities, stock footage libraries, technology hubs, schools, art scenes, and government agencies, along with its diverse array of ethnic communities, made it a nurturing environment for both mainstream and alternative documentary. Los Angeles filmmakers played an integral role in shaping the social consciousness of the nation as well as in contributing to the discourse of documentary as a pedagogical cultural form. For just as Hollywood was not coterminous with the breadth of film production taking place in Los Angeles, Hollywood was also not itself a monolithic system of capitalist entertainment.

Los Angeles Documentary follows two main narrative strands. The first concentrates on Wolper Productions' narratives about extraordinary citizens and influential politicians. "Understanding," "collaboration," "dialogue," "integration," and faith in "expertise" were key liberal themes. The studio projected images of a smoothly functioning pluralist democracy, but also masked disagreements within liberal democratic politics during this time, for example hesitancy with legislating civil rights reform, differing views on a top-down or a locally controlled approach to neighborhood initiatives, debates about whether to generate jobs through public works projects, and a lack of consensus surrounding America's military involvement in Southeast Asia.[12] The second strand of this book concentrates on filmmakers laboring independently, on the fringes of the mainstream, or in an array of noncommercial institutions. These filmmakers embraced documentary as a means to expose the contradictions and inadequacies of liberal governance, castigate the persistence of socioeconomic inequities, and empower minority communities. Incorporating both strands within this book shows the dynamic association between these two kinds of documentary. Vernacular folkways, grassroots political movements, and nonconventional filmmaking techniques "trickled up" and were absorbed by Hollywood. Marginalized filmmakers also used resources from commercial employers toward their own agenda. New forms of institutional support such as public television stations and interdisciplinary university filmmaking departments helped these documentarians to assert their presence in front of and behind the camera.

THE SCOPE AND SCALE OF PUBLIC HISTORY

The documentaries of Wolper Productions and the alternative films produced in Los Angeles at this time constituted divergent forms of what came to be called "public history." There was scattered mention of the phrase "public history" in the press over the course of the 1950s, 1960s, and early to mid-1970s, and filmmakers rarely used the term. It was not until the late 1970s that "public history" began to surface in intellectual circles and gain currency across the humanities. Its popularization thus coincided uncomfortably with the national shift toward the privatization of the economy, the deregulation of the telecommunications industries, and the defunding of humanities institutions under President Ronald Reagan. The graduate program in Public Historical Studies at the University of California, Santa Barbara (1976–) and the professional association of the National Council on Public History (1980–) used the term to describe the application of the disciplinary methodology of history to professional endeavors beyond the university. In the first issue of *Public Historian* (1978–) the editorial team noted that "historical skills and method are needed now *outside* of the academy."[13] More broadly, public history came to designate the diverse ways that history informed public life in the present, for example through museum exhibitions, television programs, or heritage parks. Public history also constituted a field of contestation in which different practices and representations existed in ideological contrast to one another. The editors of *Radical History Review* wrote about how the commercial culture industries tended to fashion public history according to a top-down model, "packaging" the past in an easily digestible fashion that bolstered dominant values. Artists and left-leaning activists endeavored to craft an oppositional, bottom-up form of public history, focusing on resistant narratives that gave voice to underrepresented communities and advocated for social justice.[14]

It is no coincidence that there was spirited discussion about public history during this time. The term came to name something that had already been happening in practice for more than two decades. This earlier period was when the creation of public history was at its most robust. The late 1950s saw the democratization of media production, circulation, and exhibition. Liberal and more radical forms of documentary comprised compelling and widely seen types of public history. Filmmaking practice varied considerably, as did filmmakers' views on their role in the process. Some were avid enthusiasts of cinema verité; others were interested in exploring the possibilities of layering voice-over narration onto archival footage, sound fragments, or photographs. Still, their methods of production often entailed shooting footage, gathering together audiovisual materials directly related to the existing social world, and shaping these elements into a film that advanced a distinct point of view. This process of creatively shaping nonfiction media around a central argument had been a persistent feature of documentary practice since the 1930s. It is what—according to classical documentary theorists such as John Grierson—distinguished social documentary from the broader field of newsreels, journalistic reportage, and photographs. As film theorist Philip Rosen would later write, "If shots as indexical traces of past reality may be treated as documents in the broad sense, documentary can be treated as a conversion from the document. This conversion involves a synthesizing knowledge claim, by virtue of a sequence that sublates an undoubtable referential field of pastness into meaning."[15]

Even as filmmakers revised older forms of documentary thanks to innovations in recording equipment and access to a wider range of "documents" during the 1950s, 1960s, and 1970s, the historicist dimension and rhetorical charge described by Rosen endured. What made the work of so many committed filmmakers in this period public history was not simply a technological capability, but the broader cultural context that informed how documentaries were designed and interpreted. The convergence of Cold War politics, social movements, and shifts in the media industries resulted in lively debates about the strategic uses of history for either liberal governance or left-leaning forms of protest. Filmmakers wrestled with conceptions of American identity, the country's place in the world, and individuals' rights to a place in the polity. Government agencies, schools, television stations, film studios, and independent cooperatives all had a stake in documentaries. Television broadcasting and 16mm film projection enabled their exhibition in peoples' homes, theaters, and civic venues. Filmmakers gravitated to documentary as a way to historicize contemporary experience as well as to provide a rhetorical perspective on the more distant past. The intent was not to hermetically seal the present off from the past, but to position the two in dialogue. In this way, documentaries created a usable past from which viewers could draw to see themselves as active agents influencing their contemporary environment.

Documentaries addressed viewers as members of a collectivity and oriented them to the world beyond the screen. Documentaries did not just aim for criticism or affirmation; they sought to mobilize spectators toward particular goals. For example, cinema scholar Jonathan Kahana demonstrates that independent leftist filmmaking by Newsreel, Winterfilm Collective, and Emile de Antonio organized viewers against such prolonged government actions as the Vietnam War.[16] Kahana shows that the sonic elements of this kind of cinema, whether in the form of voice-over narration, on-screen interviews, or ambient noise, vehemently countered official state perspectives. At the same time, sound design was essential to giving voice to student activists, aggrieved war veterans, and movement leaders. *Los Angeles Documentary* builds on Kahana's analysis, exploring how nonprofit institutions, government policies, commercial outlets, and intellectuals played a major role in the creation of both liberal and more radical forms of documentary, as well as how documentaries engaged viewers in the public sphere. The formation of the Corporation for Public Broadcasting, the release of the Kerner Commission Report, the availability of government grants, and the expansion of the university were all vital for documentary. They made available technical and economic resources for production, new channels for distribution, and venues for exhibition.

Nowhere was the terrain of documentary more dynamic and contentious than in Los Angeles. As the city was both a national hub for the culture industries and a multiracial metropolis, the construction of public history became simultaneously a business enterprise, a civic duty, and an activist endeavor. Representing the top-down model, Wolper Productions was America's leading producer of commercial documentary for theatrical release and network television. The Hollywood studio trumpeted America's "exceptional" role in leading the "free world" and romanticized capitalist democracy as a benevolent force. Their documentaries did not so much encourage intellectual debate as posit answers to clearly articulated, streamlined questions. Locally, Wolper Productions showcased Los Angeles as a cosmopolitan, egalitarian metropolis, but ignored its long history of exclusion and prejudice that continued into the present.

Representing the bottom-up perspective, filmmakers working at the PBS station KCET, in association with universities, or in independent factions made their own documentaries that adamantly challenged the status quo in a city plagued by severe class stratification and racial segregation. Documentarians sought to advance the liberation movements they depicted, forging a political consciousness for marginalized communities. Their films addressed workplace sexism and racism, police brutality, school reform, urban renewal, community arts, the Vietnam War, and amnesiac visions of the Los Angeles social landscape. If these documentaries did not necessarily enjoy large audiences or turn a significant profit, they nonetheless resonated strongly with Angelenos and viewers across the country.

In order to understand the production context and impact of these films, I examine a wide breadth of primary documents, including articles from the trade press, news periodicals, memoirs, correspondence, and interviews. These rich sources nourish an in-depth historical investigation of Los Angeles and its place in post–World War II American culture.[17] This period of public history resulted in a more inclusive understanding of American identity, but there was not a simple or singular outcome. Wolper Productions' celebratory bicentennial programming ultimately prepared the ground for a conservative political culture predicated on the sanctity of the individual, privatization, and a reinvigorated Cold War nationalism. The bicentennial was in many ways the dress rehearsal for the 1984 Olympics. At the same time, the efforts of alternative documentarians bolstered a lasting, progressive sense of racial and ethnic pride and community awareness that would continue into the future. They also created flexible models of production that would be of use to later filmmakers. Furthermore, they established a foothold in universities and festivals that helped sustain left-leaning social causes and local activism in Los Angeles, even as struggles for rights and recognition were absorbed within the discourse of multiculturalism and faced opposition from the New Right.

PARALLEL DEVELOPMENTS AND EPOCHAL CHANGES

Los Angeles Documentary designates three major periods of public history making, with each period comprising a section with two or three parallel chapters. In the first part, "New Frontier Visions in the Light and Shadow of Hollywood, 1958–1964," the Sputnik launch, the network quiz show scandals, and the presidential election of John F. Kennedy inspired the desire to strengthen the body politic by means of educational forms of mass media. Chapter 1 argues that Wolper Productions occupied an essential position on the cultural front of Kennedy's New Frontier. Documentaries about citizens, politicians, and military conflicts functioned as narratives of assurance. With the assassination of Kennedy, Wolper Productions became the preeminent custodian of the fallen president's memory. The studio's films on Kennedy's rise to the highest office (*The Making of the President: 1960* [1963]) and his death (*Four Days in November* [1964]) performed an important social function during a period of transition to the Johnson administration.

At the same time that Wolper was building his studio and staffing it with producers Mel Stuart, Alan Landsburg, and Jack Haley Jr., film school graduates were looking for employment in the city. Chapter 2 focuses on Kent Mackenzie, who, like other talented, university-trained filmmakers, worked for Wolper Productions, the United States Information Agency, and film firms that catered to the educational and business sectors. These jobs offered rewarding work outside of studio fiction but also entailed ideological and formal constraints. Mackenzie drew on the resources of his day jobs, along with the pro bono efforts of his colleagues, to make *The Exiles*. Examining the major thrust of Mackenzie's career reveals the professional challenges and opportunities for young filmmakers interested in making socially engaged documentary. His trajectory also signaled the rumblings of a resistant minority cinema in Los Angeles.

The book's second part, "After the Watts Uprising: Community Media from the Top Down and the Bottom Up, 1965–1973," frames the rise of minority liberation movements and the fracturing of Cold War liberalism. Chapter 3 explores filmmaking in Watts, East Los Angeles, and Little Tokyo. These areas appeared on-screen as complex communities, not simply as "slums" or sites of loss. Prominent filmmakers included Joe Saltzman (*Black on Black* [1968]), Lynne Littman (*Womanhouse Is Not a Home* [1972]), Robert Nakamura (*Manzanar* [1971]), Sue Booker (*Doin' It at the Storefront* [1972–73]), and Jesús Salvador Treviño (*América Tropical* [1971]). A combination of grassroots activism and government legislation inflected the training and production practices of these documentarians over the course of their time at commercial broadcasting stations, institutions of higher education, and public television outlets.

As Wolper Productions continued to make documentaries and experiment with fiction, the studio provided a professional entry point for promising talent and off-and-on employment for individuals involved with the cinema of New Hollywood. Chapter 4 investigates Wolper Productions' output during a period in which the film and television industries faced a precarious financial situation. The studio's forays into programs with the French oceanographer Jacques Cousteau charted a fresh path for nonfiction. In contrast, packaging American history or capturing recent political events would prove to be a troublesome venture. Wolper Productions' prospective adaptation of William Styron's novel *The Confessions of Nat Turner* (1967) was one of the earliest attempts by a major studio to make a commercial film about Black Power themes and figures. Widespread opposition to the film, however, resulted in a public relations disaster for Wolper Productions. Wolper and his circle came to understand the importance of having community support from the minority group the studio sought to represent.

The studio acted on this knowledge when the black record label Stax contacted Wolper about coproducing a film about the final concert of the 1972 Watts Summer Festival. Chapter 5 focuses on *Wattstax* (1973) and the different players involved with its creation. The film's verité-style footage of Stax artists and fans in the Los Angeles Memorial Coliseum, residents in the surrounding neighborhood, and testimony from comedian Richard Pryor constituted far more than a standard concert film. The documentary showed a feedback loop between everyday black experience and cultural expression. *Wattstax* also served as the crucial pivot project for Wolper's push toward minority subjects, Stax's attempt to become a film studio, and numerous crew members' personal efforts to advance their careers.

The events surrounding the 1976 American bicentennial performed the same kind of identity building on a national scale that *Wattstax* performed locally. *Los Angeles Documentary*'s third part, "Bicentennial Screens, 1974–1977" looks at the two-hundred-year anniversary of the nation's independence as a constellation of media-generated narratives around which the country either rallied or revolted. Bicentennial events in Los Angeles spoke to black mayor Tom Bradley's plan for shaping the city into a business-friendly, multicultural metropolis—a plan that would reach fruition in the next decade. Chapter 6 looks at Wolper Productions' principal role as an architect of patriotic culture of national commemoration. Without a cinematic record of early American history, the studio turned to "docudrama" as the solution to a narrative problem of documentary historiography. Combining the form and style of period fiction with the truth-telling charge of documentary, docudramas such as *Sandburg's Lincoln* (1974–76) and *I Will Fight No More Forever* (1975) were a novel kind of prestige programming. Docudrama could command high ratings and claim the pedagogical intent of educating viewers. Wolper Productions made network series and specials on American history that culminated with the studio's eight-part miniseries *Roots* (1977).

Chapter 7 considers resistant forms of national remembrance. As Hollywood docudrama incorporated minorities into a streamlined vision of the American social fabric, alternative films depicted a contentious relationship between a historic present and past. This chapter argues for the persistence of filmmakers' interest in documentary, even as they experimented with other media or blended fiction and nonfiction. Long-form films and photo-books by the collective Visual Communications (*Wataridori: Birds of Passage* [1976], *In Movement: A Pictorial History of Asian America* [1977]), a documentary made from a collaboration between anthropologist Barbara Myerhoff and director Lynne Littman (*Number Our Days* [1976]), and the artisanal filmmaking of Charles Burnett (*Killer of Sheep* [1977]) presented nuanced stories about the resilience of the city's marginalized communities. Their work on Asian Americans in Little Tokyo, elderly Jews in Venice, and African Americans in Watts denounced national myths of bootstrap individualism and upward mobility, as well as industrial decentralization and uneven downtown development under the Bradley administration. The conclusion explores the branding of Los Angeles as a "world city" along with the deregulation of the media industries and the further retrenchment of the welfare state under President Reagan. Los Angeles would be prominently on display as the home city for the 1984 Olympics.

PART ONE

New Frontier Visions in the Light and Shadow of Hollywood, 1958–1964

1

Studio Documentary in
the Kennedy Era

Wolper Productions Begins

*Praises be to Newton Minow.... He's our best press agent and I feel as if I
should send him a weekly check.*
—PRODUCER DAVID WOLPER, 1961[1]

On December 7, 1962, a *Time* magazine article assigned the title "Mr. Documentary" to David Wolper, the thirty-four-year-old film distributor turned documentary producer. The piece praised the variety and style of his well-crafted television
documentaries and the influence of Wolper Productions, a company that rivaled
the documentary output of CBS and NBC. Wolper was, *Time* announced, "the
youngest, and often the most vigorous, of the three. His offices on Hollywood's
Sunset Strip have grown in the past 42 months from a five-man [bucket] shop to a
200-employee corporation with [a] bright white neo-Palladian façade and 40 cutting rooms—some of which are already crammed with the 8,000,000 ft. of film
that Wolper is condensing into *The Making of the President: 1960*."[2]

The article connected Wolper to a place, a particular filmmaking process, and a
product. The confident producer—framed in a thumbnail portrait in a neat black
suit and comfortably holding a cigar in one hand and what appears to be a script
in the other—had located his studio on one of Los Angeles's hippest and busiest
commercial thoroughfares. Another article in the same issue highlighted the mul-
titasking capacity of President John F. Kennedy, able to preside over the military,
economic, and cultural life of the nation while still making time for his friends,
family, and outdoor recreation.[3] *Time* commended Wolper for exhibiting many of
the same traits, which the magazine associated with effective and likable leadership. His ability to work on multiple projects at once while still making time to see
the Dodgers play or meet one of his show-business friends for a round of golf
reflected what the article called his "go-go dynamism." It hardly seems coincidental

that the *Time* profile used the word "vigorous," a term frequently used by and to describe Kennedy, to talk about "Mr. Documentary."

Social reformers, politicians, major news periodicals, and the trade press shared *Time*'s enthusiasm for Wolper Productions. They applauded the studio's films, and especially their reach into living rooms, theaters, and schools. Curiously, despite being praised at the time, the organization has received scant attention in scholarly accounts of post–World War II documentary. Instead, cinema and media scholars have focused on the New York–based network news divisions or the small cluster of American cinema verité filmmakers. Los Angeles, it is often assumed, was dominated by the economic imperatives of studio features and entertainment television, invariably defined as the media center against which filmmakers in the Northeast tried to position their work.[4]

Wolper Productions, however, was a prominent player in what had become a national trend of nonfiction programming. Examining how the studio drew on the city's resources as well as collaborated with individuals and institutions across the country reveals a critical and underexplored relationship between Hollywood and the cultural Cold War. The studio focused on the recent and more distant American past, making films about military campaigns, the daily lives of citizens, and the pursuits of civic leaders and politicians. These documentaries portrayed American democracy as vibrant and emphasized the government's staunch stance against Communism, all the while smoothing over or sidestepping contentious debates surrounding civil rights, class inequality, and the use of military force overseas. Wolper Productions presented a romantic vision of liberal reform at home and geopolitical power abroad.

CAPTURING THE SPACE RACE

Wolper made a name for himself by carefully navigating the changing film and television industries. His first major film, *The Race for Space* (1958), exploited the national desire for audiovisual media that could educate a mass audience about pressing social concerns. The October 4, 1957, launch of the Sputnik satellite galvanized a new anxiety about Soviet scientific superiority and intensified America's competitive relationship with its adversary. Sputnik's launch and traceable flight, coming six weeks after the Soviets' successful testing of an intercontinental ballistic missile (ICBM), stoked hyperbolic speculation about the militaristic uses of advanced rocketry. The launch resulted in government reaction—the formation of the civilian-oriented National Aeronautics and Space Administration (1958) and the military-oriented Defense Advanced Research Projects Agency (1958)—as well as responses from the mainstream media.[5] Just as old space films were rerun on television, reissued for the classroom market, and rereleased in theaters and drive-ins, new films about intergalactic possibilities and the perils of space-age technology likewise proliferated in these settings. *Variety* was quick to proclaim that Hollywood was in a "'Sputnik Spurt.'"[6] Members of the broadcasting industry in particular looked for shows that would teach audiences about the implications of the space race. Stations and network heads were well aware of how suburban expansion and a boom in consumer spending had transformed television from a novelty into a cultural fixture in American living rooms. So, too, were they aware of the Sputnik launch providing an occasion to link programming to their vaguely defined FCC obligation to program in the "public interest."[7]

The quiz show scandals of 1956–59 further increased the appetite for educational television. The bombshell exposure of the rigging of *Twenty-One* (1956–58), *The $64,000 Question* (1955–58), and *Dotto* (1958) drew attention to corporate greed and fraud within the entertainment industry. Critics raised questions about the ethical responsibilities of the networks and the corrupting role of commercial sponsors, declaring the need for more honest and edifying shows.[8] Documentaries could satisfy the reformist initiative and improve the image of the film studios and networks. The wide variety of documentary formats, run times, and styles offered a flexible way to teach Americans about social issues and explain the country's geopolitical place in world affairs.

The Race for Space brought together Wolper's interests in show business, new media, and pedagogy. In interviews he would recall being transfixed by the early display of television at the RCA Pavilion at the New York World's Fair in 1939. As an undergraduate at USC in the late 1940s, he avidly watched movies, took photographs for the school newspaper, the *Daily Trojan*, and was head of publicity for campus functions. He left USC one semester shy of graduation to cofound Flamingo Films. *Broadcasting* called Flamingo a standout in the "big business" of "film bartering." The company distributed documentaries, serials, travelogues, and animation to independent television stations and network affiliates.[9] Wolper was the organization's principal salesman and developed eclectic tastes through its catalog. Over the course of his travels, he became familiar with local television stations. He eventually settled in Hollywood to run West Coast operations.[10] A serendipitous encounter with an old colleague, Nicholas Napoli, during a trip to New York provided the spark for an original documentary.[11] Napoli was a former Communist Party USA member and cofounder and president of Artkino Pictures, the main distributor for Soviet films in the United States. From Napoli, Wolper purchased rare footage of the Soviet space program, including footage of the first Sputnik launch.[12] The young producer saw an opportunity to make a film about a popular topic and to boost America's place in the race. Wolper separated from Flamingo Films and created his own company, Wolper Inc., in 1958. He soon changed the name to Wolper Productions. Wolper then recruited a small team, including Mel Stuart, who after studying music at New York University edited films for the avant-garde filmmaker Mary Ellen Bute. Stuart also worked on the documentary series *Project XX* (1954–70) and *The Twentieth Century* (1957–70). He had recently started his own footage-location company called Film Finders. Another key figure was Jack Haley Jr., who studied filmmaking at USC and the University of California, Los Angeles, before directing air force training documentaries during the 1950s. As the son of actor Jack Haley and former Ziegfeld dancer Florence McFadden, he had numerous Hollywood connections, which would become important for later projects.[13]

Wolper distinguished *The Race for Space* from other accounts of the space race by adopting a broader historical perspective and aggressively drawing on tropes from television journalism and classical Hollywood storytelling. Wolper's team consulted with aerospace experts and acquired footage from North American Aviation and Caltech's Jet Propulsion Laboratory, as well as government institutions in Washington, DC, London, and Moscow. They created a chronological narrative of global rocket development, binding it together with an authoritative voice-over and a dramatic orchestral score. The film aimed to inform audiences of the history of humanity's fascination with rocketry, but also to establish the United States as a longtime pioneer in the field and to sketch the Cold War stakes of the competition. In so doing, the film assumed a less political stance than some of the alarmist news reports in the days immediately following the launch of Sputnik 1, such as CBS's *Special Report: Sputnik 1* (1957). Still, the adversarial positioning of the American and Soviet space programs—indeed, the framing of the relationship in terms of a "race"—set *The Race for Space* apart from entertainment-oriented programs. These included Disney's "science factual" documentaries, which presented science as a kind of magical craft that seemed to exist independently of the Cold War.

The Race for Space opens with images of the launching of Sputnik 1 and the voice-over of broadcasting personality Mike Wallace. The suspenseful score by famed composer Elmer Bernstein draws the viewer into the audiovisual flow of information. Commenting on footage and photographs from the Department of Defense, the Library of Congress, Sovexport, and Artkino, Wallace defines rocketry as a way for the United States, the Soviet Union, and Germany to showcase national growth in the science of flight over the course of the nineteenth and twentieth centuries. Wallace pays homage to the Soviet scientist-philosopher Konstantin Tsiolkovsky's imaginative theories of space exploration; however, he proclaims that it is the American Robert Goddard, holder of 214 rocketry-related patents between the 1910s and the 1940s, who is "the pioneering genius of the new twentieth-century science."

With the militarization of rocketry during World War II, the United States appears vulnerable in the Cold War. *The Race for Space* highlights this vulnerability in its contrasting portrayals of Americans and Soviets. While the former enjoy suburban amenities and leisure-time activities, their Soviet counterparts make math and science top priorities through instructional programs and by funding research. The launching of Soviet rockets, satellites, and even live animals into space does not necessarily convey Soviet superiority but nonetheless visualizes these accomplishments as tangible threats with unforeseen consequences that in turn compel a response. The United States then pursues a coordinated effort among federal officials, universities, and private industry to make up for lost ground in the race. After a failed Cape Canaveral launch, the flight of Explorer 1 shows the United States rising to the satellite challenge. The closing declaration in *The Race for Space* that the scientist-as-hero has found his revered place in American culture and will go on to explore the "new frontier" resonates with the familiar American narrative of expansion as a means to both social and technological progress. Anticipating Kennedy's own "New Frontier" rhetoric, *The Race for Space* uses space as a way to define national purpose and a horizon of opportunity.

The roadblocks the film met on its way to exhibition helped inflate its reputation and generate a buzz in the press. After it played overseas and won awards at film festivals in Edinburgh, Venice, and San Francisco, Wolper courted the triumvirate of networks. Despite the film's achievements, ABC, NBC, and CBS all refused to show it because the program was not made by their news departments. The rejection was as much about network concern over possible inaccuracies as it was about the networks' desire to retain a monopolistic position as producers of the news. Undeterred, Wolper used his extensive personal associations with individual stations to build an ad hoc network. He used KTTV in Los Angeles, WPIX in New York, and WGN-TV in Chicago to give the show a presence in significant markets. More than one hundred stations agreed to run the program. The story of Wolper's difficulties obtaining network exposure even surfaced on the front pages of many periodicals.[14] Journalists expressed their enthusiasm for the film and dismay that the networks had barred its exhibition. Marie Torre of the *New York Herald Tribune* wrote:

> It is not without irony that while the networks are intensifying public affairs programming to show that they're answering the call of duty, perhaps THE best documentary ever made on the vital subject of space flight is being withheld from the television audience by network decree. Or, should we say, network whim? . . . In the case of "The Race for Space," which this viewer saw at a private showing, the rejection is akin to a literary magazine turning down an Ernest Hemingway original because he's not a member of the magazine staff.[15]

The Race for Space went on to be nominated for an Oscar, exhibited at libraries, and shown as part of the curriculum at the US Military Academy at West Point.[16] W. H. Pickering, director of the Jet Propulsion Laboratory at Caltech, wrote Wolper a letter thanking him for creating a valuable object of study for scientists that would ultimately aid in the security of the country. A Los Angeles newspaper later noted that Kennedy himself commended *The Race for Space* for "clearly establishing the importance of America's space program to a mass audience."[17] A shrewd showman and talented producer, Wolper would continue to cultivate a brand identity as an independent while solidifying his bonds with television stations, government institutions, and the entertainment industry. This strategy proved essential to the growth of Wolper Productions as it moved with full force into the field of documentary.

CROSSING INDUSTRIAL DIVIDES

Wolper Productions' specialization in documentary and its method of manufacture capitalized on the shifting state of film and television production. Mass suburbanization, the 1948 Supreme Court antitrust decision in United States v. Paramount Pictures Inc., and the increasing presence of television in homes and 16mm film in libraries, offices, and classrooms ensured the demise of the old studio system. No longer would Hollywood be an oligopolistic system predicated on long-term contract labor, control over exhibition venues, and a relatively guaranteed audience. Geographers Susan Christopherson and Michael Storper argue that the old majors responded to these "shocks" through a number of actions: they decreased their total output, invested in large-scale spectacular films, exploited foreign markets, and supplied programs for the big three networks or hired independents to do so for them.[18] Newly created small studios such as Ziv Television Programs and American International Pictures focused specifically on niche areas of television or created theatrically released films for the youth audience. Production became "flexibly specialized," as larger numbers of smaller firms in subsectors of the industry worked on a variety of projects.[19]

Wolper Productions grew during this period of transition, making documentaries on the space race, compilation films on Hollywood history, specials on important figures and events of the twentieth century, and series about the professional routines of American citizens. The company hired more employees and eventually occupied a cluster of buildings on the Sunset Strip. According to a special issue of the glossy trade publication *Television*, the studio helped make Hollywood the center of television production.[20] Wolper's company was within the general proximity of the foremost television studios but nearer to other commercial sites. The converted rock 'n' roll club Ciro's, the elegant Scandinavian restaurant Scandia, and the hip lounge and restaurant Dino's Lodge, which appeared as a backdrop on *77 Sunset Strip* (1958–64), were all close by.[21] Wolper would later write in 1966 that the organization's location afforded them the chance to be "in the midst of leading laboratories, unparalleled sound stages, vast studios and every variety of camera and movie making equipment."[22] The organization also relied on filmmakers who could be hired on a project-by-project basis.

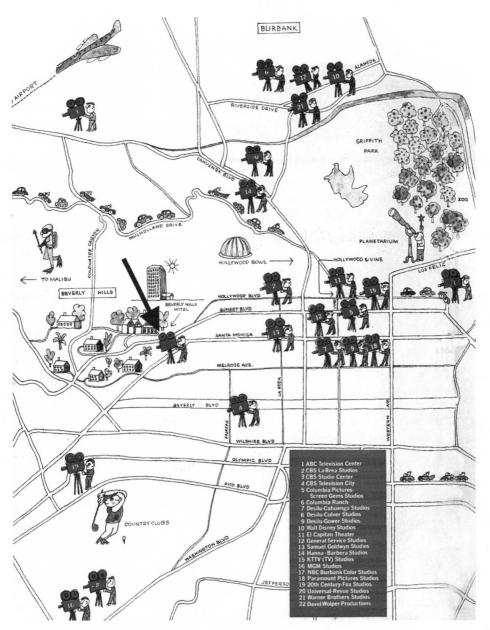

FIGURE 1: Map from Morris J. Gelman, "The Hollywood Story," *Television*, September 1963, 34–35. Wolper Productions is the studio indicated by the arrow.

FIGURE 2: Left to right: Alan Landsburg, David Wolper, Mel Stuart, and Jack Haley Jr., from Raymond Rohauer, *A Tribute to David L. Wolper* (New York: Huntington Hartford Gallery of Modern Art, 1966), 1. Courtesy of the Danish Film Institute.

The studio courted young talent and veteran members of the film and television industries. Wolper had already recruited Stuart and Haley to work on *The Race for Space*. The two stayed on at the company, assuming producer-director roles. This inner circle also added Alan Landsburg, who worked for the Army Radio Network throughout the Korean War and had made public affairs programs for the flagship NBC and CBS radio stations in New York.[23] Beyond this inner core was an array of craftspeople and technicians who moved fluidly within the city's media ecosystem. These film school graduates earned a paycheck at Wolper Productions but also found jobs working on "teensploitation" features, industrial films, United States Information Agency (USIA) documentaries, and independent projects. Cinematographer Vilis Lapenieks was principal cameraman at Wolper Productions, while also crewing on Curtis Harrington's *Night Tide* (1961), Kent Mackenzie's *The Exiles* (1961), Arch Hall's *Eegah!* (1962), and Samuel Z. Arkoff's *Queen of Blood* (1966). An additional outer pool consisted of individuals who worked for Wolper as well as on major Hollywood films. Elmer Bernstein, for example, composed music for Wolper Productions while also scoring big studio features including *To Kill a Mockingbird* (1962) and *Hud* (1963).

The attention Los Angeles drew from journalists, businesspeople, and academics at this time heightened the visibility of Wolper Productions. The city was seen as a trailblazer in the entertainment, manufacturing, petroleum, and defense industries. Its decentralizing growth pattern, observers believed, was proleptic, anticipating the fate of other American cities.[24] *Los Angeles Magazine* frequently promoted the urban area's commercial and residential expansion and downtown redevelopment. A special issue of the travel magazine *Holiday* called Los Angeles "a world in the making, a dazzlingly unconventional world which is busily creating its own and, very possibly, the entire country's future."[25] Absent from these boosterist accounts was the fact that freeway construction displaced working class citizens and heightened segregation in the city. The 1960 Democratic National Convention further advanced Los Angeles's reputation for innovation and linked the city to a vision of Cold War internationalism. Delegates traveled to the metropolis on jumbo jets that could cross the country in about five hours, half the time previously required, and congregated at the Los Angeles Memorial Coliseum.[26] In his convention speech accepting his party's nomination, Kennedy used Los Angeles as a symbolic site to unveil his administration's New Frontier platform:

> I stand here tonight facing west on what was once the last frontier. From the lands that stretch three thousand miles behind us, the pioneers gave up their safety, their comfort and sometimes their lives to build our new West. . . . We stand today on the edge of a New Frontier—the frontier of the 1960s, the frontier of unknown opportunities and perils, the frontier of unfilled hopes and unfilled threats.[27]

Put into practice, the New Frontier of opportunities and challenges extended in multiple directions: inward to plans for renovated cities, proposed antipoverty legislation, and civil rights reform; outward to a geopolitical landscape divided between a Western contingent of democratic countries, a Communist Soviet Union, and the nonaligned countries across Africa, Southeast Asia, and Latin America. The administration framed this period as one where big government would have a more direct role in influencing the lives of Americans, and individuals in turn would have a major role in contributing to the country's sociopolitical infrastructure.

Beyond helping to place Los Angeles on a national stage at the dawn of a new decade, Kennedy and his circle boosted the cultural capital of Wolper Productions and influenced the media environment in which the studio would find its stride. The photogenic Kennedy eagerly devoured films as a child, socialized with starlets over the course of his adolescence, and made appearances on television programs such as *Person to Person* as a Massachusetts senator. He performed with grace as a candidate in the first televised presidential debates against Republican opponent Richard Nixon. The cinema and media scholars Mary Ann Watson, Joseph P. Berry Jr., and J. Hoberman have found that Kennedy had a particular fondness for film and especially television, which had the ability to reach Americans directly in their homes.[28] In a guest editorial for *TV Guide*, Kennedy asserted that television could be a vehicle to advocate for the government's positive role in the lives of the country's citizenry and to educate the populace about policies, the views and actions of politicians, and national accomplishments. Kennedy understood that television

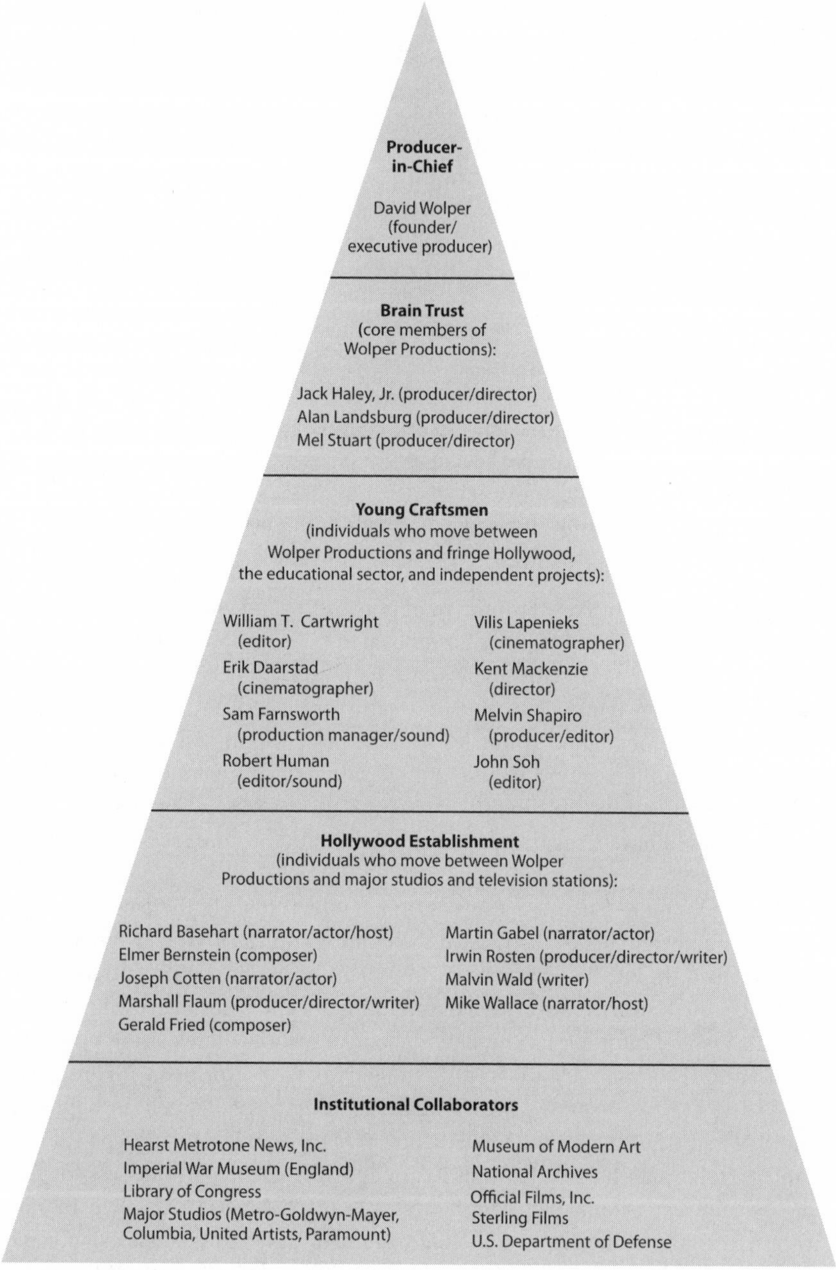

Producer-in-Chief

David Wolper
(founder/
executive producer)

Brain Trust
(core members of
Wolper Productions):

Jack Haley, Jr. (producer/director)
Alan Landsburg (producer/director)
Mel Stuart (producer/director)

Young Craftsmen
(individuals who move between
Wolper Productions and fringe Hollywood,
the educational sector, and independent projects):

William T. Cartwright
(editor)

Erik Daarstad
(cinematographer)

Sam Farnsworth
(production manager/sound)

Robert Human
(editor/sound)

Vilis Lapenieks
(cinematographer)

Kent Mackenzie
(director)

Melvin Shapiro
(producer/editor)

John Soh
(editor)

Hollywood Establishment
(individuals who move between Wolper
Productions and major studios and television stations):

Richard Basehart (narrator/actor/host)
Elmer Bernstein (composer)
Joseph Cotten (narrator/actor)
Marshall Flaum (producer/director/writer)
Gerald Fried (composer)

Martin Gabel (narrator/actor)
Irwin Rosten (producer/director/writer)
Malvin Wald (writer)
Mike Wallace (narrator/host)

Institutional Collaborators

Hearst Metrotone News, Inc.
Imperial War Museum (England)
Library of Congress
Major Studios (Metro-Goldwyn-Mayer,
Columbia, United Artists, Paramount)

Museum of Modern Art
National Archives
Official Films, Inc.
Sterling Films
U.S. Department of Defense

FIGURE 3: Wolper Productions labor network of key individuals and organizations, 1960–64. Designed by Bill Nelson.

could bolster communications between the government and its citizens and build consensus around legislation.[29] When FCC chairman Newton Minow stood before the National Association of Broadcasters and criticized the "vast wasteland" of quickly made Hollywood action-adventure serials, crime dramas, and comedies, he made it clear that he did not view the television medium itself as antithetical to the ideals of the New Frontier. He explained: "Your industry possesses the most powerful voice in America. It has an inescapable duty to make that voice ring with intelligence and with leadership. In a few years this exciting industry has grown from a novelty to an instrument of overwhelming impact on the American people."[30]

The increased cooperation between Kennedy's administration, socially engaged filmmakers, and the film and television industries was very different from some of the sociopolitical alignments of people and institutions that created television during the late 1940s and 1950s. Cultural studies scholar Anna McCarthy demonstrates that during this earlier period, corporations, philanthropic groups, reformers, labor organizers, intellectuals, and sectors of the entertainment industry prioritized the creation of programs that would educate Americans about the virtues of the free market and the rights of individuals. A large welfare state was not seen as having a critical, hands-on role in shaping Americans' day-to-day lives. With political and cultural changes toward the turn of the decade, the big three networks and independent filmmakers such as Wolper not only began to assert themselves as creative producers, but made documentaries to promote an involved relationship between an active US government and the nation's citizenry.[31]

At the turn of the decade, networks saw international politics as prime material for prestige news programming. Global media scholar Michael Curtin shows that the New York–based flagship public affairs series *CBS Reports*, *NBC White Paper*, and *ABC's Bell and Howell Close-Up!* helped build support for the country's foreign policy initiatives. He outlines how these programs depicted three main topics: the direct threat posed by the Soviet Union and the People's Republic of China to the "free world"; the struggles of nonaligned countries in Africa, Latin America, and Southeast Asia as they negotiated the prospects of capitalist democracy versus what was seen as monolithic Communism; and the connections between "home front" issues such as civil rights, American foreign policy, and the global "image" of the United States. Curtin situates these programs against the deluge of entertainment programs coming from major Hollywood studios in the early 1960s. Yet while he acknowledges public affairs documentaries' indebtedness to classical Hollywood form, he underestimates the presence of educational modes of filmmaking in Los Angeles.[32] The city proved to be an ideal place for the production of distinct and innovative modes of documentary. Wolper Productions made the expanding metropolis one of its central subjects. Indeed, the studio would gain its greatest recognition for its ability to instrumentalize both recent and more distant American history for the purpose of the Cold War.

PROGRAMMING ON THE CULTURAL FRONT

Wolper Productions' programs can be organized into two categories, what *Los Angeles Times* critic Cecil Smith referred to as Wolper's "two hats": the "porkpie" and the "sober Homburg."[33] The bulk of the former was often considered the lighter side of Wolper fare. These series and specials, for instance *Hollywood: The Golden Years* (1960) and *Hollywood: The Fabulous Era* (1962), celebrated American culture by means of a panegyric account of the film industry. These programs depicted moving pictures as a homegrown art form combining individual effort, free creative expression, and commercial acumen. Partnering with Sterling Television for their archival footage, Wolper Productions wove together clips of old films and layered the sequences with voice-overs to tell a story of how the medium developed and matured.

Both *The Golden Years* and *The Fabulous Era* featured a star-as-narrator who guided the viewer through major shifts in the film industry by using excerpts, behind-the-scenes footage to illustrate the production process, actors' screen tests, and scenes of stars enjoying their time away from work. These nostalgic "screen memories" imagined Hollywood as a story of entrepreneurial ambition, technological invention, and beloved storytelling. They also silenced or obscured labor disputes between craft personnel and management as well as racist and sexist representations and hiring practices. In *The Golden Years*, narrator Gene Kelly begins with film's emergence as a New York–based novelty, then moves to its evolution into a form of storytelling with Edwin S. Porter's *The Great Train Robbery* (1903). Kelly explains that motion pictures became affordable entertainment with the advent of the nickelodeon, D. W. Griffith's experiments with narrative form, and the post–World War I growth of the studio system. Kelly concludes with the arrival of sound film heralded by *The Jazz Singer* (1927).

In *The Fabulous Era*, narrator Henry Fonda begins where the previous program left off. After revisiting the transition to the talkies in the late 1920s, the show shifts from the Busby Berkeley musicals, Edward G. Robinson gangster films, and Mae West comedies of the 1930s to the onset of the Hays Code. *The Fabulous Era* also looks at World War II efforts on the part of Hollywood stars to serve in the armed services, participate in bond drives, and entertain troops. There is an emphasis on how plots and star performances during the Great Depression hit home with widespread frustrations of viewers around the country, but no in-depth depiction of the Cold War purging of liberalism and free speech by the House Un-American Activities Committee that occurred during the late 1940s and 1950s. *The Fabulous Era* ends with cinema's rebirth by way of new genres of big-budget historical epics and teen films, as well as alluring technologies such as Cinerama and 3D. The message is that even as television disrupts traditional patterns of film production and exhibition, industry creativity as well as audience desire for a spectacular, theater-based experience will keep Hollywood vibrant as it continues into the second half of the century. *The Fabulous Era* even demonstrates that television can teach audiences about the history of cinema and allow them to revisit their favorite films.

Hollywood: The Great Stars (1962) and the subsequent thirty-one episodes of *Hollywood and the Stars* (1963) recycled much of the previously used footage in emphasizing the appeal of charismatic actors and actresses. Occasional episodes relied heavily on observational cinematography by Vilis Lapenieks and David Blewitt. *Hollywood USA* (1963) offered spectators a drive-by tour of mansions in Beverly Hills, beach communities in Malibu, private polo fields, swimming pools, and racetracks all over the region, as well as the iconic Brown Derby restaurant and Grauman's Chinese Theatre in Hollywood.

The Rafer Johnson Story (1961) and *Biography of a Rookie: The Willie Davis Story* (1961) existed under the brim of the "sober Homburg." They developed many of the narrative techniques and themes that would be taken up in later Wolper Productions films. The Schaefer Brewing Company had asked the studio to make two short films featuring black athletes, a subject not often seen on television. The films expressed civil rights–era optimism in the idea that once black and white people recognize that they share the same aspirations, they can build toward the peaceful and productive integration of American institutions. At the same time, the films ignored the fact that systemic racism continued to function as a force excluding African Americans from educational, residential, and professional opportunities. The documentaries thus represented Pollyannaish liberal ideals rather than a wider-angle view of the on-the-ground struggle for racial equality.

In *The Rafer Johnson Story*, home-movie footage and newsreels, combined with a Mike Wallace voice-over, original interviews, and observational sequences, demonstrate Johnson's athletic and civic maturation. The African American Olympian is seen as a leader and a member of a number of interlinked communities. In high school in his hometown of Kingsburg, California, Johnson excels on the football field, on the track, and in the classroom. At UCLA in 1954, he trains as an Olympic decathlete while also becoming student body president and the first black member of the university's Pi Lambda Phi fraternity. UCLA's general manager of associated students speaks confidently about Johnson as one of the best student body presidents UCLA has ever had. His coach "Ducky" Drake says that, off the track, Johnson is "one of the finest gentlemen" he has ever known.

Preparing for the 1960 Olympics, Johnson trains at UCLA with one of his main competitors, C. K. Yang of Taiwan. Training is an athletic partnership, but here, on a symbolic level, also a partnership between Cold War allies. Their preparation touts the resources available to Yang in the United States and illustrates a process of acculturation. Putting on display collegiate life at Los Angeles's premier public institution of higher learning, Johnson and Yang shoot pool, go bowling, eat in cafés, and work out under Drake's tutelage. Johnson's victory over both Yang and

Vasily Kuznetsov in the 1960 Olympics in Rome is seen as the result of both his own individual hard work and the system that supported and encouraged him. Rather than focusing on Johnson's post-Olympic work in the entertainment business, the documentary ends with him in Washington, DC, joining the Peace Corps. Sargent Shriver awards him the special appointment of recruiter, and he is shown happily committing to formalized public service.[34] The USIA purchased twenty-five copies of the film for exhibition overseas in Nigeria and Ghana. The film also facilitated additional collaborations between Wolper Productions and the USIA. The latter hired the studio to create *Escape to Freedom* (1963), promoted as an "anticommunist feature about the Iron and Bamboo Curtains." On-location footage and émigré testimony attempt to persuade viewers that the promises of prosperity under Communist rule in East Berlin and China were a big ruse. According to *Variety*, the documentary was slated to play in 106 countries in thirty languages.[35]

Less explicitly internationalist in scope and featuring more verité-style cinematography, *Biography of a Rookie: The Willie Davis Story* is nonetheless about democracy in action, depicting a citizen's achievements within a supportive American enterprise. The documentary follows the African American baseball player Willie Davis—born in Arkansas and raised in the Los Angeles neighborhood of Boyle Heights—on his journey to secure a starting spot on the Los Angeles Dodgers. Called a "masterful, candid study" by the *Los Angeles Times*, the film begins with footage of Davis's career as a three-sport, record-holding athlete at Theodore Roosevelt High School, before tracking Davis through his extensive training sessions with scout Kenny Myers and then playing with the Dodgers farm teams.[36] The camerawork of Academy Award–winning cinematographer James Wong Howe and his assistant, Vilis Lapenieks, places the viewer alongside Davis in the dugout, the locker room, the press box, the field of competition with his teammates, and spring training at Vero Beach, Florida. Elmer Bernstein's jazz score and Mike Wallace's narration dramatize the climactic moments of Davis's performance with the Reno Silver Sox and the Spokane Indians. With each success, he makes it one step closer to the major leagues. Coaches, family, and friends discuss Davis as a passionate and devoted teammate. Davis is a rising star of America's favorite pastime and the Dodgers franchise. The documentary models how individual talent forms a complementary relationship with the technocratic prowess of a well-run organization. In a review of *Biography of a Rookie, Variety* described the Dodgers as operating with the "IBM precision" of a modern American corporation.[37]

The fact that the Dodgers would soon be playing in a state-of-the-art, automobile-friendly arena carved into the hill of Chavez Ravine contributed to the team's modern identity. The stadium could seat fifty-six thousand people—more than any other baseball stadium in the country. Important to many fans was the fact that Davis was a black athlete who was both a standout and an essential member of the team. In reviewing the film, local black sports columnist A. S. "Doc" Young wrote, "There can be no greater testimonial to Davis's titanic natural ability and guttiness [sic] than the fact that within three years, he leaped from Roosevelt High into the major leagues. . . . [He] seemed to belong from the moment he set foot into the Coliseum this year."[38] In the film, Davis climbs the company ranks through his own abilities and ambition, but is also guided by the benevolent yet demanding Dodgers staff. Trainers, coaches, statisticians, and executives track, measure, and analyze every aspect of each player's game in an attempt to maximize their performance. Davis ultimately beats the competition, rallies after he makes mistakes, and earns a spot on the team. The film concludes with Davis starting the season opener, cracking the ball and taking off in a sprint.

The focus in *The Rafer Johnson Story* and *Biography of a Rookie* on individuals excelling in noteworthy professions, rather than the subject of race relations, shaped two series that followed. Both series were not only largely created by white men, but gave the impression that white men served as the primary agents of change in the world. The sixty-five-episode *Biography* (1962–63) drew on archival footage to tell stories about well-known individuals who had influenced the course of Western civilization. The studio boasted that it had tapped archives in England, Russia, Italy, Norway, and Germany to make it. The series differentiated itself from programs like NBC's *Project XX* and CBS's *The Twentieth Century* by means of its emphasis on the personality of the featured individual and insights into his or her private life. *Biography* tended to either celebrate people as freedom-fighting military commanders, skilled artists, and generous entrepreneurs, or disparage them as fascist or communist aggressors. For example, Harry S. Truman was depicted as a soft-spoken "ordinary" man from Missouri who learned to embrace the responsibilities of government leadership. He helped win World War II and ensure a lasting peace by working with like-minded nations in the establishment of the North Atlantic Treaty Organization. The lonely and workaholic Thomas Edison suffered hardships as a child, but went on to revolutionize American life in the twentieth century. His pioneering work with the telegraph, electric lightbulb, phonograph, and kineto-scope made an indelible impact on business and leisure culture. Adolf Hitler, Fidel Castro, and Joseph Stalin were power-hungry, ruthless criminals who oppressed populations around the world. It was *Biography*'s human-interest touch and its clear delineation between the forces of good and evil that contributed to its popularity among television viewers, winning it a George Foster Peabody Award.[39]

The second series was the thirty-eight-episode *Story of . . .* (1962–64). *Story of . . .* observed the job-related endeavors of individuals, often over the course of a day. Elmer Bernstein, Gerald Fried, or Ruby Raksin's score, and the voice-over and on-location presence of television personality John Willis, guided the viewer on a tour of the individual's activities, which usually involved some kind of obstacle. As a full-page *Variety* advertisement stated, *Story of . . .* emphasized "real stories" of "real people" in "real dramatic situations."[40] It represented the breadth of professions in

American society, stressing that people are free to choose their careers and that their successes can have a social impact. *Story of . . .* also had a Los Angeles accent. This focus stemmed from the intense production schedule, which necessitated local subjects, as well as Wolper Productions' desire to spotlight citizens in its home city. The studio featured the Los Angeles philanthropist Minna Coe (*Story of a Patroness* [1963]), Lockheed Martin's test pilot Herman "Fish" Salmon (*Story of a Test Pilot* [1962]), Ferus Gallery cofounder Ed Kienholz (*Story of an Artist* [1962]), Los Angeles Fire Department chief Allen Evansen (*Story of a Fireman* [1963]), Lakers coach Fred Schaus (*Story of a Basketball Coach* [1963]), Rams halfback Jon Arnett (*Story of a Football Player* [1963]), Cheviot Hills–based writer Ray Bradbury (*Story of a Writer* [1963]), and Democratic congressman James Corman as he campaigned in Los Angeles's Twenty-Second District (*Story of a Congressman* [1963]). The series showcased Los Angeles as containing a mix of private and public enterprise and providing a welcome home for people pursuing jobs ranging from business to government to the arts.

Wolper Productions also created event-centered documentaries. *D-Day*, which appeared as DuPont's "Show of the Week" in 1962, portrays the United States in a fight against fascism. Given the shift in the geopolitical terrain between 1944 and 1962, *D-Day* was not intended as an allegory of contemporary foreign policy. In light of the thwarted Bay of Pigs invasion, another US-backed beach assault would not appear as the most successful combat strategy. And Germany was no longer a threatening fascist force. Still, in a broader sense, Wolper's depiction of D-Day as, essentially, a courageous fight in which the United States led other nations to free citizens from an oppressive regime spoke to the early-1960s Cold War outlook. The documentary begins with Dwight D. Eisenhower and allied officials at the tense planning summit in Tehran, before moving on to the battle preparations in the camps along the English coast, and then to the assault and victory at Normandy. Press releases and news articles flaunted the fact that a team of researchers had examined more than one million feet of film acquired from sources in the United States, France, and Germany. However, it was a heated debate with the old Hollywood mogul Darryl F. Zanuck over the existence of D-Day footage that most strongly established the program's factual credibility.[41]

In contrast to Wolper's use of footage, Zanuck adapted Cornelius Ryan's 1959 book *The Longest Day* into a three-hour historical fiction film—one of the most elaborate and expensive international productions to date. The decision to shoot the film in black and white and pursue Ryan's twenty-four-hour story of soldiers on opposing sides resulted in a gritty, fine-grained view of the conflict. The gargantuan scale of Zanuck's project dwarfed Wolper's television program; still, Wolper Productions' use of archival footage put Zanuck on the defensive. To justify his grandiose filmmaking practice to the public, Zanuck went on the record in a front-page *Variety* article: "I have no intention of cheating the public. . . . I will not use library footage claiming to be D-Day combat coverage because no such films exist. . . . No film camera covered the assault. I have had three editors go through all available material with a fine-tooth comb and they found nothing of an authentic nature."[42] Wolper counterattacked in the following issue, arguing that Zanuck was "entirely inaccurate" and that there was indeed footage shot that day and that Mel Stuart had acquired it. The article presented a string of supporting points that sided with Wolper. Even Jack Warner Jr., an assistant photographic officer in the United States Army who had helped plan D-Day coverage, backed Wolper's assertions.[43]

Not only did *D-Day* lay claim to a superior realism, but the films differed in both rhetoric and tone. *The Longest Day* reveals the cause and motivation for the Allied fighting over the course of the succession of skirmishes. The duty-conscious characters played by the film's forty-two stars, including the iconic cinematic war hero John Wayne, help sustain an aura of courage around World War II. *D-Day* is more pedagogical, making the political stakes and consequences of the invasion overt, but also more intimate in address. At the documentary's onset, narrator Richard Basehart appears on location in Normandy and tells the viewer that D-Day involved the greatest armada ever assembled in the fight to "liberate" an "enslaved continent." The documentary's conclusion features Franklin D. Roosevelt's June 6 radio broadcast of "Let Our Hearts Be Stout," echoing Basehart's sentiments and communicating the concept of a just war and purposeful sacrifice. Additionally, footage of the invasion showing a soldier slowly moving inland onto Omaha Beach before suddenly collapsing onto the sand in a heap provides a subtly chilling sense of the vulnerability and contingency of human life in battle.

The Longest Day was released in theaters four months after *D-Day*'s run on NBC. Both portrayals of D-Day were easy to rally behind. *The Longest Day* went on to win two Oscars and gave an economic boost to Twentieth Century–Fox. Running on a prestigious network television slot and later playing in Europe, Wolper Productions' documentary also did well. *Variety* stated that *D-Day* "proved a happy wedding of visual eloquence and narrative honesty and directness, resulting in a recollective experience that captured the spirit and significance of the original event." *Time* called it one of the ten best television programs of 1962 and opined that *D-Day* made "Hollywood war movies look like so much stagecraft."[44]

Ongoing media coverage of Wolper Productions continued to create a popular awareness of the studio. *Television* spotlighted it as "among the busiest and most prominent TV producing fixtures on the Hollywood scene." The *Santa Monica Evening Outlook* commended Wolper as a tenacious independent whose "documentaries have consistently commanded high respect from the hierarchy of television's nonfiction devotees."[45] Wolper's prominent role in various organizations complemented his New Frontiersman status. He was a board member of the Thalians charity and a founding member of Community Television of Southern California (CTSC), which lobbied to bring Los Angeles its first educational television station. A *Los Angeles Times* piece on the fight for the station featured a pencil-sketched double portrait of Wolper and CTSC executive secretary Rose Blyth. The caption refers to Wolper as an "educational TV expert." Wolper's support for educational TV reflected positively on the producer as a proponent of progressive broadcasting.[46] In the article "Will 1962 Be Documentary Year?," *Broadcasting* discussed Wolper Productions as a trailblazer in the field.[47]

At first glance, Wolper Productions appears quite different from the other renowned independent documentary organization at the time, Drew Associates. The latter company was based in New York and led by *Life* journalist-turned-producer Robert Drew. Drew Associates consisted of a small-staffed unit that included Richard Leacock, James Lipscomb, Albert Maysles, D. A. Pennebaker, Hope Ryden, and Gregory Shuker. Drew set up the projects and oversaw their development. Individuals each had areas of expertise but assumed fluid roles in the process of shooting, editing, and sound recording. Wolper Productions, on the other hand, was based on a studio model that involved a wider pool of specialized talent contributing to a larger volume of films. Beyond the different organizational models, members of Drew Associates were primarily interested in how new, lightweight, mobile cameras and advances in the synchronous recording of sound and image could intimately capture professional routines and political events. In a roundtable interview with Drew, Pennebaker, and Leacock for *Film Culture*, Drew said that what made his team's practice different from standard news reporting and documentary filmmaking is that they followed individuals as they "c[a]me against moments of tension, and pressure, and revelation, and decision." Drew Associates viewed filming as a process of quietly observing rather than intervening in the action. They edited according to a "dramatic logic" that emerged organically over the course of the shoot rather than overtly trying to shape the material to convey a pedagogical message.[48] This approach to observational cinema was becoming increasingly referred to by filmmakers as well as international film journals as an American version of cinema verité or "direct cinema."

Wolper and his circle didn't claim a noninterventionist approach. They viewed their films as expository narratives created by means of the joint efforts of technicians, craftspeople, administrators, and subject experts. Mobile, observational cinematography would often be used as a stylistic flourish or interwoven into a story told through a combination of archival footage, voice-over, non-diegetic music, an on-screen narrator, and interviews. There was an overt charge to teach and entertain people about a given topic. However, a number of strong similarities connected Drew Associates to Wolper Productions. Led by charismatic producers-in-chief, both enterprises were invested in filming people in real-life situations (rather than actors in imagined scenarios) and saw their documentaries as offering a truthful perspective on a subject. Additionally, both companies rose to prominence around the turn of the decade and occupied distinct but complementary positions on the cultural front of the New Frontier. Wolper Productions and Drew Associates both tried to maintain creative autonomy over their work, and both outfits created documentaries for television that resonated with the Cold War liberal values of the current presidential administration. Drew Associates' films frequently concentrated on gifted citizens overcoming a hurdle in their professional endeavors or members of the Kennedy inner circle successfully navigating their way through political crises. Some of Wolper Productions' documentaries focused on the contemporary experiences of Americans in demanding professions, but the studio more often specialized in digging deeper into the American past.[49]

As Wolper Productions increased its output, it created new narratives based on prior programs. The acquisition rather than the renting of footage proved essential to the company's practice of creating history for the small screen. In 1963 Wolper Productions purchased Paramount News and its news film library, giving the studio ten million feet of film shot between 1927 and 1957.[50] Specials on historic events, profiles of entertainers such as *The Legend of Marilyn Monroe* (1964), and the *Men in Crisis* (1964–65) series expanded on familiar subjects. With the assassination of Kennedy, the studio's films on the president stood out as prestige productions. They performed an important social function during a critical period of transition in political leadership.

MEMORY MANAGEMENT AND THE IMAGE OF JFK

The shooting of President Kennedy on November 22, 1963, created a logistical and epistemological challenge for the television networks. News anchors based in New York struggled to cover the disaster in Dallas; limited by technological capability as well as by the fact that the action was unfolding in real time, they had difficulty creating a coherent account of what had happened. As documentary theorist Philip Rosen writes, news anchors received and relayed pieces of information from disparate sources—fragmentary "documents" in the form of newspaper wire service reports, sound recordings, and photographs. These newscasts, Rosen argues, help to highlight the difference between television reportage and documentary. The latter requires enough "production time and cultural time" to integrate "documents" into a stable narrative with a "synthesizing knowledge claim."[51] As initial news coverage of the Kennedy assassination registered a sense of shock and trauma, the "Black Weekend" reporting provided a way for spectators to feel deeply connected to and even present at the funerary procession and ceremonies that followed.[52] But documentaries, too, quickly served a social function. Created in the aftermath of the assassination, Wolper Productions' *The Making of the President: 1960* (1963) and *Four Days in November* (1964) were crucial to the mourning process. Documentary scholar P. J. O'Connell shows that Drew Associates tracked Kennedy's rise to the presidency in *Primary* (1960), captured his administration in action in *Crisis: Behind a Presidential Commitment* (1963), and even documented his funeral in the twelve-minute *Faces of November* (1964).[53] But Wolper Productions was the true custodian of the Kennedy memory. The studio contributed to the effort by the government, the Kennedy family, and factions of the press to mythologize the fallen president's life. The Bay of Pigs debacle, Kennedy's weak stance on civil rights, his marital infidelities, and his use of political power overseas to advance US economic interests were all hidden from the public eye. These films were narratives of assurance for a shaken nation and helped establish a bridge between Kennedy and Lyndon B. Johnson.

Plans for *The Making of the President: 1960* began in 1962. Theodore H. White's Pulitzer Prize–winning campaign-trail account of Kennedy's 1960 presidential election was a work of political boosterism. His book stood in contrast to Norman Mailer's *Esquire* piece on Kennedy at the 1960 Democratic Convention, "Superman Comes to the Supermarket." Mailer assumed a critical and at times ironic relationship with his subject. The article describes the collective American psyche teetering between elation and anxiety on the eve of nominating the "movie star" candidate in Los Angeles, where "one has the feeling [that the city] was built by television sets giving orders to men."[54] White, for his part, saw politics as a series of dramatic confrontations between competitors jostling for power. His liberal anticommunist beliefs and narrative style aligned his work with America's Cold War aims and conjured an eager audience for his writing. Describing in florid detail the intricate network of establishments, gathering spaces, and personalities that comprised the election of 1960, White praised the democratic qualities of American elections as well as Kennedy's charisma and leadership abilities.[55]

Wolper Productions acquired the rights to White's book and hired the author to write the narration. Elmer Bernstein was brought in for the score, and crime film actor Martin Gabel (*Deadline-U.S.A.* [1952], *M* [1951]) was hired as narrator. William Cartwright, who had studied with montage artist Slavko Vorkapić at USC in the early 1950s, edited the film. Adapting close to four hundred pages to fit a ninety-minute TV slot, White greatly reduced the detail devoted to each town, rally, and hotel along the campaign routes. Still, the documentary format was well suited for recording Kennedy's camera-friendly persona, which White determined to be so vital to the election. According to White, the first Kennedy-Nixon debate gave "voters of a great democracy a living portrait of two men under stress and let the voters decide, by instinct and emotion, which style and pattern of behavior under stress they preferred in their leader."[56] In the film, one becomes aware of how the staging of the debate for the mass media—what cultural theorist Daniel J. Boorstin called a "pseudo-event"—placed emphasis less on discussion between candidates and more on each candidate's relationship to his surroundings in the studio and to the American public.[57] One sees producer Don Hewitt instruct technicians in preparation for the debate. Gabel's voice-over comments on the respective performances. With the debate under way, Kennedy shrewdly directs his opening address outward to viewers rather than to his opponent. Although Nixon had prior experience with television, he treats the exchange as if there are no cameras. He has a poor conception of address, tone, and stage presence. He disregards his appearance and responds directly to Kennedy and thus alienates himself from the audience. Gabel states, "Ill at ease, under strain, dressed in a suit of gray that blends into the background, Nixon in this first debate leaves a disappointing image in the minds of millions of Americans."

The film does more than just register the Kennedy effect. Like its textual counterpart, it spotlights American politics itself as participatory and riveting to watch. The documentary's movement through key events guides the spectator along the path of the campaign trail, from stump speeches over the course of the Democratic and Republican primaries, to the respective conventions in Los Angeles and Chicago, to the first round of the debates, and, finally, to the showdown between Kennedy and Nixon on election night. Fleshing out this footage, much of which was taken from broadcasters, is an array of candid shots drawn from campaign press departments or other documentary organizations. For example, Wolper used a scene charged with quiet intensity from the Drew Associates film *Primary*. The scene shows Kennedy and his staff in Milwaukee's Pfister Hotel the night of the Wisconsin primary. The integration of the scene into *The Making of the President* emphasizes the contrast between the two documentaries. With sparse voice-over, *Primary* provides viewers with an embodied experience of looking at the inner workings of a high-pressure campaign and conjures a magnetic image of Kennedy by means of fluid handheld shots and close-ups. *The Making of the President* positions direct cinema-style sequences into a rigid expository structure that teaches viewers about the allegiances of groups of voters, the implications of Kennedy's margin of victory, and the candidates' course of action for the next round of primaries.[58]

The Making of the President was in postproduction at the moment of Kennedy's death. The decision to not alter the film or delay its premiere was both practical and strategic. An earlier airdate made the film seem timelier. Additionally, changing the narrative would have proved costly. White, who was the intellectual face of the project, offered an on-screen preface to the documentary, telling viewers that because Kennedy "loved American politics" it was fitting to tell the story of the election of 1960 in "candid recollection." "Candid recollection" did not so much involve debating Kennedy's policy initiatives or personal conduct. Rather, the unaltered film placed Kennedy and the political process of which he was a part in a virtuous light. It echoed White's recent elegiac articles in *Life* that discussed Kennedy as a "man of gallantry and of action, of motion and of the trumpet," and his presidency as "Camelot."[59] *The Making of the President* pressed the theme of continuity. The film depicts democratic politics as an open, dynamic dialogue and as a process that continues beyond the leadership of any one individual. This affirmation of stability and

FIGURE 4: Still from *The Making of the President: 1960*, 1963, 16mm;
directed by Mel Stuart; produced by David L. Wolper Productions;
broadcast on ABC. Courtesy of Matthew Windsor, private collection.

cohesiveness within a system encouraged a smooth sense of transition in a time of
social rupture. In the film's closing scene Kennedy shakes hands with Eisenhower on
the day of his inauguration, and Gabel declares, "So power passes." The alliterative
phrase refers to the move from Eisenhower to Kennedy but can also be interpreted
as having a broader resonance—that the passing of power within the electoral process is a constitutive ritual of American democracy.

Even though Wolper was taking a look back at the former president's ascend-
ancy to office, all Kennedy-related topics were considered sensitive news. Therefore, Wolper had difficulty getting a network release. All three networks initially
declined the pitch. However, after ABC president Leonard Goldenson saw the program, he liked it so much that he agreed to run it. *The Making of the President* aired
on December 29, 1963, and won Emmy Awards for Outstanding Achievement in
Documentary Programs, Best Editing, and Best Musical Score. *Los Angeles Times*
journalist Cecil Smith wrote, "The show is a remarkable slab of history, perhaps
the most remarkable in electronic journalism," and emphasized that "the production was assembled by David L. Wolper's enterprising organization . . . the only
major independent producer of documentaries in television."[60] Publisher and
journalist John Tebbel praised the documentary for its ability to lay bare the mechanisms of American democracy and make viewers feel that they were welcomed
members of this inclusive system.[61]

Arthur Krim, chairman of United Artists and advisor to President Johnson,
summoned Wolper to the White House about the prospects of making two documentaries for the Democratic National Convention in Atlantic City in August.

In consultation with Krim, Johnson, and special aide Jack Valenti, Wolper Productions made *The Quest for Peace* (1964). The film highlights Johnson as a skilled diplomat and shrewd mediator of global conflicts. The studio also made *A Thousand Days: A Tribute to John F. Kennedy* (1964), which recounts Kennedy's achievements and character. Together, these films built support for a forward-looking Johnson by emphasizing the theme of continuity between the two administrations.

Wolper soon began planning a film on the Kennedy assassination itself. *Four Days in November* was an adaptation of the joint United Press International–American Heritage Magazine national best seller *Four Days: The Historical Record of the Death of President Kennedy*. Both organizations signed on as coproducers of the film and supplied many of the primary documents that analyst Jeff Myrow, editor Bill Cartwright, and director Mel Stuart used to make the feature-length documentary. Wolper brought the idea of the film to Krim, who suggested a theatrical release. This move from the small to the big screen would allow the studio to reach audiences via a new platform and help distinguish *Four Days in November* from television documentaries and news coverage.

The film complemented the Warren Commission Report, the government's official summary judgment of the assassination. The report, which affirmed that Lee Harvey Oswald acted alone in killing Kennedy, and that Jack Ruby also acted alone in killing Oswald, was released just nine days prior to the premiere of *Four Days in November* on October 6, 1964, at RKO Keith's Theatre in Washington, DC. The film was shown to seventeen hundred politicians, journalists, and members of the entertainment community.[62] According to the *Chicago Tribune*'s Marlyn E. Aycock, the script was even "read for accuracy by the Warren commission counsel."[63] *Variety* noted that Wolper was making adjustments to the film up until its release to account for the report's findings.[64] *Four Days in November* gained credibility from the official state perspective, but it also lent credibility to this perspective, making it more palatable to the public. Myrow flaunted the studio's research effort in the *Boston Globe*:

> Up to the last minute, we were on the phone with Chief Curry in Dallas; also talking to members of the White House staff, and to other people who had factual knowledge of events. At last count, we had clipped articles from some 700 magazines, domestic and foreign. Every word that such papers as the *New York Times* printed on it. Every book that was published was covered word by word.[65]

Wolper Productions foregrounded its sources in the film's prologue, listing many of them in the opening shots. Myrow, Stuart, and Cartwright molded their source material into a narrative that follows Kennedy's movements, beginning with his trip to San Antonio and Houston to inspect aerospace installations and to attempt to restore party unity. The film then shifts to the shooting in Dallas, the transport of Kennedy's body from Parkland Hospital to the Bethesda naval hospital, its display in the Capitol rotunda, the funerary procession down Pennsylvania Avenue, and, finally, the burial at Arlington National Cemetery. Another narrative strand follows Lee Harvey Oswald. Cinematographer Vilis Lapenieks's first-person perspective retraces Oswald's path of action, beginning with his commute from the suburb of Irving. He then moves to his hideout position in the Texas School Book Depository, takes a taxi back to his rooming house, is arrested in a movie theater, and is shot and killed by Jack Ruby. The details of the crime are explained through photographs, local news footage, and pertinent testimony from Oswald's cabdriver, police officers, and coworkers at the Depository who spoke with Oswald on the day of the killing.

The two narrative strands converge at Mary Moorman's grainy black-and-white photograph and Orville Nix's 8mm footage of the motorcade capturing the fatal gunshot. In the buildup to the shooting, long shots of the motorcade moving along its downtown route are crosscut with the simulated point of view of Oswald from his perch in the Depository. Bernstein's score overlays the radio narration of the procession, infusing the scene with a feeling of anticipation. With the music coming to a halt, the sound of a gunshot rings out. One sees an extreme close-up of Moorman's image of a convulsing Kennedy and his wife, Jacqueline, reaching for him. For four seconds the image is stilled and all sound is stopped. Subsequently, a siren blares as Orville Nix's footage shows Secret Service agent Clint Hill climbing aboard the back of the Lincoln as the motorcade speeds away. This reflexive moment calls attention to both still photographs and moving-image footage as material forms of representation able to retain the indexical trace of "the real." This is also a moment of dramatic climax, as the pregnant silence and arresting photograph evoke the ending of a life. The prolonged image that registers the physical impact of the bullet resonates with the emotional impact of the assassination felt by the world.

Following Kennedy's death, *Four Days in November* provided a kind of therapy for film viewers by socializing their grief. The scenes of the funeral make visible an eclectic array of people filing into the darkened Capitol rotunda to see the coffin and crowding Pennsylvania Avenue. Newscasters, politicians, and everyday citizens talk about Kennedy as a great man, what he stood for, and how deeply hurt and frustrated they feel for the loss. In Drew Associates' *Faces of November*, the montage of sorrowful faces along with images of flags at half-mast surrounding the Washington Monument grounds the grieving in a distinct, almost hallowed, sense of place. *Four Days in November* uses this sentiment as a way to sketch an expansive narrative of Kennedy's life and death. Kennedy is seen as the embodiment of youth and cosmopolitan style, possessing a vision for the United States' leadership of the "free world." Oswald is not portrayed as a pure embodiment of evil per se but rather as disturbed, a person who wrongly devoted himself to the opposite of the American values that Kennedy espoused.

Like the Warren Commission Report, *Four Days in November* closes down alternative narrative possibilities concerning the assassination and seeks to confine ambiguity to the troubled psyches of Oswald and Ruby. Journalists echoed the studio's goal of providing the authoritative historical record on the assassination. Advertisements announced that the documentary gave a "minute-by-minute, hour-by-hour, day-by-day story—with every detail revealed, every question answered."[66] The *Chicago Tribune* announced: "Every moment of this two-hour documentary is tragic history on film." Alex Freeman of the *Hartford Courant* proclaimed that *Four Days in November* is in the "great tradition of Wolper documentaries" and that materials gathered are "spliced into a breath-taking visual offering of evidence to confirm many conclusions arrived at by the Warren Commission."[67] Together, Wolper Productions' two Kennedy films made vivid the state's official perspective of the president's death and played a significant role in his commemoration. The studio contributed to what the left-leaning public intellectual Carey McWilliams had by 1964 designated as a pervasive media trend toward the mythologizing of Kennedy.[68] The immediate years to come saw the appearance of hagiographic biographies such as *Kennedy* (1965) and *A Thousand Days: John F. Kennedy in the White House* (1965) along with the documentaries *The Age of Kennedy* (1966) and the USIA-commissioned *John F. Kennedy: Years of Lightning, Day of Drums* (1964/66).

Wolper Productions had been a vital force in the cultural Cold War. The studio stood poised to continue crafting presidential portraits and documentaries about high-achieving citizens, the entertainment industry, and the perils of communism and fascism. But these were not the only works of nonfiction emanating from Los Angeles during the early 1960s. Local, university-trained filmmakers, some of whom were affiliated with Wolper Productions, struggled in the shadow of Hollywood to create more personal, resistant forms of documentary that conjoined art and social protest.

Downtown Development and the Endeavors of Filmmaker Kent Mackenzie

We were fascinated by this complex and rapidly changing life we saw around us and felt it was our duty to examine it.
—FILMMAKER KENT MACKENZIE, 1964[1]

Making the cover of the spring 1962 "Hollywood" issue of *Film Quarterly* gave the acclaimed documentary *The Exiles* (1961) and its creator Kent Mackenzie substantial visibility and renown.[2] Taken from the film's title and closing image, the journal's cover features an extreme long shot of a small group of American Indians in early-morning Bunker Hill. Framed by the Sunshine Apartments to the right and the Angels Flight funicular railway above and in front of them, they walk down Clay Street. Their previous night in downtown Los Angeles began in a clapboard apartment on the same block before moving to the bars on Main Street, then on to Hill X overlooking Chavez Ravine (soon to be Dodger Stadium), and then back to their respective homes. *Film Quarterly*'s decision to highlight an experimental documentary made by a white liberal filmmaker about the daily lives of minority Angelenos in a working-class part of the city was not as strange as it might initially seem. Besides the fact that Mackenzie's former mentor at USC, Andries Deinum, served as an advisor to the publication, *Film Quarterly* had always been a forum where a wide spectrum of cinema was discussed. Throughout the journal's previous iterations it had remained dedicated to examining film and television in Los Angeles and how filmmakers struggled to express themselves from within, draw on the resources of, and attempt to separate themselves from mainstream Hollywood. Interviews with directors, reviews of new technology, and essays on contemporary films exposed readers to recent trends in American moviemaking as well as global New Wave cinema and festivals.[3] In this issue journalist Benjamin Jackson praised *The Exiles* in a review and Mackenzie himself participated in a roundtable discussion titled "Personal Creation in Hollywood: Can It Be Done?"

FIGURE 5: Cover, *Film Quarterly* 15, no. 3 (Spring 1962). Courtesy of University of California Press.

Filmmaker Thom Andersen's excavation of Hollywood's selective memory of its home metropolis, *Los Angeles Plays Itself* (2003), gave special notice to *The Exiles* as representing what was often hidden or obscured from view in studio-created fiction. Andersen sees the film as a testament to the more human-scale and walkable city that preceded downtown's flashy hotels, office buildings, and parking lots: "Better than any other movie, it proves that there once was a city here, before they tore it down and built a simulacrum." Andersen would later write in *Film Comment* that "*The Exiles* is the most concrete and detailed record we have of these doomed spaces."[4] *Los Angeles Plays Itself* helped put Mackenzie's documentary on the radar of scholars, preservationists, and cinephiles. In 2008 Milestone Films, USC, and UCLA joined forces to restore *The Exiles*. It was rereleased in theaters that same year, and was selected for the National Film Registry by the Library of Congress in 2009. As a result, *The Exiles* has found enthusiastic audiences within and beyond the academy. Despite this second life, however, little attention has been paid to the cultural context in which it emerged and the project's relationship to Mackenzie's other filmmaking endeavors.

Like Mackenzie's student documentary on elderly pensioners in Bunker Hill, *The Exiles* countered popular understandings of the area's social identity and defied urban planners' vision of a lucrative downtown. *The Exiles* demonstrated that downtown was not simply a blighted landscape in need of sweeping demolition and redevelopment, but a populated area in which marginalized communities lived. The film also challenged the lofty tenets of President John F. Kennedy's "New Frontier" platform by engaging with the conflicted legacy of America's old frontier mythology. Showing American Indians' daily routines critiqued the stereotypes of them as historical peoples of the past who were no longer part of the national polity, or as a victimized people of the present, suffering in impoverished reservations and urban slums.

Mackenzie brought great passion to the project, but its construction was nonetheless arduous. In the same *Film Quarterly* issue that featured *The Exiles* on the cover, he expressed his frustrations during the roundtable led by the journal's Los Angeles editor and UCLA professor Colin Young and critic Pauline Kael. Fellow roundtable filmmakers John Houseman (*Lust for Life* [1956], *All Fall Down* [1962]), Irvin Kershner (*Stakeout on Dope Street* [1958], *The Hoodlum Priest* [1961]), and Terry Sanders (*Crime and Punishment, USA* [1959], *War Hunt* [1962]) talked about strategies for retaining one's artistic integrity in a money-driven and risk-averse industry.[5] Mackenzie declared his personal discomfort with the task of trying to carve out a space for himself in a large studio and the difficultly of working outside the commercial system. He was disheartened by how long *The Exiles* had taken to complete, the uncertainty of its future, and the fact that it did not model a path forward for future endeavors. He had hoped that the project would appeal to an art cinema audience interested in topical issues. However, after a year of planning and research, three years of shooting and editing, and a year on the festival circuit, the documentary was badly in need of distribution.

As *The Exiles* continued to garner attention and play in festivals and small venues in the 1960s, Mackenzie worked in the city's growing documentary sector. Like many of his colleagues, he made films for Wolper Productions and the United States Information Agency (USIA), both of which played leading roles in America's cultural Cold War against the Soviet Union. These jobs offered the chance to make films about charismatic human subjects and afforded a degree of creative autonomy, but they also required that the films conform to the ideological strictures of their parent organizations. Mackenzie's career is illustrative in this regard, shaped as it was by a powerful combination of political forces as well as critical shifts in the film and television industries.

THE POLITICS OF PEDAGOGY

Mackenzie first studied film at Dartmouth College with Benfield Pressey, an English professor whose interests in teaching cinema had led him to Hollywood to observe production up close.[6] After graduating in 1951 and serving for two years as an aircraft control officer in the US Air Force, Mackenzie went to Los Angeles in search of training that would prepare him for a career in motion pictures. He enrolled in the cinema department at USC during a time when university film education was booming. This trend was the consequence of three factors: the GI Bill, which enabled veterans to attend college for little to no cost; the post–Paramount Decree restructuring of major studios, which dissolved the traditional pattern of mentor-based systems of training; and the diversifying market for film and television, which required local skilled labor that could be hired on a short-term basis. Programs at UCLA, Boston University, Northwestern University, New York University, and especially USC were geared toward technical training as well as providing coursework in film theory, history, and style.[7]

Editor Melvin Sloan, cinematographer Ralph Woolsey, and sound technician Dan Wiegand taught Mackenzie to use the equipment and to effectively collaborate with a crew. The aspiring filmmaker gained a socially conscious orientation to the medium through the documentary and cultural history courses of Andries Deinum. The Dutch left-liberal émigré served as a production clerk and director for Twentieth Century–Fox, a research director for Douglas Sirk's *A Scandal in Paris* (1946), and a technical advisor for Fritz Lang's *Cloak and Dagger* (1946). Deinum was an advocate for progressive causes and the increased presence of minorities in the film and television industries. He was close friends with John Kinloch, managing editor of the black newspaper the *California Eagle*, and the Dutch filmmaker Joris Ivens, whom he hosted whenever Ivens visited the city.[8] When the House Un-American Activities Committee came to Los Angeles in 1947, Deinum stood up to the Red Scare. He helped build a case to defend the "unfriendly witnesses" subpoenaed to testify before the committee about their relationship to the Communist Party and suspected dissident actions. He later stated that he was "deeply involved in organizing conferences, meetings, and broadcasts around the issue, and kept materials relating to [the Hollywood 19]."[9] Deinum's involvement with the hearings and his association with Ivens resulted in his being blacklisted by the studios. He managed to find a sympathetic employer in USC professor Lester Beck, who hired him to teach cinema studies courses beginning in the early 1950s.

Aware of what Red-baiting could do to careers, Deinum was no activist in the classroom, but taught a liberal humanist approach to film. He recognized motion picture technology as possessing the ability to capture people in a distinct way. As he would later write in *Speaking for Myself: A Humanist Approach to Adult Education for a Technical Age*: "Film, alone of the arts, can display fully rounded, infinitely complicated human beings within their actual environment, interacting with it, and with each other; thus, it can show us the very processes of contemporary living as they occur."[10] When used effectively, film could lead to an in-depth understanding of human experience and the social and material conditions that impact peoples' lives. Recalling his time in Deinum's seminars, Mackenzie noted that he and classmates Erik Daarstad, John Morrill, Warren Brown, Robert Kaufman, Sam Farnsworth, and Vilis Lapenieks discussed these issues in relation to several key films: Robert Flaherty's ethnographic *Nanook of the North* (1922) and *Moana* (1926), Joris Ivens's Popular Front–themed *The Spanish Earth* (1937) and *Power and the Land* (1940), Jean Renoir's poetic *Grand Illusion* (1937), George Stoney's instructional *All My Babies: A Midwife's Own Story* (1953), Vittorio De Sica's neorealist *Bicycle Thieves* (1948), and Sidney Meyers's social documentary *The Quiet One* (1949).[11]

USC proved to be intellectually nourishing for Mackenzie and his peers. Unfortunately, it failed to provide a safe haven for Deinum. HUAC called Deinum to testify in 1955, at which point he admitted to having once been a member of the Communist Party, but refused to name his compatriots: "I could not bring upon people who were to my knowledge innocent of any subversive intent the mental suffering that has befallen me. . . . The mentioning of names would have saved me a great deal of trouble, but it would have smashed me inside and ruined me as a man."[12] When USC president Fred D. Fagg Jr. suspended Deinum, Mackenzie and his friends formed a protest committee and sent a student petition to the president to try and get their mentor reinstated.[13] Despite this effort, the un-tenured Deinum was summarily dismissed. Commenting on the incident, Martin Hall's article for the *American Socialist*, "Decline of a University," concluded with the statement: "Perhaps [Fagg] was too busy with preparations for the highly publicized 75th anniversary of the University to realize that by cheating students of their right to academic freedom he was writing another chapter in the process of decline of a once free university."[14] Barred from jobs in Los Angeles, Deinum joined the faculty at Portland State University, where he made his intellectual presence felt as a teacher in the classroom, organizer in the community, and member of *Film Quarterly*'s advisory board.[15]

Deinum's teachings continued to influence his students at USC after his departure. Mackenzie's fifteen-minute 16mm documentary *Bunker Hill–1956* (1956) took a stand against redevelopment in downtown Los Angeles by spotlighting those threatened with displacement. The documentary looked specifically at a group of elderly pensioners living in Bunker Hill, a neighborhood loosely bordered by First Street (north), Hill Street (east), Fifth Street (south), and the Harbor Freeway (west).[16] For years the area had been the subject of heated municipal planning debates. Bunker Hill was once the nineteenth-century stronghold of rich and powerful Angelenos, such as USC founder Judge R. M. Widney and mining and real estate magnate Lewis L. Bradbury. Beginning in the 1910s and accelerating post–World War I, the area's wealthy white inhabitants followed the city's expansion westward and working-class blacks, Mexicans, Italians, artists, single women, and the elderly streamed into the neighborhood. With Bunker Hill's demographic shift, aging housing stock, and low tax base, the locale quickly developed a reputation as dangerous and decrepit. The crime novels of Raymond Chandler and low-budget Hollywood detective films frequently featured Bunker Hill, amplifying this reputation. Cultural historian Eric Avila notes that "film noir cast Bunker Hill as Southern California's heart of darkness, a site that harbored crime, fear, and psychosis."[17] Drawing on the zeal of New Deal housing reform and aware of the need to accommodate the city's expanding population, urban planners, politicians, and civic organizations proposed that the government should clear areas containing substandard buildings, revamp the commercial infrastructure, and create low-cost housing options for the area's residents.[18]

The city's Community Redevelopment Agency considered several options along these lines. Following the passage of the 1949 Housing Act, the Los Angeles Housing Authority entered into a federal contract for the creation of ten thousand units. Special assistant to the Housing Authority Frank Wilkinson led the charge to sell the concept, pushing for clearance of blighted areas as well as the creation of new (and in some cases integrated) public housing complexes complete with indoor plumbing, ventilation, and green space. Wilkinson and the Housing Authority teamed up with USC students Algernon G. Walker and Gene Petersen on the documentary *And Ten Thousand More* (1951) to build support for public housing. Taking cues from the British social documentary *Housing Problems* (1935), the film focused on a peripatetic reporter investigating the so-called "slums" around Chavez Ravine, Bunker Hill, and First Street and Alameda, then declaring the need for modern and spacious public housing units.[19] The documentary, like Wilkinson's other efforts, showed concern for providing affordable housing for the city's low-income residents, but also demonstrated a lack of understanding regarding their local geographic ties. The Red Scare ultimately crippled the cause for public housing initiatives. *Los Angeles Times* publisher Norman Chandler and chief of police William Parker stoked hysteria surrounding collective living as socialist and anti-American. The election of business-backed, conservative mayor Norris Poulson in 1953 marked a decidedly anti–public housing and pro-corporate direction for the city.

At the time when Mackenzie began making his student film in 1955, city officials were fast embracing urban renewal plans that benefited private interests and the civic elite rather than the public welfare. As seen from City Hall, the vision involved restructuring Bunker Hill in order to integrate it with the metropolis and facilitate a fluid expansion of the central business district. Organizations such as Greater Los Angeles Plans Incorporated and the Downtown Businessmen's Association advocated that the city move in this direction. Hotels, cultural institutions, and office buildings, along with accompanying parking lots, roads, and plazas,

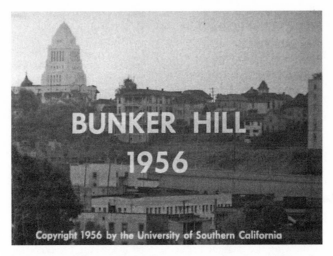

FIGURE 6: Still from *Bunker Hill–1956*, 1956, 16mm; written, directed, and edited by Kent Mackenzie; photographed and edited by Robert Kaufman. Courtesy of the University of Southern California School of Cinematic Arts' Hugh M. Hefner Moving Image Archive.

were the hallmarks of the prospective plans.[20] In contrast, Mackenzie's *Bunker Hill–1956* was boldly voiced dissent against the proposed top-down transformation of downtown. The documentary records how residents feel about their neighborhood and shows their efforts to sustain their community in the face of displacement. The film's title shot signals this threat. A spectral City Hall looms over swaths of razed hillside and old buildings such as the Brousseau Mansion, the Earl Cliffe, and the Alta Vista. The opening voice-over, read against an extreme long shot of downtown, sketches the stakes surrounding redevelopment:

> Close to the city center in downtown Los Angeles is a small residential area known as Bunker Hill. The Community Redevelopment Agency, a city agency created to clear slums, has selected Bunker Hill for a multimillion-dollar redevelopment project. The Community Redevelopment Agency hopes to condemn and buy all the property from the present owners, to move the eight thousand residents out, to demolish the buildings, and then to sell the cleared land to individuals and corporations who can afford to build in accordance with the agency's master plan.

This statement sets the terms of contest. Present-day residents are being moved out by forces beyond their control to make way for a new and modern downtown.

After several newspaper headlines show the redevelopment plans, the film shifts from a bird's-eye perspective to an on-the-ground exploration of Bunker Hill. Testimony from druggist Louis Mellon, cobbler William Varney, and doctor James

Green, coupled with a range of views of domestic interiors and scenes of commerce and interpersonal interaction, register how residents are rooted in place. Mellon opens his Angels Flight Pharmacy and a customer makes a purchase. Working in his shoe repair shop, Varney files down a heel and then goes home for lunch. Dr. Green checks the blood pressure of a patient. The Angels Flight railway brings residents to the bustling Grand Central Market. People gather for drinks and conversation at the Montana Cafe and Bar (where Mackenzie himself is in the crowd) or sit for a quiet respite on street-side benches lining Third Street and Grand Avenue. Emily Mills shapes little clay sculptures at her desk while listening to her radio. Besides periodic pans or tilts, the generally static position of the camera during these scenes of everyday life contributes to the sense of strongly willed desire for stability. The residents state that they are not opposed to change as such, but want a municipal strategy that favors rehabilitation over displacement. Mellon announces:

> If they really had an equitable plan for the benefit of the majority, they would come up with an idea to rehabilitate this area and let the same people that live here now stay here. . . . Their method of going about it is to not only clear the slums, but clear all the people out, and re-beautify the whole thing, put an opera house up here, make a picture area out of it, without keeping the inhabitants in mind at all.

Other residents echo this sentiment. They are in favor of a revitalization effort that seeks to renovate aging housing stock (most of it created before 1920), connect inhabitants to public services, and build up the commercial and residential infrastructure. Residents want to have some input as to the present and future of their own neighborhood. And if they have to move, they want to be part of the decision-making process, both for the practical reason of ensuring that they can afford a new home, and to feel that they are playing an active role in deciding their own future. Relocation conjures angst about the severing of bonds, and fears as to where the next move will take them and how much it will cost.

USC made *Bunker Hill–1956* available to the educational film sector as a way to promote discussion about urban revitalization. Journalists also praised the documentary as a well-made and moving film. *Variety* and USC's newspaper, the *Daily Trojan*, enthusiastically noted that Mackenzie's documentary played at the Edinburgh and Venice film festivals. The *Los Angeles Times* ran a picture of Mackenzie when he won the Silver Medallion award from the Screen Producers Guild and *Look* magazine. USC department head Robert Hall submitted the documentary to Margaret Herrick to be considered for an Academy Award, including in his submission letter that the film was successfully screened at the Flaherty Seminar.[21] Despite this positive reception, *Bunker Hill–1956* did not alter the immediate course of redevelopment planning. It did, however, give voice to a community that was rarely seen or heard, and led to Mackenzie's future filmmaking endeavors in downtown Los Angeles.

EXILES ON MAIN STREET

At the same time that Hollywood documentarian David Wolper was shifting from distribution to production, Mackenzie began working in educational film firms scattered across Sunset Boulevard, Las Palmas Avenue, and Temple Street. These companies catered primarily to schools, corporations, and religious organizations looking to use 16mm nonfiction as a teaching tool. The combination of the Sputnik launch, scandals in the broadcasting industry, and the Kennedy administration's attentiveness to the pedagogical power of audiovisual technology would soon increase nonfiction opportunities, especially as the television market expanded over the course of the decade. Making an award-winning film at USC facilitated Mackenzie's employment. Laboring in the educational sector offered a steady stream of jobs, the ability to continue pursuing nonfiction media, and the chance to develop his own projects in his free time. Beyond serving as an editor and cinematographer for the Frederick K. Rockett Company, Modernage Photos, Telecast Productions, and the William Brown Company, Mackenzie led the documentary unit for Parthenon Pictures. Catering to clients such as Bell Telephone Laboratories, the American Petroleum Institute, and Merrill Lynch, Parthenon styled itself as a boutique firm, proudly stating in *Business Screen Magazine* that it made films that were "handled personally and with quality by its key group" rather than generating mass-produced "commercials."[22]

Early on in his tenure at Parthenon, Mackenzie read a *Harper's Magazine* article that piqued his curiosity about a promising topic. "The Raid on the Reservations" castigated House Concurrent Resolution 108, a policy that essentially terminated the treaties and legal rights of American Indian tribes. The piece reserved hard judgment for the Bureau of Indian Affairs (BIA) relocation program, which provided subsidies and the promise of job training as a way to encourage American Indians to leave their reservations and live in big cities.[23] The article had particular relevance for Los Angeles, since more American Indians had moved or were moving from the Midwest and Southwest to that city than to Chicago, Denver, Oklahoma City, Seattle, or Tulsa. Between 1950 and 1960, the American Indian population in Los Angeles swelled from 1,671 to 8,109.[24]

Government officials and business leaders during this era championed Los Angeles as the epicenter of professional and leisure opportunities, supported by means of new highways, residential tracts, university campuses, cultural institutions, and industrial plants and factories. Still, metropolitan expansion did not benefit all residents. Some American Indian veterans did attend college on the GI Bill, and others managed to acquire training and found good jobs in the automotive or aerospace industries. But most earned money in commercial or domestic service jobs or served as short-term laborers in construction. Finding steady employment was hard, and discrimination on the job as well as in the housing market was rampant.

As the government shifted from resource-poor, termination-focused policies toward an assimilationist approach to relocation, Mackenzie remained fascinated by the issue. The BIA expressed little regard for having American Indians themselves contribute to policy or the implementation of relocation initiatives.

The agency understood moving to the city as an act of separation from life on the reservation, which, in turn, only contributed to feelings of alienation. As historian Ned Blackhawk explains, these programs "tried to force individual American Indians to choose between competing and, in the government's view, incompatible lifestyles."[25] Despite organizations such as the Indian Center located on Sixth Street in the Westlake District near downtown, which served as a communal hub, there was negligible public financial support for Native culture in these new locales. The government made it onerous for American Indians to visit their families back on the reservations and gave insufficient economic assistance to help program participants adjust to life in the metropolis.[26]

Mackenzie originally conceived of a documentary that would portray an Apache family's migration from an Arizona reservation to Los Angeles. The prospective film would offer policy recommendations to the BIA. Mackenzie's boss, Charles "Cap" Palmer, was supportive of the project and gave Mackenzie time off to conduct research with tribal leaders and government officials at the San Carlos Indian Reservation near Globe, Arizona. Mackenzie promised in his funding proposal:

> With three months' detailed research split between San Carlos and Los Angeles, and then ten weeks' shooting, as previously estimated, Cap and I can pin this down and deliver a 40 minute film for general non-theatrical release which will analyze the situation with honesty, dimension, and passion. . . . We will work in the tradition of the human and social documentary, and the Indian point of view will be paramount. We do not pretend that this will be easy, and feel that the pressure may force the development of new techniques.[27]

The project's conceptual blueprint shifted when Mackenzie began socializing with a group of American Indians he met at bars around Third and Main Streets. He turned away from wanting to create an expository account of a migratory journey and moved closer to an intimate look at a group of Bunker Hill residents. The film, as Mackenzie was now imagining it, would explore the gap between how journalists, Hollywood producers, and state institutions understood American Indians, and how American Indians lived in Los Angeles. The goal was not to create a didactic narrative, but rather to show the everyday interactions of a community systematically given short shrift in both commercial media outlets and the civic life of the city.[28]

Mackenzie's approach was shaped by his affinity for 1930s-era social documentary and the recent international New Waves, as well as by the practical constraints

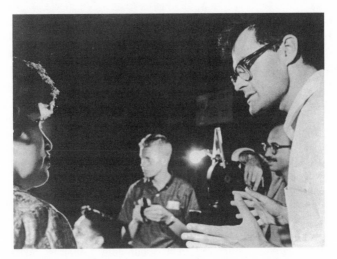

FIGURE 7: Foreground to background: Kent Mackenzie, Robert
Kaufman, and Erik Daarstad, on-location production photograph for
The Exiles, 1961, 35mm; written, produced, and directed by Kent
Mackenzie; photographed by Erik Daarstad, Robert Kaufman, and
John Morrill. Courtesy of Milestone Films and the Mackenzie Family.

he encountered during filming. His film school friends Daarstad, Morrill, Kaufman,
Lapenieks, and Farnsworth joined his crew without salary. Mackenzie put his life
savings of $539 into the film as starting funds, with friends, acquaintances, and arts
patrons contributing additional money. The Screen Directors Guild of America
extended a $1,200 grant and left-liberal Hollywood cinematographer Haskell Wex-
ler and producer Benjamin Berg donated a crucial $8,000 to bring the film to com-
pletion. The crew relied on cheap equipment or whatever could be borrowed from
employers at their other jobs. This involved shooting with a 35mm Arriflex on stu-
dio-donated "short ends." They used a combination of Masterlites, clip lights, and
car headlights to illuminate interiors and many exterior scenes. When experiments
with synchronizing the camera for sound quickly proved too expensive and difficult, they used a Magnecorder and a Magnasync Recorder for capturing sound on
location. They also relied on Parthenon soundstages for recording dialogue, singular voices, and sonic effects.[29] Following on the ideas of film theorists from the 1920s
and 1930s such as Paul Rotha, Mackenzie saw staging, artificial lighting, and dub-
bing sound as useful for rendering social reality intelligible and engaging.[30] Commenting on this method in his thesis, Mackenzie wrote that the subjects in the film
"were playing themselves in locations which were the locations of their everyday
lives, wearing the costumes they always wore, and surrounded by the friends they
were always with."[31] He went on to elaborate that the crew elicited constant input

from the people they filmed. The production and editing involved a dialogue about the structure of the film and the cultural meaning of the daily rituals. The sound-track was not scripted ahead of time, but emerged from informal conversations and interviews with American Indians.

While *The Exiles* was a collective undertaking, there were definitely limits to the collaboration. At times referring to himself as the "film author," Mackenzie saw his role as the film's artistic compass, influencing its overall tone, tempo, and themes by asserting his editorial opinion during each phase of production. This view came less from the teachings of Deinum and more from the emerging cinemas of Europe and Japan, where the role of the director was recast as an auteur, an artist-craft-sperson realizing a personal vision through the filmmaking process. When they were not making their own films, Mackenzie and his circle admiringly watched the films of François Truffaut, Jean-Luc Godard, Michelangelo Antonioni, and Akira Kurosawa at the Linda Lea on Main Street, the Vagabond on Wilshire, the Coronet on La Cienega, and the Pantages and the Egyptian on Hollywood Boulevard.[32] Mackenzie's artful approach to *The Exiles* raised its profile as an accomplished work of cinema, but also separated it from the community that it represented as well as from the educational film sector.

The arc of the seventy-minute documentary captures approximately twelve hours of a Friday night with Yvonne Williams (Apache), her husband, Homer Nish (Hualapai), and Homer's friend Tommy Reynolds (Mexican and Indian).[33] Yvonne spends her evening watching films at a sparsely populated Roxie Theatre on Broad-way and then strolls the sidewalks. She looks longingly at lavish displays of cos-metics, jewelry, and clothing in shop windows and storefronts. She reflects on how a wayward partner and economic hardship have caused her to reject as a fantasy the idea of a religious, happily married life; however, the prospect of a child gives her hope for a meaningful family life going forward.

Yvonne's husband, Homer, drifts with different friends between the Ritz and the Columbine bars on Main Street and a poker game at their friend Rico's nearby apartment on First Street. Tommy dances, mooches, and flirts his way through the night at many of the same watering holes as Homer. Whereas Tommy and Homer end the evening with a group of other American Indians on Hill X, located a short drive from Bunker Hill, Yvonne meets with her friend Marilyn, whose husband similarly stays out late. They tell stories in Marilyn's home in the Sunshine Apart-ments and keep each other company until morning. Monologues that fade in and out of the ambient noise, dialogue, and the blistering rock 'n' roll soundtrack by the Revels add a degree of psychological depth and realism to each of these narra-tive strands, connecting the individuals' inner thoughts to their social actions.

Tommy, the most happy-go-lucky of the three male friends, says that he avoids thinking about larger goals by living in the moment and surrounding himself with people who share his attitude. Yvonne conveys her frustrations with her

FIGURE 8: Still from *The Exiles*, 1961, 35mm; written, produced, and directed by Kent Mackenzie; photographed by Erik Daarstad, Robert Kaufman, and John Morrill. 1920 × 1080 ProRes 422 (HQ) transfer from the UCLA Film & Television Archive's restored 35mm interpositive, courtesy of Milestone Films and the Mackenzie Family.

perpetually absent husband and the bar scene that draws him away. She speaks with a quiet confidence about her ability to raise her soon-to-be-born child with the hope that the baby will be able to realize the kind of educational and professional opportunities denied to her. Homer ruminates on his disillusionment with school in Valentine, Arizona, and recalls the antipathy he felt for camera-toting tourists. Around the same time, Homer receives a letter and photograph from his family on the Hualapai Reservation in Peach Springs, Arizona. The letter evokes a tender domestic scene that is either Homer's personal memory or an event referenced by the note: A dissolve moves the scene from city to country. Slow pans reveal a sparse, windswept rural landscape. A woman, presumably Homer's mother, teases his father as he sings a song about a rabbit under a tree. This scene underscores how geographically and culturally far Homer is from his family. The camera's momentary pause on the small letter and photograph signal his connection to his family via correspondence. Homer expresses boredom with his friends' nightly drinking and the perpetual carousing and grandstanding. He is uncomfortable and unfulfilled with the bar scene on Main Street, but speaks appreciatively of Hill X. After a gathering on the outskirts of downtown, Homer and his friends return to Bunker Hill. The film's early-morning ending suggests finality, as the night wanderings are over and the characters return to their respective homes.

Even though *The Exiles* moved away from the kind of advocacy-oriented tone of Mackenzie's student project, it nonetheless denounced the preponderant perspective on the area as an unlivable slum in need of sweeping redevelopment. *The Exiles* sharply contrasted with the account of Los Angeles advanced by urban theorist Kevin Lynch in his widely read book *The Image of the City* (1960), in which he argues that people navigate cities by means of an interpretive "reading" of memorable landmarks, spatial patterns, and sensory cues. He goes on to claim that downtown Los Angeles, as opposed to Boston, is disorienting, "alien" and even "menacing."[34] Countering this view, *The Exiles* made downtown legible, demonstrating that it was dotted with meaningful landmarks and that small groups of people were able to comfortably navigate its landscape.

Mackenzie's film constitutes a symbolic resistance to the course of downtown urban change. While *Bunker Hill–1956* explored Bunker Hill at a time when the fate of the neighborhood was not necessarily sealed, *The Exiles* depicted the area at a time when plans for demolition were already being put into effect. On March 31, 1959, a little more than a year into the shooting of *The Exiles*, the Los Angeles City Council approved the $315 million, 136-acre Bunker Hill Urban Renewal Plan. The plan put into motion the razing of Bunker Hill properties and the leveling of the hill itself. Between 1959 and 1964, close to ten thousand people were forced out of their homes. Many American Indians moved to Los Angeles Street to live in the Baltimore, Roslyn, and King Edward residency hotels. Others moved to industrial districts such as Long Beach, Huntington Park, and Bell Gardens.

Mackenzie could have amplified the sense of injustice by foregrounding the demolition that was already underway and interviewing American Indians about the displacement. Still, his decision to bracket off these issues helps keep attention focused on the presence of American Indians in this area and their close ties to their routines. Cinema and media historians point to *The Exiles*'s depiction of a soon-to-be-demolished neighborhood as a significant indication of its value. David James asserts that the film is "a unique record of lost civic vitality and demotic architectural richness." Norman Klein writes that *The Exiles* comprises "the most complete body of imagery that exists of Bunker Hill's daily rhythm." Catherine Russell discusses the film in terms of the "expressive phantasmagoria of 'everyday'" in a neighborhood that was fast being leveled.[35]

The social charge of the film extends beyond the politics of urban planning and its own status as a historical record. *The Exiles* troubles the cultural discourses surrounding American Indians during the period. Since the 1910s, Hollywood Westerns had depicted American Indians (who were often played by red-faced white performers) in violent, nineteenth-century confrontations with white lawmen, soldiers, migrants, and townspeople. Seen as a menacing threat or as possessing a primitive innocence, Indians were portrayed as a people whose culture was being erased by the advance of white civilization and the promise of modernity. In the early 1960s, Westerns appeared with renewed vigor on theater screens and home television monitors. The cultural historian Richard Slotkin argues that the early-1960s "cult of the cavalry" subgenre treated the Indian Wars of the nineteenth century as allegories of counterinsurgency scenarios in the Third World.[36]

The diegetic settings of *The Exiles*'s private and public spaces remind viewers of the ubiquity of the Western imaginary in American life. When Yvonne is dropped off at the local movie theater, she apathetically watches what is being exhibited that evening: *The Iron Sheriff* (1957). And when Homer goes with Rico to his apartment before their poker game, the sound of a six-shooter pistol reverberates from the television and a character says, "I reckon that'll teach the moon-faced 'Injun' to have more respect for his betters." Other forms of popular culture amplified this image of American Indians as a primitive people of the past. Disneyland's Frontierland opened in 1955 in Anaheim, California, offering "authentic" powwows and tribal dances; five years later on the East Coast, the Bronx-based Freedomland opened, featuring canoe rides, "Indian attacks," and handicrafts displays. In his 1961 introduction to William Brandon's *The American Heritage Book of Indians*, President Kennedy observed, "For a subject worked and reworked so often in novels, motion pictures, and television, American Indians remain probably the least understood and most misunderstood Americans of us all." Unfortunately, the four hundred ensuing pages failed to deliver a contemporary perspective on their entrenched presence in the country.[37] The seemingly endless stream of maps, glossy portraits, and pastoral prose fossilized the voices and faces of American Indians, and completely buried Brandon's claim that "the once 'Vanishing American' is far from vanished."[38] Even the image on the title page is infused with a rhetoric of pastness: a progression of American Indians move from left to right and from foreground to background across an expanse of water. The progression reveals a shift from bodies, to abstract shades, to absence. The image visualizes what the text implicitly narrates: that American Indians have essentially vanished.

From its opening moments *The Exiles* adamantly challenged this framework. A montage of Edward Curtis photographs culled from his *North American Indian* project cuts to still images and then short scenes of the film's main characters in and around Bunker Hill. They appear near the exteriors of apartments on Clay Street, the Angels Flight railway, and the Grand Central Market. This sequence marks a discursive shift from a "vanishing" people to a minority community's effort to sustain their culture within the post–World War II metropolis.

The scene on Hill X gives evidence to this struggle. The location appears as a haven, safe from constant police harassment and unjust arrests. Homer's voice-over where he explains, "Indians like to get together where they won't be bothered, you know, watched or nothing like that," plays against shots of police twirling their billy clubs as they patrol the sidewalks. Officers punch a man, then tackle him to the ground and drag him into a squad car. Hill X serves as a crucial albeit temporary social site where American Indians can congregate under the cloak of darkness and away from the discriminatory eye of law enforcement. As Homer illustrates, people can maintain connections to reservation life by circulating news and telling stories. The late-night gatherings can mitigate feelings of alienation by way of socializing. People drink, talk, fight, and also join in the drumming, singing, and dancing known as a "49." The informal performance atop Hill X is a focal point of the meeting. It features Mescalero Apache Indians Eddie Sunrise Gallerito, Frankie Red Elk, and Chris Surefoot leading a "Social Dance" and a song derived from a Sioux "Grass Dance" for a gathering of individuals of diverse tribal affiliations.[39] The hybridity of the act combined with the collective investment in its perform-ance speaks to Los Angeles as a city where new culture is continuously drawn from different pasts, giving fresh purpose to old rituals.

The fact that this gathering overlooks Chavez Ravine emphasizes the sense of instability shared by multiple minority communities in Los Angeles. In the 1940s, almost four thousand mainly Mexican American residents called the three close-knit rural neighborhoods of Chavez Ravine home. With housing conditions poor and access to basic utilities extremely limited, the site was originally slated for redevelop-ment as the Elysian Park Heights housing project. When plans for public housing were eliminated, the city's pro-growth coalition thought that the site could be better used for creating car-accessible, middle-class entertainment. Bringing the Brooklyn Dodgers to Chavez Ravine would give the city its first major league baseball franchise, bolster its national reputation, and contribute to the restructuring of downtown as a cultural destination. Only months into the production of *The Exiles*, television station KTTV broadcast a Hollywood-hosted "Dodgerthon" to sway the public to embrace this plan and move ahead with creating a fifty-six-thousand-person stadium. Citizen opposition to Dodger Stadium was dismissed, and residents were removed from their homes. Soon after the shooting of the Bunker Hill scene in *The Exiles*, police started barring access to the area around Hill X as stadium plans moved forward, forcing American Indians to find alternative gathering places in the city.[40]

Just as *The Exiles* rejects the idea of American Indians as simply a people of the past, it also criticizes stereotypes of American Indians as a social problem. John Frankenheimer's Sunday Showcase television special *The American* (1960) and Delbert Mann's theatrically released *The Outsider* (1961) were two of the most prominent films to represent American Indians in this negative light. Both biopics broke new ground in their presentation of Pima Indian and World War II hero Ira Hayes living in tension with a white society that fails to acknowledge his griev-ances. But both productions contained a white star (Lee Marvin and Tony Curtis, respectively) performing in red face. Additionally, both films present Hays as a stand-in for the American Indian, an essentially victimized figure. Unlike *The Exiles*, these biopics had little patience for, or interest in, exploring the domestic interiors and social spaces in which American Indians lived. The broader media coverage of American Indian relocation also ignored this latter point of view. Instead, television reports and newspaper editorials tended to focus on statistics, policy decisions, and the opinions of government officials.

The Exiles's festival success stemmed from its stylized approach to capturing quotidian reality, combined with the fact that it was made by a young filmmaker outside the Hollywood system. Covering the 1961 Venice Film Festival, *Variety* called Mackenzie "another budding indie U.S. filmmaking talent," and praised *The Exiles* for having the "tingle of life and a polish in technical qualities and visual presentation." *Variety* also described Mackenzie as part of a coterie of independent filmmakers that included Morris Engel and Ruth Orkin (*Little Fugitive* [1953]), Lionel Rogosin (*On the Bowery* [1956]), Bert Stern (*Jazz on a Summer's Day* [1960]), Sidney Meyers (*The Savage Eye* [1960]), John Cassavetes (*Shadows* [1959]), and Shirley Clarke (*The Connection* [1961]).[41]

There was good reason to place Mackenzie and *The Exiles* within the pantheon of independent American film. Mackenzie, like his contemporaries, was considered part of a groundswell of homegrown auteurist cinema. *The Exiles* and other New Wave American films discussed in the festival reviews shared some thematic concerns and stylistic tendencies. These films captured commonplace interactions in working-class parts of cities within a short span of time. Although Cassavetes worked with professional actors for *Shadows*, the film chronicles a group of young black and white writers and jazz musicians in the streets, apartments, and clubs of Manhattan. Rogosin's *On the Bowery* explores the bar culture of the working poor and the homeless men living on the Bowery in Manhattan. Closer to home, *The Savage Eye* captures the anxious strolls of divorcee Judith McGuire (Barbara Baxley) as she attempts to escape loneliness and search for companionship among Los Angeles's leisure establishments. Stream-of-consciousness voice-over banter between McGuire and a heard but never seen "poet" narrator (Gary Merrill) accompanies shots of McGuire meandering around department stores, beauty salons, bars, sports arenas, strip clubs, and lounges. USC professor and educational film innovator Sy Wexler, who served on Mackenzie's master's thesis committee, was a cinematographer for the film. Additionally, Warren Brown, who was an editor for *The Exiles* (and became Mackenzie's brother-in-law) was credited as a cameraman on *The Savage Eye*. Haskell Wexler, who, as noted, provided Mackenzie with the completion funds, was another cinematographer on *The Savage Eye*.[42]

While *The Exiles* was considered part of this American New Wave, it was also admired for its distinct subject and style. Individuals ranging from William J. Speed, director of the audiovisual department of the Los Angeles Public Library, to *Film Quarterly*'s Benjamin Jackson commended the film for highlighting the complexity of the American Indians' experiences in Los Angeles. One of the film's key strengths, Jackson wrote, was how it cited past nonfiction precedents but charted an original path. Jackson declared that the film skillfully depicts real American

Indians and rejects the sentimentalizing tendencies of Robert Flaherty's ethnographies, the technocratic didacticism of John Grierson's state-backed social documentaries, and the "hyper-formalism" of city symphonies.[43] When Mackenzie showed *The Exiles* to American Indians, including those who appeared in the film, he commented that they responded to it as to a "family album," taking pleasure in the intimate experience of watching their lives with their relatives and close friends. They enjoyed a feeling of recognition and identification, even as some expressed concern that it did not cover a broad enough range of American Indians or that some might interpret the film as negative.[44]

The Exiles's subject and style attracted the attention of individual journalists and film festivals, but greatly diminished the prospects of a wide release. The fact that *The Exiles* was a documentary about a minority community that most people did not know existed in Los Angeles undoubtedly hurt its chances for finding a larger audience. In describing the process of trying to get the film into theaters or on television, Mackenzie said that distributors simply found *The Exiles* extremely "difficult." His former USC teacher, the Hollywood screenwriter Malvin Wald, confessed, "Perhaps [*The Exiles*] will never be known as anything more than a unique experimental film." In a locally syndicated AP article, Bob Thomas reported that *The Exiles* played to a packed Royce Hall at UCLA, but that it was having trouble reaching a mainstream audience.[45] *The Exiles*'s length, along with its refusal to conform to a rigorous pedagogical structure or a tight narrative, barred it from being considered a desirable film for the commercial entertainment, art house, or noncommercial sectors. While theaters around the country were beginning to more frequently exhibit documentaries, European art cinema, and the experimental work of Stan Brakhage, Jack Smith, and Kenneth Anger, they were uncomfortable with a slowly paced film focused on the lives of American Indians.

The fact that *The Exiles* was not on the radar of many within the American film vanguard further inhibited its chances of distribution. The New York journal *Film Culture*'s anticommercial stance translated to an anti–Los Angeles bias and a zealous championing of New York as the sole American center for independent filmmaking and criticism. In an article for its summer 1960 issue, journal founder Jonas Mekas proclaimed:

> New York has always been in opposition to Hollywood, not only geographically but ideologically as well. It is here that the most perceptive American film critics and film historians live and work. . . . It has to be stated here that the role of the Hollywood independents has been greatly exaggerated. The best Hollywood tradition movies (*Anatomy of a Murder, Giant, Ben Hur*) still come from the larger Hollywood producers. The best anti-Hollywood movies, however, have little to do with Independents. They come from individual East Coast filmmakers, from those filmmakers who came under the direct influence of the East Coast cinematic climate (*Shadows; Weddings and Babies; On the Bowery*).[46]

But distribution was not the only impediment to the film's success. The project had been expensive to create and every aspect of it had moved lethargically. Looking at job prospects, Mackenzie felt that going to work for a major studio to create fiction films or crime, comedy, or dramatic television did not seem particularly appealing. In an interview for *Los Angeles Magazine* devoted to the vicissitudes of film financing, Mackenzie spoke on behalf of independent filmmakers when he said, "We have decided there is no place for any of us in the industry to make the kind of films we want to do here in Hollywood. Methods of production are so stilted and conventional it's death for us here."[47]

Thus the concept of "exile" resonates in multiple ways with Mackenzie's film. Restorationist and theorist Ross Lipman has detailed how "exile" points to the American Indians' feeling of living as outcasts from both reservation and urban life, as well as to Mackenzie's pursuit of a film language that was unlike either classical fiction storytelling or sync-sound documentaries. Additionally, "exile" could be seen as relating to Mackenzie's ousted mentor Andries Deinum, and to his own feeling that he must operate outside of major Hollywood studios.[48] Unable to replicate *The Exiles*, Mackenzie continued to support its public life at festivals while working in the educational film sector. He found employment at new organizations devoted to documentary. His films for Wolper Productions and the USIA would come with some enticing freedoms and some severe restrictions.

THE WAY OF WOLPER

As Wolper Productions rapidly expanded in the early 1960s, becoming the largest producer of documentaries in Los Angeles (and rivaling the output of ABC, NBC, and CBS), the studio sought to employ the young talent around town. Although making television documentaries for Wolper gave Mackenzie a paycheck, the chance to work with compelling subjects, and an audience for his films, the streamlined style and themes of the projects contrasted with *Bunker Hill–1956* and *The Exiles*. The studio drew on classical Hollywood storytelling techniques along with tropes from network news to entertain and educate television audiences about cultural trends, politicians, major twentieth-century events, and the professional lives of American citizens. Wolper and his inner circle of executive craftsmen— Mel Stuart, Jack Haley Jr., and Alan Landsburg—ensured that the structuring story arcs and themes of these programs affirmed an upbeat image of the country as free and democratic while also critiquing communist and fascist systems of government. There was little room within Wolper Productions for interrogating the aspirations, limitations, and pitfalls of Cold War liberalism.

Like numerous film school graduates in the city, Mackenzie's USC-classmates-turned-*Exiles*-collaborators made documentaries for Wolper. Some joined immediately following graduation. Others held jobs at the studio in conjunction with crewing on other films, and still others used the studio as a springboard to work on theatrically released features or documentaries at bigger companies. It was not uncommon for a Wolper employee to also make short films for corporate clients, telefilms for the networks, documentaries for the government, and fiction films for major studios or producers on the fringes of Hollywood. Vilis Lapenieks helped shoot Roger Corman's *The Little Shop of Horrors* (1960) and Curtis Harrington's *Night Tide* (1961) before joining Wolper as an assistant to James Wong Howe on *Biography of a Rookie* (1961). Lapenieks then went on to serve as one of Wolper Productions' core camera operators in addition to crewing on projects such as Donn Harling's *Fallguy* (1962). Eventually he worked on New Hollywood productions such as *Cisco Pike* (1972). Erik Daarstad shot science and nature shorts for Pat Dowling Pictures, and Burt Topper's B-action film *Hell Squad* (1958), before being hired at Wolper Productions. Daarstad also made the Academy Award–nominated *The Spirit of America* (1963), and films on the Democratic and Republican conventions. Malvin Wald had a robust career writing acclaimed Hollywood films (*The Naked City* [1948]) and television (*Playhouse 90* [1957]). Wald went on to become one of the major writers for Wolper Productions. His scripts for *Hollywood—The Golden Years* (1960), *Biography of a Rookie* (1961), and *The Rafer Johnson Story* (1961)—each launched a series.

Wolper Productions consecutively hired Mackenzie for a number of jobs. He edited three episodes of *Story of . . .*, a series that followed the activities of different professionals. An April 18, 1962, *Variety* advertisement for *Story of . . .* highlighted the series' documentary appeal for a mainstream audience:

> (a) outstanding quality and style (b) real stories of real people in real, challenging situations (c) adventure, suspense, surprises, emotional impact (d) a lot of appeal for every part of the audience, regardless of taste, income, age, background, viewing habits (e) it ushers in a new wave of programming that people will talk about.[49]

Mackenzie's programs for the series included *Story of a Test Pilot* (1962), which profiled Lockheed Martin's chief test pilot Herman "Fish" Salmon, who had proved the viability of the F-104 training vehicle; *Story of a Jockey* (1962), featuring the jockey Bill Harmatz spending time at his home, in his real estate office, and at the Santa Anita racetrack; and *Story of an Intern* (1962), accompanying the doctor Bill Farrell on his rounds at San Francisco General Hospital. Mackenzie also edited *The Way Out Men* (1965), a program that profiled men breaking barriers in science and art, including surgeon Michael DeBakey, physician and psychoanalyst John Lilly, architect Paolo Soleri, and composer Lukas Foss.[50] That same year, Mackenzie edited *Prelude to War* (1965), which explored the years of German military aggression leading up to World War II, from the reoccupation of the Rhineland in 1936 to the attack on Poland in 1939.

Mackenzie took a prominent role as the director, producer, editor, and cowriter for *Story of a Rodeo Cowboy* (1962). With the aid of his old collaborators Daarstad (director of photography), Farnsworth (production manager), and Nicholas Clapp (associate editor), Mackenzie documented third-ranking world champion saddle-bronc rider Bill Martinelli and his fellow riders Bob Edison and Jim Charles as they attempt to win prize money at the Salinas Valley Rodeo. As in his past independent productions, Mackenzie filmed a subculture up close over a short period of time. The film looks at the rodeo cowboys over the course of their professional routine: getting dressed in their spurred boots, blue jeans, plaid shirts, and hats in their motel room; inquiring about their respective animals before the event at the stadium; riding in the competition; dancing at the 5-High Club honky-tonk during their free time; and departing for another rodeo. The immersive cinematography positions the spectator in close proximity to the cowboys throughout their journey.

Dramatic moments punctuate these observational scenes. For example, in Martinelli's last ride an extreme long shot captures his body in slow motion accompanied by Gerald Fried's Americana orchestral score. Martinelli looks balletic as he struggles to stay on the horse, clutching the rope with his left hand while his right hand waves in the air, and then perfectly dismounts and lands on his feet. At various points in the film, Martinelli ruminates on how rodeo riding offers him freedoms denied to those who work in nine-to-five office jobs, as well as close-knit camaraderie with his fellow competitors. The riders do not appear to fall into lockstep with white-collar America, but their rugged individualism is nonetheless tailored to match the ambitions of the series and the studio that produced it. For all of the rodeo cowboys' bravura, they labor in highly regulated settings and play by the prescribed rules of the competition. They are athletes, not outlaws, and apply themselves to what is seen as a meritocratic contest that rewards diligence and individual skill. The periodic commentary of John Willis familiarizes the viewer with Martinelli's sport, suggesting that rodeo riding is a profession that requires talent, ambition, and perseverance.

Mackenzie's other major Wolper Productions project was *The Teenage Revolution* (1965), in which he investigated teenagers in two related ways: first, as an empowered group of twenty-three million consumers, and, second, as young citizens learning to navigate evolving relationships with their peers, school, family, and government. In part one, narrator and on-screen host Van Heflin moves like an amateur anthropologist through the schools, homes, and commercial establishments of white, middle-class Southern California. He interviews teenagers about their use of clothing, music, and cars to fashion individual identities. Testimony from market researchers, fashion designers, and tastemakers such as music producer Phil Spector depicts teenagers as a volatile market demographic whose preferences are constantly changing. The relationship between producers and consumers of culture is seen as dynamic and symbiotic, resulting in a seemingly unlimited set of expressive possibilities. The second half of *The Teenage Revolution* profiles academic achievers. National Science Award–winning high school student

John Link receives mentorship from his teachers, support and assistance from his peers, supplies and resources from industrial companies, and purpose and recognition from the Atomic Energy Commission. Mackenzie also profiles the Job Corps, whose members work with underprivileged children in community-based summer programs in Los Angeles and other metropolitan cities. A counter–case study in *The Teenage Revolution* looks at Henry Hine, who despite his desire to support himself and his family dropped out of high school early and is frustrated, has low self-esteem, and has difficulty finding a job.

American youth appear armed with the power of choice in *The Teenage Revolution*. If they can make the right choices, the documentary implies, they can thrive within a society being transformed by new aesthetic sensibilities, technological inventions, and educational opportunities. All discussion of factors that influence the opportunities available to them such as race, gender, and class remain noticeably absent from the program, as if every teenager is in a position to make similar decisions. Furthermore, *The Teenage Revolution* amplifies the civic ends to which creativity and intellectual labor can be applied while also ignoring how fashion, music, and art can be used as possible means of social resistance.[51]

DOCUMENTARY DIPLOMACY

The USIA's program of state-backed auteurism enabled Mackenzie to create his own film about a topic that would otherwise not have been commercially viable. Filmmaker George Stevens Jr., who led the organization's film operations, tapped Mackenzie to make a documentary about a government-sponsored job training program. This was a common entrée into employment for the USIA, which recruited heavily out of Los Angeles. Mackenzie's fifteen-minute, 16mm *A Skill for Molina* (1964) follows a day in the life of Arnold Molina, a welder in training of Pima Indian and Mexican descent living in Fresno, California. Mackenzie had a greater amount of artistic freedom than at Wolper Productions, but his film still had to conform to the agency's overt Cold War mission.

Founded under President Dwight Eisenhower in 1953, the USIA aimed to "submit evidence to peoples of other nations by means of communication techniques that the objectives and policies of the United States are in harmony with and will advance their legitimate aspirations for freedom, progress and peace."[52] Beginning with the Kennedy administration, the USIA amped up its efforts to support American foreign policy by means of film, photography, literature, and radio. These forms of media sought to emphasize the positive impact of the United States on the world and to affirm the tenets of American democracy. The USIA also assumed an advisory role, gathering information about the reception of the United States abroad. Seasoned news anchor Edward R. Murrow directed the USIA from 1961 to 1964. Committed to the president's vision for intensifying the cultural Cold War,

Murrow proclaimed, "We are being outspent, out-published, and out-broadcast. We are a first rate power. We must speak with a first rate voice abroad."[53]

During this period, the USIA reached over one hundred countries through its seventy magazines and twenty newspapers, 180 libraries, and 789 annual hours of Voice of America radio broadcasts in thirty-six languages.[54] Motion pictures in general and documentaries in particular had a major role to play in the USIA's public relations initiatives. Murrow asked the filmmaker George Stevens Jr. to lead the International Motion Picture Service. The director had collaborated with his father on *A Place in the Sun* (1951), *Giant* (1956), and *The Diary of Anne Frank* (1959), and operated independently on *Alfred Hitchcock Presents* (1960–61). He also served in the Air Force Motion Pictures Division. Stevens would recall that he was inspired by the idea of public service after reading Theodore H. White's *The Making of the President: 1960*, the book that Wolper had adapted into an Emmy-winning documentary. The Stevens family name ensured that the agency would be infused with the aura of Hollywood as well as a good civic pedigree.

The Murrow-Stevens duo formed an American analogue to John Grierson, the documentary theorist, public relations pioneer, and savvy technocrat who helped to create strong state-backed systems of educational film in England and Canada. The USIA organized the international exhibition of big-budget American features and arranged for actors and directors to serve as cultural diplomats. According to the *Journal of the Society of Motion Picture and Television Engineers*, the USIA in 1962 created 44 films in the United States, acquired 36 titles, created 147 overseas productions, and made 197 newsreels. Each was translated into multiple languages. These films reached millions of viewers in 746 theaters and had 226 "film centers" in 106 countries.[55] As Congress did not want a government agency to be in competition with private enterprise, USIA films were not usually shown domestically but sent to theaters, museums, community centers, and schools in cities and towns across the globe, especially in nonaligned countries in Africa, Southeast Asia, and Latin America. Press coverage of the organization created a public awareness of recent films, the personnel involved, and the organization's broader aims. Exhibition of USIA productions at the Edinburgh, Venice, Moscow, and Bilbao film festivals promoted American film achievements and boosted the international profiles of the filmmakers.

This was not the first time the government had strategically used nonfiction. Film historian Richard Dyer MacCann writes that the Office of War Information's practice of reaching out to directors during World War II provided a foundation for how the government could work productively with individual filmmakers on a short-term basis for an international cause. However, unlike in the past, USIA documentaries were not crafted with the purpose of preparing both a civilian population and troops for an active war with fixed fronts and an enemy to destroy. Rather, they intended to project a positive impression of American democracy and expose the weaknesses of alternative systems of governance. Commenting on the delicacy of this task, Stevens proclaimed, "Ideas are fragile things, and they can't be turned out on an assembly line like sausages or jeeps."[56]

The USIA made films advertising Kennedy's Alliance for Progress initiatives to increase economic cooperation with Latin America (*United in Progress* [1963]), the lasting impact of civil rights reform in the South (*Nine from Little Rock* [1964]), the congenial, bridge-building diplomatic travels of Jacqueline Kennedy (*Invitation to India* [1962]), and respect for American labor (*Harvest* [1967]). Stevens understood that a well-made, compelling narrative that engaged with people emotionally could be more persuasive to spectators than a dry catalog of facts: "We are not interested in making travelogues. . . . We are trying to show how democracy works and how people can help themselves in developing nations. . . . Our country has developed a marvelous mechanism in its movies, and it must use this wonderful tool to explain its way of life to other countries. But such movies, to be successful, must have quality and vitality."[57]

Although based in his USIA office in the nation's capital, Stevens looked beyond Washington, DC, for gifted filmmakers. USIA filmmaker Gary Goldsmith (*The True Story of an Election* [1963], *Born a Man* [1964]) would later recall that Stevens really "had the sense to recruit the best young filmmakers that he could," rather than just seek the "low bidder." Stevens would often contact an individual upon seeing his or her film at a festival or on television. A positive reputation in the industry could also attract the attention of the agency. Stevens would then reach out to the individual about the possibilities of working on a particular project and invite the submission of a treatment that would need to be approved before filmmaking began.[58] The USIA sponsored nationwide competitions for student filmmakers and took on interns whose abilities could be cultivated, used, and then connected to the mainstream industry. Given that Los Angeles was home to prestigious film schools and was also the nation's center for the film and television industries, the city appealed as a talent pool. The conservative Hollywood director Bruce Herschensohn, Cold War liberal documentarian David Wolper, left-leaning intellectuals Haskell Wexler and James Blue, and fresh-out-of-film-school, socially minded graduates of UCLA and USC such as Mackenzie, Daarstad, and Carroll Ballard all made films for the USIA during the early to mid-1960s.[59]

The agency embraced a wide range of subject matter and formal variation. Stevens told *Film Comment*, "The important thing is to have an individual's mark on the film rather than just going to a manufacturer of film and saying: 'Make this film for us.'"[60] The idea was to show how American artists, unlike artists working within a completely state-controlled framework, possessed a greater degree of individual freedom. The USIA's desire to promote filmmakers as independent, free-thinking artists, combined with the lack of a singular directive for the organization, made for a less restrictive production environment than most commercial studios. Media historian Jennifer Horne writes that the freedoms filmmakers enjoyed at times even enabled their critique of American foreign policy and the USIA itself. James Blue's trio of documentaries about American-Colombian relations, in which he visualizes the human consequences of industrialization and satirizes the staid form of a governmental newsreel, "could be thought of as ambassadors who do not hesitate to speak out of turn, subverting their diplomatic mission."[61] Nonetheless, even as the USIA provided filmmakers the chance to creatively address topical issues that Hollywood studios and commercial news networks refused, subversion or overt criticism was uncommon. The USIA's insistence on promoting pro-American, pro-democracy, or anticommunist sentiment, as well as the fact that the agency retained the right to the final cut, resulted in broad ideological cohesion across its vast output.

Mackenzie directed and produced *A Skill for Molina* (1964) with collaborators Daarstad and Morrill, who handled the cinematography. The film depicts Molina as an indefatigable student, father, and husband, committed to raising his family's socioeconomic standing through learning a skill in the special program at Fresno City College. In a series of connected scenes that chronicle the unfolding of a day, Molina studies diligently at the dining room table before his children awake, appears thoroughly invested in his classes, plays dominoes with his peers, and spends time with his wife and nine children in the evening. Voice-over narration from Molina combined with a montage sequence of small photographs offer backstory concerning the economic and emotional hardships he endured growing up poor in Chandler, Arizona, and laboring as a seasonal farmworker prior to his arrival in Fresno. He also talks about his frustrations with looking for a job after having served in the navy during World War II and the Korean War. The narration at times has an expository function that informs viewers about Molina's schedule. At other times it comprises an interior monologue of Molina's thoughts. As he reads with his children, cuts their hair, or asks them questions about school, his narration communicates his desire for his children to study hard and attend the local city college so as not to endure what he went through. Formal education, he implies, is important to gaining the skills that will lead to full-time, stable employment. Toward the end of the film, extended takes show the family bonding over tortillas at the dining room table. The Bolivian American composer Jaime Mendoza-Nava, who had worked on everything from the *Mister Magoo* television series (1960–61) to the theatrically released *Fallguy* (1962) and *The Quick and the Dead* (1963), wrote the score for the documentary. The music imbues both the voice-over and the observational sequences with varying degrees of levity and gravity, conveying that Molina is enjoying life with his family and taking his education and prospects for steady employment seriously.

A Skill for Molina reflected Mackenzie's devotion to crafting poetic day-in-the-life portraits of people marginalized within or distorted by popular culture. The commission of Mendoza-Nava involved reaching outside the predominantly white film and television music divisions, echoing Mackenzie's old mentor Andries Deinum's fight to bring minority talent into the media industries. Additionally, Mackenzie's compassionate depiction of Molina as industrious and resilient opposed stereotypes in magazine articles, cartoons, and Hollywood films of the Mexican and Indian as a transient, lazy, poor farm laborer. Scenes that show Molina working and socializing with other minorities as well as white students also foreground the shared aspirations for economic mobility and job security that exist across racial and ethnic lines. Molina's children and grandchildren didn't see the film as propaganda, but as a "home movie" created by a compassionate stranger. Family members felt that Mackenzie captured both the heartfelt intimacy and the high energy pace of their group dynamic. The documentary would later serve as an occasion for the extended family to gather together and tell stories about the lives of the individuals depicted on-screen.

A Skill for Molina also spoke to the USIA's interests in promoting the state as a benevolent and caring presence in the lives of citizens, spotlighting how public programs could smoothly incorporate industrious minorities into the American workforce. Molina is essentially the protagonist in an "American dream" success narrative circa 1964, one based on realizing opportunities given to him by public institutions. The film's title signals that Molina is receiving a means to mobility. The film does not address contemporary discrimination in hiring practices or the impact of race prejudice on residential life in the region. It presents an idyllic state of harmony, showing black, brown, and white welders learning together, living near one another, playing dominoes, carpooling, and joking around in the locker room. Daarstad and Morrill's verité-style camerawork captures the details of Molina's tasks, helping to personalize his story and show that he is a productive member of a larger welfare initiative. Shots of Molina up early studying in his kitchen, concentrating on his welding exercises at school, and happily eating and doing homework with his kids in the evening demonstrate the success of the program in action. The importance of secondary-school education is seen as both useful knowledge that Molina is passing on to his family and a way of validating the institutions in which he now receives training.

Mackenzie's film embodied the USIA's eagerness to encourage filmmakers to take ownership over their projects, as well as the agency's tendency to showcase high-functioning relationships between the government and its diverse populace. *A Skill for Molina* circulated globally and played at select venues in the United States, such as the School of Visual Arts in New York, where it had a special screening and accompanying panel discussion.[62] Over the course of the 1960s, the agency continued to embrace motion pictures as a means to promote Lyndon B. Johnson's vision of the Great Society abroad. Bruce Herschensohn's *John F. Kennedy: Years of Lightning, Day of Drums* (1964) was even released theatrically to an American

audience in 1966. The documentary touted the fallen president's policy achievements and claimed their ongoing vitality within the Johnson administration.
However, the rise of minority liberation movements within US cities, along with
growing opposition to the country's aggressive foreign policies, would soon give
way to a crisis in Cold War liberalism. These tensions reached a flash point in Los
Angeles, discouraging plans (at least for the moment) for the sweeping redevelopment of downtown, and energizing grassroots organizing in working-class minority neighborhoods. Mackenzie's films in Bunker Hill anticipated the efforts of
other white liberal filmmakers. At the same time, his documentary practice would
itself become the object of contentious debate, as marginalized groups sought to
directly represent their own communities.[63]

PART TWO

After the Watts Uprising

*Community Media from the Top Down and
the Bottom Up, 1965–1973*

The Rise of Minority Storytelling

Network News, Public Television, and
Independent Collectives

Television coverage of the 1965 Watts Uprising broadcast an image of Los Angeles unfamiliar to most Americans. Scenes of urban chaos appeared in living rooms across the city and around the country, shattering the popular image of Los Angeles as a placid West Coast metropolitan paradise. In KTLA's compilation film *Hell in the City of Angels* (1965), newscaster Hugh Brundage discussed how the August 11 altercation between police and the family of Marquette Frye on the corner of 116th Street and Avalon Boulevard escalated into a week of chaos. He spoke of "hoodlums" committing "indiscriminate" acts of "violence" that brought about rampant destruction.[1] Aerial views from the station's telecopter surveyed burning commercial establishments along Avalon, police officers trying to disperse crowds and making arrests, and individuals carrying stolen objects moving quickly down alleys and sidewalks. Close-up shots of damaged news vehicles and debris-strewn streets were meant to convey the danger journalists faced covering the event and the generally unsettling atmosphere. In an interview, cameraman Ed Clark described Watts as a "war zone" that was "worse than Korea" and mayor Sam Yorty confidently declared that the only effective way to meet the "mob" was with "overwhelming power." The documentary primarily framed and edited Watts residents running, yelling, and looting, advancing the mainstream media's perspective that the unrest was simply a hateful and confused expression of rage. KTLA's coverage was consistent with the alarmist headlines in the *Los Angeles Times*, leading stories in *Time* and *Newsweek*, and Universal Newsreel's *Troops Patrol L.A.* (1965).

The geographic reach of the conflagration in Watts effectively halted mid-1960s plans for significant downtown development, as investors moved to the white Westside instead.[2] Nationally, as the Watts Uprising occurred only five days after the signing of president Lyndon B. Johnson's Voting Rights Act, which outlawed discriminatory practices that disenfranchised minorities, it signaled a rupture in the Great Society, a plan that the president had been trying to strengthen and expand. Johnson declared in a speech at the University of Michigan and then wrote in his book *My Hope for America*, "The Great Society rests on abundance and liberty for all. . . . It is a place where every child can find knowledge to enrich his mind and to enlarge his talents."[3]

This idea of the Great Society did not end after the Watts Uprising. Johnson's administration moved to address the urban strife as part of its effort to actualize its broader vision of what the expanded welfare state could achieve. The Great Society consisted of a multipronged policy initiative comprised of: race relations (the Civil Rights Act of 1964 and Voting Rights Act of 1965); community-based antipoverty programs (the Economic Opportunity Act of 1964); education (the Elementary and Secondary Education Act of 1965); health care (the Social Security Act of 1965); and arts and culture (the National Foundation on the Arts and the Humanities Act of 1965 and the Public Broadcasting Act of 1967). Poverty, racial tension, and all forms of socioeconomic inequality could be fixed, the administration confidently thought, through creative forms of legislation, an increase in opportunities for able and willing citizens, and a spirit of public service.

Politicians, entrepreneurs, and civic leaders were eager to explain "the problem" of Watts and urged the city to move forward. The *CBS Reports* documentary *Watts: Riot or Revolt* (1965) provided a stage for "experts" to pontificate on the meaning of the event. It reinforced the recently published *Violence in the City—An End or a Beginning?* authored by governor Edmund Brown's Commission on the Los Angeles Riots.[4] Members of the commission, led by the conservative former CIA director John McCone, contended that there was a fractious relationship between the black community and police and considered the uprising a detestable act of anger rather than a protest. In the documentary, Police Chief William Parker blames members of the black community for the current crisis. He states that a criminal element in Watts, stirred up by civil rights leaders, was creating unreasonable demands and promoting widespread disrespect for police. The film also reinforced secretary of labor Daniel Patrick Moynihan's *The Negro Family: The Case for National Action* (1965), which claimed that the disintegration of the black family was at the heart of problems in Watts and that improving male employment was the clear way to strengthen families and uplift the blighted neighborhood.[5] Amid the talking heads, the faces and voices of Watts residents appear as fleeting images or sound bites.

Participants in the uprising, however, were not simply hoodlums, nor was the neighborhood in which they lived simply a problem to be solved. The unrest stemmed from the persistence of police prejudice and use of excessive force, the neighborhood's severely limited access to public utilities, exploitation by business owners, and the lack of employment opportunities for both men and women. Los

Angeles's support for the ballot initiative Proposition 14 (1964), which sought to negate antidiscriminatory housing legislation, revealed the entrenched racism in the city. Compounding these problems was the fact that mayor Sam Yorty remained intransigent about the prospect of federal money alleviating poverty in Los Angeles.

In the aftermath of the uprising, white liberals made films within commercial broadcasting that peered beneath the sensational facade obscuring many people's understanding of South Central. Stuart Schulberg and Joe Saltzman were dissatisfied with the conventions of public affairs programming. They aimed to create greater awareness among white viewers concerning some of the challenges that black Angelenos faced, increasing constructive channels for interracial dialogue. Schulberg and Saltzman's films did succeed in registering a profound sense of frustration and conveyed some of the motivations behind the Watts Uprising. Nevertheless, they were primarily aimed at white audiences and did not engage in depth with Black Power as a political movement.

As the 1960s progressed, other minorities and women drew inspiration from black liberation struggles. They shared some of the same criticisms of the limitations and inadequacies of the discourse of liberal integration as well as the desire for self-determination. Documentary media was essential to the black, brown, yellow, and women's movements. Their presence was acutely felt in Los Angeles—the film and television capital of the country and the most racially diverse postwar American metropolis. Marginalized people of the city demanded the right to assert their voices from behind the camera, arguing that self-representation was crucial to self-determination. With cinema being such a resource-intensive craft, many citizen groups, filmmakers, activists, and intellectuals fought for increased access to money, equipment, and training. Others went outside, and indeed positioned their work against, commercial or public systems of production.

In an attempt to provide a space for a greater plurality of voices to be heard within an increasingly fraught democracy, the shell-shocked mandarins of the Great Society were compelled to respond, without always the clearest idea of what providing increased access to education, equipment, distribution channels, and exhibition venues would entail. While schools such as UCLA played a crucial role in cultivating filmmakers' interests and providing training, the university was one among numerous institutional frameworks that had an impact on local production. Filmmakers drew heavily on an expanding array of schools, workshops, foundations, studios, and broadcasting facilities. They gravitated to documentary out of practical necessity, but also because of its distinct social utility. Documentary offered filmmakers an economical form of reportage while also enabling them to interpret the sociopolitical geography of the city. They aligned their films with the fight against police brutality, the whitewashing of school curricula, egregious pop culture stereotypes, political disenfranchisement, systemic racism and sexism in the workplace, and the US imperial involvement in Southeast Asia. The documentaries they produced were viewed in libraries, theaters, private homes, neighborhood centers, schools, churches, and union halls. Such films claimed both physical space in the city and discursive space within contemporary liberation movements. In so doing, these documentaries helped forge the political consciousness of marginalized communities across the country and constituted a form of community advocacy that engendered lasting social change within Los Angeles.

NETWORK RENEGADES

The two television documentaries by Stuart Schulberg were early interventions into how the mainstream media represented South Central Los Angeles. Stuart and his brother Budd grew up in Beverly Hills and had numerous ties to Hollywood. Their father was the New Deal–supporting Paramount mogul B. P. Schulberg. Stuart could have pursued a more traditional career making studio fiction, but instead went into public affairs documentary. His Cold War liberal outlook was informed by his experiences making educational films for the Office of Strategic Services during World War II, the US military government in Berlin, and the Marshall Plan Economic Cooperation Administration in Paris. He believed that film could perform a valuable social service and assist in stabilizing democratic societies. His documentaries promoted advances in modern technology, industrial expansion, collective security, and international trade and business, all while reinforcing the image of the pro-democracy, pro-capitalism United States as a decisive force for good. Stuart returned to the United States in the mid-1950s and worked in NBC's Washington, DC, offices as a producer for *David Brinkley's Journal* (1961–64).[6]

His films about Watts emerged out of his brother's literary outreach after the uprising. As the cultural studies scholar Daniel Widener writes, Budd Schulberg's Watts Writers Workshop was motivated by concern for his home city, guilt for being naive about the hardships facing his fellow Angelenos, and hope that creating a cultural outlet could calm racial tensions and provide professional guidance for aspiring writers.[7] The workshop attracted around twenty individuals who met at the Westminster Neighborhood Association at 10125 Beach Street in Watts. They soon expanded and relocated to the nearby Watts Happening Coffee House and then the nine-room Frederick Douglass House. Budd led sessions where he encouraged workshop members to share their feelings of alienation from white America by means of poetry, prose, and plays. His brother proposed making a documentary on the workshop that would allow a national audience to understand the thoughts and frustrations of black residents as well as create a bridge for local talent to the nearby film, television, and publishing industries. Stuart, like Budd, felt confident that his good intentions and expertise in strategic communication could aid the process of racial integration. NBC News vice president Don Meaney calculated that the Schulberg brothers' production would generate a lot of attention, given the family's prominence, and demonstrate that the network was invested in socially conscious programming.[8]

The Angry Voices of Watts: An NBC News Inquiry was filmed in ten days during the summer of 1966. The documentary adhered to the standard network convention of a trusted, white male interpreter framing the subject matter. It begins with Budd, as narrator and guide, driving down 103rd Street, past the vacant lots, the ABC Loan store, the Giant Food Market, and Block's Yardage. He comments that he is working "in a ghetto, within a ghetto, within a ghetto," but that he has been able to make a unique and positive impact on residents' lives through his workshop. Inside the Watts Happening Coffee House, he gives a brief profile of some of the writers before introducing sample works. The individuals' dramatic readings play against on-location images that resonate with their words.[9] Harry Dolan's short autobiographical piece "The Sand-Clock Day" focuses on the difficulty and fatigue of searching for a job in the city. Dolan gets up in the morning and leaves his home in Watts, takes one bus to downtown and another to Van Nuys before arriving late to his interview. Sadly, he does not get the job. Shots of pile drivers and close-ups of conveyer belts accompany Jimmie Sherman's poem "The Workin' Machine" to convey anxieties about automation and the possibilities of unemployment. Black adolescents play baseball for Birdell Chew's "A Black Mother's Plea," a manifesto-like prose poem about the desire for her son to grow up free from self-doubt and the threat of discrimination. In between readings, Budd assumes the role of host, mentor, editor, and therapist. He conducts the flow of the workshop, gives advice to the participants, commends their productivity, and offers comfort to Dolan when he is momentarily overcome with grief.

Upon the film's airing on the anniversary of the uprising, Percy Shain from the *Boston Globe* wrote that it provided "an outlet for seared feelings."[10] The *New York Amsterdam News*'s Poppy Cannon White remarked that while the program's title was sensationalistic, the show was "freighted with drama—the curious, but almost incredible drama of a vision made visible."[11] The program generated interest in the anthology of the workshop's writing, *From the Ashes: Voices of Watts*, and had additional professional payoffs. Johnie Scott placed a poem in *Harper's Magazine*. Television personality and composer Steve Allen set Jimmie Sherman's poetry to music, and he was later hired as a screenwriter at Universal.[12] NBC purchased Dolan's script for the teledrama *Losers Weepers* (1967). The program portrayed a father who returns from prison to his 92nd Street home to reestablish a relationship with his children, as well as to retrieve some money he stashed away after a robbery.[13] *The Angry Voices of Watts* also helped the workshop attract the financial backing of Steve Allen, Art Buchwald, James Baldwin, Robert F. Kennedy, and John Steinbeck.[14]

An article Stuart Schulberg penned for *Variety* reflected his optimism as well as his arrogance and naïveté concerning what he thought his film had achieved. He called himself "the leading authority on Watts TV production" and asserted that "white technicians who considered Watts north of the demarcation line soon felt as much at home there as they did in Burbank or Beverly Hills. Negro cast and (mainly) white crew, uptown pros and downtown hopefuls, merged into one happy if hard-working family."[15] Schulberg's follow-up program, *The New Voices of Watts* (1968), mainly featured dramatic readings in the neighborhood.[16] "Nobody loves the song out of captivity" exclaims Fredericka White, reading from her poem "Something of Mine" in front of the Watts Towers. "I am a black phoenix," recites James Thomas Jackson, reading from his poem "Blues for Black" in front of a large junk heap. At a rehearsal for the domestic drama *A House Divided*, author Jeanne Taylor talks about the thrill of seeing others perform her work, how she draws on her own familial experiences in her art, and the satisfaction of sharing the "true" experience of growing up in Watts with a larger audience. The program's other major segment consists of Birdell Chew's teledrama *The Time of the Blue Jay*, which follows two black children who become curious about school following their chance encounter with an inspiring black teacher.

Despite the continuities between *Angry Voices* and *New Voices*, Stuart Schulberg's *New York Times* article "Watts '68: So Young, So Angry" revealed widening ideological rifts within the workshop. In the article, Stuart details his and Budd's frustrated attempts to limit nationalist rhetoric and shape the literary style of some of the members: "We were confronted by four Black Nationalist poets so young, so angry and so proud that they overpowered our ability to communicate."[17] Stuart noted that the Four Furies poetry ensemble refused to censor their "four-letter words," which prevented them from participating: "We tried to explain that they couldn't say ——— and ——— on the air, at least not while *this* generation of fuddy-duddy Establishment whites still controls the airwaves."[18] But the trouble with *New Voices* extended to other aspects of the program as well. The black residents of Johns Island, South Carolina, where Chew's film was shot, disrupted the production; they were dissatisfied that white personnel were in charge of the program. This was not the first time that the workshop faced public disapproval.[19] Nonetheless, the difficulties besetting *New Voices* were symptomatic of growing opposition to the organization's professionalizing mission which connected black talent to an exploitative entertainment industry. They also pointed to dissatisfaction with outside white "experts" claiming to be authorities on minority experiences. As the workshop attempted to reinvent itself, Budd Schulberg returned to novel writing. His brother continued on as a producer for NBC.

Stuart Schulberg's documentaries in Watts anticipated the work of the white liberal documentarian Joe Saltzman for the CBS-owned-and-operated Los Angeles station KNXT; however, Saltzman's *Black on Black* (1968) skirted the traditional role of the white newscaster. Born in Alhambra in suburban Los Angeles, Saltzman studied cinema at USC and served as the editor in chief of the school newspaper, the *Daily Trojan*. He then earned a graduate journalism degree from Columbia University. Returning to Los Angeles, he began his career in broadcasting as a reporter for KNXT's *Ralph Story's Los Angeles* (1964–69), a popular magazine-style series that covered the city's cultural milieu. In the aftermath of the Watts Uprising, Saltzman proposed to station heads a documentary on Watts residents in which the film's subjects would be the only voices heard. Saltzman believed that this format would create a sorely needed platform for black residents to speak honestly about their lives. In turn, the program would be educational for white viewers and result in more open and constructive channels for interracial dialogue in Los Angeles. KNXT rejected the idea, arguing that the absence of an in-house anchor would give viewers the impression that the station lacked control over its program content. Flagrant racism within the newsroom also initially stalled the program.[20]

Two factors in a nationwide climate of media reform eventually swayed KNXT to greenlight the project. First, a report issued by the National Advisory Commission on Civil Disorders, chaired by Illinois governor Otto Kerner Jr., sent shock waves through television stations across the country. The report was the upshot of the Johnson administration's July 27, 1967, mandate to explore the reasons behind four years of urban strife.[21] The Kerner Commission researched the mass media's interpretation of these events as well as the response of minorities to the media's coverage. The document indicated that these outlets have "not communicated to the majority of their audience—which is white—a sense of the degradation, misery, and hopelessness of living in the ghetto. . . . They have not shown understanding or appreciation of—and thus have not communicated—a sense of Negro culture, thought, or history." It detailed the need to bring a greater amount of minority personnel into the film, television, and newspaper industries and also claimed, "The news media must find ways of exploring the problems of the Negro and the ghetto more deeply and more meaningfully."[22] The commission's findings had many proponents. In his front-page *Variety* editorial, FCC commissioner Nicholas Johnson wrote, "The media must get the Negro's side of a story—not just that of the Welfare Dept. or the Police Chief . . . not just through the 'filter' of a responsible 'spokesman' or reporter."[23] The conflagrations in American cities following the April 4, 1968, assassination of Dr. Martin Luther King Jr. intensified the need for an inclusive approach to film and television.

The second major factor involved the efforts of lawyers, advocacy groups, civil rights leaders, and entertainment personnel to make television stations responsive to their minority constituencies. Their battle led to a 1966 court case against the station WLBT in Jackson, Mississippi, that established the right of citizens to participate in a station's license renewal proceedings. A groundbreaking 1969 court decision stripped the same station of its license because of its failure to address the views of the area's black community. Media historian Allison Perlman argues that the WLBT case showed that a station's racist programming policies and lack of attention to minority audiences could serve as cause for revocation. The case also provided a precedent for future legal efforts to hold stations responsible to their viewers.[24] Under pressure to respond to issues facing Angelenos, and distant from the New York–based oversight of the CBS network, KNXT executives shifted their position on Saltzman's program from rejection to reluctant acceptance.

Saltzman and a small crew spent three months working on *Black on Black*, including three weeks on location during the spring and early summer of 1968. Saltzman's liaison with Watts was Truman Jacques, a community organizer building his career in television. By way of Jacques, Saltzman met Donnell Petetan, a resident who worked for the Concentrated Employment Program helping to provide services to job seekers. Petetan became Saltzman's main interlocutor with the neighborhood.[25] Saltzman worked with KNX radio engineers for the editing of ambient noises, individual testimony, and music. "I was far more concerned with audio than video" Saltzman would later recall, for sound could document "the things that were happening inside the heart and the mind of the people."[26]

Petetan appears at the beginning of the film, driving past small homes, the Watts Towers, children playing, housing projects, weed-filled vacant lots, and adult men and women walking down the street. He explains that Watts at once shares the salient characteristics of other black, urban, working-class neighborhoods and is also distinct in its makeup and relationship to its metropolitan area. He contends that although there is very little home ownership, and landlords are most often absentee, Watts is not simply a blighted terrain. Residents feel affection for and draw psychological support from the environment. The film then examines topics that coalesce around black identity, cultural practices, oppression, and hopes and anxieties for the future. Saltzman explores these subjects in one-on-one interviews. The spectator never hears Saltzman's voice, and his own presence remains beyond the frame. While the interviewees speak, the camera frequently cuts away to observational sequences that match the content of what has now become voice-over narration. Speaking from his bedroom at his East 112th Street home, Petetan says that popular culture has for too long attached negative connotations to the adjective "black" and positive connotations to the adjective "white." He argues that it is important to resituate the former as essentially affirmative and beautiful. Male and female interviewees then extend the discussion of identity, reflecting on the significance of wearing clothing that relates to their ancestral heritage or styling their hair to express racial pride. Speaking in his own shop, barber Walter Butler explains how at one time black people were urged by the cosmetics industry to process, curl, and straighten their hair, emulating that of whites. He claims that wearing "a natural" allows black people to develop a more authentic sense of self.

In additional scenes, individuals insist that conflict is part of everyday life, including television's psychological attack on people of color. "Why does TV make fool[s] out of other races?" Petetan asks. Conflict can also be associated with

FIGURE 9: Still from *Black on Black*, 1968, 16mm; directed by Joe Saltzman; executive produced by Dan Gingold; broadcast on KNXT, Los Angeles. DVD courtesy of Joe Saltzman.

face-to-face indignities. One young woman shares an aggravating story of a time when her boss discouraged her from applying for a higher-paying position. He thought she wouldn't "enjoy working in this office where there are all white people." Providing a sweeping critique of a racially divided workforce, Petetan's mother Ethel looks directly at the camera and says, "I tell you why the white man is a snake in the grass. The white man will train you for any kind of job that he wants you to do. . . . He won't train you for the better jobs."

Black on Black does not try to build consensus or present a monolithic view of Watts. Religion, for example, is a divisive issue. Inside a service at the Garden of Eden Church of God in Christ, a woman shares with the congregation her belief that the church offers a safe and nurturing space for children. In contrast, Petetan says that religion is "the biggest hustle of all." Household income is another debated topic. One mother says that she and her husband both work full time, as this is a necessary step toward home ownership and financial stability. Another woman says that it is important to have one parent stay home with the children in order to provide them with guidance. *Black on Black* stays focused on individual voices through its conclusion, where it presents residents' desires and predictions for the future. While one woman declares that integration should be a goal for black people and that violence never yields tangible benefits, Petetan and his friend argue that violence is an American tradition that stretches back to the country's founding. Presenting these voices as stand-alone, personal opinions arguably made Black Power seem less threatening for spectators of the documentary, presenting it as an outlook held by particular individuals rather than a mass political movement.

Following *Black on Black*'s July 18 premiere, *Television* critic Sherman Brodey wrote that the emphasis on Petetan-as-guide made *Black on Black* both part of, and different from, television's recent turn to covering inner cities across the country. *Variety* stressed that *Black on Black* "transcended any previous effort to picture the black people as they are, without the embellishments of extraneous dramatization." The *Los Angeles Sentinel* commented that most news programs provide a "recitation of statistics on crime, violence, poverty and despair," but that *Black on Black* showed residents "articulat[ing] what it's like to be black as it is to them."[27] The documentary won two local Emmys and various national broadcasting awards. Other CBS-owned-and-operated stations in St. Louis, Chicago, New York, and Philadelphia showed *Black on Black*. Letters of praise sent to KNXT headquarters at 6121 Sunset Boulevard spoke to the show's popularity, especially among white liberals. San Pedro resident Barbara Wasser wrote that "*Black on Black*, which appeared last night, offered me more insights into Negro problems than any show I've seen to date." The film was even used to teach race relations at Horace Mann Elementary School in Glendale. But *Black on Black* was also subject to a conservative backlash. Saltzman recounted that after the program first aired, calls came in through the CBS switchboard denigrating the documentary as little more than liberal propaganda. A copy of *Black on Black* was mutilated by a patron within days of its being donated to the Los Angeles Public Library.[28]

Saltzman spoke extensively with residents in Watts about the documentary. In an early-August memo to his producer Dan Gingold, he communicated that although some people were extremely positive about the show, others lamented that it was an isolated program created by outsiders, that it did not represent enough voices, and that it would not lead to progressive change within the neighborhood.[29] These were some of the same criticisms made about Stuart Schulberg's films. They also revealed dissatisfaction and skepticism regarding the idea that making a mainstream audience aware of issues facing African Americans would have an incisive and lasting socioeconomic impact on that community. It was around this time that filmmakers began to look beyond commercial broadcasting in order to cultivate a militant political cinema. Los Angeles Newsreel viewed liberal film practice as incapable of altering the status quo, and thus decidedly ineffectual when it came to radical social change. They believed that to truly empower minorities and the working class, a militant leftist cinema needed to exist outside of, and indeed take a strong position against, the commercial culture industries.

RADICAL NEWS

Newsreel began in New York but soon had a branch in Los Angeles. The organization emerged out of a meeting called by avant-garde impresario Jonas Mekas and the filmmaker Melvin Margolis in late 1967 at the Film-Makers' Cinematheque. They talked about the need for films to counter the mainstream media's representation of the antiwar March on the Pentagon. Network news and newspapers failed to take seriously the grievances of the protestors and the abuses they suffered. The core of New York Newsreel consisted of activists from Students for a Democratic Society and experimental filmmakers. Most of them were white, middle-class men. Local branches formed in Boston, Albuquerque, Detroit, Seattle, Atlanta,

San Francisco, and Los Angeles.[30] Newsreel contributed to what the documentary theorist Michael Renov calls the "political imaginary for the New Left."[31] Members sought to disrupt the consciences of spectators in an effort to politicize them, move them toward acts of resistance, and project the possibilities of what their actions might achieve. Newsreel's purview included the related struggles of the New Left: campus protests against the corporatization of the university; antiwar demonstrations; the committed endeavors of Third World nations to break free of colonial rule and influence; and grassroots protests by women and communities of color to fight systemic discrimination at home. Newsreel was opposed to commercial film, television, and publishing, which they saw as extensions of the ruling class's attempts to bolster economic and racial hierarchies.

San Francisco Newsreel's Marilyn Buck and Karen Ross articulated the group's hard battle lines in the winter 1968–69 issue of *Film Quarterly*. They described Newsreel as

> a way for film-makers and radical organizer-agitators to break into the consciousness of people. A chance to say something different . . . to say that people don't have to be spectator-puppets. In our hands film is not an anesthetic, a sterile, smooth-talking apparatus of control. It is a weapon to counter, to talk back to and to crack the façade of the lying media of capitalism.[32]

Early Newsreel films were short, 16mm, black-and-white productions and mainly came from the New York and San Francisco branches. Films were often conceived by collective debate, but those individuals with the financial means to create them held significantly more sway. Communal funds made available to filmmakers by the organization were, in reality, quite meager. On-location recorded sounds and images conveyed the immediacy and intensity of the action. Voice-over narration taught viewers about the meaning of the depicted confrontation. Editing, too, emphasized the tension between activists and oppressive institutions of the capitalist state. New York Newsreel's Robert Kramer claimed: "Our films remind some people of battle footage: grainy, camera weaving around trying to get the material and still not get beaten/trapped. Well, we, and many others, are at war."[33] Introductions and post-screening discussions made viewing interactive, expanding audience comprehension of the film's arguments. In its first two years, Newsreel covered a range of topics. *Columbia Revolt* (1968) concentrated on the student protests against the university's expansion into Harlem; *Off the Pig* (1968) presented key principles of the Black Panthers and the need for the organization to take a stand against racist police and the judicial system; *Garbage* (1968) looked at the dumping of garbage in the plaza at Lincoln Center by the anarchist collective Up Against the Wall Motherfucker; and *America* (1969) explored the antiwar movement.

Los Angeles became a hub for the exhibition of Newsreel films, along with documentaries from Third Cinema filmmakers such as Santiago Álvarez. Films were

available to rent from Los Angeles Students for a Democratic Society leader Jim
Fite. The underground newspaper the *Los Angeles Free Press* advertised screenings
and interviews with branch leaders.[34] In his article "Guerrilla Newsreels," the critic
Gene Youngblood heralded Newsreel as "the most important mass communication
development in this country in decades."[35] Los Angeles Newsreel began following
an October 1968 screening of *Off the Pig* and established a small office at 1331 West
Washington Boulevard in the unpretentious bohemian enclave of Venice. Approximately fifty people attended the first meeting, but the organization soon pared
down to a smaller contingent composed of Ron Abrams, Jonathan Aurthur, Judy
Belsito, Peter Belsito, Bill Floyd, Christine Hansen, Dennis Hicks, Mike Murphy,
Barbara Rose, Elinor Schiffrin, and Stephanie Waxman. Like other branches, Los
Angeles Newsreel was mainly white, middle class, and college educated. However,
there was a more even gender balance. Also, the Marxist orientation of the members, along with their strong interest in organizing, steered the chapter toward exhibition rather than production. The collective worked with political groups to host
screenings. Films supported these groups' goals, raised the political consciousness
of viewers, and served as catalysts for conversation. Los Angeles Newsreel showed
films at rallies, union halls, welfare and unemployment offices, and branches of the
Los Angeles Public Library. UCLA, California State College, Valley College, and
City College were also popular venues for Newsreel films. Beyond Los Angeles,
Hicks and Waxman screened *Salt of the Earth* (1954), a blacklisted film about a
Mexican American zinc miners' strike in New Mexico, for Chicano activist Rodolfo
"Corky" Gonzales's "Crusade for Justice" event in Denver.

Los Angeles Newsreel collaborated closely with the Black Panthers, who drew
extensively from the city's black working class and unemployed youth. Bobby
Seale and Huey Newton started the Black Panther Party in Oakland in October
1966. They saw self-determination as both a process and an objective for achieving
the collective liberation of black Americans. Chapters formed in Baltimore, Chicago, Seattle, and Cleveland. Former Slauson Avenue gang member Alprentice
"Bunchy" Carter established the Southern California chapter in 1968. The base of
operations was Forty-First Street and Central Avenue. Geographer Laura Pulido
describes the chapter as "notable for its size, commitment to self-defense, intense
police repression, and leadership."[36] Carter embraced the Panthers' revolutionary
nationalism, and pursued an agenda of armed patrol, a free breakfast for children
program, and a health care clinic. For recruitment and community education, Los
Angeles Newsreel frequently screened *Off the Pig* at Panther headquarters. They
also screened films with the Panthers for special events, including an antiwar picnic and teach-in at Fairmont Park in Riverside. The filmmaking collective's initial
four projects were never completed. These included documentaries about the Panthers' free breakfast program, urban development in Venice, political unrest in
Mexico, and the Lamaze method of childbirth.[37] Los Angeles Newsreel moved

adamantly toward production around the turn of the decade, just as the break-down of unity inside Students for a Democratic Society, along with the FBI's nationwide assault on the Black Panthers, inhibited the sustainability of the collective. Los Angeles Newsreel struck a defiant position. They became increasingly radical in the face of state violence in the streets and the persistence of the government's war in Southeast Asia. *Repression* (1970), which was primarily shot and edited by Hicks and Murphy, decisively called for the cross-racial organizing of working-class people toward armed resistance.

A montage of photographs and archival footage at the film's onset likens black labor to a form of imprisonment within the United States. The searing saxophone of Ornette Coleman's "Sadness" plays against scenes of African Americans collecting garbage, picking cotton, working in a factory, and walking as part of a chain gang and in handcuffs flanked by police. The testimony of minister of education Masai Hewitt makes explicit the connection between race and economic exploitation, contending that minorities come to the United States from all over the world for the purpose of the white ruling class's economic gain. Hewitt explains that racism is used to maintain an oppressive global capitalist system. The close-up on Margaret Bourke-White's 1937 photograph *Kentucky Flood* contrasts the mainstream media's whitewashed fantasy of the American dream with a stark Great Depression–era lived experience. The photograph shows black men and women standing in line for food and clothing under a billboard showing a white family happily driving in a car. The banner text reads, "World's Highest Standard of Living: There's No Way Like the American Way." The photograph calls attention to the persistent incongruity between economic fantasy (as generated by the mass cultural industries) and grim quotidian reality. The image also highlights the idea that the freedom and mobility offered by the automobile seems to be geared toward whites only, that not all Americans can share in the thrill and practical benefits of having access to a car.

Repression then moves to the streets of South Central in the current moment. The film contends that recent attacks on the Panthers have been distorted or ignored by the mainstream press. Instead, Americans hear misinformation about the Panthers' excessive use of guns, that they are inciting violence in the streets, or that Panthers are anti-white. Footage of children eating at the free breakfast program shows one of the organization's constructive community activities, demonstrating that the Panthers give to hungry children what American businesses and the government have not been able to provide. *Repression* also spotlights the FBI and the Los Angeles Police Department's highly coordinated December 8, 1969, raid on Panther headquarters, occurring four days after the murder of deputy chairman Fred Hampton in Chicago. State authorities had been escalating their targeted assaults, arrests, and harassment of the Panthers over the past two years, resulting in the demise of Panther leadership on a local and national scale. In

Repression, footage of the dilapidated, bullet-riddled exterior of the Panther head-quarters, crowds of frustrated people milling around the entrance, and police patrolling the territory register the suffering experienced by the black community. *Repression* then declares that the Panthers are under attack from the government and black nationalist organizations collaborating with establishment politicians. Images of the funeral of Panther luminaries John Huggins and Bunchy Carter are paired with voice-over narration stating that both individuals were killed in a gun-fight with the US Organization. *Repression* asserts that Ron Karenga and the US Organization, a black cultural nationalist group, have ties to the wealthy and polit-ical Rockefeller family and are responsible for the deaths of Huggins and Carter.

The film pivots here to call for solidarity and action. With many Panther higher-ups struck down, it argues, there is a need for new ones to come forward (as Elaine Brown's song "The End of Silence" intones). *Repression*'s message is on one level an attempt to help rebuild the battered Los Angeles chapter. It is also an attempt to mobilize oppressed people across the United States. Panther leader David Hilliard and Los Angeles Newsreel's Elinor Schiffrin and Jonathan Aurthur assert that viewers of *Repression*—black, brown, yellow, red, and white, male and female—should look not just to the Panthers for inspiration, but also to liberation move-ments in Guinea-Bissau, Mozambique, and Angola as well as in Asia and Latin America. *Repression* claims that rebellion against capitalist institutions and the creation of an alternative, socialist system of labor is necessary to bring about a sweeping redistribution of power to the working class and the poor. Los Angeles Newsreel screened the film to Panthers, fellow radicals, and filmmakers at UCLA, but it was deemed too militant and ideologically loaded for organizing. It advo-cated for a path of leftist action that the collective and its allies were not prepared to pursue, nor was the confrontation it promoted practicably feasible. *Repression* was more revolutionary reverie than battle plan or blueprint.

The very same political shifts that Los Angeles Newsreel documented ultimately caused the collective to disintegrate. With the Panthers reeling from sustained attacks and internal tensions, the film collective lost the political organization with which it had aligned its operations. So, too, did sectarian infighting and the partici-pation of the California Communist League compound its inability to function. Numerous members moved into factory work at the General Motors plant in South Gate or participated in local activism throughout the city. Film scholar David James argues that the city's long-standing opposition to left-liberal organizations, as well as its fragmented social geography, inhibited the populist working-class cin-ema Los Angeles Newsreel envisioned and prevented the realization of *Repression*'s revolutionary aspirations.[38] Also weighing against the possibility of imagining a future for Los Angeles Newsreel were growing pressures for minority access to the means of media production. Debates surrounding authorship and editorial control essentially fractured the production-focused New York Newsreel. In Los Angeles, people of color and women were beginning to make their voices heard from behind and in front of the camera, resulting in alternative models for politically engaged cinema. Filmmakers frequently struck a critical stance against government institutions and corporate power, but did not necessarily advocate for sweeping revolutionary change. Instead, they saw cinema as a means to build, strengthen, and politicize their communities.

HUMAN AFFAIRS AT PBS

Los Angeles had been slow to invest in noncommercial television, but Community Television of Southern California eventually established KCET in 1964. Hollywood insiders (David Wolper and Bob Hope), business leaders (Jesse Tapp of Bank of America and James Doolittle of Space Technology Laboratories), as well as communications conglomerate Metromedia were vocal supporters and contributed financial resources to its launch. KCET affiliated with the Ford Foundation–backed National Educational Television network and set up shop at 1313 Vine Street. Referencing how former FCC chair Newton Minow had famously disparaged Hollywood's penchant for creating mass-produced entertainment television, critic Cecil Smith claimed KCET would give the Los Angeles "wasteland a shot in [the] arm."[39] However, financial setbacks and allegations that the station was too conservative in its programing led to a change in administration in 1967.[40] Government support for public television legislation set KCET on a fresh path. As broadcasting scholar James L. Baughman writes, support for an expansive system of public television stemmed from the perceived failure of commercial broadcasting to address the concerns of diverse constituencies and to create programs with educational value.[41] Lyndon B. Johnson, in his speech for the signing of the Public Broadcasting Act that same year, declared that public television "announces to the world that our nation wants more than just material wealth. . . . While we work every day to produce new goods and to create new wealth, we want most of all to enrich man's spirit." Public television, he hoped, could be used for "education and knowledge" for the nation's citizenry.[42] In many cases, public television reflected the Cold War liberalism and elitist tastes of its architects. Thus, programming meant documenting the high arts of classical music and ballet, teaching world history from a Western perspective, or offering instruction in practical skills.[43] And yet, there was a strong, albeit vague, desire to create an inclusive media platform for people who were usually marginalized within American society. The Carnegie Commission on Educational Television's seminal 1967 report *Public Television: A Program for Action* recommended that the government should play an active role in noncommercial television:

Public Television programming can deepen a sense of community in local life. It should show us our community as it really is. It should be a forum for debate and controversy. It should bring into the home meetings, now generally untelevised, where major public decisions are hammered out, and occasions where people of the community express their hopes, their protests, their enthusiasms, and their will. It should provide a voice for groups in the community that may otherwise be unheard.[44]

The Kerner Commission Report, in concert with progressive filmmakers, cultural administrators, and grassroots advocacy groups influenced the practical applications of public television's programming mandate. This was especially true at the local level. At KCET, program director Charles Allen was committed to creating Los Angeles–centered, socially conscious shows. He recognized that the diverse communities of the city needed and demanded this kind of programming. In 1967 the station received part of a $3.5 million grant to help create the telenovela-style series *Canción de la Raza* (1968–70). The success of the show facilitated a follow-up Mexican American–themed series, *¡Ahora!* (1969–70).[45] KCET soon hired the young Mexican American filmmaker Jesús Salvador Treviño to work on the show.

Born in El Paso, Texas, Treviño grew up in the East Los Angeles neighborhoods of Boyle Heights and Lincoln Heights. He studied philosophy and cinema at Occidental College and became increasingly interested in politics. After graduating in 1968, he joined the Chicano movement, which coalesced around a number of issues: resistance to the Vietnam War, in which Mexican Americans were disproportionately killed; the 1968 walkouts by Mexican American students from East Los Angeles high schools protesting the city's deplorable public school conditions and tendency to bar Mexican culture from the general curriculum; and the Cesar Chavez and Dolores Huerta–led labor protests in the Central Valley.[46]

Writer and community leader Frank Sifuentes brought Treviño into the recently established minority training program New Communicators. The Office of Economic Opportunity provided necessary funds and USC cinema professor Mel Sloan, filmmaker Jack Dunbar, and producer Mae Churchill oversaw the training sessions.[47] Treviño attended classes at a converted bank located at 6211 Hollywood Boulevard. Fellow students Martín Quiroz and Esperanza Vásquez would become lifelong collaborators. Treviño first made the drama *Ya Basta!* (1968) about a Chicano student expelled from school and killed on the way home. Second, he made the newsreel *La Raza Nueva* (1969), which contextualized the recent school walkouts, the arrest of the "L.A. Thirteen," and the sit-in at Lincoln High School in protest of the suspension of teacher Sal Castro. Third, he created a documentary about the National Chicano Youth Liberation Conference in Denver, where the poetic manifesto "El Plan Espiritual de Aztlán" was read aloud.

Treviño landed a job at KCET working with producer Ed Moreno on *¡Ahora!*. He quickly advanced from assistant to associate producer to cohost. Rather than shoot the program at the station in Hollywood, Treviño and Moreno set up a satellite studio on 5237 Beverly Boulevard in East Los Angeles. In contrast to standard news and public affairs reporting, they actively sought a direct dialogue with the city's Mexican American residents. KCET's September 1969 program guide, which featured *¡Ahora!* on its cover, announced that the series covered "the Mexican American community in all its aspects: art, music, economics, politics, problems, accomplishments and aspirations." Moreno later emphasized in a *Los Angeles Times* article that the series stressed the city's Mexican American roots as well as Chicanos' contemporary contributions to public life: "Our heritage isn't just Olvera Street, Sepulveda Boulevard, and enchiladas. It goes much deeper than that."[48] *¡Ahora!*'s first episode comprised a cross-section of topical issues. Community organizers discussed the recent high school walkouts. Children from a Head Start program performed movement songs. Chicano painter Gilbert "Magú" Luján presented his artwork. And members of the League of Mexican American Women gave a talk. In later episodes, Treviño and Luis Torres introduced *La Raza History*, a weekly series of five- to ten-minute vignettes on Chicano history spanning hundreds of years.[49] Treviño also produced the three-part documentary *Image: The Mexican American in Motion Pictures and Television* (1970). The first part attends to the different ways Mexican Americans have been stereotyped. The second part exposes discriminatory hiring practices against Mexican Americans in the entertainment industry. The third part argues for the need to increase the number of Mexican American producers, directors, and writers.

Treviño recalled that local residents frequently told him how much they appreciated *¡Ahora!*. Following the screening of an episode at an Educational Issues Coordinating Committee meeting, the audience gave him a standing ovation.[50] Notwithstanding the show's appeal, *¡Ahora!* was brought to a standstill in the spring of 1970 due to the costs of the large staff combined with an inability to secure additional funds from outside donors.[51] Still, as film scholar Chon Noriega points out, the series served as a catalyst, encouraging the station toward Chicano-themed programming.[52] The establishment of the Human Affairs department constituted an umbrella framework under which marginalized voices in the city gained a platform to speak. The department pooled financial and technical resources. Éclair cameras and Nagra recorders allowed for mobile, on-location shooting. Filmmakers crewed on one another's projects and shared common topics and questions of interest, while still creating their own documentaries from distinct points of view. Their documentaries were penetrating forms of public history, bolstering a feeling of ethnic pride and dignity within their respective communities, and helping residents to talk to themselves about themselves. At the same time, their documentaries mobilized support against systemic forces of injustice. When Human Affairs evolved into the L.A. Collective (which brought together different nonfiction divisions within KCET) in the early 1970s, filmmakers continued to make stand-alone documentaries and series with the same ethos.

Treviño's *Chicano Moratorium: The Aftermath* (also titled *The Salazar Inquest*, 1970) depicted the August 29, 1970, Chicano Moratorium march down Whittier Boulevard to Laguna Park. The mass demonstration against the Vietnam War brought twenty thousand Chicanos from Texas, Arizona, and New Mexico. Many journalists mischaracterized the protestors as violent and disorganized. When the *Los Angeles Times* columnist and KMEX news chief Rubén Salazar was fatally shot by a sheriff's deputy with a tear-gas projectile at the Silver Dollar Bar, the mainstream media sided with the courts and law enforcement and deemed his death an accident. Treviño's nationally broadcast documentary provided a perspective from the Chicano community that countered "official" accounts. The film walks the viewer through the sixteen days of the inquest, by means of footage of the peaceful marchers, clashes with police, and court proceedings. KCET's legal consultant Howard Miller explains how eyewitness testimony concerning the deliberate forcing of Salazar into the bar, along with his targeted killing at the hands of police officers, had been strategically silenced. The film played nationally on PBS and won the San Francisco Broadcasting Industry Award for Best News Program. Diana Loercher of the *Christian Science Monitor* wrote, "The Program's most creative effect lay in instilling enough knowledge in the viewer's consciousness, and conscience, to enable him to evaluate the factors for himself. The evident Chicano bias seemed more an attempt to give fair presentation to an underdog position than a departure from objectivity."[53]

América Tropical (1971) explored the distant Mexican American past as essential to the construction of contemporary Chicano identity. Treviño's film is at once a narrative account of the creation of a 1932 mural by David Alfaro Siqueiros, and a symbolic examination of the recent resurfacing of Chicano culture. *América Tropical* begins by looking at Siqueiros's work in the city through sepia-toned photographs and interviews with the artist, his former collaborators, and art historian Shifra Goldman. Siqueiros was a committed socialist who frequently painted scenes of labor in his art. *Workers' Meeting* (1932), the mural he created with students at the Chouinard Art Institute, portrayed an image of black, white, and brown manual laborers gathered together for passionate dialogue with a union organizer. The provocative image supported class solidarity to strengthen the strikes then taking place in California's Central Valley, and condemned the forced repatriation of Mexican Americans. The owner of the Plaza Arts Center on Olvera Street subsequently wanted Siqueiros to paint a large mural of a tropical paradise. Siqueiros, the film explains, instead painted *América Tropical*, an image of violent oppression measuring eighteen by eighty feet. In the mural, an Indian is tied to a double cross, atop which a threatening eagle—the same that appears on the back of the US quarter—is prominently perched. The ruined Mayan temple in the background cements the theme of Western imperial violence toward indigenous peoples. The mural was quickly whitewashed over, and with the renewal of Siqueiros's US visa denied, he had to leave the country.

FIGURE 10: Still from *América Tropical*, 1971, 16mm; directed by Jesús Salvador Treviño; photographed by Barry Nye; broadcast on KCET, Los Angeles. DVD, Cinema Guild, New York, 2006.

América Tropical then shifts to the present. It portrays Olvera Street in the early 1970s as a quaint thoroughfare where tourists purchase sombreros and listen to mariachi music. Observational shots of the mural show Mexican art restorers discussing the possibilities of stripping away the whitewash, a material metaphor for cultural recovery. Commenting on the film at the time, Treviño asserted that the mural is "symbolic of the treatment the Chicano has had in the United States. . . . It reminds us that there have been other whitewashings, and that we are faced with some of the same feelings that were there in the early 1930s."[54] Contemporary artists in the film echo Treviño's claims and announce that Siqueiros is being brought back into public awareness through the mural and lives on in the street art of a new generation of practitioners. The resurfacing of Siqueiros is part of an effort to build a collective identity for Chicanos and ensure they are seen and heard within the city. *América Tropical's* local exhibition, combined with it winning the Silver Medallion award at the International Film and Television Festival in New York, heightened awareness of the mural and began the long campaign to restore the work of art and make it publicly accessible.

Treviño expanded upon *América Tropical's* theme of historical recovery in *Yo Soy Chicano* (1972). The documentary took up questions posed by Rubén Salazar in his polemical February 6, 1970, *Los Angeles Times* column "Who Is a Chicano? And What Is It the Chicanos Want?" by presenting the histories of Chicano people from pre-Columbian times to the present.[55] The film juxtaposes a past made out of archival photographs, maps, paintings, voice-over, and staged reenactments, with a present captured through verité-style footage shot by Barry Nye and Martín Quiroz. The structure serves a twofold rhetorical purpose. First, it declares that the Chicano civil rights movement is part of a hundred-year-long fight against dispossession and prejudice. For example, after a description of the 1848 Treaty of Guadalupe Hidalgo and the steady seizing of territory and refusal to honor citizenship rights, recent footage of Reies López Tijerina shows his determination to win back the New Mexico land-grant territories. Shots of Tijerina speaking at New Mexico Highlands University and West Las Vegas High School depict him as a charismatic and revered leader. At another point in the film, photographs that illustrate the

plight of Central Valley migrant farm labor in the early twentieth century are jux-
taposed with footage from United Farm Workers rallies and interviews with
Dolores Huerta. She speaks proudly about the formation of the union in 1962,
the strike of 1965, and the five-year Delano Grape Strike that ended victoriously in
July 1970.

Second, *Yo Soy Chicano* demonstrates that culture is essential to how Chicanos
understand themselves. The documentary traces a historical line from the art,
music, and literature of postrevolutionary Mexico through to the Denver-based
poet Rodolfo "Corky" Gonzales, author of the poem "Yo Soy Joaquín." Even the
film's title song, composed and performed by El Teatro Campesino, is an adaptation of the popular corrido from the Mexican Revolution, "La Rielera." Culture
becomes a repository of collective memory and a way to sustain group identity
across time and space. Critic Cecil Smith wrote that the film "would segue from
the political and social situations here and along the Texas border towns . . . into
the historical context, where the people came from, their presence on this land
long before the Anglos took over."[56] Treviño told the *Los Angeles Times*, "In the
schools, Chicanos are not taught their history, I really went into the historical
experience in order to start filling in the gaps." The documentary was first shown
on KCET and around Los Angeles, including a community premiere at the new
KCET studio. The film then played nationally.[57]

Treviño, together with Chicana activist and filmmaker Rosamaria Marquez,
produced the public affairs series *Acción Chicano* (1972–74). The first episode took
place at the impressive Plaza de la Raza, the recently constructed library, art center,
museum, auditorium, and classroom space in Lincoln Park. The site was an accessible, mixed-use communal space for Chicanos, constructed by means of a combination of federal Model Cities funds and funds from organizations such as the East
Los Angeles Community Union. Other *Acción Chicano* episodes included a profile
of the Mexican American women's organization Comisión Femenil Mexicana
Nacional and a deliberation among Chicano professors about the struggle to
establish Chicano studies at universities.

An important episode covered the first national convention of La Raza Unida
Party. The event was held in El Paso September 1 through 5, 1972. The party was
established in 1970 in Crystal City, Texas, as a deliberate alternative to the country's two-party system, one that could directly serve the sociopolitical and economic needs of Chicanos. With electoral victories of local candidates, La Raza
Unida expanded throughout Texas and into the Southwest and West Coast states.
Movement luminaries Reies López Tijerina, Rodolfo "Corky" Gonzales, and José
Angel Gutiérrez convened a national convention to unify the party, establish a
platform, and determine its leadership. Treviño was in charge of media relations
for the convention and also documented its unfolding. The *Acción Chicano* episode depicted a debate among representatives about goals for the party and the

prospects of cross-racial and transnational coalition building. The differences between Gonzales's militant nationalism and Gutiérrez's ambition to grow broad-based support were evident. The film also explored tenets of the party platform, backing the United Farm Workers Union, equitable salaries, school reform, the acquisition of land-grant territories, and maintaining an independent position from Democratic and Republican Parties. After Gutiérrez is elected party chairperson in an intense election, the film ends with a call for shared ethno-cultural identity and political purpose.

The African American filmmaker Sue Booker was another key member of KCET. Born in Chicago, Booker studied film, journalism, and creative writing at the University of Illinois. At Columbia's Graduate School of Journalism, she took classes with Fred Friendly and participated in campus protests. She graduated in 1968 and worked with Jon Stone and Samuel Y. Gibbon Jr. at the Children's Television Workshop, developing what would become *Sesame Street* (launched in 1969). She then joined Nebraska's public television station KUON for the series *The Black Frontier* (1969–70), which depicted the experiences of nineteenth-century black traders, soldiers, and cowboys.[58] Charles Allen recruited Booker to KCET. Booker later recounted that she desired to "document the history and present moment of the African American people. Our lives were invisible and I wanted to make us visible, in all our beauty and dignity."[59] One of her first programs, *Cleophus Adair* (1970), concentrated on the problem of drugs in Watts. The documentary followed a reformed addict who went on to serve as a senior counselor at the House of Uhuru clinic and social services center. Both Adair and House of Uhuru were depicted as badly needed and much beloved by the community. Booker used Adair's recorded voice as well as on-screen scenes of him giving an informal tour of the area to explore the sociological conditions that made Watts vulnerable to drugs.[60] The documentary was nominated for a local Emmy.

Booker and Treviño's collaborative project *Soledad* (1971) investigated California's infamous Soledad State Prison. It was alleged that prison authorities had framed three African American inmates for killing a white guard. The prison was known for mistreating inmates of color, especially those who were politically outspoken. Booker, Treviño, and cameraman Barry Nye got permission to film inside the prison and were led by deputy warden Jerry Enomoto on a series of interviews with inmates on their way to parole. Distracting the prison authorities, the team managed to conduct on-the-fly interviews with inmates. Otis Tugwell spoke about the "hole," a solitary confinement "prison within the prison" in which inmates were placed and sometimes found dead. Tugwell decried the racist mistreatment of minorities and censorship regarding the expression of leftist political opinions. In a heated moment in *Soledad*, a befuddled Enomoto is unable to respond to black inmate Chris Walker's statements about racism in the facility. The documentary won first prize and a jury award at the Atlanta International Film Festival.[61]

Subsequently, Booker created a series of nationally broadcast, black-themed programs under the title *Doin' It!* (1972). The series was broken down into nine episodes, with each installment lasting thirty minutes. The first show, the Emmy-nominated "Victory Will Be My Moan" (1972), examined the radical politicization of black inmates made to live in horrific conditions. In the program, actors dramatize the real-life experiences of incarcerated individuals. Big Man plays a self-taught revolutionary who tries to educate his fellow inmates. He shares a cell with a drug addict, an ex-hustler, and a newly arrived convict. For the soundtrack, the Watts Prophets perform poetry written by prisoners.[62] Booker turned *Doin' It!* into the locally broadcast series *Doin' It at the Storefront* (1972–73). She insisted on having a studio in South Central, enabling the series to have a strong presence within the community. Booker set up a "storefront" studio at 4211 South Broadway. In an interview with *Essence*, she explained: "Because we're regarded as a part of the community, people walk in off the streets with news stories for us. This aids us in presenting news that receives very little, if any, coverage in the general mass media. White media has a crisis coverage mentality and, therefore, ignores our daily lives and struggles, which seem minor but are really major events that lead to the changes of tomorrow."[63]

The studio was a space from which to broadcast as well as a social destination. Booker encouraged people to drop in off the street to share story ideas. The studio was also used as a meeting center to discuss health, education, and arts outreach. With the facility's open-door policy, Booker was able to formulate a community calendar. The series' community coordinator, Agnes McClain, would read the schedule of upcoming events during each program. Booker also frequently appeared to introduce the topics of the program as well as the staff. This established an intimate rapport with viewers and signaled her investment in the lineup of topics. She even proudly introduced interns, whose labor is often invisible in the television industry. Journalist Maury Green wrote that the show's embedded studio made it "more than a news bureau," and that "Booker concerns herself with the things that matter to the black community."[64] The *New York Amsterdam News* called the concept "unique" because of how it functioned as a "community center as well as a news-gathering office." *Doin' It at the Storefront* directly tended to local needs. For example, Booker's staff took families of inmates to California prisons for visits. John Outterbridge's Compton Communicative Arts Academy gave Booker an award for her pioneering work in community engagement.[65]

The series' episodes can be classified into three major clusters. The first focused on direct activism, which included events like the November 1972 strike at the William Mead public housing project or Angela Davis's speeches against Richard Nixon's attack on minority rights. The second looked at neighborhood culture, which included topics such as the Yo' People rhythm and blues ensemble, Horace Tapscott's Pan Afrikan Peoples Arkestra, or Mayme Clayton's Third World Ethnic Bookstore. And the third examined national debates that reverberated locally, such as illiteracy and blaxploitation cinema's impact on spectators.[66] The format for each individual program consisted of a mix of performances, interviews, speeches, and conversations. For example, "Soul Radio and the Black Community" (1973) described the creative skills and important function of black DJs. In the program DJs appear in their broadcasting booths like artists in studios. Their manipulations of the microphone, records, switches, and levers make for an elegant performance. The DJs comment on daily life, while also creating a soundboard for listeners to phone in and voice their opinions. The charismatic KGFJ DJ Magnificent Montague, whose signature shout-out was "Burn, Baby! Burn!" exclaims into the microphone and out to his listeners: "Put your hand on the radio and reach out and touch me this morning." Or, in the beginning of the episode "The Church" (1973), Operation Breadbasket Choir sings "Go Down Moses" on a soundstage, before Booker appears in front of the camera to provide an introduction. She talks about the history of the black church in the United States as an establishment that upheld the humanity of its members and assisted in their ability to maintain a connection to their African roots. Paul Kidd Jr., who serves as the gospel DJ for KGFJ, then guides the viewer through a timeline of African American religious history. He begins with the Free African Society in the late eighteenth century, speaks about the role played by preachers in helping their congregations deal with the promise and disappointments of black freedom during Reconstruction, and affirms the importance of religious teachings to the civil rights movement. The show concludes by surveying contemporary nationalist perspectives on religion, for example Reverend Albert Cleage's Black Christian Nationalism and Malcolm X and Elijah Muhammad's Nation of Islam. The Operation Breadbasket Choir provides lyrical commentary on the history that Kidd narrates, at times singing hymns or gospel tunes such as "Steal Away Home," "I Want to Be a Worker for the Lord," or "Come, Let Us Walk This Road Together." Booker's series and stand-alone documentaries made black Angelenos more aware of themselves as possessing shared life experiences, cultural rituals, and sociopolitical concerns.

Lynne Littman was another essential Human Affairs member, creating a niche for herself in documenting the burgeoning women's liberation movement. Born in the Bronx, New York, Littman studied French and philosophy with Susan Sontag at Sarah Lawrence College and spent her junior year abroad in Paris, where she developed a love for European New Wave cinema. After graduating from college in 1962, she returned to New York motivated to find employment in the film and television industries. She found opportunities for women extremely limited, but worked her way up from a secretarial position at WNET to jobs where she was directly involved in production. She became a photographic researcher for Wolper Productions and an associate producer for William Greaves's series *Black Journal* (1968–78), the first nationally syndicated black public affairs show. She also crewed as an editor and associate producer on individual *NET Journal* documentaries.

Diary of a Student Revolution (1969) investigated the University of Connecticut students' opposition to on-campus recruitment by corporations. Some of the companies had connections to weapons being used in Vietnam. *What Harvest for the Reaper* (1968) explored the lives of migrant African American laborers in agricultural camps in Cutchogue, Long Island, where they picked beans for low wages and were housed in ramshackle lodgings.

The French filmmaker Agnès Varda recruited Littman to come to Los Angeles to work as an assistant on the art-house fiction film *Lions Love* (1969). Littman had met Varda at the New York Film Festival through their mutual friend and colleague, the Canadian cinematographer Guy Borremans. Littman would later recall heated conversations with Varda about the dynamic state of world cinema, the challenges to creating socially engaged art, and the need for more women directors. *Lions Love* looked at the antics of New York underground performers Viva, Jim Rado, and Jerry Ragni. They play struggling actors who spend much of their time in a house and backyard pool on St. Ives Street above the Sunset Strip. The trio tries on and takes off different identities: strung-out hippies, celebrities, a nuclear family with kids. The satirical performances poke fun at the artifice of the entertainment industry and the glamour associated with the health-conscious, affluent Los Angeles lifestyle.[67]

Littman found that she was interested in the lives of the city's diverse inhabitants rather than in deconstructing the dream factory: "Journalism and documentary were different than fiction film. They were a way to really learn about the world . . . and in documentary, you find that everyday people have important, heartfelt things to say."[68] Determined to create her own films, Littman made UCLA-sponsored medical documentaries about drug addiction and counseling. With the formation of Human Affairs at KCET, she landed a job in public television. Her films advanced the cause of women's liberation, demonstrating that "private" and "personal" issues associated with domestic life, the family, and the body were indeed public and political.

Littman was connected to Los Angeles's National Organization for Women (NOW) chapter, which organized around gender equality in the workplace, increasing access to education and job training, as well as the expansion of childcare and maternity leave. Fighting for progressive legislation, participating in protests and consciousness-raising circles, as well as the fashioning of self-representations in the media were all important. *In the Matter of Kenneth* (1973) concentrated on the efforts of state officials to take a poor black child away from his mother due to charges of abuse, with lawyers advocating that they be allowed to stay together; *Airwoman* (1972) exposed the abuses suffered by airline stewardesses; *Come Out Singing* (1972) captured an in-studio performance by the feminist folk singers Holly Near, Cris Williamson, Margi Adam, and Meg Christian; *Fortune in Singles* (1972) chastised the parents who profited from a child's acting career as well as other entertainment industry affiliates who made money from the labor of children; *Power to the Playgroup* (1972) profiled a much-loved playgroup that was being pushed out of its Silver Lake neighborhood facility because of a minor building violation.

Womanhouse Is Not a Home (1972) was Littman's largest project of the period and most directly intersected with the creative endeavors of other feminists. The film focused on the seminal art installation and collaborative performance space *Womanhouse*, organized by artists Judy Chicago and Miriam Schapiro. The documentary is an extraordinary record of the ephemeral installation and affirms the value of art as a community-building social practice. One of the motivating forces for *Womanhouse* was to create a space for female cultural production that could stand against a male-dominated art establishment. The same year that the Los Angeles Council of Women Artists protested the 1971 Los Angeles County Museum of Art's *Art and Technology* exhibition for excluding women from its roster, Chicago began one of the first feminist art programs at Fresno State College. When the administration insisted that she shut it down, she started the Feminist Art Program at CalArts in Valencia. With the new facility under construction, Chicago, Schapiro, and art historian Paula Harper planned an independent exhibition. They created *Womanhouse* with their students in a soon-to-be-demolished seventy-five-year-old mansion at 533 North Mariposa Street in Hollywood. Students transformed each of the seventeen rooms into a themed space that spoke to different aspects of the female experience. The artists deliberated together on the direction of each room.

Littman had met the artists of *Womanhouse* as well as one of the founders of the Feminist Art Program at CalArts, Sheila de Bretteville, through her participation in consciousness-raising circles hosted by individuals in living rooms across Los Angeles. *Womanhouse Is Not a Home* captures the themed spaces, performances that took place on the premises, and visitors' reactions and conversations with one another. The documentary's title announces that the "house" in which the art is exhibited is not simply a "home," nor a traditional museum or a gallery. As the film makes clear, *Womanhouse* was intended to destabilize viewers' assumptions about the separation between art and life, public and private realms of experience. After a piano performance by Debby Quinn in which she sings a ballad in praise of female independence, "Do You Think That It Would Matter," Littman takes the viewer to the building's front door. People walking in and out give their initial impressions. One woman says that men should definitely come to the exhibition, because they would learn a lot. Another says that it is a wonderful commentary on the female experience. A man's gripe that *Womanhouse* should be "redecorated" appears as a condescending sound bite, diminished by the testimonies of praise that surround it.

Moving inside the house, longer interviews with the artists lend insight into their processes and provide an interpretation of each room. Vicki Hodgetts and Robin Weltsch discuss their *Nurturant Kitchen*, which features sunny-side-up eggs on the ceiling that slowly morph into rubber breasts on the walls. They talk about the room as registering the sense of angst and frustration with a woman's domestic role, but also the sense of warmth women may feel within the space. Hodgetts and Weltsch share that their fellow artists urged them to think about representing food and the body together. In *The Nursery*, large furniture and androgynous dolls fill a room painted dark blue and red. Artist Shawnee Wollenman reflects on the idea that the room is designed to simulate the experience of being a child; however, the gender-neutral toys and decor subvert traditional gender norms.

Interwoven with the film's tour of the different rooms are short performances. A silent Sandra Orgel irons a piece of fabric in *Ironing*, continuously repositioning and refolding the linen. The absence of any background noise, along with the unflinching camera, amplifies the sound of her ironing and focuses attention on the routine. The performance argues that domestic work can be a form of exacting, isolating, and monotonous labor. In *The Birth Trilogy* a group of women choreograph "birthing, mothering, and nurturing" as a series of stages. In a choreographed dance, they first simulate the act of giving birth to one another, before crawling toward and singing in one another's arms. The shift in sound from the collective cry of "push" to the lullaby-like chant gives continuity to the performance. In Judy Chicago's *Menstruation Bathroom*, a stark white bathroom contains shelves stuffed with wadded-up cotton and used tampons overflowing a trash can. The intention, as Chicago indicates, is to call attention to the contrast between the public fantasy of women's bodies as "sanitized" and "pure" and their actual experiences. Menstruation is often not talked about, but rather treated as invisible or taboo. The installation foregrounds a sense of frustration with women feeling as though they must keep themselves hidden behind literal and symbolic closed doors, and the desire to make visible the facts of the female body.

Interviews also lend insight into how the members of the class felt about the installation. Judy Huddleston states of her *Personal Environment* that working collaboratively was at first hard, but that she quickly found her classmates a source of constant encouragement and camaraderie. One scene features Chicago, Schapiro, and Gloria Steinem debating how the *Womanhouse* installation positions the women's liberation movement vis-à-vis artistic practice, thus counteracting the commonplace suppression of female experience in art school. The women also debate whether male understanding should be considered extraneous to the project's core goals. Littman's film does not seek to arrive at fixed conclusions about these issues, but rather to bring attention to the discourse surrounding the creation and exhibition of feminist art.

Outside of the *Womanhouse* exhibition, Chicago along with art historian Arlene Raven and graphic designer Sheila de Bretteville created the Feminist Studio Workshop. They were buoyed by a belief that women can understand other women, as well as advocate for their rights by means of art. The workshop evolved into the

Woman's Building. The institution opened in late 1973 at 743 South Grandview near MacArthur Park, the former site of the Chouinard Art Institute.[69] It was a mixed-use facility offering theatrical productions, art displays, the Sisterhood Bookstore, a coffeehouse, and a NOW office. Littman frequently visited the Woman's Building, and the creative hub would be important for her later documentaries.

Littman, Booker, and Treviño all used the resources of KCET to advance the social movements in which they were deeply invested. And just as public television offered one kind of framework on which marginalized communities could rely to produce socially engaged films, the public university provided another.

VISUAL COMMUNICATIONS AND
THE PUBLIC UNIVERSITY

Asian American filmmakers made UCLA a home for the Yellow Power movement. The university was considered a premier public institution of higher education and was more integrated in the metropolis than private schools such as USC. Nancy Newhall wrote in her 1967 photo-book about the UC system: "UCLA is urban—not only surrounded by the city, but intimately and deeply related to it."[70] However, only recently had the university begun to seriously address the presence of minority Angelenos on campus. UCLA chancellor Charles Young's establishment of the four Ethnic Studies Centers in 1969—the Asian American Studies Center, the Center for Afro-American Studies, the Mexican American Cultural Center (changed to the Chicano Studies Center in 1971), and the American Indian Studies Center—was a response to student demand for diversifying the faculty, course offerings, and programming. Galvanized by the black and Chicano liberation movements, Asian Americans at UCLA and around the city rallied around a number of causes: combating racist discrimination in housing and schools; challenging stereotypes circulating in popular media concerning the "Oriental" as either a model minority or a dangerous criminal; participating in the antiwar movement; and confronting the lingering trauma of Japanese internment during World War II.

Robert Nakamura was a pioneering creator and theorist of Asian American media. Following the December 7, 1941, bombing of Pearl Harbor, Nakamura and his family were among the one hundred and twenty thousand Japanese residents on the West Coast who were deemed a subversive threat by the federal government's Executive Order 9066. The three-year experience of living in a small wood and tar-covered barrack in the Manzanar War Relocation Center in Owens Valley, California, haunted Nakamura and his family as they tried to start over in Venice. As Nakamura grew older, he became curious about the social function of art. He took classes at Art Center College of Design, where he studied the photography of Gordon Parks and Walker Evans as well as the documentaries of John Grierson and Basil Wright. He earned a living shooting photographs for *McCall's, Collier's,*

FIGURE 11: Installation photo of *America's Concentration Camps*
exhibition, 1970. Courtesy of the Visual Communications Photographic Archive.

Parade, and *Life.* Then, as an employee of Charles and Ray Eames's design workshop in Venice, he learned to shoot and edit film. Nakamura contributed to the
"House of Science" display for the company's 1962 World's Fair Science Pavilion in
Seattle and the *Nehru: His Life and His India* tribute exhibition commissioned by
Indira Gandhi.[71] "At Eames, they didn't take a precious view of art," Nakamura
would later recall. "They asked questions like, what do we want our object to do,
what's its function, who is it for?" Despite the positive learning experience and
steady paycheck, he found it alienating to work for corporate clients and felt discon-
nected from current social movements. He enrolled in the film program at UCLA
to bridge his political and artistic interests.[72]

Upon entering the university in 1969, Nakamura immediately joined the
graphic design staff of *Gidra,* the experimental Asian American newspaper started
by students Mike Murase, Dinora Gil, Laura Ho, Colin Watanabe, and Tracy
Okida. The monthly publication was a loudspeaker for the Yellow Power movement within the United States and also supported the liberation movements in
Southeast Asia and Latin America. Nakamura joined with professor Bob Suzuki
and the Japanese American Citizens League (JACL) in designing a traveling exhibition of photographs from the Japanese internment camps.[73] The exhibition combined photographs taken by the War Relocation Authority, which made camp life
look benign and even quaint, with ones surreptitiously taken by the interned Tōyō
Miyatake, which depicted the distress and resilience of a captive people living in
dire conditions. Both sets of images had been largely unseen by a general audience.
Internment itself was not acknowledged as America's official public memory of

World War II. The exhibition was polemically titled *America's Concentration Camps* and was part of JACL's larger campaign against Title II of the McCarran Internal Security Act. Nakamura collaborated with classmate Alan Ohashi to create a three-dimensional display of thirty-two black cubes individually enveloped by a collage of blown-up photographs. The cubes appeared as the ruins of internment camp history, memory fragments that could form the building blocks of a contemporary Asian American consciousness. The exhibition accompanied JACL events around Los Angeles, and was shown in cultural centers and churches in San Francisco and Chicago.[74]

Professor Alan Nishio recruited Nakamura into the newly created Ethno-Communications program. The initiative stemmed from the ambition and drive of the university's first black film professor, Elyseo Taylor. The Chicago-raised army veteran, intellectual, and photographer led minority students and faculty in a series of protests calling for diversity in what was an overwhelmingly white department. The advocacy group received encouragement from film faculty and university administrators and formalized itself as the Media Urban Crisis Committee. With the aid of a $17,200 grant from the Ford Foundation, the committee devoted itself to teaching cinema to minorities and eventually took the name Ethno-Communications. The program aimed to train black, Asian, Chicano, and American Indian students to make films about subjects that were meaningful to them. They would have access to expertise, equipment, and a creative environment to make films. The first major assignment was a Super 8mm short known as "Project One," and the last was a feature-length thesis film. Individuals crewed for one another, but at the same time took ownership over their films.

Ethno-Communications encouraged students to envision their personal experiences within a social context as well as in relation to contemporary liberation movements. The importation of Third Cinema into the program through Taylor's "Film and Social Change" seminar inspired students to think about the politics of cinematic form. They gained exposure to the revolutionary cinemas of Ousmane Sembène, Fernando Solanas, Tomás Gutiérrez Alea, Octavio Getino, and Julio García Espinosa. The work of these filmmakers emerged out of the anti-imperialist struggles of Latin America, Asia, and Africa and stood against the "First Cinema" of Hollywood as well as the "Second Cinema" of the European art house. The writings of Frantz Fanon, Ngugi wa Thiong'o, Richard Wright, and Malcolm X further bolstered the curriculum's leftist orientation. Ethno-Communications drew primarily from the film and ethnic studies faculty, including Taylor and cinema professor John Young. African American student Charles Burnett and Mexican American student David Garcia Jr., who were already enrolled at the university, served as teaching assistants for the courses.

While the recently established American Film Institute (AFI) backed some progressive minority initiatives such as the Community Film Workshop Council, its flagship school exacerbated rather than diminished the need for Ethno-Communications. The AFI took concrete form as a Great Society initiative in 1967. Prominent liberals, including Gregory Peck, Arthur Schlesinger Jr., and Sidney Poitier, were on the board of trustees. The former head of motion pictures at the USIA, George Stevens Jr., became the first director. Chair of the UCLA Theater Arts Department Colin Young (no relation to John Young) was an early AFI advocate, penning editorials for *Film Quarterly* during the 1960s in favor of an expansive, federally funded organization for the preservation, production, and exhibition of American cinema. But the students the AFI enrolled were almost exclusively white and male. The Conservatory for Advanced Film Studies in Beverly Hills was invested in nurturing the talent of New Hollywood to take on the art cinemas of Asia and Europe rather than assisting working-class minorities to tell their own stories. The same year that Ethno-Communications began, the AFI admitted its first class, which included Rhodes Scholar turned MIT philosophy professor Terrence Malick, Pennsylvania Academy of Fine Arts graduate David Lynch, and prolific Los Angeles film critic Paul Schrader.[75]

Nakamura joined Ethno-Communications members Eddie Wong, Duane Kubo, and Alan Ohashi to form Visual Communications (VC) in 1970. The abbreviation—identical to that for the Viet Cong—signaled the organization's opposition to the Vietnam War. Reflecting on the formation of the collective, Nakamura would later recall, "We needed to be visible," to tell Asian American history from the perspective of Asian Americans, to present views from "within."[76] To achieve this, VC aimed to connect with Asian Americans in the city, while also trying to reach mainstream audiences. The collective published an unsigned editorial in the local Japanese daily newspaper *Rafu Shimpo*, which declared, "Our materials try to develop a positive sense of ethnic identity and to formulate a larger perspective of a multi-cultural, multi-ethnic American society, where one need not sacrifice a unique ethnicity in order to become 'acceptable.' Our other audience is a broad category of non-Asians of the general public. As in the case of addressing Asian Americans, a basic production of facts and personal experiences provides background information."[77] VC members were free to generate their own film ideas, which were then developed by the group, with a particular filmmaker leading each project. As the oldest and most experienced member of the organization, Nakamura acted as a mentor and mediator between VC, UCLA, the Asian American community, and government agencies. VC opened a small office at 3222 West Jefferson Boulevard in the multiracial, culturally vibrant Crenshaw neighborhood. Because of the fact that at UCLA, unlike at USC, students were allowed to retain ownership rights of the films they created, Nakamura and his classmates tried to stay affiliated with the university and use its resources for as long as possible.[78] VC incorporated as a nonprofit in order to receive funding from the Comprehensive Employment and Training Act, the National Endowment for the Humanities, and the Emergency School Aid Act.

FIGURE 12: On-location production photograph for *Manzanar*, 1971, 8mm; directed by Robert Nakamura; an Ethno-Communications Film; produced by Visual Communications. Courtesy of the Visual Communications Photographic Archive.

Nakamura's Project One film, *Manzanar* (1971), concentrated on the experience of World War II internment. The film begins with close-ups of autumn foliage, capturing what appear to be the serene environs of Owens Valley; however, this dreamscape soon turns to a nightmare as a hazy gray line comes into focus in the foreground of the shot, resolving as a taut strand of barbed wire. Handheld shots of the infrastructural debris of the Manzanar camp are interleaved with period photographs of imposing sentry towers, stoic armed guards, anti-Japanese propaganda, and the closed storefronts of Japanese-owned businesses in Little Tokyo. The juxtaposition of the photographs and the frantic movement around the desolate camp conveys the distress of relocation. The pictures are from decades ago, yet the memories, like the broken teacups, water pumps, guard towers, barbed wire, fence posts, and stone rubble inscribed with detainees' initials, remain, serving as material evidence of what happened at this site. The closing image of the documentary focuses on the cemetery monument still present at Manzanar, painted with Japanese characters that translate to "soul consoling tower." While the psychic and physical damage of relocation can never be undone, confronting the experience is a way of coping with the grief and helps to ensure that it will not happen again.

Manzanar aided in bringing the experience of Japanese internment into public consciousness, pressuring the California legislature to grant Manzanar official landmark status in 1973. UCLA exhibited the documentary alongside other Project

One films. These screenings were public, well attended, and widely reviewed. Treviño remembered driving from East Los Angeles to UCLA to see *Manzanar* and other Ethno-Communications films.[79] *Los Angeles Times* critic Kevin Thomas highlighted *Manzanar* in his article on Project One films: "As idyllic scenery gives way to vintage stills of Japanese-Americans being forced to leave their homes and businesses, 'Manzanar' become[s] a timeless, eloquent reminder of an infamous page in American history."[80] *Manzanar*, like subsequent VC films, played at local churches, community centers, university campuses, and elementary schools in Berkeley, Pasadena, and San Diego school districts. VC members traveled with their films, showing them to disparate audiences and facilitating post-screening discussions. Little Tokyo's Koyasan Buddhist Temple proved to be a stalwart for exhibition. After seeing *Manzanar*, David Ushio of the Japanese American newspaper *Pacific Citizen* exclaimed, "I found myself living the agony of being rounded up and incarcerated in desolate camps. I could feel the despondency and futility of those that suffered the indignities of evacuation." The *Rafu Shimpo* reported that an excerpt of *Manzanar* was to be broadcast on the local CBS news program *About a Week*.[81]

Eddie Wong's Project One film, *Wong Sinsaang* (1971), took as its subject his father, Frank, and what Wong depicted as his double life. Viewers first encounter Frank as the owner of a laundry and dry cleaners in Hollywood, diligently catering to white customers who are often gruff, condescending, and rude. There are only terse verbal exchanges in which items are dropped off or picked up and paid for. Miles Davis's trumpet along with mechanical noises play on the soundtrack, setting a somber tone for the portrait. Wong explains that for a long time he never knew his father beyond the hardworking Chinese laundryman, a professional who had to put up with racist white customers, a person he thought never belonged in "Hollywood, USA." The film then reveals Frank's interior life as a painter, poet, intellectual, and father. Old photographs and documents tell the story of his immigration to the United States in 1930, his work as a shipbuilder during World War II, and the pride he finds in his ability to earn a living. Long shots show Frank practicing kung fu in the backyard. Eddie's voice-over interprets his father's personal endeavors as not so much an "escape" or "retreat," but self-empowering rituals. They are a way to cope with and resist the physical fatigue of the job and the mental abuse he endures there. Wong later mentioned that when he screened the film in Chinatown for his father and members of the community, the lively experience was akin to how a family enjoys a home movie. They could identify with the experiences represented on-screen, and the film jump-started a discussion about the joys and hardships of living in America.[82]

During this period, VC developed other kinds of documentary media to educate elementary and high school students about the United States from the perspective of Asian Americans, and to generate positive attitudes toward the study of ethnic particularity, similarity, and difference. A small picture book it produced in

1971, *Asian American People and Places*, consists of a seven-panel folding screen, each panel featuring one of nine stories about people in a variety of occupations: Mrs. Chan, a Chinese garment worker; Peter Hon, a computer and mathematics advisor from Hong Kong; Mr. Lagofaatasi Sialoi, a Samoan minister and ship worker; Mrs. Kim, a Korean junior high school teacher; Dr. Jenny Batongmalaque, a Filipino doctor; Greg Ito's family, who are Japanese strawberry farmers; Roger Wong, a Chinese adolescent who is practicing the lion dance for the New Year's celebration; Japanese shopkeepers in Little Tokyo; and Asian American produce vendors in downtown markets. A companion booklet contains a glossary of key terms, study questions, activity suggestions, discussion topics, and a timeline of significant dates in Asian American history.[83]

Additionally, VC created two slide presentations designed for lectures, one on Japanese immigration to America and the other on World War II relocation. The acquisition of a National Endowment for the Humanities grant provided the means for VC to start its Asian American photography archive. By 1972, VC had amassed more than ten thousand images and related documents. Community members, including elementary school principals, professors, JACL members, and university administrators, wrote letters to the Office of Education in Washington, DC, in support of VC's grant funding.[84] The collective continued to use the resources of a wide network of institutions as it looked to expand its purview to include a broader range of Asian Pacific peoples.[85]

THE ART AND CRAFT OF REBELLION

Black filmmakers made up a core contingent within Ethno-Communications. The program attracted local filmmakers as well as individuals from the Deep South and overseas. Charles Burnett, Ben Caldwell, Larry Clark, Jamaa Fanaka, Haile Gerima, Pamela Jones, Barbara McCullough, Thomas Penick, and John Reir did not see themselves as a formal collective or organization. They were, however, vehemently opposed to Hollywood's long history of trafficking in black stereotypes for profit. So too were they frustrated with discrimination in the film and television industries as well as with the lack of minority representation in para-industry workshops and university film schools. The black film critic and scholar Clyde Taylor would later describe these filmmakers and their output as constituting the "L.A. Rebellion." In a review of their work at the Whitney Museum of American Art in 1986, Taylor wrote that this loose formation "is recognizable in a determination to expose the irresponsibility of Hollywood portrayals of black people by developing a film language whose bold, even extravagant, innovation sought filmic equivalents of black social and cultural discourse. Every code of classical cinema was rudely smashed—conventions of editing, framing, storytelling, time, and space. Soundtracks carry needling surprises."[86]

Lessons about the history and theory of documentary and Third Cinema in Ethno-Communications encouraged students to see their films as a means for representing their communities and as a form of sociopolitical critique. Program participants explored a number of connected issues that, as cinema scholars Allyson Nadia Field, Jan-Christopher Horak, and Jacqueline Najuma Stewart argue, addressed the "distinct elements of Black culture" and the "lifeworlds of Black working-class and poor people."[87] Some common topics included black identity, police brutality and prejudice, the experience of migrating from the rural South to the urban environs of Los Angeles, Pan-Africanism, racist stereotypes circulating in the commercial film and television industry, and the legacy of the 1965 Watts Uprising. From the beginning, filmmakers embraced a mix of cinematic styles that clashed with the styles of commercial fiction as well as network broadcasting.[88] For example, Haile Gerima crafted a series of dream motifs in *Hour Glass* (1971) to show how the writings of Angela Davis and Malcolm X led to the political awakening of an African American teenage basketball player. In *A Day in the Life of Willie Faust, or Death on the Installment Plan* (1972), Jamaa Fanaka reimagines the stylized realism and conventional plot elements of blaxploitation to show the gruesome demise of a drug dealer.

Charles Burnett was a visionary teacher, mentor, and filmmaker within the L.A. Rebellion whose work exhibited a strong documentary charge. Born in 1944 in Vicksburg, Mississippi, Burnett moved with his family to Los Angeles in the late 1940s. He grew up about a mile west of Watts on Ninety-Ninth Street and Towne Avenue. Burnett attended Samuel Gompers Junior High School with Marquette Frye, whose arrest during the summer of 1965 triggered the Watts Uprising. Burnett vividly remembered the National Guard stationed near his home during the unrest.[89] A combination of factors contributed to Burnett's participation in Ethno-Communications. As a teenager, he loved the mediums of photography and cinema. He frequently visited motion picture palaces after getting off work at the downtown branch of the Los Angeles Public Library. Among his favorite films was Jean Renoir's *The Southerner* (1945). He admired its humanistic treatment of poor farmers.[90] At the same time, he was disgusted by the degradation of minority characters, and their relegation to the far corners of the frame, in most Hollywood Westerns, films noir, and romantic comedies. Burnett enrolled in electronics courses at Los Angeles Community College, but he soon gravitated to formalized study of film and writing. He earned a bachelor's degree in creative writing from UCLA in 1969 and then enrolled in the school's graduate film program. As one of the only people of color in the film department, he felt unable to identify with the class status, social freedoms, and commercial ambitions of many of his white countercultural peers.

With the creation of Ethno-Communications, Burnett joined the program as a teaching assistant and educated incoming L.A. Rebellion filmmakers as well as

Asian American, Chicano, and American Indian students. Leftist cinema and literature from Brazil, Cuba, and Senegal helped Burnett and his peers to understand the similarities between their experiences in Los Angeles and those of the peasants and working classes wrestling with the devastating impact of colonization around the world. Burnett collaborated with the Center for Afro-American Studies to bring Senegalese filmmaker Ousmane Sembène to campus for the First African Film Festival. In post-screening discussions and roundtables, filmmakers and students talked about the current state of African cinema and its contentious relationship to European and American film culture. In addition to Taylor's "Film and Social Change" course making a big impression on Burnett, Basil Wright's "Documentary Traditions" seminar emboldened him to think about the empathetic power of documentary:

> I was lucky to be taking Basil Wright's documentary class at the time. . . . I felt like I had a connection with him in terms of what I was trying to do. I told him that I felt like I didn't fit in. He told me that the most important thing is respect—for the people you work with and the subject of the film. They're human beings, and you don't exploit them. There's never a justification for exploiting the subject. There was a focus on working with your subject as a living thing that's already been hurt—you don't need to exploit them any more. It's not about you, the director; it's about the people you're focusing on—their needs, their interests. That's the purpose of documentary.[91]

It was during this period, in 1969 and 1970, that Burnett created his Project One film, *Several Friends* (1969). Analyzing the L.A. Rebellion's Project One films, scholar Allyson Field writes that they "functioned like a laboratory for experimenting with the medium of film as a means of expression, and the films demonstrate this sense of formal experimentation that would be foundational for the filmmakers' later work."[92] This would be especially true for Burnett. His Project One focused on a small cluster of moments drawn from the daily lives of members of his community. The short film is deeply indebted to British and American social documentary from the 1930s, in which people perform their habits, rituals, and routines for the camera; it relies on staging and loose scripting rather than the direct cinema practice of observing people through immersive, mobile perspectives. The scenes in *Several Friends* do not so much follow the logic of a melodramatic story. They unfold elliptically, existing as snapshots of Watts that add up to a micro-history of a contemporary Los Angeles working-class neighborhood. The film is a kind of vernacular play put on by residents. There is no action-driven plot, no grand solution to problems, and there are no charismatic heroes: just a community surviving. Burnett would later reflect on this kind of filmmaking in terms of "recording an experience that had a narrative inherent in it."[93]

The opening of *Several Friends* signals disquiet. The sound of breaking glass plays against a gray title card with the printed tagline "A Film by Charles Burnett."

FIGURE 13: Still from *Several Friends*, 1969, 16mm; directed by Charles Burnett; photographed by Jim Watkins; sound by Rodolfo Restifo. 1920 × 1080 ProRes 422 (HQ) transfer from the UCLA Film & Television Archive's restored 35mm interpositive, courtesy of Milestone Films.

The image shifts to a little girl standing on a sidewalk that adjoins the house where Burnett himself grew up. She faces a drunken, distraught soldier. In awkward silence they look at each other. When friends Andy Burnett, Eugene Cherry, and Charles Bracy drive by and ask the girl about the whereabouts of her father, the man collapses. It is unclear whether he was, in fact, struck by the car. It is as if the man's unacknowledged presence mirrors his invisibility within his own community and American society more generally; or perhaps the distraught, staggering man suggests a possible despairing future for the child. The next scenes follow a chronological sequence of interactions. Parked outside a liquor store, Andy, Cherry, Bracy, and another friend of theirs named Deloras Robinson talk about purchasing a bottle of wine but never gather the necessary funds. Their conversation does not advance the storyline, but involves playful banter about the desire to gather the money and Robinson's eccentric outfit. Their voices overlap and at times blend in with a soundscape of diegetic noises. Next, in a conversation at Andy's house, Cherry shares that his young daughter needs surgery. When Cherry leaves, Andy and his wife Cassandra Wright get into a minor argument. Their exchange is periodically interrupted by the voice of a boxing announcer emanating from the television or the R&B song "I Only Get This Feeling" from the record player.

After Wright asks Andy to go to the meat market, the film transitions to the site of slaughter. Duke Ellington's "Jeep's Blues" accompanies a butcher slitting the throat of a chicken, then cleaning it and putting it against a spinning cylinder to pluck the feathers. The sounds of a whining, muted trumpet and clarinet provide an eerie impression of the chicken's plight. What seems like the next day, Andy and Cherry try to work on Andy's car but cannot figure out the exact problem, let alone how to fix it. Bracy and his wealthy white girlfriend then come by the house. When she uses the bathroom, Bracy makes derogatory comments concerning his taking advantage of all the gifts and affection that she is giving him. At the film's conclusion, the three men attempt to move and install a heavy washing machine before going to a club in Hollywood. Ultimately, the task proves too onerous and time consuming, so they never make it.

Certainly, *Several Friends* is a record of time spent among "several friends." Burnett captures the rhythm and cadence of their quotidian life. But the film's mise-en-scène, editing, and structure also reflect Burnett's Third Cinema interests in film as an expressive form of social critique. Technology takes on a symbolic dimension in *Several Friends*. On one level, technology is a source of constant adversity for these characters. The Southern California dream of mobility and access to professional opportunities and pleasurable experiences, so often represented in popular culture through the icon of the smooth-running automobile, does not apply to the residents of Watts. The scene depicting Andy and Cherry working on their car shows the automobile as a sculptural mass, rooted in place, not a sleek vehicle for upward mobility. Andy lies on his back under the chassis, as Eugene leans in to look at the engine beneath the vaulted hood. They hope to get the machine moving again, but cannot seem to identify the problem. They only know that screws are loose or missing. With public buses chronically underfunded and the mass transit streetcar system decimated by the 1960s, the characters will undoubtedly face additional challenges as the result of this car trouble. The car's undiagnosed ailment confirms that the characters are stuck in place.

Later in the day, when the three friends try to install the washing machine, the cumbersome unit brings the evening's plans to a halt. The machine is so heavy and bulky that they can barely move it. Handheld shots of the men surrounding the large object and trying to inch it forward emphasize the arduousness of the job along with their frustrations. When the machine gets stuck in the hallway, preventing the three from pushing it in any direction, they appear to momentarily give up. Trying in vain to install the washing machine results in their missing their dates in Hollywood that Bracy had set up. For them, technology is something that demands labor and eats away the day, not something that saves time and alleviates stress. In *Several Friends*, technology appears as a structuring mechanism for the narrative. There is no impression of propulsive movement for the characters. And yet they do share a tender camaraderie, taking comfort in one another's company. They draw emotional strength from their interactions. *Several Friends* contrasts with the kind of slick forward motion of classical Hollywood narrative, and resembles a social reality more true to the residents' lives. Burnett honed his cinematic voice through this Project One film. It became an important blueprint for his later thesis film, *Killer of Sheep* (1977). Burnett, like his classmates, would continue to create images in opposition to Hollywood film and television as well as the low-budget, studio-produced blaxploitation films that were beginning to build momentum.

Several Friends was a benchmark achievement within a vibrant period of grass-roots media. Marginalized peoples in the city authored representations of their own neighborhoods and communicated their own perspectives on issues deeply important to them. Documentaries advanced the black, brown, yellow, and women's movements and facilitated new ways in which viewers could see themselves as part of a community. They also reached wider audiences, and served as effective forms of advocacy. Constituting diverse forms of public history, the films were never simply intended for posterity, but aimed to actively shape the present.

Meanwhile, on Sunset Boulevard, Hollywood liberals were struggling to reconcile their conventional documentary practice with the changing political climate. Wolper Productions was particularly vulnerable. With liberalism and the commercial film and television industries in a state of crisis, what it meant to make progressive, commercially profitable films was rapidly evolving. The studio that had initially crafted an image of the New Frontier and screened the first glimpses of the Great Society found itself on shaky ground.

4

Hard Lessons in Hollywood Civics

Managing the Crisis of the Liberal Consensus

"The Confessions of Nat Turner," both the book and the proposed film, are symptoms of a tragic racial problem. I'm rocking the boat because I have grave fears about the future. . . . Why use the motion picture camera, the most powerful method of communication known in the world, to perpetuate a mythical Nat Turner, when the real Turner was a better man? We're stuck with too many myths in this country.

—ACTOR OSSIE DAVIS, 1968[1]

The 1965 Watts Uprising in South Central Los Angeles did not immediately affect Wolper Productions' output. The Hollywood studio was busy settling into its new home at the Metromedia headquarters on the Sunset Strip. David Wolper thought that selling his company in 1964 to the fastest-growing communications conglomerate in the country was not so much a matter of selling out as of buying in, an opportunity to continue making documentaries and also move into fiction features, live performance, and short-format sponsored films. Under the leadership of entrepreneur John Kluge, Metromedia had developed from a two-station television company to a large entity with broadcasting, out-of-home media, publishing, mail marketing, and local entertainment divisions. Moving from New York to Los Angeles, Kluge expanded the KTTV station to build a massive home base for his communications empire. Metromedia's development anticipated a trend toward corporate diversification where film and television production constituted one part of a conglomerate's varied business pursuits.[2] Kluge was one of the major donors to Community Television of Southern California, the nonprofit that helped launch the public television station KCET. He saw Wolper Productions as both a commercial investment and a way to build the company's reputation for intelligent programming. He said he was trying to create a "thinking man's network."[3] Wolper assumed the role of vice president of Metromedia and retained his position as leader of the studio he built from scratch. In the aftermath of John F. Kennedy's assassination on November 22, 1963, his organization's documentaries smoothed the transition from the presidency of Kennedy to that of Lyndon B. Johnson, from the constellation of policy initiatives and tenets that constituted the New Frontier to the new president's vision of an expanded welfare state, increased technological innovation, and aggressive foreign policy that made up the Great Society. Transforming Johnson's policies into streamlined, character-focused narratives, these documentaries asserted that a partnership between an active government and a motivated citizenry could solve any problem, including what Johnson perceived to be particularly complex situations like domestic poverty and the global spread of communism.

As the 1960s progressed, Wolper Productions' partnership with Metromedia turned out to not be as fruitful as originally anticipated. The studio split with the conglomerate in late 1968. But even as Hollywood experienced a seismic economic downturn toward the end of the decade, Wolper's pivot to independence proved an easier challenge to navigate than trying to retain his studio's claim to relevance as a civically engaged producer of documentaries. The conventional Cold War narratives on which the studio had built its reputation seemed increasingly out of sync with calls to Black Power, protests against the entrenchment of corporations in public life, and growing opposition to American military interventions in Southeast Asia. Wolper Productions tried to find its footing within a shifting social landscape. The studio's attempts to document the country's relationship to electoral politics indexed a pervasive crisis in cultural liberalism and resulted in some instructive failures.

FLEETING IMAGES OF THE GREAT SOCIETY

Wolper Productions' three clusters of Great Society documentaries included presidential portraits, programs on contemporary American culture, and historical compilation films. These documentaries were geared toward exhibition on commercial television, at select festivals, and in venues such as schools, libraries, and community centers. The core brain trust of Wolper, Mel Stuart, Alan Landsburg, and Jack Haley Jr. designed the programs in collaboration with the old guard of the entertainment industry, young up-and-coming filmmakers, the Washington, DC, intelligentsia, and archives around the world. Similar to the studio's past programs, the documentaries were relentlessly affirmative, showing individuals seizing opportunities and overcoming obstacles by working hard and relying on a supportive government. They depicted a rosy vision of American democracy that rhymed with Lyndon B. Johnson's photo-book *This America* (1966). Acknowledging the challenges—automation, distribution of resources to a large population, environmental fallout—that threaten a growing society, the president wrote in the preface, "I believe that a great society can master its dilemmas" before going on to proclaim, "All our domestic programs and policies converge on a common set of

aims: to enrich the quality of American life; to provide a living place which liber-
ates rather than constricts the human spirit; to give each of us the opportunity to
stretch his talents; and to permit all to share in the enterprise of our society."[4]
Wolper Productions' films argued that strong presidential leadership and a robust
policy agenda were necessary for creating a dynamic America, and made visible
the lives of individuals who were building this society.

Programs in the first cluster tried to ingratiate Johnson, who came across to many
as a rough-hewn Texan, to the public. The task was all the more necessary given his
predecessor's movie-star looks and charismatic personality. These documentaries
also reinforced the idea that a democratically elected chief executive would act wisely
on behalf of the populace. *The Making of the President: 1964* (1965) begins with radio
dramatist and Hollywood actor Martin Gabel's booming narration, "Power in
America is carried by no assassin's bullet. It must be freely given, freely won." In addition to the documentary including the familiar voice of Gabel, who had served as
narrator for the previous *The Making of the President* film, this latest installment
once again involved Theodore H. White adapting the script from his recently published book. Telling the story of the 1964 presidential campaign with a distinct focus
on Johnson, the documentary provides quick flashes of backstory for each candidate, and describes the competition of the primaries, the national conventions, the
final election, and its immediate aftermath. Gabel's voice-over, set against newsreel
footage, still photographs, and television reports, recounts Johnson's political maturation. Following his stint teaching underprivileged children in the hill country of
his home state, Johnson enters politics as secretary to Democratic congressman
Richard Kleberg in Washington, DC. He then returns to Texas to become head of
Franklin D. Roosevelt's National Youth Administration. His political career moves
from senator, to vice president under Kennedy, and then to president, where his race
for the highest office results in his defeating the bigoted, trigger-happy, antigovern-
ment Arizonan Barry Goldwater. *The Making of the President*'s support of civil rights
legislation is seen as encapsulating what the Johnson administration viewed as a
constructive path toward progressive social change: nonviolent rather than violent,
integrationist rather than separatist, grounded in the mechanisms of the liberal state
rather than aligned with radical grassroots activism.

Seven Days in the Life of the President (1965) further fleshes out Johnson's character and demonstrates that the administration's beliefs have led to concrete
actions. Produced in association with Time-Life Inc., it was the most anticipated
episode in the studio's eight-part *March of Time* series (1965–66).[5] Unlike the
original theatrically released *March of Time* films (1935–51), which dramatically
staged historical events, the newer version relied on archival footage as well as on-
location shooting. For *Seven Days*, a small crew, including cinematographer Vilis
Lapenieks, shadowed Johnson for a week to try to place viewers in the president's
shoes. At the beginning of the episode, noir actor and radio announcer William

Conrad's voice-over intones: "In his vision, he is sure, he would desalt the sea and heal the sick, rebuild the cities and enrich the farms, retrain the old and educate the young. . . . He has given the dream a name, the Great Society." The bulk of the program looks at the president and his administration as they try to locate this "dream" in policies that square with domestic and international goals. So, too, does the program show Johnson's comportment as embodying the stability and resolve of the nation. The documentary takes the viewer inside the West Wing, on a stroll around the White House grounds, to press corps briefings, aboard Air Force One, and to Johnson's Texas ranch. Lapenieks captures the everyday act of Johnson eating breakfast and reading the newspaper; press secretary Bill Moyers and special assistant Jack Valenti communicating with journalists, politicians, and administrative staff; the diplomatic gestures of Johnson formally greeting foreign dignitaries; and the political ceremony of the swearing in of officials. The president's ability to ceaselessly work and make resolute decisions, the film implies, has led to policy achievements in education, civil rights, and the arts. His passing of the Elementary and Secondary Education Act is one of the climactic moments of the film. The ceremonial signing of the legislation is itself an occasion to cinematically document the inner workings of the Johnson administration.

The latter part of the episode concentrates on the question of whether the United States should send additional troops to, and increase aerial strikes on, Vietnam. While the ramping up of US involvement in Southeast Asia was hardly news by the time *Seven Days* aired, the documentary wanted to showcase the administration's process of decision-making under pressure. In this way, *Seven Days* resonated with Drew Associates' television documentaries on Kennedy, which were built around the representation of the successful negotiation of a contemporary crisis. This is exemplified in *Crisis: Behind a Presidential Commitment* (1963), which focused on the controversy surrounding the racial integration of the University of Alabama. In *Seven Days* presidential decision-making involves consulting an inner circle of trusted experts. Johnson meets with his foreign policy experts, secretary of state Dean Rusk, secretary of defense Robert McNamara, and national security advisor McGeorge Bundy. He also reads over briefings, consults with outside military officers, and retreats to the Oval Office for quiet contemplation. *Seven Days* casts the official government position to escalate involvement in Vietnam in a positive light, presenting it as a careful decision to confront the communist threat of the Viet Cong. In a news conference, Johnson claims, "Retreat does not bring safety and weakness does not bring peace."

A second cluster of documentaries centered on civic achievements. *The Race for the Moon* (1965) looks at the next step of what the program calls the "great adventure" of space travel: the training of US astronauts for a mission to the Moon. The show considers whether Project Apollo ought to strive for Kennedy's initial goal of a lunar landing before the end of the decade, or instead follow a gradual and perhaps less costly timeline. Slanting toward trying to meet the 1970 objective, the documentary surveys the expanding infrastructure in cities such as Houston and situates space travel within a Cold War context of competition with the Soviet Union. Princeton professor of astronomy Martin Schwarzschild enthusiastically asks interviewer Bill Stout: "Do we want to be a great nation, accepting a challenge and the opportunities that are given to us, or do we want to relax in lethargy?"

Another program in this cluster, *The Way Out Men* (1965), profiles professionals loosely connected through their drive to push boundaries and to amplify the social impact of their work. Scientists, engineers, and artists are seen excelling in surgery, theoretical physics, abstract painting, musical composition, computer processing, and urban planning. Citing the ambitious state of American invention, narrator Van Heflin tells viewers, "Never before has man's horizon widened so far." The program visits theoretical physicist Murray Gell-Mann at Caltech, avant-garde classical music composer Lukas Foss in Buffalo, New York, and experimental biologist and psychologist James McConnell at the University of Michigan.

Revolution in the Three R's (1965) examines the reimagining of the classroom as a creative laboratory to cultivate dedicated teachers and curious students. The program takes its title from the multipronged initiative in education. The *Los Angeles Times* noted that the "revolution" sought to update curricular reform in "reading, writing and arithmetic" to more effectively connect different levels of schooling, promote interactive forms of student learning across the humanities and sciences, and support teacher training.[6] The documentary ventured into schools in Los Angeles, St. Louis, and Harlem to investigate collaborative approaches to problem solving and computer-based instruction. Special notice was paid to new classroom patterns designed to increase social cohesion and enhance student productivity.

As in previous years, a steady stream of new talent flowed to Wolper Productions. The studio offered employment to young editors, cinematographers, sound technicians, and aspiring directors, giving them the chance to hone their craft while also earning a paycheck and at times taking a lead role on a production. Filmmakers, however, were denied complete editorial control, which remained the purview of Stuart, Landsburg, Haley, and Wolper. In some cases people found employment at Wolper Productions by way of a personal connection or interest in documentaries. In other cases, Wolper recruited talent for the purpose of innovating the studio's line of films and to meet the demands of an expanding organization. For example, he brought the twenty-nine-year-old Chicagoan William Friedkin to Los Angeles after seeing his award-winning television documentary *The People vs. Paul Crump* (1962) at the San Francisco International Film Festival. Friedkin had worked his way up from the mail room of Chicago's WGN to direct live programs. His chilling documentary about the wrongly convicted Crump, who was on death row for the alleged killing of a police officer in a robbery at the Libby, McNeil and Libby packing plant, led to the eventual commutation of Crump's sentence.[7]

Friedkin was excited about bringing his love for European art cinema and investigative reporting to Los Angeles, but quickly found that he had to redesign the style and message of his films when working for Wolper. In his memoir, *The Friedkin Connection*, he recalls his difficulty incorporating "subliminal cuts, jump cuts, unexpected transitions" into his film *The Bold Men* (1965), a documentary about people in life-threatening professions who exhibit mental fortitude and physical strength. He shot a welder on skyscrapers, a high-diving stuntman, a fire-fighter of oil and gas fires, and a racecar driver. Friedkin's rough cut emphasized the characters' vulnerabilities and their complex emotional relationships to their jobs. Upon seeing Friedkin's finished documentary in a viewing session, Wolper allegedly threw his shoe at the screen and shouted, "This is the worst piece of shit I've ever seen!" and demanded that Mel Stuart step in to do an overhaul edit. The final cut, complete with what Friedkin called "wall-to-wall" narration, eschews vulnerabilities in favor of heroic depictions of confident professionals.

Friedkin's *The Thin Blue Line* (1966) explores (then) state-of-the-art policing in Chicago, Los Angeles, and Rochester. Minimizing any mention of police brutality or systematic discrimination against the minority communities they are supposed to be serving, the show commends police officers as ethical public servants. Friedkin depicts them using sophisticated audio equipment to coordinate and dispatch officers to high-tension situations. Throughout the program, law enforcement personnel allege that police are the ones threatened by the so-called "crime epidemic." Van Heflin's voice-over emphasizes that police officers are involved in a battle of good against evil, protecting the innocent and catching criminals. Observations of a drug bust in downtown Los Angeles, a place that the show proclaims to be a home for "pushers and addicts," document a performance of swift justice, from the beginning stages of planning, to the stakeout, to the moment of intervention, to the arrests, to the sentencing.

Historical compilation documentaries that cast the United States in the role of benevolent peacemaker and leader of the "free world" comprised the third cluster. The one-hour films *France: Conquest to Liberation* (1965), *Prelude to War* (1965), *The General* (1965), and the three-part *The Rise and Fall of the Third Reich* (1967–68) delineate the Allied fight against Germany and Japan during World War II. *Korea: The 38th Parallel* (1965), *Japan: A New Dawn over Asia* (1965), and *China: The Roots of Madness* (1967) separate old regimes from contemporary geopolitical realities. The documentaries map Asia according to its willingness to cooperate with the West: friendly democratic societies provide economic and political support versus communist powers that are portrayed as domineering and resistant to diplomatic ties. Traditions of technological accomplishment made up a subgenre within this cluster. *And Away We Go* (1965) examines the cultural history of the automobile in the United States, from the introduction of the horseless carriage around the turn of the century, to the post–World War I Henry Ford era, to the current moment of high-speed driving on highways crisscrossing the nation. *The Epic of Flight* (1966) traces the twentieth-century development of the aircraft, beginning with the Wright Brothers and ending with modern jet-engine planes.

These three groups of Great Society films were generally well received by news periodicals, the industry trade press, and entertainment magazines. They won Peabodys, Emmys, and USIA Cine Golden Eagle awards at festivals. In 1966, Wolper Productions was the focus of a five-week tribute exhibition at the Huntington Hartford Gallery of Modern Art in New York. The curator, Raymond Rohauer, wrote in the accompanying catalogue that Wolper "has explored nearly every facet of contemporary American life and created a vivid history of the country and its people that will be viewed by millions in the future."[8] New programs that moved away from politics and toward cutting-edge entertainment would continue to garner praise from journalists and members of the film and television establishment.

Underwater documentaries with famed oceanographer Jacques Cousteau and subsequent nature films pushed the techno-aesthetic horizon of nonfiction and impressed critics. Wolper collaborated with Cousteau for the final installment of a four-part National Geographic series for CBS. *The World of Jacques-Yves Cousteau* (1966) expands on the oceanographer's Oscar-winning *World without Sun* (1964), and follows him and his team of six "oceanauts" as they harvest natural resources for three weeks at Conshelf III at the bottom of the Mediterranean Sea, off the southern coast of France. Living in a spherical undersea vessel, Cousteau and his crew conduct a series of experiments and demonstrations to prove the efficiency of operating on an oil rig, marine stock farming, and hydroarchaeology. Wolper then orchestrated a deal between his studio, Cousteau, and ABC for the twelve-program *The Undersea World of Jacques-Yves Cousteau* (1968). The show was less about the pursuit of science than the desire to craft floating, underwater views of the Red Sea, the Indian Ocean, and the Gulf of Aden using a sophisticated array of color photography cameras, sound recorders, and lighting equipment. The programs were well suited for television, with the small screen akin to the porthole window of a ship— or what Wolper once claimed to be a fishbowl in the living room. Cousteau's personable charm increased the programs' appeal; the Frenchman made the ocean alluring.[9] *New York Times* journalist Jack Gould commented on the follow-up broadcast, *Savage World of the Coral Jungle*: "His remarkable equipment for photographing what happens beneath the depths is a continuing source of revelation and fascination. Last night he reported on the interdependence of fish and a coral reef, a strange and absorbing underwater city where the dead polyps raise the reef's height and the fish seek the shelter of the reef's protection."[10]

As the 1960s progressed, the praise given to some of Wolper Productions' documentaries seemed to provide a distorted sense of the studio's representation of pressing social realities. At home, minority street protests in cities such as Los Angeles, Detroit, Chicago, Baltimore, and Newark, along with the assassinations of Dr. Martin Luther King Jr. and Robert Kennedy, intensified a crisis in the integrationist vision of racial harmony espoused by civil rights leaders and architects of the Great Society. With calls for Black Power as well as the rising brown, yellow, red, and women's liberation movements, minorities saw self-determination as decisive for claiming their rights as citizens, combating institutionalized racism, and lifting their economic standing. Overseas, the escalation of US involvement in Vietnam inspired demonstrations against the Johnson administration and its drafting of young adults to fight an unpopular and unjust war. Even the government's official position on the assassination of John F. Kennedy, which Wolper Productions had used to solidify its civic reputation, was called into doubt. In 1966, *Esquire* published "A Primer of Assassination Theories," which included thirty-five versions of Kennedy's murder. That same year, the books *Inquest: The Warren Commission and the Establishment of Truth* and *The Second Oswald* along with the book and documentary *Rush to Judgment* critiqued the decision-making process of the Warren Commission and its findings.[11] During this period, Wolper Productions navigated a shifting position within the film and television industries and struggled to maintain its social relevance.

STATE OF FRACTURE

In late 1968 Wolper Productions separated from Metromedia. The conglomerate faced antitrust litigation due to its proposed merger with the Transamerica Corporation, which owned United Artists. Wolper was satisfied with the move to independence. He felt that he was being spread too thin across a number of administrative tasks and did not have enough time to devote to nurturing individual films and series.[12] The departure went against the current trend toward studio mergers, which were caused by the financial downturn in the film and television industries as well as by changing models of production and distribution. The old majors suffered from a declining theater audience, competing forms of entertainment, and unanticipated box office flops. MGM, Paramount, and Warner Bros. sought financial stability with larger corporate parents. Studios adjusted their production calculus toward stylistically innovative narratives that engaged topical issues. Given that Wolper Productions was a smaller studio working in multiple sectors of film and television, it found it advantageous, at least for the immediate future, to retain its semi-independent status and partner with media organizations and personnel to work on its varied projects.[13]

Individuals would frequently work for Wolper Productions as well as contribute to the low-budget, countercultural features of the emerging "New Hollywood." For example, after *The Thin Blue Line*, Friedkin went on to direct the burlesque comedy *The Night They Raided Minsky's* (1968), the queer drama *The Boys in the Band* (1970), and the police thriller *The French Connection* (1971). Vilmos Zsigmond worked as a cinematographer for Wolper Productions on *The Story of . . .* series, and then shot the teen horror film *The Incredibly Strange Creatures Who Stopped Living and Became Mixed-Up Zombies* (1964) as well as the revisionist Western *McCabe & Mrs. Miller* (1971) and the Southern drama *Deliverance* (1972). Walon Green wrote and directed nature documentaries for Wolper Productions and also penned the Western *The Wild Bunch* (1969). John Alonzo shot nature and social documentaries for Wolper, the Roger Corman bandit film *Bloody Mama* (1970), and the road film *Vanishing Point* (1971). But while Wolper Productions personnel labored on the front lines of New Hollywood, for the most part the studio's output followed the story arcs and themes of its past films. The documentaries projected nostalgia for an era when it seemed as though liberal governance could unify the country.

Wolper Productions tried to make the American military, which had long fascinated the studio, the subject of captivating cinema. But even as Wolper gave World War II an elaborate fictional treatment, complete with high production values and a star-studded cast, his features fell flat. They didn't necessarily attract the kind of ire and controversy that John Wayne's ode to counterinsurgency, *The Green Berets* (1968), garnered from major journalists and intellectuals. However, they were often described as stale and out of touch.[14] Wolper Productions first adapted to the screen a literary account of the American-Canadian First Special Service Force, which during World War II captured the Nazi mountain outpost Monte la Difensa. This became *The Devil's Brigade* (1968), made with United Artists and starring longtime military actor William Holden and Cliff Robertson, who had played John F. Kennedy in *PT 109* (1963). Journalists panned the film as a tired rehashing of World War II movie tropes. Vincent Canby's *New York Times* review opined: "There is hardly a character, a situation or a line of dialogue in *The Devil's Brigade* that has not served a useful purpose in some earlier movie or television show. Now, with the passage of time, the characters, the situations and the lines have begun to look very tired and very empty, like William Holden's eyes."[15] Not only was the film considered cliché, it exuded a wistful longing for past military glory while remaining unengaged with the climate of protest against the Vietnam War. Charles Champlin of the *Los Angeles Times* called it "dull, inept and offensive." George McKinnon of the *Boston Globe* wrote that "the two-hour film seems old-fashioned. It tends to romanticize war at a time when the whole nation nightly views a real war on television."[16]

The Bridge at Remagen (1969), the studio's follow-up to *The Devil's Brigade*, fared no better. The underlying story deals with the Allied seizure of the Ludendorff Bridge, which helped bring the war to an end in 1945. Production fell apart soon after on-location shooting began at the Davle Bridge in Czechoslovakia. Wolper had to defend the film against claims from the East German press and the Soviet official newspaper *Pravda* that the production was a front for CIA intervention in Czech political affairs and surveillance of the Dubček government. These charges resulted in restrictions placed on the use of military resources during shooting. The presence of Warsaw Pact tanks rolling through city streets—the effective end to the Prague Spring—forced the film crew's hasty retreat out of the country. They first went to Hamburg and then to Rome to finish shooting.

Wolper attempted to leverage these difficulties for publicity, including a two-page *Variety* spread containing a shot log of the vicissitudes of production, but this advertising campaign backfired. It took attention away from the film itself and made audiences more aware of the disconnect between the movie and the contemporary moment. Gary Arnold of the *Washington Post* wrote that *The Bridge at Remagen* was a "combat melodrama" that filled a Hollywood quota of World War II fare: "If Wolper isn't filling the quota, another producer will be along to take his place." The *Chicago Tribune*'s Clifford Terry commented that the film was an "extravagant, glossy exercise of soldiers in simulated combat" and a "shamefully wasteful" use of resources.[17] Clear-cut representations of American military heroics no longer constituted a sturdy tent pole around which liberal ideology could coalesce.

Wolper Productions' *Los Angeles: Where It's At* (1969) failed to relate to a rising tide of public opinion, this time on a local scale. The documentary reflected the studio's past portrayals of Los Angeles as an expanding metropolis filled with professional and leisure opportunities. However, against a backdrop of urban unrest, it came off as an effort to manage the incendiary images of the city circulating in the mainstream media. Backed by mayor Sam Yorty and the Economic Development Board, the documentary tried to sell Los Angeles back to its disenchanted citizens and potential tourists. As city officials hoped to reinvigorate the reputation of Los Angeles as a place where residential developments, industrial sites, natural landscapes, and cultural establishments coexist in harmony, so too did the film take up the theme of cohesion. The documentary's boosterist charge echoed the prose of glossy guidebooks such as *Los Angeles: Portrait of an Extraordinary City* (1968). This travel book declared greater Los Angeles "a scattering of communities that has evolved into a great urban complex, unified by ties of social, cultural and economic interest and laced together by a unique mode of transportation that enables people to pursue far-flung interests with little concern for time or distance."[18]

The film's opening spotlights the Port of Los Angeles as a major hub for global imports and exports of merchandise, produce, and raw materials. Inland lie the high-tech aerospace and defense industries, a public school system to educate the city's youth, and beaches, hiking trails, art museums, galleries, bars, and movie theaters for recreation. In Natalie Wood's quick cameo appearance, she proudly turns to the camera and says, "I like Los Angeles because I can go to the beach, the desert, the mountains, and the theater, all in the same day. Where else can you do that?" The film also details the proximity of Los Angeles to other enticing locales. By car, Angelenos are thirty-five minutes from Marineland, forty-five minutes from Disneyland, and three hours from Mexico. By plane, they are five hours from Hawaii and "two fast cocktails" from San Francisco. At the film's conclusion, Yorty shares his thoughts while hovering high above the city in a helicopter. Los Angeles, he claims, is a city full of "beauty," "hustle bustle," and "excitement." Such hyperbolic speech mirrors the documentary's refusal to acknowledge the city's deep social divisions and the ways racial discrimination and economic status directly impact access to the kinds of professional and recreational experiences it celebrates. In a speech Yorty delivered at UCLA on November 21, 1968, the crowd of students began to jeer when he mentioned that the "magnificent film" would be shown regionally as well as on airplanes and steamships to "advertise" Los Angeles.[19] *Van Nuys Valley News* reporter Ali Sar reported that politician Alphonzo Bell Jr. "blasted the work as a puff film about Los Angeles" and that Bell's aide mentioned that the "money might have been better spent."[20]

Wolper Productions' documentaries about national politics not only signaled growing rifts between state leaders and frustrated Angelenos, but also amplified the studio's own struggle to remain a relevant chronicler of the country. With Johnson under increasing attack from inside and outside the Democratic Party, culminating in his March 31, 1968, television announcement that he would not seek reelection, the Democratic National Committee pulled Wolper's documentary *Promises Made, Promises Kept* (1968) from the Chicago convention in August. The committee-funded film was intended as a highlight reel of the president's policy achievements, but was eliminated by convention managers fearing "it might set off hostile demonstrations."[21]

The film's removal and Johnson's absence from the ticket were symptomatic of a breakdown in American liberalism, a crisis more fully felt in Wolper Productions' account of the 1968 presidential election, *The Making of the President: 1968* (1969). Like the first two films, the third installment centered on the presidential election, observing the campaigns of the Democratic and Republican candidates. But *The Making of the President: 1968* was more interested in surveying conflicts than in concentrating on either the virtues of a specific individual or electoral politics as an effective democratic process. Theodore H. White, the patron saint of consensus reportage, delivers introductory remarks just as he had at the beginning of the other *The Making of the President* films. On this occasion he appears anxious:

> Some people called 1968 the year of the grotesque, and it was. Lunatic events hammered us. . . . Somewhere along the way the old politics died, an era ended. The old politics had somehow given us the illusion of control. A presidential campaign . . . gave people a clear choice of direction. . . . Nineteen sixty-eight was the year we lost that sense of control. Not only the people, but our leaders too, leaders who tried to control the instruments of government and failed, failed overseas in Vietnam, failed in the streets of Chicago and Washington, failed in the streets of a dozen ghettos.

An array of television footage depicts a despondent Johnson, concerned about his administration's investment in asserting control in Southeast Asia and the realities of the opposition to the campaign. Compounding Johnson's worries are what he shares as the growing "communication gap" between his presidency and the American people, a gap widened by the contentious association between his administration and the press. Beyond the falling popularity of Johnson, narrator Joseph Campanella explains that Republican candidates Nelson Rockefeller, George Romney, Richard Nixon, and Ronald Reagan as well as Democrats George McGovern, Eugene McCarthy, and Hubert Humphrey are candidates at war with one another. Campanella further argues that these men are speaking to targeted constituencies rather than to "the nation as a whole." They are unable to unite the country within a context of assassinations, clashes of minorities with police, protests on college campuses such as Columbia, heavy losses in Vietnam, and dissent within the Democratic National Convention. Nixon wins not because of his visionary abilities to chart a new path for the United States, but because of an epochal breakdown in American electoral politics. The film offers no tools with which to repair the body politic, only an expression of its fracture.

The Making of the President: 1968's implication that an absence of strong leadership has resulted in so much discontent doesn't take seriously the motivations of people who have taken to the streets. As the New Left analogue to White's moderate voice, Norman Mailer helped elucidate demonstrations such as the October 21, 1967, anti-Vietnam march to the Pentagon as socially significant and symbolic. His 1968 "nonfiction novel" *The Armies of the Night* focused on the experiences of the protestors and their fight against what he viewed to be authoritative state power (labeled "technology land" or "corporation land") that controlled its citizenry through "packaged education, packaged politics" and plunged it ever deeper into war.[22] *The Making of the President: 1968* refused to comprehend why young Americans gravitated toward varying forms of confrontational protests against state power on the local and national level.

The Journey of Robert F. Kennedy (1970), written by the official Kennedy family historian, Arthur Schlesinger Jr., intensified *The Making of the President: 1968*'s elegiac tone. The *Boston Globe*'s Percy Shain wrote that the film "summed up the tragedy and turbulence of the 60s."[23] The combination of home movies, newsreel footage of Robert Kennedy campaigning for public office, and interviews with Charles Evers, Robert McNamara, Art Buchwald, and Frank Mankiewicz gave rise to an image of Robert Kennedy as an erudite statesman and passionate supporter of integration, endowed with a gift for de-escalating domestic and international conflicts, and for bringing people together across racial and class lines to understand their common humanity. Los Angeles, once the city that had anointed John F. Kennedy at the 1960 Democratic National Convention as he announced his vision of the New Frontier, had become the city where Robert Kennedy was assassinated. Rafer Johnson, who campaigned for Robert Kennedy and was also the subject of an early Wolper Productions documentary, *The Rafer Johnson Story*

(1961), wrestled the gun away from the assassin. Unlike the ending of *The Making of the President: 1960* (1963), where the "passing of power" from Eisenhower to John F. Kennedy also signaled the passing of power from John F. Kennedy to Johnson, the conclusion of *The Journey of Robert F. Kennedy* offers no solace. There is no clear sense of either the future of the American welfare state or the country's status as a leader in global affairs.

In a highly limited capacity, Wolper Productions did begin to experiment with trying to recalibrate its liberal posture to directly address the contemporary climate of protest. Responding to the Black Power movement's reclaiming of American history and the growing dissatisfaction with integrationist comedies and dramas, Wolper Productions attempted a collaboration with Twentieth Century–Fox. The project focused on an adaptation of William Styron's best-selling novel about a Virginia slave revolt, *The Confessions of Nat Turner* (1967).[24]

THE TROUBLE WITH HISTORY

From the outset, Wolper Productions and Twentieth Century–Fox imagined the novel's adaptation as a progressive prestige picture. Styron's book was published in early October 1967, and Wolper shortly thereafter bought the screen rights.[25] As film historian Christopher Sieving argues, the film was one of the earliest, most elaborate, and most widely covered studio efforts to try to capitalize on the Black Power movement. The opposition to the project and the inability to create the film revealed, according to Sieving, "the chasm separating the best intentions of white liberal filmmakers from the values of African American critics and spokespersons in the 1960s."[26] Certainly the project exposed the arrogance and prejudices of establishment filmmakers and the systemic racism that existed in the entertainment business. But debates concerning the politics of representation resonated beyond the scope of the project. The film's turbulent preproduction life also highlighted a larger tension between the value of social history to the minority liberation movements and the profit motive of the culture industries. Furthermore, it underscored a localized conflict between white Hollywood producers and black intellectuals and activists in Los Angeles.

From Wolper's perspective, the adaptation looked promising. The mainstream media and literary establishment had already vetted the book. Styron was considered a proud liberal of elite pedigree. The recipient of the distinguished Rome Prize for *Lie Down in Darkness* (1951), he had garnered acclaim for the antiwar novel *The Long March* (1952), which drew on his experience serving in World War II and the Korean War. In addition, he was an editor for the *Paris Review*. He thought of himself as a keen observer of the black experience and an authority on African American history. Styron, who was born and raised in Newport News, Virginia (not far from the site of Turner's nineteenth-century slave rebellion), was eager to write about Nat Turner. Encouraged by his friend James Baldwin to pursue the project, he felt confident in his ability to navigate the relationship between fact and fiction.

Turner was a slave from Southampton County, Virginia, who, in the early morning of August 22, 1831, led a slave revolt against white oppression in which he killed his master and the master's family, along with other white men, women, and children in the region. The insurrection was suppressed within two days and participating members as well as a number of slaves thought to be part of it were captured, tried, and executed. Turner avoided capture until late October, after which he was hanged. The lawyer Thomas Gray created a summary of these events based on his interview with Turner before his execution and published it as *The Confessions of Nat Turner, the Leader of the Late Insurrection in Southampton, VA* (1831). The kind of fantastic and contradictory portrait of Turner that appears in Gray's book was itself a topic of debate, obscuring as much as clarifying Turner's actions. Aspects of Turner's life, motivations, and the event itself went unaddressed in this text. Styron saw his own book as a "meditation" on history, an imagined account of Turner that would nonetheless seek to convey certain truths about Turner's life as well as about the historical circumstances and effects of slavery. In his prefatory author's note, Styron made clear that he sought to cleave to the "known facts about Nat Turner," while also employing a novelist's creative license and the "freedom of imagination" within the "bounds" of history to reconstruct events and "re-create a man and his era."[27]

Styron's meditation became an immediate best seller. Journalists commended the author for placing the deplorable system of slavery before the American public at a time when slavery was not often a subject of popular literature, film, or television. National news periodicals commented that by assuming the first-person perspective of Turner, Styron was able to explore the human experience of slavery in an imaginative and psychologically complex way; it was as if readers could inhabit the consciousness of Turner.[28] Historian Arthur Schlesinger Jr. deemed the book "the finest American novel in many years." He went on to write that Styron, "without departing from the external realities of character and setting, . . . has perceived this episode with a clarity and penetration, at once loving and terrible, which gives it a timeless and even mythic quality."[29] Featuring Styron's book as its October 16, 1967, cover story, *Newsweek* praised it for giving Americans a valuable time machine: "Styron lifts us up and puts us down in the Virginia tidewater, 1831, and makes us think as a brilliant slave, we are convinced, must have thought."[30] Baldwin said that Styron was productively starting an inclusive conversation about America's past: "He has begun the common history—Ours."[31] When *The Confessions of Nat Turner* won the Pulitzer Prize in 1968, Wolper and Twentieth Century–Fox were quick to congratulate Styron on the prize for the "distinguished novel" by taking out a large advertisement in *Variety*.[32] Looking to move ahead with the adaptation, the Hollywood team hired director Norman Jewison, who had recently directed the Oscar-winning *In the Heat of the Night* (1967) starring Sidney Poitier.

Even as the book sold widely and attracted favorable reviews, a critical backlash began to foment. Prominent black as well as white critics took aim at Styron for having relied too little on historical sources and too heavily on his racist imagination. They argued that Styron's literary license did not simply provoke scholarly quibbles, but had distorted history and had contemporary consequences for understanding both Turner and the world he lived in. For example, Styron wrote that the Turner revolt was the "only effective, sustained revolt in the annals of American Negro slavery," a grossly inaccurate assertion that Twentieth Century–Fox nevertheless circulated in its press releases for the film.[33] This contention contradicted documented accounts of other rebellions leading up to and beyond the Turner revolt as well as daily forms of resistance to slavery that occurred on a smaller scale. Styron's book denied that opposition was constitutive of the experience of slavery. Another contentious issue revolved around Styron's avowal that Turner did not have a wife, which, journalists claimed, led to his characterization of Turner as a repressed celibate with sexual longings for white women. This contradicted nineteenth-century newspaper articles stating that Turner did in fact have a spouse. The *New York Amsterdam News*'s Gertrude Wilson remarked that Styron's depictions of Turner's fictitious desires for white women perpetuated some of the oldest and most damaging myths about black people and anxieties about racial integration.[34]

A topical critique of the book and prospective film had to do with Styron's failure to understand Turner's present-day significance. The edited volume *William Styron's Nat Turner: Ten Black Writers Respond* (1968) argued that Styron's novelization of Turner blunted the radicalism of his actions and created a weak figure. Writers in the anthology claimed that Turner was not simply a conflicted psychology and a vehicle to understand the cruelties of slavery; he was a socially motivated person who led a charge against an oppressive system. Historian Lerone Bennett Jr. wrote, "We are objecting to a deliberate attempt to steal the meaning of a man's life." Writer and Schomberg Collection librarian Ernest Kaiser professed, "[Styron's] writing is impervious to Negro social change and struggle and to the facts of Negro history."[35] Examining the situation from a symptomatic perspective, Hollywood publicist and sports journalist A.S. "Doc" Young called the hype around the book and film a result of the "truth gap" separating black experience from the readers and viewers of white-controlled mainstream media.[36] These criticisms gained force as Nat Turner was increasingly looked to as a unique kind of hero. Styron's Turner clashed with how Black Panthers leader Eldridge Cleaver, historian William Aptheker, literary scholar Addison Gayle Jr., and poet Robert Hayden saw Turner: namely, as a revolutionary whose role in a courageous struggle against slavery made him an inspiring figure for the current post–civil rights era of Black Power militancy.

At first, those involved with the book and the adaptation assumed a range of defensive positions. Styron participated in a heated debate with black actor and activist Ossie Davis at the Los Angeles "political cabaret," Eugene West, where he explained his motivations and defended the interpretive strategies he chose. The moderator, James Baldwin, defended Styron's right to assume the voice of a black man as part of the freedom entitled to a writer; at the same time, Baldwin acknowledged both the ethical responsibilities of a writer to his material, and the likelihood that the film would reach a far greater audience than the book: "Bill's novel is a private act, but what happens when it's onscreen and disseminated at this time in our history? There's a possibility that thousands of black people will die."[37] Wolper rejected the allegations brought forth against Styron and cited the positive press surrounding the project, stating, "I don't see why they should challenge a book that has withstood the test of a critical press since last October."[38] While more sympathetic to the protests, and committed to presenting Turner as a "black Gideon and a hero,"[39] Jewison nonetheless brandished his auteurist shield, declaring that he would not be swayed by the tide of public opinion: "I'll make the film my way . . . and nobody is going to tell me how to do it. I'll listen to all the people involved, but it will be done my way, and my way alone. That goes for the studio as well as for protest groups."[40]

The black left-liberal creative community in Los Angeles led the opposition to the film. Two former Universal employees, Vantile Whitfield and Louise Meriwether, who worked with the Performing Arts Society of Los Angeles and the Watts Writers Workshop, joined forces with Ossie Davis to create the Black Anti-Defamation Association.[41] They set up an office in the mixed-class African American neighborhood of Leimert Park. The organization gained the support of poets H. Rap Brown and Amiri Baraka (LeRoi Jones), actor Godfrey Cambridge, congressman Adam Clayton Powell Jr., the Black Panthers of Los Angeles, members of the Southern Christian Leadership Conference, the US Organization, and the Los Angeles branch of the National Association for the Advancement of Colored People. Protests took the form of letters sent to Jewison, Wolper, and Jack Valenti, a petition against the production that ran in the pages of the *Hollywood Reporter*, and editorials in the mainstream and minority press.

It was not that protestors opposed *any* kind of film about Turner. Rather, they reacted to the specific way he would become a living person on the big screen and the implications of the representation. In the *Los Angeles Sentinel* Vantile Whitfield was quoted as saying, "Our goal is to create a mammoth movement protesting this crap, to make Hollywood aware of this tide of black power."[42] Echoing Whitfield's criticism, Davis spoke out against the myths the adaptation would perpetuate:

The book does little more than help the attitude of unsophisticated readers. . . . The mass reception of this book makes me fear a need in the general white community to justify possibly brutal retaliation to the upheavals in our cities. I can accept a black slave being in love with a white woman on a southern plantation, that's within truth. I cannot accept the fact that this kind of thought has become so predominant that since freedom over 3,000 black men have been lynched and castrated because some ignorant white[s] believed they were after their lily white women.[43]

Despite the various initial defensive positions held by above-the-line labor involved with the production, the steady stream of essays, editorials, and news articles that condemned the book and the proposed film persuaded them to see the project in a new light. Other factors also influenced the course of production. Petitions, lawsuits, and demonstrations by civic groups pressured the film and television industries to construct new platforms for minority voices both in front of and behind the camera. Furthermore, the Johnson administration's widely discussed report by the National Advisory Commission on Civil Disorders had concluded that the news and entertainment media had failed to provide professional opportunities for people of color, and had also failed to address topical subjects of interest to minority viewers. It was in this period, as Wolper and Twentieth Century–Fox were struggling with the Nat Turner project, that minority filmmakers in Los Angeles made inroads within public television and universities. It was also at this time that they began to create independent collectives in order to produce films about their own communities.

Moved by the protests against the film and understanding that the production needed to change, Wolper told the *New York Times*, "Every legitimate black organization in America came out against certain parts of the book, and I felt something had to be done. . . . You don't go forward and make a film about a black hero if the entire black community feels it is wrong, any more than you'd make a film of 'Exodus' if the Jewish community felt it was wrong."[44] Two adjustments involved hiring black personnel and agreeing to expand the film's source material. Wolper brought on black playwright-screenwriter Louis Peterson to write the script. Peterson was a celebrated author who attended Morehouse College before going on to pursue graduate training at the Yale School of Drama and New York University. Peterson was also used to working across media, having written the Broadway play *Take a Giant Step* (1953) and adapted the stage production for the screen in 1959.[45] The title of the film was changed to *Nat Turner*, distancing it from Styron's book, and actor James Earl Jones was hired for the lead role.

Following a meeting in late December of 1968, Meriwether reported: "Both Wolper and Jewison have assured us that they will project a positive image of Nat Turner as a black revolutionary, and that such things as slaves lusting after white women and raping them, slaves putting down the rebellion, homosexual incidents and other figments of Styron's imagination, will not be included in the screenplay."[46]

But Peterson's work on the script did not involve wholesale reconstruction. Peterson toned down Turner's sexual longings for white women, but kept his obsession with the young girl, Margaret Whitehead. He replaced a scene where Turner witnessed a sexual encounter between his mother and a drunken Irish overseer with one of his mother denying a black sailor. Peterson also omitted scenes of rape, and made Whitehead's death an accident rather than a climactic act of aggression on Turner's part.

Social service outreach to African Americans in Los Angeles served as another strategy to mend the public relations crisis. Wife-and-husband teams involved with the film, including Dixie and Norman Jewison, Bea and Mark Miller, Suzanne and Lawrence Turman, and Dawn and David Wolper, started the coalition Neighbors of Watts (NOW) to raise funds to construct a childcare center in South Central. As outlined in a *Los Angeles Times* article, "NOW—A Good Neighbor Policy for Beverly Hills," the center had a threefold purpose, providing childcare for working mothers, immunizations and nutrition courses, and a Head Start operation for early education.[47] The center provided much-needed social services, as Watts had a mortality rate for children that was 70 percent higher than for the rest of Southern California, and 46 percent of all families were single-parent homes. NOW raised money by raffling off tickets to Hollywood premieres and hosting benefits.

To be sure, social outreach was nothing new to liberal Hollywood, but it had assumed a heightened importance and visibility in the aftermath of the Watts Uprising. Budd Schulberg's Watts Writers Workshop constituted an early effort to use artistic expression as a form of social uplift and as a way to mediate the fractious state of race relations in the city. NOW's fundraising and advisory board involved a mix of individuals connected to the entertainment industry, as well as health care and legal specialists who worked in the South Central area. Sponsors included an illustrious list of Hollywood insiders, some of whom had been involved with the Watts Writers Workshop. NOW's big April 1969 charity concert took place at the Aquarius Theater in Hollywood and featured Frank Sinatra, Bill Cosby, Nancy Sinatra, Nelson Riddle's big band, and Tom Smothers as emcee. Black mayoral candidate Tom Bradley, actors Martin Landau and Ricardo Montalbán, and journalist Shana Alexander were all in attendance.[48]

Despite the changes in production and outreach for *Nat Turner*, the start of principal photography was postponed. The controversy that continued to swirl around the adaptation made Twentieth Century–Fox hesitant to move forward. Jewison soon dropped out to fulfill his contractual obligation to shoot *Gaily, Gaily* (1969) and *Fiddler on the Roof* (1971) for United Artists. A reluctant Sidney Lumet stepped into the directorial role.[49] He was focused on an array of practical problems associated with the production and appeared aloof concerning the project's political resonance:

FIGURE 14: Advertisement for *Nat Turner*, *Variety*, July 30, 1969, 80.

It's going to be difficult technically. . . . We have to show cotton, tobacco and corn crops at different times—at planting, full-grown, at harvesting. Art director Gene Callahan and I will just have to arrange for some out-of-season rotation farming to be ready for our 10-week location schedule. I don't know the first thing about it, being a Jewish city boy. The first question I asked 20th [Century] research was "How do you plant corn?"[50]

Advertisements for the film proclaimed a March 1970 start to production, but delays combined with the poor financial state of Twentieth Century–Fox after a series of disastrous big-budget film investments left the Nat Turner project in a stalled state.[51] NOW's activities continued into the next decade, but the film that indirectly engendered its creation was nothing but a memory by the early 1970s.[52]

As Christopher Sieving insightfully notes, the late-1960s Nat Turner film debacle discouraged Hollywood from pursuing well-funded black-themed features about controversial topics. Following the success of *Cotton Comes to Harlem* (1970), *Sweet Sweetback's Baadasssss Song* (1971), and *Shaft* (1971), the majors looked instead to low-budget, black-cast crime dramas.[53] The Nat Turner project was thus instructive for Hollywood. Significantly, however, Wolper learned something different from what the other studios did. His company looked to refashion the minority prestige picture into a new kind of film. This was to a large extent due to Wolper and his colleagues' recent experience of working on the Nat Turner project in such a charged climate of protest. They became more aware of the past struggles and contemporary political movements of black communities within and beyond Los Angeles, and interested in how cinematically addressing these issues could potentially attract large audiences. Wolper Productions also realized that a film about a minority subject needed to have the direct investment of minority participants. Successful films begin with productive partnerships. The studio would get a chance to exercise its newfound wisdom when the black-owned-and-operated record label Stax contacted Wolper about documenting the concluding concert of the 1972 Watts Summer Festival.

5

Wattstax and the Transmedia Soul Economy

*The action itself is the art form, and is described in aesthetic terms:
"A very imaginative deal," they say, or, "He writes the most creative deals in
the business."*

—WRITER JOAN DIDION, 1973[1]

*I enjoyed every bit of Wattstax. The people were being themselves, and I felt
like I was there in the movie. Some parts of it just brought tears to my eyes
because it was so beautiful.*

—MOTHER IN CHICAGO, 1973[2]

When the soul music label Stax Records joined forces with Wolper Productions to
make a documentary about the concluding concert of the 1972 Watts Summer Festival, the result was no ordinary concert film. The event in the Los Angeles Memorial Coliseum consisted of a showcase of Stax artists, including Isaac Hayes, the
Staple Singers, Albert King, and Rufus and Carla Thomas. The 112,000 attendees,
most of whom were black, were eager to see many of their favorite performers and
to participate in the festival's larger effort to commemorate the 1965 Watts Uprising.
Making a film about a concert that honored a street protest was a particularly
complex undertaking. The documentary brought together a wide-reaching cast of
characters. Stax executives Al Bell, Larry Shaw, and Forest Hamilton supplied the
musicians for the show and retained editorial control over the documentary.
Wolper Productions' David Wolper and Mel Stuart coordinated the filmmaking
operations. Up-and-coming comic Richard Pryor provided the narrative commentary. And neighborhood residents appeared as interviewees in front of the camera
and, in some cases, helped shoot the event.

For years *Wattstax* was treated as just a minor episode within the rise-and-fall
story of Stax, but recently, increasing interest in comparative media studies and
cultural histories of Los Angeles has led to a flurry of scholarship on the film.
Interpretations of the documentary sort into three general positions. The first

contends that *Wattstax* was a fresh way to display the record label's talent, but that the project failed to successfully launch Stax into film.[3] The second maintains that *Wattstax* documented creative stylizations of black experience that spoke to a sense of self-respect and optimism for future prospects in Los Angeles.[4] The third argues that the documentary aimed to present a non-stereotypical view of Watts, but that its financial imperatives and its romantic depictions of the area distanced it from both the communities it ostensibly sought to represent and the audiences it sought to reach.[5]

These three interpretations have either under-theorized the role of the film's different players or overemphasized their profit motive. Only through analyzing *Wattstax* as a collaborative project can we understand the full scope of the film's economic and social ambitions. This approach also makes evident the increasing intersection between disparate figures and institutions in the film, television, and record industries during this period, and highlights the ephemeral nature of these partnerships. The distinct efforts of Stax, Wolper Productions, and local filmmakers and residents enabled the documentary's innovative exploration of black cultural nationalism. Drawing on, but adamantly differentiating itself from popular black action features and concert documentaries, *Wattstax* portrayed music as an empowering language of individual and collective expression, connecting the performances heard in the coliseum to the social landscape of the surrounding neighborhood. The documentary's multilayered approach to black music made penetrating the commercial market difficult, but ultimately led to its positive reception in black communities.

GROOVING WEST

The concept for *Wattstax* grew out of the Watts Summer Festival, which began in August 1966. As historian Bruce M. Tyler has written, organizers intended for the festival to commemorate the uprising the year before, but were more invested in celebrating black creativity and increasing access to social services than advocating for another mass protest.[6] Key planners included Tommy Jacquette, founder of Self-Leadership for All Nationalities Today (SLANT), Maulana Ron Karenga, leader of the US Organization, and Booker Griffin, prominent radio commentator and newspaper columnist. Reflecting the festival's cultural-nationalist goals, participants showcased present-day folkways as well as African heritage by means of music, art, and dance. Six blocks of 103rd Street as well as Jordan High School became home to entrepreneurs, outreach organizations, a jazz festival, and a parade. The Watts Happening Coffee House served as a theater and music venue. In its first editions, the festival occasionally became a site of violent contestation. Attendees clashed with police, who were against the idea of honoring the uprising.[7] So too did organizers clash with militant radicals, who claimed that the festival was an escapist carnival with no direct political effect.[8] Still, the multiday event sustained momentum and gained greater visibility with each year.

Stax saw the creation of a concert and an accompanying film at the 1972 festival as the culmination of a recent period of transition. Stax had shifted significantly since 1957, when the white record producer Jim Stewart started the small company in a recording studio in Memphis's Capitol Theatre. By the late 1960s, Stax was a large organization intent on diversifying, expanding its roster of artists, and cultivating a more socially conscious image.[9] The black producer Al Bell became Stax's creative compass and guided the label through this period of change. Bell had worked as a student teacher with the Southern Christian Leadership Conference in Atlanta and as a DJ and record producer in Little Rock and Washington, DC. He was drawn to the intellectual and affective power of music to move listeners. Bell joined Stax as the national promotions director in 1965 and advanced to vice president in 1967. By the turn of the decade he was a co-owner and by 1972 the sole owner.[10]

Artists drew inspiration from the cultural milieu of the Mid South Delta region in which the company was founded. Stax's unofficial name, "Soulsville U.S.A.," pointed to the label's secularization of sacred black music traditions. Artists combined the call-and-response patterns and "vocal freedom" of gospel with the musical virtuosity, danceable tempo, and storytelling of rhythm and blues.[11] The name also gestured toward the label's passion for capturing raw performances rather than highly produced routines. Martin Luther King Jr.'s assassination at the Lorraine Motel in Memphis and the concomitant rise of the Black Power movement were important to Bell's ascent within Stax and inflected the company's expansion. Stax hired more black advertising, marketing, and secretarial personnel. Artists backed health care and educational initiatives in minority communities. Bell supported artists as their songs began to directly embrace themes of black empowerment and looked to build musical bridges between American and African composition. New subsidiary labels that featured John KaSandra's raps and Jesse Jackson's popular litany "I Am Somebody" were marketed to schools and churches.[12]

It would be plausible to see the label's expansion as dovetailing with President Richard Nixon's support of "black capitalism." In the months leading up to and immediately following his 1968 presidential campaign, Nixon vocalized his support for "more black ownership, for from this can flow the rest—black pride, black jobs, black opportunity and, yes, black power." He went on to stress, "What is needed is an imaginative enlistment of private funds, private energies and private talent."[13] However, as historians Laura Warren Hill and Julia Rabig argue, the "business of black power" was a topic of debate long before Nixon began using the phrase to co-opt black militancy for a Republican Party platform and to woo liberals and minorities from the other side of the aisle. Black economic empowerment included a wide range of positions: Earl Ofari Hutchinson's critique of capitalism as essentially racially and economically exploitive; Andrew Brimmer's assertion that a separatist black economy could not be sustained within the realities of the market; publications such as *Essence* supporting blacks in leadership positions in major corporations; James Forman's demand for reparations for slavery; and Stokely Carmichael's proposal of co-op business models in which community members have a stake and the profits go back to the community.[14] While Stax was not a grassroots organization, it also was not an entirely profit-driven corporation. Bell saw minority empowerment as something that required collective effort and social benefit. It could not be simply achieved by individual drive and the free market. Aligning Stax too closely with Nixon's pronouncements obscures the complexity of the organization and the relationship between the label, its projects, and its multiple audiences.

One of Stax's central goals was to build a profile in motion pictures. The company's sale to Gulf and Western in 1968 was motivated by the prospects of working with the conglomerate's film subsidiary Paramount Pictures and setting up a studio in Los Angeles. The films Stax artists worked on in the late 1960s and 1970s did not coalesce around a particular view of race relations or a conception of a new black cinema. In fact, the white auteur Jules Dassin's black-cast film *Uptight* (1968), the black artist Melvin Van Peebles's independent production *Sweet Sweetback's Baadasssss Song* (1971), and the black commercial photographer and filmmaker Gordon Parks Sr.'s studio feature *Shaft* (1971) clashed with one another ideologically and inspired differing criticism and praise. All these productions nonetheless explored post-1968 racial politics and rejected the liberal integrationist "social problem" film. Stax saw the soundtrack as a new vehicle to promote its music, an imaginative medium for its artists, and a commercial product in its own right. The label also sought to rival Motown, its main competitor. Motown president Berry Gordy had recently expanded his Detroit-based pop–R&B label to Los Angeles, hoping to showcase its stars in both television variety programs and feature films.[15] Motown was known to the country as "Hitsville USA," and the Motor City label's sound—characterized by a clean, smooth balance between vocals and instruments along with catchy melodies—appealed to a crossover teenage audience. *Los Angeles Magazine* declared that Gordy was creating a "commercial empire" in Hollywood.[16]

For the Paramount film *Uptight*, Stax's leading session musician Booker T. Jones composed the score and performed it with his MGs ensemble. *Uptight* focuses on Tank Williams (Julian Mayfield), a black ex-convict and former steel mill employee living in Cleveland. Distraught by King's assassination, Tank is unable to join his fellow radicals on an arms raid. His absence causes hiccups in their plan and the police pursuit of the group's leader, Tank's close friend Johnny Wells (Max Julien). Ostracized by his friends for refusing to join them, Tank becomes a police informant, which results in Johnny being killed by lawmen. Tank's guilt-ridden wandering through the streets of Cleveland concludes with his death at the hands of his former friends.

Booker T.'s compositions are overtly intertwined with the on-screen action. The ballad "Johnny I Love You" plays at the film's opening against a series of watercolor paintings assembled in storyboard fashion. The impressionistic images show an adolescent Tank and Johnny playing on the streets of Cleveland. The lyrics speak to Tank's affection for Johnny as a brother and also communicate a shared desire to "fix" a city that "ain't right." The optimism conveyed by the song is quickly ruptured by the immediate transition to documentary footage of King's funeral cortege on the streets of Atlanta, and reenactments of street protests by black crowds in Cleveland. It is as if nonviolent resistance and the desire for integration exist in the past, unable to confront the realities of the present.

"Time Is Tight" plays at the film's conclusion during the chase scene when Tank first runs from, and then tries to attract, the attention of his former friends. The driving electric guitar and drums charge the scene with nervous energy, but the transition to the slow wail of the organ creates the feeling of a funerary dirge as Tank hangs from a crane and then drops to a pile of dirt and iron ore below—laid to rest in the mill where he had worked for twenty years before being fired.

The success of *Uptight's* soundtrack motivated Stax to pursue film opportunities and soon after to take a major role in distributing Van Peebles's *Sweet Sweetback's Baadasssss Song* as well as its accompanying album.[17] The story follows Sweetback (Van Peebles), a black orphan turned sex show performer who is arrested on a bogus charge. He escapes his captors by beating them with his handcuffs before they kill a Black Panther. Sweetback then spends the rest of the film running from the law and making a narrow escape across the border to Mexico. *Sweet Sweetback's* "musical pastiche," according to historian Amy Abugo Ongiri, involves gospel, spoken-word performance, African-style drumming, and the funk stylings of Earth, Wind & Fire.[18] In the book *The Making of Sweet Sweetback's Baadasssss Song*, Van Peebles wrote that he wanted to experiment with sound to "help tell the story."[19] Free jazz playing against the contrapuntal editing sets a fast-paced tempo for Sweetback's flight across train yards, freeways, pump fields, and the Los Angeles River. Van Peebles's voice-over raps, interwoven with the soundtrack, comment on Sweetback's physical and mental state as he fights exhaustion, injury, and the police. Stax's vice president of publicity, Larry Shaw, handled the targeted distribution of both the film and the soundtrack to black audiences in major cities. Viewers could even buy the LP in theater lobbies.[20]

Shaft would come to be the most visible Stax-related feature film. MGM commissioned Stax artist Isaac Hayes, who had recently achieved worldwide popularity with his album *Hot Buttered Soul* (1969), to do the music. The film tells the story of John Shaft (Richard Roundtree), a black detective working out of Harlem. Black gangster Bumpy Jonas (Moses Gunn) commissions Shaft to find his kidnapped daughter Marcy (Sherri Brewer). Bumpy deceptively leads Shaft to collaborate with the black militant Lumumbas, of which Shaft's old friend Ben Buford

(Christopher St. John) is a member. Together they fight the downtown Italian mafia, who are trying to muscle in on Bumpy's illegal business dealings, and rescue Marcy. As in *Uptight* and *Sweet Sweetback*, the soundtrack plays a key role in character development. Starting with the opening credits, the music of Hayes and the Bar-Kays establishes the personality of the protagonist as a man of action. Sixteenth notes played on the hi-hat cymbal are in sync with Shaft's steps as he emerges from a subway station in midtown Manhattan. Recurring wah-wah-pedal guitar riffs, strings, and horns set a fast pace for Shaft's purposeful strides. He swiftly moves past pedestrians and weaves through oncoming traffic.

The critical attention to and high box office returns of *Sweet Sweetback* and *Shaft*, along with recently released films such as *Cotton Comes to Harlem* (1970), led to a deluge of studio-made black action features. Set in inner-city locales, these films typically center on black male detectives, vigilantes, and gangsters seeking retribution, revenge, or order—in opposition to a white villain. At a time when major studios were desperately trying to stave off declining theater attendance, films targeting black viewers were beginning to be considered a significant revenue generator. For much of the classical era, studios had written off trying to explicitly court minority viewers. Hollywood's shift toward black action features was also a response to pressures to create professional opportunities for African Americans and to represent a greater breadth of black experience on-screen. *Newsweek* announced a veritable "Black Movie Boom," and the Black Arts magazine *Black Creation* declared that there was an "explosion" of black cinema.[21] Warner Bros.' *Super Fly*, Paramount's *The Legend of Nigger Charley*, American International Pictures' *Blacula*, and MGM's *Melinda* and *Cool Breeze* are just a sampling of the films that came out in 1972. The cycle's popularity stemmed from its foregrounding of strong black characters who proudly challenge white authority, the involvement of black personnel in the production process, on-location shooting in black communities, and nationwide distribution to black audiences.

Still, critics offered scathing reviews of these films. Claiming that they were a form of "black exploitation," Junius Griffin led the Los Angeles–based Coalition Against Blaxploitation, which criticized the cycle for promoting negative stereotypes and primarily benefiting white Hollywood power brokers.[22] Without weighing in too heavily on specific debates regarding the plots or themes of the films, Stax's Al Bell voiced his support for the individuals working on the productions. In a front-page *Billboard* article he stated that *Sweet Sweetback* and *Shaft* were valuable because they involved black artists coming together to work collaboratively: "A major film with a black director, a black star and a sound by a black composer . . . is an enormous source of pride to the black community. It's more than just a movie—it's a special event."[23] In its future endeavors, Stax would forgo trying to replicate *Shaft*'s success, focusing instead on creating an alternative kind of community-focused cinema.

THE STAX-WOLPER ALLIANCE

Jim Taylor and Richard Dedeaux of the Mafundi Institute approached Forest Hamilton with the idea of Stax staging a concert to conclude the Watts Summer Festival. Mafundi was a local cultural-nationalist arts space and social service center on 103rd Street. It had been a crucial contributor to previous festivals. Hamilton had worked in film distribution and as an entertainment and sports promoter before helping to establish Stax's Southern California satellite, Stax West. Eager to migrate Stax's music across media, Hamilton developed the concept of filming the show. Bell loved the idea. The Joseph Schlitz Brewing Company agreed to serve as a sponsor, the artists agreed to play for free, and Stax decided to charge only one dollar per ticket. The proceeds would go to the Martin Luther King Jr. General Hospital, the Sickle Cell Anemia Foundation, and the Watts Labor Community Action Committee.[24] Giving the concert a celluloid afterlife would project the sounds of Stax much farther than the coliseum's loudspeakers. This strategy would also guarantee access to black communities as well as white liberals, college students, and the art cinema crowd. Importantly, Stax anticipated that *Wattstax* would provide a strong counterpunch to what the *Los Angeles Sentinel* described as the "Motown Entertainment Complex."[25]

When Bell sent Hamilton to find the "very best documentary producer," he went to see David Wolper, who signed on for the film.[26] Beyond the jazz background of one of Wolper Productions' main directors, Mel Stuart, the studio possessed three highly desirable qualities that made it the ideal choice for Stax. First, Wolper Productions had been making an eclectic range of documentaries for more than ten years—everything from historical compilation films about military conflicts to verité-style portraits of politicians. Second, Wolper Productions was based in Los Angeles and consistently worked with different talent pools. Observational filmmakers such as D. A. Pennebaker, Richard Leacock, or the Maysles brothers were well known for documenting musicians, but they were based in the Northeast and lacked familiarity with Los Angeles; further downsides included their strong auteurist sensibilities, resistance to exposition in their films, and distaste for working within large organizations. Third, Wolper Productions knew how to cover large affairs. Recently the studio had collaborated with the Olympic Committee, the Bavaria-Geiselgasteig organization, and eight international directors to create *Visions of Eight* (1973) about the Munich Games.[27]

Wolper Productions had much to gain from the partnership. The studio had made documentaries that addressed race relations since the early 1960s, but was looking for the chance to create a new kind of film that could directly engage with minority viewers. Wolper's *Biography of a Rookie: The Willie Davis Story* (1961) and *The Rafer Johnson Story* (1961) were nonfiction television analogues to the civil rights–era Sidney Poitier features such as *All the Young Men* (1960), *Lilies of the*

Field (1963), and *To Sir, with Love* (1967). Through the optic of sports, Wolper's television documentaries presented black Angelenos achieving an equal place in American society by means of hard work, individual performance, and integrated team play. Later in the decade, Wolper believed that adapting novelist William Styron's self-labeled "meditation on history," *The Confessions of Nat Turner*, would be a progressive undertaking. Ultimately his attempts to make the adaptation revealed major ideological tensions between liberal Hollywood and the Black Power movement. Black entertainers and intellectuals alike objected to the film's racist source text as well as the film's lack of black labor both below and above the line. The production never made it past the planning stage. But working on the project made Wolper and his circle more conscientious about the history of race prejudice and the contemporary black struggle for self-determination. They had also become eager to reach minority viewers, and knew that films that focused on African Americans needed to directly involve the people being represented.

Although Stax and Wolper Productions were confident about filming the Wattstax concert, they were unsure about the best way to build a film around the performance. By the late 1960s, concert documentaries had emerged as a popular film subgenre and provided a possible model. *Monterey Pop* (1968) and *Woodstock* (1970) were extensions of their respective festivals' commercial initiatives and, as film scholar Keith Beattie argues, registered the immersive experience of attending the show.[28] *Soul to Soul* (1971) also provided food for thought. The documentary depicted a concert in Ghana's Black Star Square in Accra on the fourteenth anniversary of the country's independence from Britain. R&B artist Wilson Pickett, beloved in Ghana, headlined the festival, and Ike and Tina Turner, the West African Kumasi Drummers, and Amoa Azangio were part of the lineup. An advertisement for the film read, "America to Africa: Where It All Came From / Bonds Tightly Tied—Musical Fire—Sound to Sound—Soul to Soul."[29] Much of *Soul to Soul* captures the ecstatic fifteen-hour, all-night concert. Brief cutaways highlight the American artists' enthusiastic reception at the Kotoka Airport and their visits to the nearby village of Aburi and the Elmina slave castle.[30]

Stax and Wolper ultimately wanted to pursue a different kind of documentary, one that cogently addressed the relationship between music and social context. The Wolper Productions in-house director Mel Stuart, in particular, felt that films like *Monterey Pop* were overly "simple" and "boring," akin to a basic newsreel. He told Forest Hamilton, "I don't do newsreels." In his estimation, the documentary would need to have a strong expository aspect.[31] Stax and Wolper resolved to interweave concert footage with interviews and observational scenes of South Central, emphasizing the association between the performances on the bandstand and people's everyday lives.

An eclectic mix of personnel and institutions signed on to help create *Wattstax*. Columbia Pictures handled distribution, ensuring a wide release. Despite having

FIGURE 15: Jesse Jackson and Larry Shaw, publicity photograph for
Wattstax, 1973, 35mm; directed by Mel Stuart; produced by Stax
Records and Wolper Productions; distributed by Columbia Pictures.
Courtesy of the Stax Museum of American Soul Music Archives.

recently distributed a series of money-making, award-winning films, including
the New Hollywood road movie *Easy Rider* (1969), the studio was in financial
trouble at the turn of the decade. Its attempts to diversify into television, radio, and
real estate coupled with poor box office returns on its recent roster of films had put
it in the red.[32] Mel Stuart agreed to direct the movie. He, along with producers
Hamilton and Shaw, recruited the film's black crew from the immediate area. Many
came from universities and arts organizations.[33] Included in this group were Larry
Clark and Roderick Young, both of whom were involved with the L.A. Rebellion
film movement around UCLA. Clark had worked with Charles Burnett on what
would become *Killer of Sheep* (1977). Young had crewed on the Hollywood black
action feature *The Final Comedown* (1972) and exhibited his nonfiction photography at the Los Angeles Festival of the Performing Arts. The Mexican American
cinematographer John Alonzo was hired as a cameraman. His lyrical pans and
sweeping tracking shots in *Vanishing Point* (1971) and *Sounder* (1972) had made
him a noteworthy New Hollywood technician.

Wolper Productions coordinated production, but Stax assumed editorial control over the content. This was a contractual move that separated *Wattstax* from
many studio pictures of the time. According to Clause 2.4 of the contract, Stax
would

> have the absolute right of prior approval of film or narration which is included in the
> Picture which relates to Black relationships and feelings; words or phrases having a

special Black connotation; and, if the Picture has a narrator, approval of the narrator and the accuracy of the narration script as to the music contained in the Picture. You [Stax] shall have the right of reasonable approval of the writer of the narration script, and you [Stax] agree to exercise said right in good faith.[34]

Comedian Richard Pryor joined the film to serve as a one-man Greek chorus. Stuart recalls that when Hamilton took him to see Pryor perform at the Summit Club on La Brea in Baldwin Hills, "within three minutes I knew that he was the greatest comedian of our time."[35] Pryor played Billie Holiday's endearing, reserved piano player in Motown's *Lady Sings the Blues* (1972). Now performing as himself in *Wattstax*, his barbed quips supplied the connective tissue holding the film's disparate elements together.

COMMUNITY PORTRAITURE

Wattstax's polyvocality is grounded in three kinds of performance: Stax artists on the bandstand; South Central residents on steps, sidewalks, cafés, and barbershops; and Pryor backstage at the Summit Club. Together, they establish how everyday life and music are in dialogue, each influencing the other. The film consciously aims to document the self-presentation and self-narration of both residents and artists, showing that performativity is integral to both informal interactions and formal, aesthetic expression. The film opens with Pryor seated against a solid black backdrop. Speaking directly to the viewer, his prefatory statements convey that the concert is a political act of commemoration. As the camera slowly zooms in on his face, he explains:

> All of us have something to say, but some are never heard. Over seven years ago, the people of Watts stood together and demanded to be heard. On a Sunday this past August in the Los Angeles Coliseum, over one hundred thousand black people came together to commemorate that moment in American history. For over six hours the audience heard, felt, sang, danced, and shouted the living word in a soulful expression of the black experience. This is a film of that experience, and what some of the people have to say.

Pryor's comments direct the viewer's attention toward the people of Watts who protested together in 1965 and the crowd that gathered at the coliseum seven years later. What happened in Watts, Pryor states, was not a casual occurrence or haphazard act of violence, but a historic occasion of a people "demand[ing] to be heard." The Watts Summer Festival honored the sounding of grievances through a contemporary assertion of visibility and voice. In turn, *Wattstax* was an effort to keep the significance of past actions alive and relevant. Participants were not simply on the receiving end of a message; they were agents in creating an event that resonated with the cultural vibrancy of their community.

A quick cut transitions from the darkened interior of the Summit Club to the Watts Towers. The sculptural mass of concrete-wrapped steel, inlaid with fragments of porcelain, glass, and tile, stands tall near the intersection of 107th Street and Graham Avenue. The title "Wattstax" appears in the foreground. A screeching wail cries out as a handheld camera glides down one of the spires. These shots give way to a montage of neighborhood views, playing against the Dramatics' 1971 hit "Watcha See Is Watcha Get" on the soundtrack: "But baby I'm for real / I'm as real / as real can get / If what you're looking for is real loving / then what you see is what you get." The song goes on to accompany images of small children playing in a vacant lot, a mailman making deliveries, women waiting to board a city bus, a young couple in a romantic embrace, and teenagers walking to school, holding books. Images of Charcoal Alley ablaze from the 1965 uprising conclude the sequence.

As *Wattstax* takes the spectator into the coliseum, the concert is an occasion to reflect on the uprising as well as on the social dimensions of music. Framed in a medium shot on the bandstand with periodic cutaways to close-ups and overhead views of the crowd, Reverend Jesse Jackson is the first to address the audience before the show begins. He proclaims, "All of our people got a soul, our experience determines the *texture*, the *taste*, and the *sound* of our soul." Performing this sentiment in song, Kim Weston's rendition of the black national anthem, "Lift Every Voice and Sing," speaks to the centuries-long fight for black liberation. Originally written by James Weldon Johnson, "Lift Every Voice and Sing" was first publicly performed by schoolchildren on the occasion of Abraham Lincoln's birthday, February 12, 1900. Weston's 1968 recording inspired renewed enthusiasm for the anthem as an emblem of self-determination and unity.[36] In *Wattstax*, the song speaks evocatively to the contemporary moment as a time of possibility but also of great challenge. The position of strength from which Weston sings seems shared by the crowd. Whereas people remain seated and look distracted and bored during the singing of the "Star-Spangled Banner," they stand proud for "Lift Every Voice and Sing," elevated to their feet by the words and melody. The song then travels out of the diegetic context of the coliseum to serve as the soundtrack to a sequence of photographs and archival footage. The sequence includes an illustrated diagram of the slave ship *Brookes*, images of African Americans working in the field as sharecroppers during Jim Crow–era segregation, short newsreels depicting civil rights sit-ins, and brutal confrontations between black protestors and white police. Images of Frederick Douglass, Marcus Garvey, Malcolm X, Dr. King, Huey Newton, and Angela Davis surface throughout the still and moving images.

The sequence eschews a straight chronology of events or a simple, streamlined narrative of progress. It foregrounds the leaders who have in distinct ways fought for collective empowerment by means of leading boycotts, staging public sit-ins, waging legal battles in the courts, crafting political art, penning philosophical texts, or meeting the threat of violence with physical force. The sequence encourages viewers to see connections rather than differences among the leaders' social actions. The images reference the struggles that the song narrates. At the concert, the 112,000-strong gathering of black people freely expressing themselves was heralded by festival organizers, attendees, and journalists as an achievement in itself. The peaceful happening proved wrong racist law enforcement officials and municipal leaders who thought so large a gathering would either not materialize or would result in violence.[37]

Alternating scenes depicting local citizens' heated discussions about the meaning of the uprising and the current state of life in Watts take up the ideas raised during the anthem. In a scene in a store portraying a group of three friends debating the effects of the rebellion, one man comments, "It did something constructive for the whole community," and another person chimes in, "They've opened up a Dr. Martin Luther King Hospital; and there are more black people in Watts who were formerly on county and state aid employed right now." In a conversation in a café with a different group of people, one man states, "Up until the point when we had a riot, everybody said 'those niggers are all right, they're doing fine'; when we had a riot, the white man said 'something's *wrong*, because these suckers are burning down my store, I better give them something because I thought they were happy.'"

But just as some viewpoints affirm that the uprising has engendered constructive change, others appear dubious. Some comment that the recent addition of a handful of new facilities provides an image of progress that is shortsighted and illusory. One elderly man interviewed claims that neglect and corruption are still prevalent. Another man confidently states that the rebellion "changed some for the best, an awful lot of cases for the worse, and some, it has not changed at all. There is no difference in Watts now, from Watts '65." Filming individual testimonies communicates residents' hopes and anxieties about the future of Watts, but obscures the implications of broader economic and political forces that were shaping post-'65 daily life in the area: the increasing government crackdown on militant organizing; infighting among Black Power leaders; increasing industrial relocation to the South Bay and outlying suburbs; and the prospective electoral victory of the city's first black mayor, Tom Bradley.

And yet, *Wattstax* is more intent on capturing the persistence of a post-'65 sense of love and pride residents feel for a shared expressive culture. The documentary demonstrates that black identity and music are mutually constitutive. For example, artist Rufus Thomas's invitation to the crowd to come "Do the Funky Chicken" signals the power of the music to create its own form of social space. Clad in a hot-pink cape, shorts, and go-go boots, Thomas shimmies, sings, and struts on the bandstand while members of the audience swiftly move from their seats to the field. Grooving concertgoers transform the coliseum into a grand outdoor dance floor, performing the steps to the "Funky Chicken" in a seemingly infinite array of styles. In both long shots of the crowd and close-ups of men and

FIGURE 16: Still from *Wattstax*, 1973, 35mm; directed by Mel Stuart; produced by Stax Records and Wolper Productions; distributed by Columbia Pictures. DVD, Warner Home Video, Burbank, California, 2004.

FIGURE 17: Still from *Wattstax*, 1973, 35mm; directed by Mel Stuart; produced by Stax Records and Wolper Productions; distributed by Columbia Pictures. DVD, Warner Home Video, Burbank, California, 2004.

women, adults and children, the camera captures the collapsing distance between artist and audience, fan and celebrity. Each is ecstatically feeding off the energy of the other, coauthoring the concert, and relishing the cinematic spotlight.

Moving from inside to outside the coliseum, guitarist Albert King's performance of "I'll Play the Blues for You" plays against a series of conversations showing how the blues gives form to personal and communal lament. Gazing out at the crowd as his fingers dance on the neck of the guitar, King announces that the song is "dedicated to all of the blues lovers, and to all those that aren't hip to the blues, we're going to *learn* them to you, teach them to you, rather, because we'll be around for a while." Shots of King playing are interspersed with interviews that show people's familiarity with the blues. Men and women talk about the blues as something that "people can relate to right now, not tomorrow." They wax poetic about the blues as a melancholic sentiment and a way to convey unrequited love and frustration. Their discussion often swings out to engage the generalized condition of feeling low and depressed. King sings: "If you're down and out and you feel real hurt / come on over to the place where I work / All your loneliness, I'll try to soothe / I'll play the blues for you." One man states, "I've been down so long, that getting up hasn't even crossed my mind." Another relates the blues to being by yourself on the street at night alone, and yet another says that the blues are like "an old car, man, that keeps stopping on you. This is what I've experienced with the blues, in many ways, not just with being in love." A woman exclaims that the feeling of the blues is being left on your own with "your heart in your hand." King's *worrying* of the notes forms the instrumental counterpart to the speakers' tremulous, impassioned voices. While the voicing of such sentiments often emphasizes singularity and loneliness, the sighs, yelps, laughter, and short responses from surrounding listeners give solace to the speakers, ultimately socializing the grief.

Other performances within the coliseum are interweaved with representations of and discussions about religion. When the Staple Singers take the stage to sing "Respect Yourself" off their 1972 album *Be Altitude: Respect Yourself*, they signal soul music's connection to their gospel roots and stress its continued relevance. The family ensemble, like numerous Stax artists who grew up singing in church, did not abandon the sacred for the secular; they continued to draw on gospel instrumentation, lyrics, and performance styles in their music.[38] In the film, the electric guitar playing of Roebuck "Pops" Staples, accompanied by the hand clapping of his two daughters, Mavis and Yvonne, begins the song: "If you disrespect everybody that you run into, yea / how in the world do you think anybody is supposed to respect you / If you don't give a heck about the man with the Bible in his hand, y'all / just get out the way and let the gentleman do his thing." The refrain is sung in unison by all three: "If you don't respect yourself ain't nobody gonna give a good ca-hoot, na, na, na, na / Respect yourself, respect yourself, respect yourself, respect yourself." The song proclaims the need to treat others the way you want to be treated, a call for mutual respect that references scripture: "And as ye would that men should do to you, do ye also to them likewise" (Luke 6:31). Pops asserts that "the man with the Bible in his hand" has a role to play in helping to spread this message of self-worth and mutual admiration for strangers and friends alike.

The Staple Singers embrace the call-and-response patterns of a preacher and congregation. Their repeated address to the listener as "you" and "y'all," the imperative to "respect yourself," and the between-the-verse phrases such as "help me y'all" strengthen their bond with the audience. Mobile, handheld cameras frame the family on the stage with their fans. Unidentified members of the audience, along with prominent black celebrities such as Ossie Davis and Ruby Dee, appear enraptured by the music. They sing along, mouth the words, or tap their feet to the beat. Others stand up and dance in place. Then, the song serves as a non-diegetic accompaniment to shots of institutions in the neighborhood and in other centers for black life throughout the country. Shots of the Mafundi Institute in Watts, the Malcolm X College in Chicago, the Harlem Hospital Center, and the "Africa Is the Beginning" mural art from the YMCA Building in Roxbury, Massachusetts, illustrate what black power can achieve when people come together.

A photo montage portraying more than fifteen churches gives a sense of the presence of religion within black Los Angeles. The facades have different ornamental design schemes and signage, but all the churches appear heavily used.

Many are storefronts or converted houses. The combination of two waves of black migration from the South and Midwest, along with the media resources of the city, made Los Angeles a destination for traveling gospel singers in the early to mid-twentieth century. Churches nurtured the music all over the city.[39] In *Wattstax*, interviews with residents reveal that religious music puts people in touch with cherished memories. One woman recounts how listening to the gospel standard "Amazing Grace" is a ritual of familial remembrance: "When I hear the choir sing 'Amazing Grace' I start thinking about when my grandmother died, you know, she died of cancer. I was young, but the music just sets a *thing*." A man talks about how church music provides him with an embodied emotional and spiritual charge: "When they [the choir and band] really get going, when they really get to jamming, I used to dig that, because you know, I'd be right there with them, and when people jump up and get happy, I'd jump up and get happy, too."

A longer scene where the camera ventures inside a small church places viewers in a service. The Emotions' rendition of "Peace Be Still" in front of a packed congregation speaks to the sentiments of the recent testimonies. With tight three-part harmonies, Sheila and Wanda Hutchinson and Theresa Davis raise the emotions of the crowd. They sing about how vigilance and faith can help people survive the most tempestuous of storms. Rocking in their pews, waving hands, fans, and scarfs, and calling out to the trio, the congregants are actively involved with the performance. Shots of the congregation echo those depicting the crowd in the coliseum. Both groups keep the beat with their hands and feet, hum or sing along with the music, and call out to one another and to the performers. *Wattstax* depicts the church and the coliseum as places that bring together family, friends, and strangers. The musical architecture of the songs heard within the physical architecture of the churches and the coliseum constructs complementary frameworks for community building.

Periodic cutaways to Richard Pryor in the same backstage space as his introductory address are woven between the music in the coliseum and the testimony of the residents. He riffs about law enforcement, gambling, religious rituals, nightclub culture, and alcoholism. Pryor's intonation has a bop-prose quality. He moves at a frantic pace from anecdotes to declarations to one-man dialogues. He quickly changes the pitch, volume, and intensity of his voice as he impersonates white police officers, his parents, a drunkard, and a younger version of himself. Humor offers both a shield and a sword, an armor that allows one to laugh to keep from crying. Pryor weaponizes humor to impugn police brutality, racial discrimination in the workplace, and class privilege. His impromptu monologues are a way to combat the kinds of traumatic experiences associated with racism and economic disparity that preceded the uprising and continue within Watts.

His jokes about the intricacy of Black Power handshakes and devout religious faith are also meant to open up a space for reflection. They show how social practices work to build solidarities, but also indicate that these same practices can separate and alienate individuals from one another. As the cultural historian Scott Saul argues, Pryor's role as "trickster-in-chief" at once "hedges the film's political militancy and deepens it: hedges it in that he holds up the movement itself for mockery; deepens it in that his comedy reveals a movement capable of self-satire, willing to laugh at the games that ideology plays."[40] Pryor's monologues, together with the interviews with Watts inhabitants and observational shots of Stax artists, also deepen an understanding of the entangled relationship between cultural forms and daily life. Just as music has a community-building function within the film, Stax and Wolper Productions wanted *Wattstax* to serve a community-building function for black audiences. They also saw this targeted release of the documentary as coinciding with the attempt to package and distribute the film to a larger crossover audience.

MULTIPLE PROJECTIONS

Members of Stax and Wolper Productions worked with several affiliates to develop a twofold plan of exhibition. First, they executed a focused release in black communities, crafting a socially conscious lens through which viewers would watch the documentary. Larry Shaw told the journal *Black Creation*, "We wanted to bring the same sensitivity to our post-production activity that we used in putting the film together."[41] Hiring the black marketing firms Communiplex (Memphis/Chicago), Communicon (Chicago), Cherrytree Productions (New York), WMS Associates (Washington, DC), and Z-J Associates (Philadelphia) was instrumental to the film's niche advertising and exhibition within cities. Second, the team cultivated an aura of artistic merit around the documentary designed to excite critics and attract white liberals, college students, and the counterculture. Columbia Pictures launched a campaign for a wide theatrical and international film festival release. Shaw outlined in a letter to Columbia's Robert Ferguson and circulated to Wolper, Bell, and Hamilton that the advertising and outreach should concentrate on both black and white moviegoers. The musicians themselves would assume the role of ambassadors for the film and would appear at select screenings.[42]

Articles about *Wattstax*'s production history, along with preview screenings tied with fundraising, community organizing, and nonprofit organizations, fueled anticipation for the film's world premiere at the Ahmanson Theatre in the Los Angeles Music Center on February 4, 1973.[43] Advertisements featured the documentary's artists organized into a pyramid of talent with banner title "Wattstax" in sharp relief. *Pittsburgh Courier* journalist Larry Grant Coleman applauded the documentary's ability to connect the music to daily life as something that a nationwide black audience could identify with:

The issues they discussed were the blues, the changes of love, politics, unemployment, economics, dope, prison and a thousand more. . . . We heard the plaintive and
celebrating music of the best of contemporary black artists—and the music again
brought to us, the message of the people. It forces us to understand clearly that the
music of black people is more than mere entertainment bound up into a few rhythmic arrangements. That is, our music is really a pattern (a mosaic) of our lives and it
weaves and bobs and changes as we do.[44]

Los Angeles Sentinel entertainment editor Gertrude Gipson noted the involvement of black personnel and commended the film for "immortalizing not only
those who came to perform, but, also, those who came to witness the event and
those who live in the communities of which Watts is symbolic."[45] Ruth E. Donel-
son, who had won the "Send a Mother to the Wattstax World Premiere Contest"
when it was previewed in Chicago for a gathering of black mothers, said, "To me,
Wattstax is a family movie that I recommend to all mothers. Though some people
may not like some of the language, it is a part of everyday life, and even a part of
the beauty of Black people living."[46]

Screening a commercial documentary about black culture was a first for the Los
Angeles Music Center. Designed by the city's civic elite, the institution aimed to
make downtown more attractive to white-collar commuters, business developers,
high-culture arts patrons, and middle-class Angelenos seeking a new leisure destination. The complex was one of Los Angeles's most prestigious performance halls for
European classical music, theatrical drama, and opera. While exhibition of the film
in this venue distanced it from the vernacular culture the film represented as well as
from the people of South Central, many in the black press viewed the documentary's
display as a point of pride. *Wattstax*'s subject and the guests' flamboyant fashions
transgressed the conservative norms of the then five-year-old venue. And the inclu-
siveness of the event differentiated the premiere from standard Hollywood openings.
The 2,100 invited guests included popular entertainers, community leaders, and government officials. Attendees included black city councilman (and soon to be mayor)
Tom Bradley, executive director of the United Negro College Fund Arthur Fletcher,
founder of the Watts Summer Festival Tommy Jacquette, personnel from Stax and
Wolper Productions, famous entertainers Jim Brown, Redd Foxx, Cicely Tyson, and
Sonny and Cher, as well as mayor of Compton Douglas Dollarhide. In a cover story
for *Soul: America's Most Soulful Newspaper*, Leah Davis described the lavishness and
showbiz quality of the event, chronicling how "searchlights scanned the heavens
pointing to the direction in which a galaxy of new film stars was to be launched."
Isaac Hayes "arrived in fur in a white Rolls Royce with motorcycle escort" and "the
Luxurious Ahmanson Theater was filled with beautiful people, beautifully garbed."[47]
Congresswoman Yvonne Brathwaite-Burke began the evening by presenting a
$3,000 scholarship to Crenshaw High School student filmmaker Stanley Houseton.

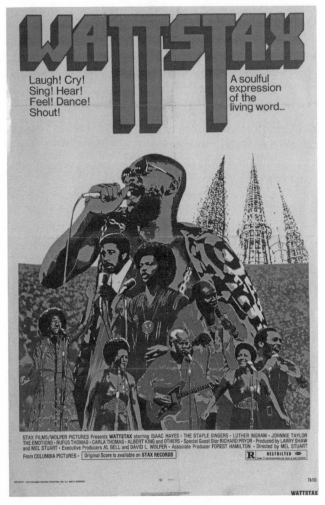

FIGURE 18: Advertisement for *Wattstax*, 1973, 35mm; directed by Mel Stuart; produced by Stax Records and Wolper Productions; distributed by Columbia Pictures. Author's collection.

Localized screenings followed that connected the film to other cultural efforts. The documentary was shown at the Watts Writers Workshop in South Central in mid-February to an enthusiastic group. A memo about the exhibition noted, "The packed house laughed, cried, sang and shouted their approval of *Wattstax* the Living Word."[48] For its New York release, *Wattstax* opened at a benefit for the Harlem-based Schomburg Collection for Research in Black Culture. As part of a benefit for Operation PUSH (People United to Save Humanity), Reverend Jesse Jackson hosted the Midwest

FIGURE 19: Cover, *Soul: America's Most Soulful Newspaper*, March 12, 1973. Author's collection.

premiere at the Oriental Theatre in Chicago. For additional screenings in Los Angeles, the *Los Angeles Sentinel* ran an advertisement with a quote from Bob Johnson's *JET* magazine article on the film: "Wattstax is rated 'R' by a Motion Picture jury, but in the black community, Wattstax is rated 'MF.'*"[49] The "MF" stood for "magnificent film." Another gauge of the documentary's positive reception was the encouraging letters sent to its producers. Crenshaw resident August Jones wrote in a letter to Wolper, "[It] is an enthralling, awe-inspiring experience to see and hear 100,000 folks, black folks, in a symphony of festive excitement and exhilarating pride."[50]

Some well-known reviewers claimed that *Wattstax* failed to relay the feeling of being at the show. Vincent Canby of the *New York Times* dismissed *Wattstax* as a "slick souvenir program rather than a motion-picture documentary on the order of *Woodstock*, a film that assumed the shape of the event recorded."[51] Dennis Hunt of the *Los Angeles Times* called *Wattstax* "fragmented" and "skittery" and accused it of not having "enough moments of interest and hilarity to offset the stretches of boredom that occur when an interviewee lapses into rhetoric or a singer lumbers through a number."[52] Yet most national news organs praised rather than faulted the film for the ways it differed from conventional rockumentaries. Joy Gould Boyum of the *Wall Street Journal* interpreted *Wattstax* as being about more than the music: "*Wattstax* emerges [as] a more revealing social document than was *Woodstock*.... *Wattstax* is, then, less about a concert than it is about black attitudes and values, with the performed music serving to establish motifs which are further orchestrated by images of the concert audience, by sequences shot in the streets, shops, and churches of Watts, and by a running commentary provided by black comedian Richard Pryor."[53] The *Hollywood Reporter* called Stax a "stand out" in "the age of mixed media" for uniquely combining diversification and community involvement.[54] In the same publication, Ron Pennington wrote two months later, "The concert was just a jumping off place and 'Wattstax' is much more than just another rock concert documentary."[55] The Los Angeles publication *Westways* championed the choice to depart from the formulaic recording of a performance.[56]

The press continued to track *Wattstax* as it gained momentum and played overseas. In May 1973, *Wattstax* artists along with Bell, Shaw, Wolper, Stuart, and Pryor accompanied the film to the Cannes Film Festival. Although *Wattstax* technically played out of competition, its opening-night screening helped boost its prestige and advanced its path toward international exhibition. Shortly after Cannes, it played at the International Jazz Festival in Montreux, Switzerland, before starting a European tour. The showing of the documentary at the United Nations for fifty dignitaries from the Organization of African Unity, hosted by the famed Senegalese actor Johnny Sekka, contributed to Stax's push to establish a greater presence in Nigeria, Algeria, Angola, Egypt, and Ethiopia.[57]

Targeting a cross-section of white viewers in the United States was motivated by both a desire for box office returns and the notion that fostering awareness of black culture would lead to increased interracial dialogue. "I hope [*Wattstax*] will be an easing of tensions," Stuart told the *Christian Science Monitor*. He went on to mention that he hoped the film could "break down unnecessary fear. Help white people get over hang-ups about black people."[58] The strategies used to package the documentary for a crossover audience, however, resulted in a conflict between the subject matter of *Wattstax* and the way audiences were at times encouraged to view the film. Many advertisements downplayed the documentary's engagement with black culture and the way it had been embraced by black moviegoers and critics, thus depoliticizing the film. An advertisement in the *New York Times* ran a quote from Bernard Drew of the *Gannett News Service* that praised the film in vague, generic terms, calling *Wattstax* "Funny, Funky, Tragic, and Triumphant." An advertisement in the *Wisconsin State Journal* posted around campus at the University of Wisconsin ran the banner line, "You Can't Judge a Movie by Its Color" and that "film critics everywhere," including the *Wall Street Journal, Saturday Review,* and *United Press International,* hailed *Wattstax* as a motion picture that will be enjoyed "by *all* movie-goers." Some advertisements went so far as to claim that *Wattstax* was intentionally created as an appealing object for white consumption. A *Los Angeles Times* advertisement for a multi-theater release in the city ran this line from a *Newsweek* article: "*Wattstax* is a welcome gift to white America!" The same quotation appeared in an announcement aimed at college students for UCLA's UA Cinema Center screening in Westwood.[59]

The fact that *Wattstax* was not a runaway box office success was due in large part to its inability to penetrate the mainstream market. Perhaps the advertisements downplaying the film's focus on black Los Angeles caused the counterculture to understand *Wattstax* as yet another concert film and thus ignore it. Or perhaps the subject matter of the documentary was seen as unappealing to white middle-class audiences who did not care to watch a film about black cultural expression and working-class Angelenos. Nonetheless, the film did generate a respectable amount of money and was well received both by critics and by black communities across the country.[60] Importantly, those who labored on the documentary anticipated that it would directly lead to additional professional opportunities.

Bell's vision of following *Wattstax* with a series of films and television programs encountered major problems. Stax chased existing genres and formats instead of playing to the strengths of the organization or tapping the depths of its creative resources; it overextended itself in motion pictures without a firm sense of direction. Stax first partnered with Paramount on the action drama *The Klansman* (1974). Despite the fact that the film was based on William Bradford Huie's Pulitzer Prize–winning novel and featured an all-star cast that included Lee Marvin, Richard Burton, and O. J. Simpson, the film was riddled with scandal during the production process and suffered numerous script alterations. In a *New York Amsterdam News* article, James P. Murray wrote:

> In spite of all the trappings of a Hollywood blockbuster, "The Klansman" is bound to leave many serious film-goers miserable. The selection of such a book on such a topic would lead observers to expect a social consciousness film within an entertaining framework. Yet "The Klansman" represents none of this. . . . With three rapes, a castration, bloody shootouts and scene after scene of unreasoned racial invective, it rapidly becomes a pointless endeavor.[61]

Stax's *Darktown Strutters* (1975) was also a disappointment. The film starred Trina Parks as leader of a female biker gang in Watts. Parks is searching for her mother, who has been abducted by a white fast-food magnate. As Parks discovers, the magnate is planning to kidnap and clone black leaders to keep the entire black population oppressed. Containing savvy criticisms of white racism through character parody and slapstick, *Darktown Strutters* was ultimately stranded between science fiction, action, and comedy. Genre conventions clashed and resulted in a pastiche of jokes, fight sequences, and brief moments of exposition. The black press wrote some complimentary articles about Parks, but the general consensus was that the film was scattered and full of tired conventions in a market oversaturated with blaxploitation.[62]

Stax expected that television would provide a fruitful route to film production in the mid-1970s, but the connection never materialized. Bell, Shaw, and Hamilton teamed up with Murray Schwartz of Merv Griffin Productions to tape a performance of Stax stars at Caesars Palace in Las Vegas in December 1972. The event was simultaneously broadcast on radio and taped for network television.[63] Despite articles in the trade press asserting that the relationship with Merv Griffin was "a solid marriage," the Vegas event did not lead to any further film or television programs.[64]

Stax's financial troubles were amplified by a disastrous distribution deal with CBS Records that essentially routed Stax albums to regional commercial outlets rather than smaller stores. This prevented the label's products from reaching their primary consumer base. Stax suffered from the industry-wide trend of conglomerates tightening their hold on the reach and creative freedom of independent companies. Charges brought against Bell for bank fraud, along with a controversy involving a payola scheme at the label, compounded Stax's troubles. By 1975 the company filed for bankruptcy.[65]

Wattstax thus represented both a high point and the beginning of the end for Stax. Some of the other contributors to the film, however, went on to work successfully in motion pictures. Pryor moved full tilt into acting, appearing in *Uptown Saturday Night* (1974) and *Silver Streak* (1976). Cinematographer John Alonzo continued to work on New Hollywood productions such as *Chinatown* (1974). Roderick Young and Larry Clark charted a different path in the 1970s. Drawing on piecemeal funds from short-term commercial film jobs, as well the technological and intellectual resources of UCLA, they created independent films about struggles against class and racial inequality in South Central Los Angeles.

For Wolper Productions, *Wattstax* constituted *the* pivot project. Wolper would later write, "[*Wattstax*] marked the beginning of my relationship with the black community in film," which in turn involved a new approach to developing projects.[66] But going forward, Wolper Productions would not use *Wattstax* as a blueprint. In addition to the logistical challenges of such an endeavor, the resistance to *Wattstax* by mainstream viewers discouraged any such effort. Rather, the studio aimed to engage crossover audiences in prestige television as America's two hundredth birthday approached. The studio's docudramas would come to constitute an inventive liberal cultural form that addressed the increasing presence of minorities in the civic life of the nation, even as the vanguard liberation movements faced political repression over the course of the 1970s. Wolper Productions' *Roots* (1977) would occupy the center of national debates concerning America's bicentennial.

PART THREE

Bicentennial Screens, 1974–1977

6

Roots/Routes of American Identity

Roots premiered on ABC over eight consecutive nights from January 23 to 30, 1977. It was the capstone media event of the American bicentennial and Wolper Productions' most ambitious public history project. The twelve-hour miniseries attracted 130 million American viewers, the largest audience up to that time for a single program in the medium's history, and played on home television screens in more than twenty countries.[1] David Wolper adapted *Roots* from author Alex Haley's family slave narrative.[2]

The story begins with the capture of Haley's ancestor Kunta Kinte (LeVar Burton) in the West African village of Juffure in the mid-eighteenth century. It ends with Kinte's descendant leading the family to a newly purchased plot of land in Henning, Tennessee, shortly after the Civil War. *Roots* drew its cultural authority and emotional power from its innovative "docudramatic" form, and was part of a larger wave of bicentennial-themed programming and merchandizing. The two hundredth anniversary of the nation's independence was not an isolated event, but a constellation of performances, parades, exhibitions, theatrically released films, and television shows around which the country rallied during a period of instability in the national economy and distrust in the power of the chief executive.

It would be corporations, entrepreneurs, filmmakers, and local politicians, rather than the federal government, that assumed responsibility for bicentennial planning. Under the leadership of Tom Bradley, Los Angeles's first African American mayor, the metropolis both reflected official bicentennial values and became a major center for the creation and display of bicentennial media. For the film and television industries, the bicentennial offered a seemingly limitless vault of experience from which patriotic moving images of a diverse American polity could be

153

constructed. Televised docudrama became the bicentennial's preeminent commercial product, and Wolper its most prolific creator and greatest supporter. Docudrama combined the truth claims of documentary with the world-creating capacity of period fiction.

Roots did internationalize American identity and confronted the controversial subject of slavery in a progressive way. At the same time, the miniseries was part of the bicentennial's broader effort to downplay the politically resistant dimensions of cultural expression and to absorb the minority liberation movements into a discourse of celebratory multiculturalism. This process of incorporation sought to package Americans' disparate historical experiences as simplistic narratives of progress. Strategic forgetting as well as remembering, silencing as well as giving voice, became integral to bicentennial culture.

The architects of the bicentennial portrayed history through a distorted lens, giving Americans a misleading perspective regarding the severe racial and class hierarchies that pervaded society in the early years of the Republic. This perception in turn obscured the persistence of injustices in the present.

BUILDING A NATION ON THE RUINS OF CONSENSUS

Arrangements for America's two hundredth birthday had been shifting for the ten years leading up to July 4, 1976. What had started as federally organized activities concentrated within one historic East Coast city had evolved into a dispersed and heavily privatized series of events. Official bicentennial preparations began in 1966 when president Lyndon B. Johnson created the American Revolution Bicentennial Commission (ARBC) by signing Public Law 89–491. Johnson envisioned the bicentennial as not only looking back but also marking the central tenets of his "Great Society" legislation. Using Cold War rhetoric, he claimed that since the writing of the Declaration of Independence, "the forces of tyranny and despotism have been in retreat throughout the world, and where men find freedom still denied, they struggle on, inspired by the ideals expressed in those words."[3] Boston, Philadelphia, and a Washington, DC-Virginia-Maryland consortium each vied to be the bicentennial epicenter. When Richard Nixon took office in 1969, he down-sized the plans for the celebration and rejected the notion that the bicentennial should be housed within any one city.

This change of direction stemmed from the new administration's decision to reduce federal funds for massive public projects. Memories of all-too-recent urban uprisings further deterred the government from locating the bicentennial in a single metropolitan area. Under Nixon's tenure, interest in a federal government–planned bicentennial continued to wane. An unjust and prolonged war in Southeast Asia heightened tensions between American citizens and their political leaders. Additionally, critics charged that the ARBC was being mismanaged and that its members were involved in conflicts of interest. Nixon eventually established the smaller American Revolution Bicentennial Administration (ARBA) in 1973. ARBA would help the federal government coordinate and promote state and municipal events and make modest financial contributions.[4] The mounting Watergate scandal coupled with an unprecedented energy crisis and rising stagflation further discouraged momentum for the bicentennial.[5] In the aftermath of Nixon's forced resignation, citizens felt profoundly suspicious of big government and were wary of its place in public life.

President Gerald Ford pursued the idea of a dispersed and locally planned bicentennial, while attempting to infuse it with a sense of patriotism and levity. Administrators anticipated a bicentennial based on the active participation of private industry as well as limited federal government support. *The Bicentennial of the United States of America: A Final Report to the People, Volume 1* announced that Watergate, Vietnam, and assassinations had put the American political system to the test, and that the Declaration of Independence, the Bill of Rights, and the Constitution aided the nation in persevering. The publication later stated, "All these events had not proven our system to be faulty. They had proven that our system works like no other. They had shown the strength of those three great documents. They had proved our Founding Fathers to be brilliant architects."[6] Three programming initiatives bolstered the bicentennial. "Heritage '76" commemorated famous leaders and events; "Festival USA" lauded "diversity" and the "traditions" of the American people; and "Horizons '76" outlined future challenges and goals that could be met by means of individual drive and technological innovation.

Many social chroniclers did not consider Los Angeles a very historical place, as the city was only incorporated as an American municipality in 1850. Robert Lawlor gave it scant mention in his cross-country tour guide, *The Bicentennial Book*.[7] Nonetheless, Los Angeles generated a vibrant array of bicentennial attractions. Mayor Bradley organized the Los Angeles City Bicentennial Committee to coordinate and promote events.[8] Bradley grew up on Central Avenue, a midcentury African American cultural hub that nurtured many of the city's great jazz musicians. At UCLA he studied education and ran track; later he rose through the ranks of the LAPD in unprecedented fashion. Bradley lost the 1969 mayoral race to incumbent Sam Yorty, who frequently resorted to racist attacks on his competitor during the election. But in 1973 Bradley defeated Yorty by mobilizing a biracial coalition of African Americans, white liberals, and Jews. His campaign pledge to "be a mayor of all of Los Angeles" involved devoting increased attention to the city's diverse populations and business interests.[9] In practice, this meant building on some of the unifying concerns advanced by the minority rights movements as well as the liberal coalition that elected him to office. Bradley courted existing federal funds for social service and job training programs. He also brought blacks, Latinos, Asian Americans, and women into public-sector jobs through commission appointments and affirmative action. Furthermore, he sought to combat systemic racism within the LAPD by instituting heightened oversight on proceedings, along with civilian review boards, which allowed greater citizen participation in the process of policing.[10]

Cultural historian Daniel Widener describes Bradley's creation of the Cultural Affairs Department (1978–81) as one of the major undertakings that engendered an era of "incorporative municipal multiculturalism." This initiative brought about greater "inclusion" of minority arts within Los Angeles; however, it also involved "containing" these cultural practices within established institutions, festival days, and sponsored events, thus severing them from their home communities and curbing their potential for social change.[11] Although the bicentennial is often overlooked in social histories of Los Angeles, it paved the way for what would later become arts administration policy. So, too, did the bicentennial begin the cultivation of Los Angeles as a "world city" that would come to fruition in the 1980s. Los Angeles's official bicentennial theme, "unity through diversity," spoke to Bradley's vision for the city as a multicultural metropolis. Urban historian Scott Kurashige argues that Bradley's policies "emblematized the new effort by civic leaders to celebrate ethnicity and reverse the postwar tendency toward assimilation."[12] Bradley also looked to mobilize the idea of diversity for the purpose of making Los Angeles a friendly home for transnational capital. In turn, the bicentennial involved two goals. First, to celebrate the city's residents by means of cultural display, promoting the message that all Angelenos possessed a heritage. Exhibitions and live performances encouraged people to see their lives and those of their ancestors as distinct, but sharing the experience of movement, struggle, and success. Bicentennial events highlighted rituals of cooking, craft, music, and religious practice as constituting ways that group identity is communicated and sustained over time. Loyola Marymount University hosted an exhibition about German immigration. At the First United Methodist Church, religious figures performed the Islamic call to prayer, Buddhist chants, Greek Orthodox hymns, and Jewish prayers. A gathering at the Ukrainian Cultural Center titled "Old Ways in the New World" featured musicians from Ghana, Italy, Japan, Lebanon, Mexico, and Panama. The International Heritage Festival at the Civic Center Mall contained one hundred kiosks filled with costumes, food, and entertainment provided by Scottish bagpipers, Swiss alpenhorn players, Chinese ribbon dancers, Samoan fire dancers, and Egyptian belly dancers. Visitors could sample Belgian waffles, French wine, German beer, and Nicaraguan tamales. The local bicentennial committee called it the "city's largest multiethnic celebration ever."[13] Bus tours advertised the city's Spanish heritage as a period of "romance" and "adventure."[14]

A second goal was to showcase Los Angeles's history and contemporary identity as deeply connected to trade, invention, and industry. Journalist Steve Harvey playfully noted that the city had given birth to the relatively contemporary "science" of cryonics, the freeway, mini-golf, and the drive-in church.[15] A large exhibition titled *Free Enterprise and How It Has Built the American Way* took place at the Convention Center. A show on commercial aviation was held at Northrop University in Inglewood. The Museum of Science and Industry brought attention to industries native to California and also hosted the multimedia extravaganza *USA '76—The First 200 Years*. Cal State Los Angeles had an open house where visitors toured the Van de Graaff atomic particle accelerator and learned about cutting-edge medical devices.[16] The Los Angeles County Museum of Art hosted a traveling exhibition by Charles and Ray Eames on "the world" of Benjamin Franklin and Thomas Jefferson. Visitors learned about how Franklin's and Jefferson's respective ideas concerning the rights of humanity, civil society, and the government mechanism of checks and balances directly influenced the early growth of American democracy. The show also looked at their breakthroughs in natural science, architecture, and communications.[17]

These bicentennial events complemented Bradley's broader efforts to expand the city's military defense, aerospace, finance, technology, and craft sectors. The creation of the Office of Economic Development in 1975 was crucial to this endeavor. Between 1972 and 1979, employment in seven high-tech clusters, including aircraft, communications equipment, electronic components, and guided missiles, grew by 50 percent. Industry became increasingly concentrated in the outlying white working- and middle-class counties of Orange, San Bernardino, Riverside, and Ventura. These shifts disadvantaged working-class minorities, many of whom lived in downtown, South Central, and East Los Angeles. As the urban historian Roger Keil details, recent immigrants and minorities were able to find jobs in the fast-growing apparel and service sectors geared toward retail, business, and social utilities. Nonetheless, these positions were often low wage, part time, and nonunion, which made for highly insecure employment.[18]

Under Bradley's leadership, downtown Los Angeles was becoming a site of corporate redevelopment with the creation of the Aon Center (1973), Broadway Plaza (1973), and Security Pacific Plaza (1974). Little was built for working class minority residents. The creation of the Century Plaza Towers (1975) strengthened the Westside as a financial and business destination. The luxurious New Otani Hotel (1977) went up in Little Tokyo, and the massive thirty-five-story Westin Bonaventure Hotel (1976) took up a city block on West Fourth Street and Figueroa. *Los Angeles Magazine* marveled at the futuristic elements of the latter, which included "an indoor park with trees, hanging gardens and even a meandering one-acre lake; twelve lighted, rocket-shaped glass elevators which lift guests through the atrium, then outdoors up the side of the cylindrical towers to guest rooms; on the very top, a revolving two-story restaurant and cocktail lounge; six shopping balconies to wrap around the atrium; and cocktail 'pods' that jut over the lake."[19]

Hollywood personnel made many contributions to the bicentennial. For example, studio luminaries took part in the city's "celebrity quilt." Each member of the thirty-square quilt got to add designs that were personally meaningful. Gene Kelly highlighted the Whiskey Rebellion and the Liberty Bell in honor of his home state of Pennsylvania. The quilt was made available for viewing in Los Angeles libraries, at Broadway Plaza, and at the United California Bank. Actors and actresses walked in the "All Nations, All Peoples Official Los Angeles County Bicentennial Parade." Four thousand participants walked for nearly eleven miles down Wilshire Boulevard, from Grand Avenue in downtown Los Angeles to the Santa Monica city limits. Mayor Bradley led the parade. Behind him were floats containing busts of the founding fathers, scenes from popular films, and boutique automobiles. Disneyland hosted its own "America on Parade" procession, in which classic animated characters in "Spirit of '76" costumes marched down Main Street USA together with pilgrims, colonists, pioneers, flappers, and suffragettes. Wolper along with other Hollywood producers planned the Los Angeles International Film Exposition. The festival's bicentennial retrospective contained Frank Capra's *Mr. Smith Goes to Washington* (1939) and John Ford's *The Grapes of Wrath* (1940), silent comedies by Buster Keaton, Charlie Chaplin, and Harry Langdon, and a series of Westerns. The opening night's theatrics involved a costumed figure dressed as George Washington riding a horse into Century City's Entertainment Center. Fireworks emblazoning the festival's logo lit up the sky.[20]

President Ford selected Wolper to join the twenty-five-person American Revolution Bicentennial Advisory Council. Wolper was then elected chair by its members. Writer Alex Haley, poet Maya Angelou, former first lady Claudia "Lady Bird" Johnson, and CBS executive Frank Stanton were also on the council.[21] The group's task was to advise the ARBA board on the approval of annual budgets, the coordination of programming, and the process of reviewing grants. Reflecting on the experience, Wolper wrote, "We saw, through the various bicentennial events, that, although we are a patchwork of different cultures, various colors, shapes and sizes, from different regions, when put together we certainly make a beautiful quilt."[22]

Businesses interpreted the bicentennial as an opportunity to combine consumerism with civics. They made it possible for people to literally buy into the bicentennial, expressing their fondness for history by purchasing a T-shirt with George Washington's face, learning about the American Revolution from a board game, or branding their home as patriotic thanks to a bald eagle–decorated doormat. Companies took pride in their contributions to commercializing the bicentennial. After all, ARBA emphasized that capitalism and principles of the free market were essentially American. As the historian Tammy S. Gordon argues, "The business world used the occasion of 1976 to re-naturalize the connection between American business and American heritage."[23] If companies paid ARBA a 20 percent royalty for a specific product, the organization would officially sanction the item.[24]

Pieces of Hollywood memorabilia were on board the American Freedom Train. Pepsi-Cola, General Motors, Prudential Life Insurance, and Kraft, as well as the commodities broker and part-time engineer Ross Rowland Jr., funded the locomotive. Departing from Wilmington, Delaware, and traveling for twenty-one months across forty-eight states, the train was an exhibition of Americana on wheels. When the train stopped in a city, it shuttled passengers along a moving walkway for the price of one or two dollars a ticket. Visitors saw Harold Lloyd's glasses, Judy Garland's dress from *The Wizard of Oz* (1939), a poster from *The Magnificent Yankee* (1950), and Cecil B. DeMille's script for *The Ten Commandments* (1956).[25]

The American Film Institute collaborated with ARBA to produce *America at the Movies* (1976), a tribute to Hollywood cinema since the mid-1910s. In the official pamphlet accompanying the film, Librarian of Congress Daniel Boorstin wrote, "Movies were an American invention" and "became the great democratic art, which naturally enough, was the characteristic American art." He went on to comment that *America at the Movies* "shows the boundless diversity of the American experience—a national family album."[26] The documentary's director (and former head of the US Information Agency film division) George Stevens Jr. used the organization's Doheny Mansion in Beverly Hills as the home base for production. Charlton Heston served as narrator. Discussing the mission of the compilation documentary, Stevens announced, "We have tried to create a mosaic of how we've seen America through the movies."[27] The film includes excerpts from eighty-three movies, divided into five thematic segments: "Land," "Cities," "Family," "War," and "Spirit."[28] At the beginning of the documentary, Heston delivers a rousing proclamation: "From the beginning, the story of America was an adventure. It began with a dream, a candle burning in the mind. Immigrants all, they crossed the seas hoping to find a new and better world." Set against images of families aboard large ships journeying toward the Statue of Liberty around the turn of the twentieth century, Heston establishes that the upward struggle of the immigrant is the overarching narrative of the American people. Wolper served as a consultant on the project and attended the film's premiere at the Kennedy Center in Washington, DC. Also in attendance were five hundred members of the American Film Institute, twenty-two senators, and 125 members of Congress. The film went on to play commercially as well as in schools, embassies, and consulates overseas.[29]

Televised docudrama engaged with the bicentennial in a unique fashion. This genre of prestige educational entertainment for the small screen embraced dramatic reenactments of past events while still claiming fidelity to truth. Docudramas constituted a more immersive and emotional form of pedagogy than the on-location reporting, interviews, and variety shows typical of NBC's *The Glorious Fourth* (1976), CBS's *In Celebration of US* (1976), and ABC's *The Great American Birthday Party* (1976).[30]

WOLPER'S DOCUDRAMATIC TURN

By the early 1970s Wolper Productions had itself become a respected and still-vibrant institution. The honors it received spoke to the history-focused charge of the studio's output as well as its affirmative and optimistic view of the nation's past. Wolper Productions had also been recalibrating its liberal posture toward post–civil rights America by means of taking an inclusive perspective on its subjects and hiring practices. Commemorating Wolper's twenty-fifth anniversary in the media profession (including distribution and production), the American Film Institute arranged a one-week retrospective in Los Angeles. Additionally, the American Embassy in London organized a three-day tribute to the studio. The Cinémathèque française in Paris even planned a thirty-day screening of Wolper documentaries; its eminent director, Henri Langlois, wrote, "As a custodian of films, I appreciate perhaps more than anyone the historical significance of documentary films, and David Wolper's outstanding contribution to recording current history on film."[31] *Los Angeles Times* journalist Marshall Berges noted in his introduction to an interview with the producer, "David Wolper is a history buff who makes history pay off. . . . He is an undisputed leader of documentary films, serving up a classroom of the air with television specials."[32] Mayor Bradley proclaimed March 17, 1976, "David Wolper Day," describing Wolper as "the most honored producer of film documentaries in the world." Around that time, the Hollywood Chamber of Commerce dedicated a star to Wolper on the Hollywood Walk of Fame at Sunset and Vine.[33]

The bicentennial seemed to trigger a commemorative impulse that rippled through the film and television industries. In 1976 CBS board chair William Paley donated $2 million to create the Museum of Broadcasting in New York, an initiative that coincided with the network's own fiftieth-anniversary celebration. Paley announced that the mission of the museum was to "collect, preserve and present the programs and historical materials of radio and television. Its purpose will be to give scholars and students an insight into broadcasting."[34] Two years later, the Library of Congress widened its archival purview to systematically include television and radio in its collection. Under the guidance of media historian Erik Barnouw, the Motion Picture, Broadcasting and Recorded Sound Division would be responsible for the "custody, processing, preservation and servicing of the library's collection of more than 252,000 motion picture reels and 711,000 sound recordings, as well as developing a new American Television and Radio Archive."[35]

During the early to mid-1970s Wolper Productions continued to move in innovative directions, even as some of the company's chief 1960s-era personnel left the organization. Of the three core members of the original Wolper brain trust, only Mel Stuart remained. Jack Haley Jr. left in 1970 and went on to become creative affairs director at MGM. In 1974 he became president of Twentieth Century–Fox Television, where he produced the compilation film *That's Entertainment* (1974).

Landsburg left in 1970 to form Alan Landsburg Productions, where he made the-atrically released fiction and documentaries.

Television docudramas were by far Wolper Productions' most highly regarded and publicly discussed genre. These shows helped to fashion a renovated liberal imaginary as well as to reaffirm the studio's brand identity as a producer of public history. The docudrama was also an alluring commercial venture. As scholars Thomas W. Hoffer and Richard Alan Nelson argue, docudrama denotes a particular kind of documentary-drama hybrid involving "accurate recreations of events in the lives of actual persons." In their definition, "accurate" and "actual" involve claims to factual evidence on which productions are based. "Re-creations" point to the full array of written dialogue, performances, sets, and special effects that are used to craft the story-world.[36] Hoffer and Nelson's framework positions doc-udrama within a tradition of film practice going back to the medium's origins. They also call special attention to the cycle of American television docudramas in the late 1960s and 1970s.[37] The early docudramas on public television such as *NET Playhouse* (1966–72) and network series such as *Saga of Western Man* (1963–69) gave way to *Continental Congress, 1976* (1971).

Hoffer and Nelson as well as other scholars of nonfiction provide a useful vocabulary for analyzing the epistemological claims and formal complexity of docudramas, but have not fully accounted for the cultural pressures and signifi-cant players that contributed to the rise of docudrama in the United States during this period. First, the horizon of the bicentennial incentivized filmmakers to devise a way to portray events and people that existed before the advent of moving-image technologies. Producers saw docudrama as capable of "creating history" along with maintaining a strong investment in "truth" and "authenticity." If fashioned in collaboration with skilled subject experts, docudrama could perform the intellec-tual labor of documentary, while venturing into the reaches of the past where con-ventional forms of documentary could not travel. Second, docudrama was an enticing way to make educational programming popular and vice versa. Its crea-tors sought to synthesize the grandeur of Hollywood historical epics with mobile, character-focused documentary. Separately, these different spheres of media pro-duction were not particularly fresh. On the one hand, a number of 1960s-era flops such as George Stevens's *The Greatest Story Ever Told* (1965) had proven that large-budget period fiction was a precarious financial investment. On the other hand, observational documentaries about well-known and everyday citizens had appeared on the small screen of television since the early 1960s. Even though they offered their producers, sponsors, and exhibitors prestige, they attracted an extremely limited viewership.

Docudramas were elaborate in production values and scope, but still possessed an intimate focus on individuals and small groups. They flaunted their relationship to "truth" within the program itself or by means of press releases, advertisements, or reviews; the sensory-rich encounter with a historical moment and locale was considered paramount. Docudramas were time machines, transporting viewers to biblical Jerusalem, the New England colonies, the antebellum South, turn-of-the-twentieth-century New York, or post–World War II suburbia. Audiences could *feel* what it was like to be a part of seismic events, to observe both major politicians and ordinary bystanders. At a 1979 symposium on docudrama (chaired by Wolper) in Ojai, California, writer Frank Swertlow praised the format for offering a holistic, historical perspective on society—one that narrowly focused, temporally constricted news and print journalism could not.[38] In practice, docudramas constituted totalizing period- and place-specific environments that looked and sounded authentic. Within these worlds individuals overcame tremendous obstacles in uplifting fashion. Spectators could relish the intimate experience of getting to know and then identifying with these characters as well as luxuriating in the period environments. Docudrama thus proved an ideal cultural form for the bicentennial. As critic David Lowenthal noted, "the past" as seen through the prism of the bicentennial was not "museumized" but actively relived.[39]

Wolper Productions had experimented with docudrama in *They've Killed President Lincoln!* (1971) and the seven-episode *Appointment with Destiny* (1971–73) that followed. Beyond these early endeavors, the studio partnered with *American Heritage* magazine for a series of docudramas for ABC. One of the show's sponsors, Texaco, communicated that the objective of the series was "to humanize our country's heroes and in so doing give Americans fresh insight and renewed pride in the story of America."[40] The first program, *The World Turned Upside Down* (1973), shines a light on the leadership of George Washington during the American Revolution. The climax is Charles Cornwallis's defeat at Yorktown. The second program, *Lincoln: Trial by Fire* (1974), portrays the conflict between the confident, pro-emancipation Lincoln and the inept, proslavery Union general George McClellan. The third program, *The Yanks Are Coming* (1974), is based on an actual archive of letters from a World War I veteran; the show recounts the misadventures of a wealthy, young, idealistic Bostonian who goes off to fight in Europe, has his dreams dashed, and is eventually killed in combat. The last installment, *The Honorable Sam Houston* (1975), traces the fruitless fight to prevent the state of Texas from seceding from the Union and Houston's own withdrawal from political office. In an interview about the series, writer-producer Robert Guenette proudly asserted that these shows "reconfirmed one's feelings that the roots of the country are very strong. You don't kill a tree by chopping off its branches. One thing the bicentennial will do is show that our roots are very strong, and we will survive. I challenge the most entrenched cynic to sit there and deny a flutter of patriotism watching these shows."[41] The mainstream press responded favorably to the period likeness of the settings as well as to the way the actors skillfully embodied their characters. Critics also praised the expansive advisory council for the series, which included James MacGregor Burns, Daniel Boorstin, Bruce Catton, Barbara Tuchman, and Arthur Schlesinger Jr.[42]

Wolper's adaptation of Carl Sandburg's multivolume biography of Abraham Lincoln embraced an episodic structure that revolved around one man. The *Washington Post* deemed Wolper's six-part NBC miniseries *Sandburg's Lincoln* (1974–76) "the best of the networks' Bicentennial offerings."[43] The series dramatized periods in Lincoln's life without the conventional aid of voice-over, stock footage, or interviews. Much of Sandburg's lyrical description of Lincoln's surroundings and the people with whom he interacted was excised from the series. What made Sandburg's multivolume project seem full of facts to critic Van Wyck Brooks in his 1926 review of the biography, or a kind of literary encyclopedia of Lincoln experiences to the contemporary historian James Hurt, was absent in the television programs.[44] Nonetheless, humanizing Lincoln was crucial to the project. The tightly framed, hour-long episodes looked at different moments in his legal and political career. They showed Lincoln as a calm, compassionate, and candid lawyer, as well as in the roles of president, father, and husband. This characterization contributed to a warm, but still commanding, image of American politics so lacking in the early 1970s.[45] The country was reeling from the disgraceful actions of the thirty-seventh president. Actor Hal Holbrook believed that a program about Lincoln might boost national morale. Holbrook wanted to make viewers "feel they're actually seeing Abraham Lincoln." He went on to say, "Lincoln was an honest man; even when he was a shrewd politician, he still had integrity. I have never seen that in Nixon."[46] Journalists echoed this juxtaposition, comparing Honest Abe to Tricky Dick.[47]

The series eschewed some iconic moments in Lincoln's life, for instance his debates with Stephen Douglas, the Gettysburg Address, and his assassination. Instead, it delivered poignant vignettes that cast Lincoln in a personable although no less virtuous light. In the first installment, *Mrs. Lincoln's Husband* (1974), a wartime Lincoln quells Union fears concerning his wife's alleged Southern loyalties and copes with the sickness and death of their young son, Willie. In *Sad Figure Laughing* (1975), Lincoln clashes with secretary of the treasury Salmon Chase over the 1864 presidential nomination, but as a believer in the free democratic process he does not discourage his opponent's efforts. The episode ends with Lincoln reading the second inaugural address. *Prairie Lawyer* (1975) is a portrait of the statesman as a young attorney in 1838. Lincoln appears as a lovesick romantic, losing Mary Owens and eventually finding Mary Todd. Additionally, he is a shrewd Illinois litigator who successfully argues for an acquittal on behalf of the accused murderer Henry Truett. The fourth program, *Unwilling Warrior* (1975), explores Lincoln's maturation as a decisive leader, his intolerance for corruption in politics, and his demand for clarity of government actions during the Civil War. He tells secretary of war Simon Cameron, "When we try to hide government business from the people, we are betraying them." The drama of political appointments makes up the fifth episode, *Crossing Fox River* (1976). This episode takes place between the 1860 election and the inauguration. Lincoln refuses to bow to pressures by his own advisors to pay back those who supported him or to appease opponents. He demonstrates his abilities as a negotiator and statesman to bring individuals of different ideologies together to serve in the same cabinet. The final installment, *Last Days* (1976), aired on the anniversary of Lincoln's assassination. The episode explores the post-Appomattox denouement of the Civil War and the challenge of how to reintegrate the South into the Union. Lincoln desires a "harmonious restoration of the Union." He supports a balanced and moderate strategy before going with his wife on a carriage ride and then on to Ford's Theatre, where he will tragically meet John Wilkes Booth's bullet. The first episode of *Sandburg's Lincoln* was previewed at Ford's Theatre, followed by a reception at the National Portrait Gallery for Washington, DC, dignitaries and the entertainment community. Critics responded warmly to Holbrook's performance and the show's redemptive image of American politics. The miniseries received three Emmy nominations, for Supporting Actress, Lead Actor, and Film Sound.[48]

In the same period, Wolper Productions created docudramas on minority subjects.[49] *I Will Fight No More Forever* (1975) depicts the resistance and defeat of Chief Joseph (Ned Romero) and his Nez Perce tribe by the US Army. The film narrates the Army's egregious effort to remove the Nez Perce tribe from their home in Wallowa Valley, Oregon, and relocate them to an Idaho reservation. It begins in 1877 with General Oliver Howard (James Whitmore) announcing Ulysses S. Grant's mandate that Chief Joseph and his tribe must relocate or they will be forced to do so.[50] After being provoked into a war when the US Army kills one of their tribespeople, the Nez Perce begin a three-month, 1,600-mile attempt to escape the American government's jurisdiction into Canada. The Indians clash with the soldiers in a series of shrewdly fought battles across Oregon, Idaho, Wyoming, and Montana. Surrounded, and with the tribe decimated, Chief Joseph surrenders less than forty miles from the Canadian border. It is here, in the concluding moments of the program, that he recites the famous lines, "Hear me, my chiefs, I am tired. My heart is sick and sad. From where the sun now stands, I will fight no more forever."

It is difficult to imagine the broadcast of *I Will Fight No More Forever* without the Red Power movement's struggle to bring the long history of American Indian displacement and dispossession to public consciousness. The Indian occupations of Alcatraz Island (1969–71) and the town of Wounded Knee (1973), along with Sacheen Littlefeather's Oscar refusal on behalf of Marlon Brando (1973) made a mainstream film like *I Will Fight No More Forever* possible. And yet, Wolper Productions' film is also self-conscious about the national wrong in a way that blunts its progressive charge. The docudrama signals the government's treatment of the Nez Perce as an injustice that will one day be rectified. This is a move that in part redeems some of the US government figures featured in the film and posits a belief that the future will entail enlightened change. The viewer's sympathies are supposed to lie with the Nez Perce, but also with Howard and his lieutenant Wood (Sam Elliott), who appear deeply conflicted and even regretful about what they have been ordered to do. These soldiers ruminate on the Nez Perce's removal, and clearly understand it to be unjust and unethical. Talking to Wood in the Army camp toward the conclusion of the pursuit, Howard mentions that "We [the US government] make massive mistakes, captain, and we pray we survive them." He sees the kindhearted Wood as having a future leadership role in government and tells the young lieutenant to "stick with it, this country really needs men like you."

I Will Fight No More Forever was nominated for two Emmys (for writing and editing) and was rebroadcast closer to the bicentennial.[51] Even though the docudrama's producer, Stan Margulies, was white, the fact that Romero was half Blackfoot Indian aided in separating the film from a long tradition of Hollywood Westerns in which the lead American Indian role was played by a white actor in red face. *Baltimore Sun* journalist Terrence O'Flaherty discussed the letters he received from viewers deeply affected by the plight of the Nez Perce. O'Flaherty quoted Chief Joseph's 1879 speech in Washington, DC, on the equality of all people before the law and the necessity for all people to be free. He concluded his review with the line, "If *I Will Fight No More Forever* caused some spectators to think about this—even for a moment—television's seldom-used power for human kindness will have been abundantly demonstrated."[52] Offscreen, the cast members participated in local events in Los Angeles. Romero was grand marshal of the 1976 Watts-Willowbrook Christmas Parade and Frank Salsedo was master of ceremonies at the American Indian Cultural Festival.[53] Wolper Productions continued to address minority social history during the creation of *Roots*, the studio's most ambitious project to date.

ROOTS AS MEDIA EVENT

Adapting Alex Haley's *Roots* ran parallel to Wolper Productions' other bicentennial projects. Cinema scholars such as Linda Williams have placed *Roots* within a long tradition of American melodrama starting with Harriet Beecher Stowe's 1852 abolitionist novel *Uncle Tom's Cabin*.[54] The television miniseries, however, had its more immediate origins in the changing media industries and political culture of the early to mid-1970s. Wolper first heard about *Roots* through Haley's friend, the actress Ruby Dee, whom he had met at the 1969 Moscow International Film Festival. The two discussed the myriad problems plaguing Wolper's controversial and never-to-be-produced Nat Turner film. Dee's husband, the actor and civil rights activist Ossie Davis, was an outspoken opponent of the Turner project. Over the course of their conversation, Dee pitched literary texts by black authors that she thought would make promising films, including Zora Neale Hurston's *Their Eyes*

FIGURE 20: Alex Haley and David Wolper, ca. 1976, in *The Man with the Dream: A Pictorial Tribute to the Life and 50-Year Career of David L. Wolper*, ed. Auriel Sanderson (Hong Kong: Warner Bros. Worldwide Publishing, 1999), 106.

Were Watching God (1937), Margaret Walker's *Jubilee* (1966), and Haley's unfinished *Roots*. Dee and Davis then discussed Haley's narrative at greater length with Wolper over dinner at his Beverly Hills home the next year. Wolper was moved by the historical sweep of Haley's genealogical research and intrigued by its docudramatic potential as a grand story about family. Wolper discovered that Columbia Pictures had already optioned the book and was planning to do a four-hour theatrically released feature. Upon learning that the deal had fallen through, he aggressively courted the book. Wolper discussed its possibilities with Haley's agent, Lou Blau; the president of ABC's Movies for Television Division, Barry Diller; and members of his own studio. An August meeting, during which Haley's retelling of the story of *Roots* allegedly left Wolper's staff and ABC executives in tears, solidified the studio's interest in bringing the book to the screen.[55]

Wolper Productions spearheaded the *Roots* adaptation, but it was the conjuncture of diverse interests that made it feasible. Haley had little experience with film and television beyond coauthoring *Super Fly T.N.T.* (1973), the minor sequel to Gordon Parks Jr.'s *Super Fly* (1972). He nonetheless wanted to reach the largest possible audience and was thus excited about the idea of a network television docudrama. Haley himself was a best-selling author famous for starting *Playboy*'s interview column in 1962 and cowriting the critically acclaimed *The Autobiography of Malcolm X* (1965). Since the mid-1960s, he had been researching his family's genealogy. This journey took him across the United States as well as to England and Africa. Haley published condensed excerpts from *Roots* in the May and June 1974 issues of *Reader's Digest*, which fueled anticipation for the release of the longer narrative scheduled for early fall 1976. Haley emphasized the connection between *Roots* and the bicentennial, noting on the dedication page that *Roots* was a "birthday offering to my country."[56]

The fact that ABC was moving in the direction of long-form narrative created an opening for *Roots*. After the high ratings and positive reviews of Leon Uris's Holocaust-themed courtroom drama *QB VII* (1974), the network wanted to expand into multipart dramas. ABC acquired the rights to Irwin Shaw's novel *Rich Man, Poor Man* (1970) about the disparate life trajectories of the German American Jordache brothers. The network also brokered a deal for John Dos Passos's *USA* trilogy, which follows twelve characters struggling against the forces of modernity in the early twentieth century.[57] ABC vice president Lou Rudolph liked the idea of programming topical subjects and drove the network's investment in this direction.[58]

Wolper and his circle were motivated by the prospects of commercial success as well as by the socially progressive dimensions of *Roots*. They were committed to having African Americans actively involved with creating the miniseries. Haley continued to work on the manuscript over the course of 1974 and 1975 from Jamaica and acted in an advisory capacity throughout the process of adaptation. Joseph Wilcots, the first African American to be admitted to the International Cinematographers Guild in 1967, served as director of photography. He had worked on *The Long Goodbye* (1973) as well as *Lady Sings the Blues* (1972) and *The Mack* (1973). Wolper tried to sign Gordon Parks (*The Learning Tree* [1969]) and Michael Schultz (*Together for Days* [1973], *Cooley High* [1975]) to direct installments of the series, but both directors were committed to other films. Willie Burton recorded sound for *Roots* at the same time that he worked on *Car Wash* (1976) and *The Bingo Long Traveling All-Stars and Motor Kings* (1976). Burton was the first African American inducted into the International Sound Technicians union. Wolper also succeeded in signing Gilbert Moses to direct three episodes; Moses had cofounded the Free Southern Theater and directed the black gangster film *Willie Dynamite* (1974).

Still, much of the editorial power concerning character, script, and story was held by white personnel. It was William Blinn who adapted Haley's writing into a continuity script that was then used to write individual episodes. Blinn had received an Emmy for writing ABC's integrationist sports drama *Brian's Song* (1971). Stan Margulies, who had produced *I Will Fight No More Forever*, served as head producer. Veteran television director David Greene set the visual tone and pace of the miniseries by directing the first episode. As one of three directors for *Rich Man, Poor Man*, Greene was familiar with the high production values of long-form commercial television. The prolific record producer, musician, and soundtrack specialist Quincy Jones was hired for the score, but ended up being replaced by Gerald Fried due to Jones's frustration with the rigid temporal and financial constraints of the miniseries format. Casting involved black and white entertainment personalities and artists well known to crossover audiences. These included Richard Roundtree, O. J. Simpson, Maya Angelou, Leslie Uggams, Ed Asner, Chuck Connors, and Carolyn Jones.

Roots took on a subject seldom seen on television. The Afrocentric narrative of American history did not shy away from the human suffering engendered by the institution of slavery. The miniseries begins with the birth of Kunta Kinte in the West African village of Juffure in 1750, his capture in 1767 by white slavers, and his transport on the *Lord Ligonier* to America. It follows the selling of Kinte at a slave auction in Annapolis, Maryland, to John Reynolds (Lorne Greene), who owns a nearby Virginia plantation. Kinte's three failed escapes result in the amputation of half of his right foot. Kinte eventually marries Bell (Madge Sinclair), a house slave who helps him recover, and the two have a daughter named Kizzy (Uggams). The narrative next tracks the separation of the family. After assisting a young slave named Noah (Lawrence Hilton-Jacobs) in an escape attempt, Kizzy is sold to a North Carolina plantation as punishment. She is raped upon arrival by her new master, Tom Moore (Connors), and gives birth to "Chicken" George (Ben Vereen). Chicken George becomes a prominent cockfighter, but is sold to an Englishman, Eric Russell (Ian McShane), to repay his master's debt. Chicken George eventually returns to the plantation, but has to relocate because of a law preventing free black men from staying in the state for longer than sixty days. His son Tom (Georg Standford Brown) participates in the Civil War, attending to the Confederate cavalry horses, and is severely abused. Contemporaneously, his family befriends and provides for a poor white couple from South Carolina, George and Martha Johnson (Brad Davis and Lane Binkley), who are looking for food and shelter. In the early years of Reconstruction Tom and his family are continuously harassed by members of the Ku Klux Klan. Tom contemplates whether they should move or become sharecroppers. The miniseries' conclusion involves a valiant Chicken George returning to defend his family and lead them on a journey to a newly purchased plot of land in Henning, Tennessee.

To be sure, *Roots*'s popularity stemmed from the ways its story could be interpreted as compelling as well as relatable to a wide range of viewers. Still, its publicity was critical to its success. Over the course of its production, the miniseries stayed in the public spotlight. Haley's book release, his speech-giving and interviews, along with Wolper's and ABC's press reports, production photographs, and print advertisements, sustained considerable buzz.[59] *Roots* was poised to be not just a program enjoyed in the privacy of one's home, but the subject of discussion in high school classrooms, college campuses, around water coolers in offices, and in neighborhood bars. *Newsweek* referenced the recent blockbuster phenomenon of theatrically released fiction in its description of *Roots*'s "*Jaws*-size publicity."[60] Some of the same techniques used to mastermind a new breed of Hollywood mega-hits on the big screen were also applied to *Roots*. The miniseries used a popular literary property as a springboard, featured a cast of well-known and emerging talent, and was subject to an aggressive, multimedia advertising campaign. Showing the docudrama over consecutive nights made it an extended event instead of a series of isolated broadcasts. What was originally a conservative network decision to mitigate the losses of a possible ratings disaster actually concentrated mass interest. The nightly rather than the weekly broadcast cycle heightened the momentum of the continuous narrative, but still allowed time for conversation to build around each episode. *Variety* advertised *Roots* as a "historic television event."[61]

The miniseries received a 44.9 rating and 66 percent audience share, thus captivating the most viewers to date for a single program in television history. *Roots* was showered with awards, including a record-setting nine Emmys, a City of Los Angeles Proclamation of Honor, and the NAACP Image Award. Colleges assigned credit for watching the miniseries, and study guides were made available for primary and secondary schools.[62] Sales of Haley's book skyrocketed in the aftermath of the broadcast. Vernon Jarrett of the *Chicago Tribune* wrote that the "shocking truths" of the African American slave experience dramatized for viewers would "replace the old, beguiling, myth-filled half-truths about slavery that have been perpetuated in scholarly works and textbooks as well as in novels and movies such as *Gone with the Wind*." The cover of the trade publication *Broadcasting* proclaimed *Roots* "the biggest event in television history." The *Washington Post*'s Sander Vanocur observed, "We have read about slavery. But we have never seen it." Donald K. Richardson of the *New Journal and Guide* noted, "[*Roots*] presented a realistic portrayal of African culture and served in its way, to dispel the notion that black Americans are void of heritage, language, and religion."[63]

Roots provided a tent pole around which the country could come together and affirm a national identity built, on the micro level, around the family, and on the macro level, around a narrative of national progress. In designating the week of January 23, 1977, "Roots Week," Mayor Bradley proclaimed, "In telling the story of [Haley's] family's heritage, he has told the story of all Americans."[64] The miniseries

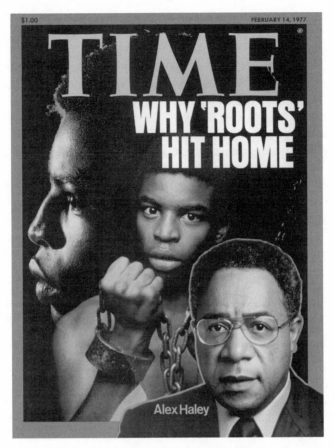

FIGURE 21: Cover, *Time*, February 14, 1977. © 1977 Time Inc., all rights reserved, reproduction in any manner in any language in whole or in part without written permission is prohibited. TIME and the TIME logo are registered trademarks of Time Inc. used under license.

was designed to appeal to Americans across racial lines. The full title of Haley's book was *Roots: The Saga of an American Family*. Tellingly, to emphasize the notion that the familial struggle resulted in achievement, the title of the miniseries was changed to *Roots: The Triumph of an American Family*. Roots "is primarily a story that deals with a family," opined ABC vice president Brandon Stoddard, "a very human story."[65] *Newsweek* asserted that "in many homes the program was an intimate family ritual, attended by serious discussion or emotional outpourings."[66] Haley said that "when you start talking about family, about lineage and ancestry, you are talking about every person on earth. We all have it; it's a great equalizer."[67] In a cover story, *Time* cited the appeal to the concept of family as a major reason

"Why Roots Hit Home" with so many Americans.[68] Viewers witness the family's oppression as field hands and day laborers, their friendships and love interests, their unwavering support of one another, and their shared investment in drawing on their past for strength. In addition, the presence of sympathetic white characters and familiar crossover stars strategically obviated moral color casting and broadened the series' appeal.

On a macro level, *Roots* portrayed American history as a narrative of progress that begins with the brutality of slavery, but ultimately leads to freedom, integration, and class mobility. The opening episodes feature Kinte spending his adolescent years in chains on a plantation. The later episodes, however, show the family not only surviving, but enjoying a series of accomplishments. Chicken George earns his freedom, and his son becomes a skilled blacksmith. The last episode depicts Kinte's descendants embarking on a wagon train migration westward from North Carolina to Tennessee. With Fried's buoyant score accompanying their journey into a lush green field, they stop atop a bluff and look out onto the land Chicken George has purchased. George gives a speech that recounts his family's genealogy and models the oral process of passing down the heritage from generation to generation. The final embrace is one of core kin, but also a larger, integrated collectivity. White compatriots and coworkers George and Martha Johnson eagerly make the journey with Chicken George's family, driven by feelings of solidarity and friendship as well as a desire for economic opportunity. George's speech, in some ways answering Dr. Martin Luther King Jr.'s "I Have a Dream" speech, serves as an optimistic end to the story. Concluding the miniseries on such a note further amplifies the sense of triumph. This ending resonated with the collective desire at the end of the bicentennial—less than two weeks after president Jimmy Carter's inauguration—to conceive of racial strife as a problem that had been solved.

Although *Roots*'s narrative and docudramatic form made it appeal to crossover audiences, these factors were also cause for intense criticism. Some intellectuals, community groups, and concerned citizens rebuked the docudrama's liberal idealism, Cold War nationalism, narrow focus, and sacrificing of strict fidelity to archival sources for the sake of entertaining storytelling. These reviews rhymed with criticism that Wolper's past programs had recently received. In writing about his *American Heritage* specials, the prominent television critic Horace Newcomb described them as more pageantry than inquiry, and attacked the programs' lack of depth.[69] On the subject of *Sandburg's Lincoln*, historian Martin Duberman wrote that the choice to show Lincoln as a unifier and compromiser diverted attention from understanding his position on slavery and the racial politics of the Civil War. Duberman also catalogued some of the episodes' inaccuracies (for example the extremely exaggerated encounter between Lincoln and his stepmother in *Crossing Fox River* that mythologizes rather than "humanizes" his image).[70] Similarly, *New York Times* critic John O'Connor and *New Yorker* critic Michael J. Arlen took aim

FIGURE 22: Still from *Roots*, 1977, 16mm; based on the book by Alex
Haley; directed by Martin J. Chomsky, John Erman, David Greene,
and Gilbert Moses; produced by Wolper Productions; broadcast on
ABC. DVD, Warner Home Video, Burbank, California, 2007.

at *I Will Fight No More Forever*'s revisionist treatment of General Oliver Howard.
The program misrepresented him as a conflicted liberal who was forced to act
against his conscience, rather than as the provocateur he actually was, a figure who
encouraged the fighting with the Nez Perce tribe.[71]

Criticisms of *Roots* coalesced around three issues. First, the miniseries foregrounded characters such as Captain Davies and George and Martha Johnson to
offset the dichotomy of white cruelty and black victimhood. This plot device was
an attempt to downplay the horror of slavery and to make the miniseries more
appealing to white viewers. Second, *Roots*'s clear moral delineation of people and
places made for a streamlined narrative but distorted the social geography and the
complexity of both African and American societies. The on-location shooting as
well as attention to period dress and decor resulted in an environment that
appeared manicured and polished. John E. Cooney from the *Wall Street Journal*
wrote that the miniseries' depiction of Kinte's African village was "so saccharine it
looked like a travelogue for Club Med. The sun always shone. Everyone seemed as
serene as transcendental meditation teachers. For the most part, unpleasantness
and hardship belonged to other tribes, other places."[72] Third, the program's steady
focus on family diverted attention from social movements, communal action,
and federal intervention. These forces were crucial to small- and large-scale acts
of resistance to slavery and the struggle for emancipation. Local and national

government are referenced as abstract entities. The Nat Turner rebellion and the Civil War remain in the background and surface only obliquely, serving as signposts rather than narrative agents driving the plot.

Furthermore, the *Roots* phenomenon revised the American myth of individual agency into a romanticized conception of the family as a social unit that is always supportive, always joining together against an outside threat. Infusing a multigenerational slave narrative of survival with the "bootstrap" mythology of struggling upward through hard work, frugality, and faith afforded the opportunity for the mass television audience of white spectators to project their own family sagas of immigration onto the screen vision of Haley's ancestors.[73] As the social historian Matthew Jacobson argues, *Roots* did not galvanize a nationwide interest in African American or minority history so much as family history as such, encouraging all Americans to discover their own "roots." He thus connects *Roots* to the ethnic white revival during the 1970s. White Americans of Irish, German, and Italian descent proudly embraced the life stories of their ancestors as narratives of perseverance against oppression. They were at once drawing on the vocabulary, structures of affiliation, and rhetorical claims of the minority liberation movements as well as rebelling against the legal and social advances made by these groups.[74] Indeed, a cottage industry of guidebooks and instructional research texts were published in the mid-1970s, encouraging people to discover their own family histories. John J. Stewart commented in the 1977 book *Finding Your Roots*, "By starting out with your mother and father, you embark on a journey to meet your ancestors. As you travel back into your family history, you are bound to experience the pleasure and excitement of discovering warm and fascinating characters whose blood flows in your veins."[75] This cultural shift toward the subjective and private reinforced the political shift involving the retrenchment of the welfare state. The rise of corporate interests in planning the nation's birthday demonstrated the business sector's increasing presence in public life. So, too, did the *Roots* phenomenon support the notion that it is individual initiative and self-reliance, independent of government assistance or social movements, that lays the successful path toward upward economic mobility.

In addition to being socially "bound" by the familial frame, *Roots* also remained temporally bound. Haley appears at the conclusion of the miniseries to explain that he is, in fact, the descendent of Kunta Kinte. He then gives a snapshot summary of the subsequent generations, positioning his own life within the *Roots* narrative. Still, his cameo does little to help spectators understand the myriad ways people live with and relate to their personal and collective pasts in the present. *Roots* revealed how far racial tolerance had come, and proved that it was no longer possible for the film and television industries to simply ignore the country's diverse population and historical traumas. At the same time, *Roots* exposed the limits of American society's ability to address pressing socioeconomic inequities. The logic of *Roots*, its fellow docudramas, and bicentennial culture in general was that race and class tensions were problems of the past that had ultimately been solved or were on a promising path toward reconciliation. The docudrama's spectacular display of familial unity masked a fractured body politic suffering in plain sight. "Difference" and "diversity" circa the mid- to late 1970s was fashioned into something to be simply celebrated rather than the subject of critical reflection and debate. The bicentennial thus appears as a proleptic cultural event that anticipated the Los Angeles–based 1984 Olympics.

While Hollywood docudrama offered people a thrilling historical encounter that left them feeling safe and secure, activist filmmakers on the fringes or outside of Hollywood found other ways to put the past in dialogue with people's present lives. Documentarians associated with Visual Communications, the L.A. Rebellion, KCET, and even commercial studios made films about the consequences of selective deindustrialization and corporate development, the community-building power of art, embattled memories of Vietnam, and the everyday struggle to survive with dignity and grace. As the cultural politics of the bicentennial anticipated the country's conservative turn to the right, activist documentarians continued to create an alternative space for the reevaluation of public history.

Numbering Our Days in
Los Angeles, USA

If you don't have history, you don't exist.
—FILMMAKER ROBERT NAKAMURA, 2010[1]

In contrast to the pageantry of the bicentennial celebrations, activist documentarians in Los Angeles cast a more critical eye on the subject of collective remembrance. They did so within the context of waning energy for the vanguard minority liberation movements, diminishing government support for community media, and the twin urban planning forces of aggressive corporate development and strategic neglect. While these filmmakers did not explicitly address the bicentennial per se, they creatively engaged with the myriad ways the present informs understandings of the past and vice versa. They captured the reverberations of traumatic events on the national psyche as well as advanced local struggles against displacement and the decisive practice of historical recovery. At times viewers even interpreted these films as sharing an unsettling relationship to the triumphant spirit of mainstream bicentennial programming. As Hollywood producers pioneered docudrama as a field of popular pedagogy, activist filmmakers—working independently or as part of collectives, within universities, or in collaboration with public media outlets or commercial studios—pushed the form and conceptual aims of documentary in new directions. They moved toward multimedia projects and stylistically hybrid features.[2] Their films transformed private memories into public history, insisting that Americans confront some hard truths.

RE-MEMBERING VIETNAM

The Vietnam documentary *Hearts and Minds* (1974) involved a collaboration between New Hollywood producers and a maverick filmmaker within the establishment New York news media. BBS Productions coordinated the project. Its founders, Bert Schneider and Bob Rafelson, had numerous family ties to the major studios, and they met while working on television programs for Screen Gems. Interested in making more alternative films that were aligned with their left-leaning political views, Schneider and Rafelson started Raybert Productions in 1965. After creating a satirical feature about the Monkees entitled *Head* (1968), they added producer Stephen Blauner and changed their name to BBS. The studio developed a reputation for coordinating low-cost, counterculture features that Columbia would distribute. Their films tended to concentrate on themes of alienation from mass society and longing for new forms of community. BBS scored a number of runaway successes, including *Easy Rider* (1969), *Five Easy Pieces* (1970), and *The Last Picture Show* (1971), but also suffered some flops, including *Drive, He Said* (1971). During this time Schneider and Rafelson gave money and publicity to anti–Vietnam War rallies and became close with both Youth International Party cofounder Abbie Hoffman and Black Panthers cofounder Huey Newton.[3]

The idea for *Hearts and Minds* emerged out of a series of conversations between Schneider, Rafelson, and CBS documentarian Peter Davis. Davis was nationally known for creating public affairs programs that pushed the social justice purview of conventional liberal politics. *Hunger in America* (1968) looked at poverty among Mexican Americans in Texas, Navajos in Arizona, and African Americans in Alabama and Washington, DC. Subsequently, the Department of Agriculture expanded its food stamp initiative. *The Battle of East St. Louis* (1969) captured a three-day retreat comprised of eighteen black and white citizens from east St. Louis. The retreat was designed to improve race relations through mediated dialogue, role playing, and group exercises. Davis's Emmy- and Peabody-winning documentary *The Selling of the Pentagon* (1971) exposed the Pentagon's massive $30 million per year propaganda effort to persuade Americans as to the virtue of US military action in Southeast Asia. The documentary detailed the Pentagon's support of film, television, and radio programs, as well as its attempts to manipulate the press's overseas war coverage.

Upon seeing *The Selling of the Pentagon*, BBS contemplated making an anti–Vietnam War film. They first envisioned doing a portrait of Daniel Ellsberg, the former Pentagon analyst who had recently leaked more than seven thousand documents detailing government efforts to escalate US involvement in Vietnam. They contacted Davis and the project quickly expanded into a long-form investigative documentary. Davis shot the film between July 1972 and August 1973, including two months on location in South Vietnam. After editing the film over the next year, the documentary approached final cut by April 1974.

According to Schneider and Davis, the project tried to address "why we went to Vietnam, what we did there and what the doing of those things did to us."[4] To be sure, *Hearts and Minds* explicitly condemns the war. The documentary combines interviews, news broadcasts, archival excerpts from Hollywood war films, photographs, and observational sequences in order to excavate America's Cold War motivations for first aiding the French and then increasingly asserting its own imperialist presence in Southeast Asia. But the film does not attempt to chart a strict chronological timeline or recount events in great detail. And although *Hearts and Minds* was part of the broader cultural front of the antiwar movement, it was made during the period of Vietnamization, in which President Richard Nixon began to withdraw US ground troops and shift the responsibility for fighting to the South Vietnamese. Davis did not imagine his film to be the same kind of social organizing tool as the late-1960s films of Emile de Antonio or Newsreel.

The rhetorical thrust of *Hearts and Minds* is centered on the war's physical and psychic impact on Americans. It sought to influence how the war lived within American culture and how it would be remembered. In the film, top military and political brass, including George Patton IV, William Westmoreland, Walt Rostow, and George Trendell, staunchly defend the war. They directly reference or gesture toward the need to "contain" the Red Menace, the domino theory of how Communism would supposedly spread, and the belief that the United States is the great liberator of oppressed people around the globe. These same individuals calmly deny the US-inflicted brutality on the Vietnamese people and appear unaware of or apathetic toward their commitment to an anti-imperialist fight for national unification. In interviews with American civilians that rhyme with these perspectives, subjects reveal a willful ignorance about the conflict, or proudly affirm the hawkish goals and defensive positions of its architects.

Many American veterans, however, express feelings of anger and sadness at having suffered as well as having been the cause of so much pain. Captain Randy Floyd from Norman, Oklahoma, speaks about the moment that the abstract, technical exercise of executing a bombing raid transformed into an alarming awareness that he was destroying entire villages. Lieutenant Robert Muller from Great Neck, Long Island, explains that the repetitive act of killing eroded the stock narratives surrounding America as a benevolent, freedom-fighting superpower. The veterans' testimonies are supplemented with footage of South Vietnam shot by cinematographer Richard Pearce and other journalists over the course of the war. The moving images give evidence of the horrors the American soldiers recount and show the consequences of US military involvement: exhausted marines in foxholes; petrified Vietnamese children whose flesh has been stripped away by napalm; the natural environment ravaged by the chemical defoliant Agent Orange; and resilient Hung Dinh villagers whose families have been killed by US bombs, and whose homes and livelihoods have been decimated.

Hearts and Minds foregrounds the fact that for a lot of individuals touched by the war, daily remembrance of the agony is inescapable. Some are forced to confront a physical loss. Pearce often first frames an individual's face, then pulls back or reframes the interview in a follow-up sequence to reveal that the veteran in question has lost the use of one or more limbs. Thus, the documentary shows over time that Muller is paralyzed from the waist down and that William Marshall has a prosthetic arm and leg. "Loss" can also be interpreted as something abstract, as Muller conveys that what hurts most is not the inability to use his legs, but that he feels absolutely no sense of pride in his country or its leaders. For David and Mary Cochran Emerson of Concord, Massachusetts, the anguish that stems from the death of their son Bing surfaces through the momentary silences in their testimony and strained expressions on their faces as they attempt to hold forth on the moral right of America's official position on Vietnam.

Hearts and Minds had a highly uneven path to exhibition. After playing at the Cannes Film Festival, where writer Rex Reed announced that the documentary was "a brutal, mind-blowing experience," it was screened at festivals in Atlanta and San Francisco.[5] Columbia Pictures, however, expressed hesitancy concerning the film's commercial release. The studio also feared that conservative viewers would stay home or even boycott Columbia's other pictures. Furthermore, studio executives were anxious of criticism from the government as well as a possible libel suit.[6] Unhappy with his interview, Rostow tried and failed to get a restraining order on the film. Columbia ended up selling the documentary to Rainbow Pictures. Warner Bros. would then handle distribution. Despite these complications, when *Hearts and Minds* finally played nationwide in both commercial theaters and noncommercial venues, it was a resounding critical success. *New York Times* reporter Stephanie Harrington confidently noted, "Unlike news photos, it does not merely present images of a collective tragedy but persistently focuses on individuals and how the war has blasted the whole of life for a particular person." *Los Angeles Times* critic Kevin Thomas claimed that the film "may well be the most important documentary of our time." Gary Arnold of the *Washington Post* observed, "Davis approaches the subject as a part of history."[7] *Hearts and Minds* won the Oscar for Best Documentary in 1975, a year when Hollywood was particularly divided on the relationship between art and politics. When Davis and Schneider took the stage to accept their award, they drew attention to the continued suffering in Vietnam and their hope for children to grow up in a world different from the one depicted in the film. They then went on to read a dispatch from the Provisional Revolutionary Government of South Vietnam affirming the Paris Peace Accords.

The action provoked a range of encouraging and disparaging comments from luminaries present at the event. Hosts Bob Hope and Frank Sinatra prepared an announcement condemning the acceptance speech and supporting "patriotism." The evening certainly revealed ideological tensions within the Hollywood community. But the fact that *Hearts and Minds* received such extensive attention was indeed significant. The recognition from intellectuals, journalists, and the Academy heightened its reach and visibility. Commenting on the centrality of the film in American culture as well as the ways in which it shrewdly interrogated long-held myths of United States exceptionalism, *New York Times* critic Vincent Canby called *Hearts and Minds* "the true film for America's bicentennial."[8] For many of the veterans interviewed, testifying to their experiences allowed them to work through their feelings of pain, shame, and frustration. Bobby Muller went on to become a lifelong peace activist. The documentary also productively served as a catalyst for framing a conversation about Vietnam, the ideologically treacherous reasons for entering into the conflict, and the war's fraught connection to American national identity in general and past military interventions and policies in particular. At the same time, the film's direct confrontation with the consequences of the war for both the Vietnamese and the American people served as a warning against taking similar action in the future.

BORDER CROSSINGS

Throughout the mid-1970s, KCET documentarian Jesús Salvador Treviño remained passionate about the power of moving images to shape Chicano identity and advocate on behalf of Chicano people. When he was invited to develop the filmmaking wing of the theater collective El Teatro Campesino in 1974, he saw this as a chance to apply his talent to a fresh and vibrant artistic environment. He was also attracted to the prospect of living in a commune, located three hundred miles north of Los Angeles in San Juan Bautista. Still, there were broader forces that influenced Treviño's decision to make a career change. He was growing disheartened about the state of La Raza Unida Party. Grassroots efforts in the early part of the decade made headway in unifying Mexican Americans across the political spectrum into a formidable political party, but the organization was having difficulty both winning campaigns at the local level and gaining a firm foothold within national democratic politics. La Raza Unida suffered from court indictments as well as infighting and ideological rifts among its leaders. José Angel Gutiérrez and Rodolfo "Corky" Gonzales each vying for power prevented the party from enacting a unified national vision. Additionally, Democrats began running Latino candidates who courted the Chicano vote, thereby diminishing La Raza Unida's base and political strength. Finally, the government's crackdown on activism through propaganda and direct acts of violence made radical organizing associated with the Chicano movement a constant challenge.

Treviño had honed his craft at KCET, but the public television outlet was beginning to shift away from community documentary and in-depth public affairs reporting and toward magazine-style news shows and prestige drama. This mirrored national trends throughout the mid- to late 1970s and would accelerate in the 1980s. Public television managed to outlast the attacks of the Nixon administration and secure federal funding under President Gerald Ford, but there was no longer the same climate of pressure to align programming with progressive grassroots social movements. PBS retreated to the cultivation of middlebrow tastes by means of spotlighting ballets, symphonies, and literary adaptations. And the search for high ratings along with the upcoming bicentennial resulted in spectacular docudramas, which began to surface on television screens during the early 1970s. The Carnegie Commission's investigation into the present and prospective future of public broadcasting between 1976 and 1978 yielded the assessment that PBS needed to be better funded, more accountable to minority viewers, and less susceptible to the desires of government and corporations.[9] While KCET produced some bold social dramas during this period, particularly through its *Visions* (1976–80) series, the station pivoted away from the kind of local, community-based nonfiction produced by the Human Affairs department. *New York Times* critic John J. O'Connor called out KCET in his critique of public television at the turn of the decade, noting, "The system has become a repository for nicely reassuring, non-minority, middle-class values and attitudes."[10]

As El Teatro Campesino's in-house filmmaker, Treviño documented the troupe's performances and collaborations with the Mexican group Los Mascarones and Peter Brook's International Centre for Theatre Research. Treviño's partnership with the collective was rewarding, but he soon found that he had difficultly squaring his own ideas about the responsibilities of individuals within the collective with how the organization functioned in practice. Not only was there an uneven distribution of duties and responsibilities in the commune, but Treviño clashed with members as to the exact role of filmmaking.[11] He found a new direction during the summer of 1974 at a conference on Latin American cinema at the Centro Universitario de Estudios Cinematográficos in Mexico. As the invited representative of Chicano cinema, Treviño met and saw the films of Mexican directors Pepe Estrada and Sergio Olhovich, Cuban directors Julio García Espinosa and Miguel Torres, and exiled Chilean filmmaker Miguel Littín. Treviño returned to the United States convinced that class issues needed to be foregrounded in his films and inspired to read liberation theology and Marxist theory. When asked by the former Mexican president Luis Echeverría Alvarez to make a feature-length fiction film about Chicanos, Treviño eagerly accepted.

Raíces de Sangre (*Roots of Blood*, 1977) highlighted the fight of exploited garment workers to form a transnational union. Treviño shot the film between June and December 1976 in San Diego and the Mexican town of Mexicali, although the story is nominally set in the Texas town of Socorro and the Mexican town of Ciudad Juárez. *Raíces de Sangre* follows the Harvard-educated Chicano lawyer Carlos Rivera (Richard Yniguez) as he comes to understand his professional relationship to the labor rights organization Barrio Unido, and his romantic relationship with one of its core leaders, Lupe Carrillo (Roxanna Bonilla-Giannini). The narrative weight of *Raíces de Sangre* rests on the lives of the people who labor in *maquiladoras* (foreign-owned manufacturing and assembly plants in towns along the Texas-Mexico border). The film spends considerable time representing the workers' material conditions and the exhausting routines they are forced to endure as employees of the Morris Shirt Company. Treviño told *Cineaste*, "I tried to tie the film as close as I could to reality."[12]

The film opens with a scene depicting Mexicans hoping to cross the border to find lucrative employment opportunities in America, only to die of asphyxiation in the back of a jam-packed truck parked on the side of an empty Texas highway. This tragic scene was based on a real incident Treviño had read about earlier in the decade. The portrayal of the skirmish between participants in the Barrio Unido rally and festival and the police in the Fourth Avenue Park resembles the police abuses Treviño witnessed at the Chicano Moratorium antiwar march in Los Angeles. Furthermore, the characters in the film speak a true-to-life mixed Spanish-English dialect known as Caló, further emphasizing the film's verisimilitude.

Raíces de Sangre includes many scenes set on the factory floor. This locale is at once a site of confrontation with management as well as a place of social bonding. When one employee becomes injured and is unable to keep pace with the required quota of shirts, her colleagues readily contribute garments to her pile. Characters toil busily at their sewing machines during the day, and have secret meetings to discuss organizational tactics at night. They talk of the need to form a union to negotiate wages, fight for job protections and safety protocols, and eliminate harassment. At their strike toward the end of the film, they cut electrical cords and dismantle machines so as to halt the flow of production.

At one moment in the film, Rivera reflects on the multigenerational Chicano experience of exploitation. He gazes out to the landscape in which he was raised and tells Carrillo that his family before him worked in the fields, struggling their whole lives to obtain economic stability. Now, he is participating in a related fight in the barrio.

The film ends on a somber yet hopeful note. Participating in a funeral march, Morris workers from both sides of the border carry the body of a killed organizer to the company officials and local police. They are honoring their fallen comrade who was killed during a rally, and making visible their rage. Separated by a barbed-wire fence, the two ranks of marchers display a fierce strength in their refusal to be broken down by corporate bullying and corrupt law enforcement. The film signals that this kind of transnational labor solidarity to fight a multinational company is a long time coming, here reaching a conceptual power that gives hope for the workers and their cause. Treviño told the *Los Angeles Times*, "The Chicano experience does not only take place on this side of the border, but it's heavily influenced by the border itself and by Mexico."[13]

Raíces de Sangre was completed in 1977, just when Treviño's previous films were being re-exhibited. For example, *Yo Soy Chicano* played at Los Angeles Mission College, at one of the first Chicano film festivals at the East Los Angeles Library, and at the Magic Lantern Basement Cinema in Washington, DC. *Raíces de Sangre* was warmly received in Mexico but at first had a difficult time getting distribution in the United States. The fact that it was a feature-length bilingual realist drama that took a hemispheric approach to American culture did not make theatrical release easy. The film premiered in the United States at the 1978 Chicano Film Festival in San Antonio and went on to play in select commercial theaters, festivals, and at special events. It was particularly popular in Spanish-language theaters in downtown Los Angeles. Following a benefit screening at the Golden Gate Theater in East Los Angeles, professor Jason Johansen of California State University, Northridge, called the film a "landmark" of Chicano cinema. *Variety* called *Raíces de Sangre* a "solidly made call to political activism."[14] Treviño wanted viewers to see that working-class people on both sides of the border are deeply affected by the growing presence of unregulated, multinational corporations, and that both grassroots organizing and progressive legislation are needed to combat globalization.

UNSUNG ACHIEVEMENTS

The African American filmmaker Sue Booker left KCET at around the same time as Treviño to pursue freelance projects. She served as the creative consultant for the two-week KNBC series *What Is It* (1973) about black achievements across the humanities and sciences. The series consisted of actors performing the roles of famous black professionals or giving accounts of their accomplishments. Louis Gossett Jr. charts a historical trajectory of blacks in medicine from James McCune Smith, the first African American to hold a medical degree, to pioneer heart surgeon Daniel Hale Williams. Actor John Amos hosted an episode on black cinema from 1916 to 1930.

Booker drew on *What Is It* for her series *The Rebels* (1976). The series was part of KNBC's bicentennial lineup and was also connected to UCLA's Extension courses. *The Rebels* spotlighted ten individuals from the American Revolution to the Civil War. Each person was played by a famous actor and was interviewed in his or her historical setting. In the series, host Dr. Keith Berwick interviews theoretician of American independence Thomas Jefferson, early feminist Abigail Adams, black female abolitionist Sojourner Truth, as well as militant antislavery activist John Brown.[15] During this period Booker also stepped into the role of a literary chronicler and social historian. She wrote poignant pieces for the *Los Angeles Times* and the *Los Angeles Sentinel* on under-recognized figures within and beyond Los Angeles: Mayme Clayton, a black rare-book dealer, archivist, and owner of the Third World Ethnic Bookstore in the West Adams neighborhood; Sidney Saltzman, prominent member of the Dedicated Older Volunteers in Educational Services; and George Washington Carver, the prolific black scientist-inventor.[16]

GRAY POWER IN VENICE

Filmmaker Lynne Littman stayed on at KCET through the mid-1970s. Even as the station began to shift its focus away from hard-hitting social documentary, Littman believed that public broadcasting still offered opportunities for women not available in the commercial sector. She told the *Los Angeles Times* in 1973, "The studios don't know how to treat you unless you are a secretary or a starlet. If you have any brains they give you a blank stare."[17] The same newspaper reported that by 1974 there were only sixteen women registered as part of the 1,390 West Coast members of the Directors Guild Association. Between 1949 and 1980, women directed 115 of the 65,000 hours of prime-time television. Entry into film schools was also a major challenge. In 1970, Women for Equality in Media organized a march on the West Coast American Film Institute headquarters to protest the small numbers of women awarded grants or offered training by the institution. Littman was one of nineteen individuals who eventually received a grant from AFI's first Directing Workshop for Women in 1974.[18] As she made films at KCET, she advocated for the increased presence and equitable treatment of women within the film and television industries.

KCET broadcast Littman's *Till Death Do Us Part* (1975) as part of an "International Women's Year" lineup of programs "by, for and about women."[19] The film concentrated on interviews with five widows, aged twenty-eight to seventy-four. They talk about their personal experiences of love and death and how they cope with the absence of their partners within a context of restrictive societal norms and economic hardship. The program foregrounds the women's courage and stamina, the solidarity they feel with other women in similar situations, and how they have created independent identities for themselves. Reviewer Linda Gross enthusiastically wrote, "Littman is a sensitive and provocative interviewer. She doesn't probe, she listens. The women reveal very intimate feelings but one doesn't feel like an intruder."[20] *Till Death Do Us Part* was rebroadcast with Joyce Chopra's *Girls at 12* (1975) as part of the series "Something Personal." The film also played theatrically at Los Angeles's Royal Theater as part of a women's film series in 1977.

Littman explored the concerns of retired, widowed, and elderly women in *Number Our Days* (1976). The documentary took as its subject Eastern European immigrant Jews living in the Venice neighborhood of Los Angeles. She made the film with her close friend and fellow feminist, USC anthropologist Barbara Myerhoff. The two had met at the Woman's Building, at a talk Myerhoff was giving on her ethnographic research on the immigrant enclave. After years of researching the Huichol Indians in northern Mexico, Myerhoff began fieldwork on Venice Jews around 1972. Her project was part of an initiative for the study of ethnicity and aging sponsored by USC and the National Science Foundation. *Number Our*

Days portrayed the daily routines and life histories of the elderly, giving voice to a community threatened by civic neglect and encroaching gentrification.

Venice at midcentury was composed of artists, working-class minorities, and elderly retirees. Beatniks as well as painters, sculptors, and graphic designers gathered at the Gas House and then at the Venice West Café. Artists Dennis Hopper, Robert Irwin, and Ed Moses had studios in the area. In the late 1960s the Peace and Freedom Party and the newspaper *Free Venice Beachhead* made Venice into a site of heated political activism, particularly for the antiwar movement. But the neighborhood's proximity to downtown, along with the possibilities of bringing some of its prime beachfront property into the fold of wealthy Santa Monica to the north and Marina del Rey to the south, informed the tenor of urban development plans. The Department of City Planning moved to condemn and raze properties deemed substandard, unsettling bohemians who resided in the canals, elderly Jews who rented near Ocean Park, and African Americans who lived in the Oakwood neighborhood.

Throughout the 1970s, absentee landowners and speculators raised rents and demolished old high-density apartment complexes to make room for luxury condos along Pacific Avenue. More middle-class Angelenos bought homes in the area, reversing the proportion of occupant-owners to renters. The Resident Homeowner Association and the Venice Canal Association sought to protect what urban historian Andrew Deener calls a "politics of quaintness," consisting of a unified home size along with beautified waterways and sidewalks.[21] *Los Angeles Magazine* reported in October 1974 that incomes per capita had risen 31 percent since 1968. In the same issue, writer Susan Squire outlined a walking tour from Pico to Washington Boulevard, where the "rapidly moving rehabilitation of Venice's commercial district promises to take the best of the old, artsy-funky, free-for-all and down-and-out Venice and combine it with the best of the new money and the high tastes filtering into the area."[22] While the elderly often had to deal with crime and insensitive hecklers, displacement posed a greater danger. Reporting on the new boutiques, rising rents, and J. Allen Radford's high-rise developments, journalist Dial Torgerson made the grim observation, "The poor shall not inherit the shoreline."[23]

At the start of Myerhoff's research, around four thousand elderly Jews lived in the area, residing within a five-mile stretch of boardwalk (and cutting inland about a mile) around the Israel Levin Senior Adult Center. The elderly senior citizens had spent their childhoods in the *shtetls* of Russia, Poland, Romania, and Lithuania, and had come to East Coast or midwestern cities around the turn of the twentieth century or just before World War II to escape religious persecution. They had spent most of their adult lives in New York, Philadelphia, Boston, Minneapolis, or Milwaukee, and then moved to Venice to spend their retirement years in a place that promised warm weather and cheap rents. They also appreciated the urban layout that catered to pedestrians, proximity to other Southern California Jews, and the chance to re-create aspects of their native culture.[24] *Number Our Days* gave the elderly the ability to share their life stories, as they felt themselves heirs to a culture that had been almost completely destroyed. In the film, Myerhoff serves as narrator as well as friend, confidant, and what poet Marc Kaminsky describes as a "cultural next-of-kin" for the community.[25]

Littman and Myerhoff opposed the ethnographic film conventions of distanced observation and authoritative voice-over. Myerhoff interacts with the elderly in front of the camera, making her encounters a central part of *Number Our Days*. She is not a fly-on-the-wall observer, but rather a participant in the action. She accompanies individuals and small groups on the boardwalk and converses with them about the process of maintaining traditions that connect their pasts to their contemporary lives. The Israel Levin Center exists as the social hub for the senior citizens. It houses Shabbat candle-lighting ceremonies, lectures and seminars, birthdays, music performances, High Holiday meals, and New Year's celebrations. The film even opens in the center with people dancing to "Hava Nagila," the traditional, upbeat Israeli folk song. The elderly enter the building as individuals, but are quickly brought together by the klezmer music being performed on the bandstand. Myerhoff, along with Littman and cameraman Neil Reichline, create a space for the viewer to share in these experiences and learn about their significance.

The senior citizens' rituals are a means of retaining their *Yiddishkeit* (Yiddish folk culture). At the same time, they are strategies of resistance, ways of asserting themselves to a surrounding urban environment that ignores their very presence. Bertha faithfully pursues her routine of "feeding pigeons, walking two miles every day, and telling and retelling a cycle of personal stories, with messages about dignity and autonomy." Talking with Myerhoff on a bench, Bertha describes the anguish of having outlived all of her children and husband, but also the companionship she feels with other center members. Shots of Bertha leading the Shabbat candle-lighting ceremony also show her as a leader of her surrogate family and a custodian of the collective memory of her people.

In another scene, Myerhoff listens to Pauline in her home as she talks about her feelings of accomplishment at having raised a family and cultivated a talent for sewing. Looking around at her prized items, Pauline mentions how her sewing machine was a means of materially providing for her family, but also a way of pursuing her hobby of making elaborate hats and dresses. She proudly talks about her ability to turn a *schmatta* (a common, often shabby article of clothing) into a fashionable garment, but regrets that she was unable to turn this hobby into a career.

Center director Morrie Rosen holds forth as a dynamic figure who teases, affirms, and supports the institution's members. As Myerhoff describes it, he "fights with the outside world for their survival." Since the early 1970s, Rosen has led the community in rent strikes and marches for affordable housing, and has remained involved in ongoing debates with business owners and government officials. Walking around the blocks surrounding the center, Rosen describes real estate developers as "profiteers" who came to Venice and are now displacing residents. He says that rising rents are forcing the senior citizens to find other accommodations in dilapidated apartments located far away.

The title *Number Our Days* references a psalm frequently recited at Jewish funerals. The activities of the elderly within the context of urban change signal that their days indeed seem to be "numbered," for they are forced to confront the twin threats of death and displacement. Nonetheless, the film's title also speaks to a deliberateness and intentionality with which the senior citizens confront each day. Their rituals are survival tactics, as they actively negotiate psychological, physical, and economic obstacles, and enjoy the community they have created for themselves. KCET's broadcast of *Number Our Days* made the lives of these Venice residents visible to a large audience.[26] The news media praised the documentary, but did not engage with the politics of place that had given rise to it. *Los Angeles Times* critic Lee Margulies described the film as a "poignant portrait of old age—the peacefulness and the loneliness, the dignity and the disregard, the pride and the pain."[27] *Number Our Days* won the Academy Award for Best Short Subject Documentary in 1977 and continued to be broadcast on television. It was also exhibited in nontheatrical venues, including the Smithsonian Institution in Washington, DC, as part of the "Kin and Communities: The People of America" symposium.[28] Members of the Israel Levin Center responded fervently to the film, relishing a kind of public recognition denied them in their daily lives. They felt like "stars" on-screen.[29]

Number Our Days also generated much-needed funds. By 1978 the institution received $25,000 in unsolicited donations and more than a thousand letters from people around the country who were moved by the film. The money helped to pay for the upkeep of the center and to subsidize the senior citizens' continued inhabitation of Venice. The film also attracted new members. Throughout the 1970s, membership grew by more than three hundred. *Number Our Days* was a catalyst for Myerhoff's book on the community, published in 1978, as well as a series of "Life Not Death in Venice"—themed exhibitions, marches, rallies, and performances that progressed into the 1980s.

Despite the film's acclaim, Littman found the prospects of continuing her documentary endeavors difficult. Describing a meeting with a major producer about creating a series of television programs based on *Number Our Days*, she recalled, "The first thing they asked was: 'Do they have to be old?' . . . Then I gathered that they shouldn't be Jews. I got the idea they wanted to do 'Number Our Days' as a series about some young WASP surfers living in Venice."[30] Looking ahead, Littman also believed that public television was fast becoming "broke" and "baroque," encouraging its filmmakers to rely on outside grants or private funds to make socially conscious films on under-recognized groups. She worried that a "17th century approach to so much television drama" was becoming a norm.[31] Littman left

KCET to work as an executive producer for ABC before crossing over into theatrically released realist fiction.

AMERICA'S ASIAN PACIFIC PEOPLES

By the mid-1970s, Ethno-Communications ceased to exist as a formal program at UCLA, and one of its chief architects, Elyseo Taylor, had to leave when he was not awarded tenure. Still, the film department and affiliated area studies centers at UCLA endeavored to sustain minority media at the university. The Ethiopian writer and filmmaker Teshome Gabriel was one of the central lifelines for this initiative. Shortly after beginning graduate study in film at UCLA, he started teaching as a lecturer in 1974 and brought filmmakers from Africa and Latin America to campus for screenings and conferences. He went on to earn his master's degree in 1976 and his doctorate in 1979, and he was hired as an assistant professor in 1981.

Students who started in Ethno-Communications in the late 1960s maintained their affiliation with the university throughout much of the next decade in order to use the department's editing suites, camera equipment, and screening facilities. Visual Communications (VC) kept close ties to UCLA as well as to the city's Asian American communities. The organization also relied on grant funding from the National Endowment for the Humanities, the Emergency School Aid Act, the Japanese American Citizens League, and the Rosenberg Foundation. VC documentaries positioned personal experiences often not addressed in mainstream media within a sociopolitical context. The collective's films concentrated on exclusionary immigration laws, coalition building across ethnic and racial lines, art as a performance of memory, and the struggle to maintain communal bonds over time and across geography.

Robert Nakamura's *Wataridori: Birds of Passage* (1976) looks at the immigrant experiences of three Japanese Americans in Southern California. The fisherman Koshiro Miura talks about how he, along with other *issei* fishermen, helped pioneer the West Coast fishing industry and how they value the camaraderie of working among skilled, dedicated professionals from their home country. They had thirty ships that sailed from their headquarters in Turtle Bay. Miura shares that they were financially successful in the years leading up to World War II, but that their livelihood was destroyed when the US Navy confiscated their boats and the government began interning Japanese Americans. Sepia-toned photographs of family members as well as on-location shots from Manzanar fill in the oral history with concrete images, as Miura laments that these traumatic experiences are still with him today.

Nakamura's father, Harukichi Nakamura, tells of how he left Oshima, Japan, with high hopes of coming to the United States, a place where, he had heard, "money was scattered like winter leaves." Given the stringent immigration laws, he

FIGURE 23: Still from *Wataridori: Birds of Passage*, 1976, 16mm; directed by Robert Nakamura. DVD, Third World Newsreel, New York, 2012.

was forced to enter illegally through Mexico, and then started a one-man gardening business in Los Angeles. He recalls long hours on the job, the cumbersome commute of riding a bicycle while holding his lawn mower and rake, and the prejudice expressed by people in the neighborhoods in which he gardened: "Very often, little boys would throw stones and chant 'Jap, Jap,' as I rode down the street." His voice-over plays against images of his routine mowing lawns and trimming hedges. Nonetheless, Harukichi speaks enthusiastically about how he made enough to live on and cherished his friendships with fellow Japanese gardeners. There are indeed moments of levity and solidarity. Observational scenes show the friends playing cards, telling jokes, and swapping stories. Harukichi says that they offer one another emotional and financial support. Similarly shot scenes also show Harukichi taking pleasure in his hobbies such as judo, an activity that allows him to pass down knowledge to future generations.

Nakamura's third subject, Haruno Sumi, arrived in the United States on the day of the San Francisco earthquake in 1906 and immediately moved to Los Angeles. She recounts what it was like growing up in Little Tokyo and the bustling commerce of the emerging business district. She goes on to describe the difficulties of being one of two Asian girls at Polytechnic High School. She was constantly made to feel isolated and lonely. Later, she recounts how her husband leased land in the Imperial Valley but lost everything in the 1920s cotton crash and was forced to move to a small farm in Del Mar, near San Diego. The narration is intimate, as her voice-over accompanies footage of her preparing tea in her kitchen, as well as displaying photographs of her family, Little Tokyo streets, and neighborhood institutions. The camera constantly explores the surface of the photographs, suggesting a memory coming into focus. Presently confined to her house due to bad health, Haruno finds solace in the radio, her dog, and painting. A large picnic of the Kagoshima Kenjinkai mutual aid society concludes the film, revealing a joyful intergenerational gathering. Children, teenagers, parents, and elders pass around prepared food, talk, and play games. Harukichi claims that although he has his roots in Japan, his home is here in the United States.

VC also looked to pan-Asian topics and shared working-class experiences among Third World peoples. Eddie Wong's *Pieces of a Dream* (1974) examines generations of produce farmers in the Sacramento River Delta. The documentary shows that the first to locate there were the Chinese, beginning in the 1860s. Around the turn of the twentieth century, the Japanese came to farm the land. Recently, Filipinos have called the area home. *Pieces of a Dream* addresses both individual and collective forms of hardship faced by the immigrants: Chinese discuss the effects of the Exclusion Acts and the Alien Land Laws; Japanese recall the cell-like conditions of immigrating through Angel Island and the abuse they later suffered as farmers working under white property owners; and Filipinos talk about deteriorating infrastructure, economic competition from big agribusiness, and a depleting population. And yet, *Pieces of A Dream* does not simply catalogue hardships, but also depicts evolving forms of social affiliation within the domestic and commercial enclaves of the Delta region. Festivals and religious institutions are major gathering centers, and there is a pride people feel when interacting directly with the land. The documentary also devotes time to tensions within and across different Asian communities. Elders discuss how members of the younger generation leave the Delta for cities and never return. Filipinos denounce their exploitation by the Chinese and Japanese. *Pieces of a Dream* ultimately represents peoples' complex relationships to a place, from feelings of protection and loyalty, to nostalgia and happiness, to animosity and heartache.

Wong's *Chinatown Two-Step* (1975) offers a more contemporary look at maintaining urban social ties. The film profiles the Imperial Dragons, a drum and bugle corps that draws from primarily middle-class Chinese American youth. The camera follows the Imperial Dragons during rehearsals and competitions. It is as if the spectator can train with the ensemble rather than just watch them. Participating members and their parents talk about the history of the drum corps and praise the organization's ability to bring Chinese families together in a fragmented metropolis; the Imperial Dragons is a way to teach their children about vernacular traditions. As many of the residents profiled in the documentary have moved out of Chinatown proper to surrounding suburban enclaves, the music brings geographically disparate groups together.

The Japanese American jazz-fusion band Hiroshima is at the center of Duane Kubo's *Cruisin' J-Town* (1975). Band members Dan Kuramoto (flute, saxophone, bandleader), Peter Hata (guitar), June Kuramoto (koto), Johnny Mori (percussion and *taiko*), Dave Iwataki (keyboards), and Danny Yamamoto (drums) composed much of the music for VC films. Hiroshima combined Latin, African American, and Japanese musical styles and attracted fans from these traditions. As the film opens, Hiroshima provides a rhythmic sonic backdrop for observing the street life

FIGURE 24: Still from *Cruisin' J-Town*, 1975, 16mm; directed by Duane Kubo, with Hiroshima; produced by Visual Communications. Courtesy of Visual Communications Photographic Archive.

of Little Tokyo. The music sets the tempo for walking among the vegetable markets, fruit stands, the Daimaru Hotel, and the Amerasia Bookstore. *Cruisin' J-Town* then shifts between interviews with musicians and shots of their performances. Individuals talk about how learning to play the traditional Japanese instruments involved a musical maturation as well as a political and cultural awakening. June Kuramoto says that her love of her deceased grandmother's string instrument, the koto, was met with scorn from her Anglo classmates and skepticism from some members of her own family. The latter encouraged her to assimilate by playing the piano. Nonetheless, she is pleased with how playing the koto puts her in touch with her ancestors. Dan Kuramoto states that his musical pursuits defy stereotypes of a "traditional" Japanese profession. He elaborates on music as a way to share culture with his own Asian American community as well as with a broader audience who might not know anything about the history or identity of his people. A scene of an energetic *taiko* performance shows three generations of Asian Americans gathered at the Senshin Buddhist Temple. Verité-style camerawork positions the viewer next to the drummers as they seem to bounce around the stage, quickly rotating between drums.

A scene that captures Hiroshima performing with El Teatro Campesino musical director Daniel Valdez at the Embassy Auditorium demonstrates the bridge-building power of music. Prior to the concert, members speak with Valdez about the importance of music to their respective cultures. They affirm that music is so beloved by the masses because it is so common, so nourishing, so rooted in daily life. Their onstage collaboration does more than reveal a new kind of polymorphic

FIGURE 25: On-location production photograph for *I Told You So*,
1974, 16mm; directed by Alan Kondo with Lawson Inada; produced by
Visual Communications. Courtesy of the Visual Communications
Photographic Archive.

sound; it models the socializing power of music and the possibilities for other,
political solidarities that could extend beyond the concert hall.

The Japanese American poet Lawson Inada is the focus of Alan Kondo's *I Told
You So* (1974). Inada's impassioned reading of his verse, interviews with his friends
and family, and observational sequences on the streets of his multiethnic hometown of Fresno, California, all create an understanding of how the Chicano, African American, and Japanese communities informed Inada's upbringing and continue to enrich his career as a poet and teacher. Kondo captures Inada sharing his
works in progress with fellow writers as they discuss the volume that will become
the famous *Aiiieeeee!: An Anthology of Asian-American Writers* (1974).[32]

As in the initial years of the collective, VC exhibited their films individually at
elementary and high schools, Japanese American Citizens League chapters, branch
libraries, East Los Angeles College, UCLA, and the Koyasan Hall in Little Tokyo.[33]
VC also created special events, such as a series of screenings in May 1976 at the
Theater Vanguard in West Hollywood—"Asian America: Films by Visual Communications"—which included *Chinatown Two-Step, To Be Me: Tony Quon, Pieces
of a Dream, Kites and Other Tales, Crusin' J-Town*, and *Wataridori: Birds of Passage*.[34] *Los Angeles Times* critic Linda Gross summarized each of the films and
commented that they were "meticulous, and moving studies of Americans who
own a dual heritage."[35]

VC expanded on its documentary practice of arranging text and photographs
that they had begun in the early part of the decade. In addition to creating the

FIGURE 26: Advertisement for Asian America film screenings at the
Theater Vanguard, West Hollywood, May 16 and 23, 1976. Courtesy of
the Visual Communications Photographic Archive.

photo-block display *America's Concentration Camps* (1970), they published the
anthology *ROOTS: An Asian American Reader* (1971). Nakamura coordinated the
photographs and Eddie Wong edited the accompanying writing. The volume was
broken down into three sections, "Identity," "History," and "Community," and contained short essays and images from academics, activists, artists, and civic leaders.
In his preface, Franklin Odo emphasized the importance of the grassroots

perspective when narrating the social character of a people: "There is, however, equal emphasis on the contemporary expression of the Asian American condition by the people themselves. *ROOTS* is, therefore, not only a handy repository of secondary writings on the subject but a documentary collection from our time."[36]

A selection of images drawn from VC's vast archive of photographs on the Chinese, Japanese, Korean, Filipino, and Samoan experience in the United States appear in their 1977 photo-book *In Movement: A Pictorial History of Asian America*. As stated in its opening, the book is "visual evidence of the trials and hardships of immigration and resettlement; racist exclusion and exploitation; the building of communities which provide for Asian minorities a measure of pride and appreciation for their own ethnicity in an unfamiliar and at times hostile environment." *In Movement* places images of Japanese tuna fishermen, Korean apricot farmers, Filipino bartenders, Chinese herbalists, and Korean grocers within accounts of their coming to the United States and constructing homes, commercial establishments, and neighborhoods. *In Movement* foregrounds VC's own origins along with its mission: "By gaining knowledge of our history as a community, as a people, we can participate in the determination of our own destinies."[37]

VC members committed themselves to local forms of direct activism, fighting back against the corporate reshaping of selective parts of the metropolis under mayor Tom Bradley. They participated in the Little Tokyo People's Rights Organization, protesting the public-private partnerships spearheading aggressive redevelopment plans in the area. Duane Kubo galvanized residents to combat the city's efforts to raze the long-standing network of local establishments within a small, dense, mixed-use area known as the Weller Street triangle; eviction notices had gone out to 124 individuals and families, 19 businesses, and 21 cultural organizations. Particularly sensitive was the prospective demolition of the cherished Sun Hotel, which housed retirees and community groups. VC's film *Something's Rotten in Little Tokyo* (1975–77) attacks the Kajima International Corporation's plans to build the New Otani Hotel as well as an adjoining parking lot and upscale businesses on the Weller Street triangle. Kajima had recently built the nearby Sumitomo Bank building that loomed over Little Tokyo. The corporation, along with the Community Redevelopment Agency, imagined that the $30 million, twenty-one-story luxury hotel complex would cater to tourists and wealthy businesspeople as well as make Little Tokyo an attractive place for international capital.[38]

In partnership with LTPRO, VC members attempted to halt evictions, preserve the existing commercial infrastructure, and persuade the government and private entities of the need for new affordable housing units. They staged sit-ins, stormed City Council sessions, and picketed construction sites. They also made films about their efforts to garner attention and support for their struggle. Furthermore, activists debated local shop owners who reasoned that revamping the area would lead to a boost in business. Ultimately, Kajima created the New Otani hotel, and many

Weller Street organizations and residents were displaced. Still, VC's involvement was instrumental in creating an organizational base for citizen participation for future developments in the area. This became particularly important for the creation of the Little Tokyo Service Center, government-subsidized affordable housing units, and eventually the Japanese American Cultural and Community Center.

SOUNDING SOUTH CENTRAL

Like the members of VC, the black filmmakers who informally comprised the L.A. Rebellion also maintained ties to UCLA as well as to their home communities. Charles Burnett continued to be interested in social documentary even as he was increasingly drawn to the creative control he could have with scripting and staging. The stylistically hybrid Third Cinema of Latin America and Africa was also a considerable influence on Burnett. In 1974 he helped organize the Third World Film Club, where students watched the films of Sergio Giral (Cuba), Pastor Vega (Cuba), Miguel Littín (Chile), Jorge Sanjinés (Bolivia), and Glauber Rocha (Brazil). The club advocated for the US government to facilitate greater cultural exchange with Cuba. In creating a political cinema that connected to their own experiences, Burnett and his circle consciously positioned their practice against Hollywood entertainment, most of which either excluded people of color from the plots, relegated them to the far corners of the frame, or portrayed them with demeaning stereotypes. However, L.A. Rebellion filmmakers did not necessarily completely reject the low-budget cycle of black studio action films that by the early 1970s had come to be known as blaxploitation. Many despised the studios' pursuit of profit and the ways in which blaxploitation features sensationalized the social tensions that they addressed. And yet, these films provided employment opportunities for minority talent, represented working-class black experiences given scant attention in commercial cinema, and defied saccharine models of classical Hollywood storytelling.

Furthermore, in creating their own productions, UCLA-trained filmmakers critically engaged with the characters, themes, and settings of this film cycle. As cinema studies scholar Jan-Christopher Horak argues, "The L.A. Rebellion's aesthetic strategies and ethics emerged as a direct reaction to Blaxploitation's amplification of particular signs and symbols of African American life (e.g., the urban, the criminal), but the Rebellion films also referenced those 'false' images in order to work toward a more nuanced and comprehensive view of Black experience." In his analysis of the films by Jamaa Fanaka, Horak claims that "while Fanaka mimics, parodies, subverts, and critiques Blaxploitation genre conventions and expectations more closely than any of his Rebellion compatriots, he also constructs an explicitly political text that deconstructs Blaxploitation cinema's male chauvinist and often racist narratives."[39]

Burnett worked on an eclectic mix of films during his time teaching at UCLA and reading scripts at the Westwood-based casting agency Chasin, Park & Citron. He directed, edited, produced, and wrote the short film *The Horse* (1973), about a black child on a deteriorating Southern farm who witnesses the killing of a cherished colt. Burnett also crewed, along with the talented *Wattstax* cameraman and photographer Roderick Young, on Haile Gerima's MFA feature *Bush Mama* (1975). The naturalist film centers on Dorothy (Barbara O. Jones), a pregnant welfare recipient living in Watts, and her husband T.C. (Johnny Weathers), a recently returned Vietnam veteran who is imprisoned under false charges. The film depicts the oppression and radical political awakening of Dorothy as well as the torment experienced by T.C. as a result of his time in combat. Additionally, Burnett was a cinematographer for Fanaka's *Welcome Home Brother Charles* (1975), about an ex-convict who wields his superpowered genitalia like a weapon as he takes revenge on the people responsible for sending him to jail. And for Jacqueline Frazier's drama *Hidden Memories* (1977), about the stresses and anxieties of teen pregnancy, Burnett recorded sound.[40]

Burnett's MFA project, *Killer of Sheep* (1977), is a subtle portrait of daily life in South Central. The film concentrates on Stan (Henry Sanders), a slaughterhouse employee, Watts resident, husband, and father of two children. Burnett shot *Killer of Sheep* over a series of weekends in 1971 and 1972 and began editing the film shortly thereafter. The intricate sound mix was finally completed (with music rights cleared) by 1977. A $3,000 Louis B. Mayer grant, which ended up being a little less than a third of the film's total budget, helped finish the project.[41] *Killer of Sheep* expanded on Burnett's *Several Friends* (1969). Even though he penned a loose script and the film's protagonist had experience as an actor, Burnett did not simply invent a fictional story. The project retained the documentary charge of his previous projects. Burnett wanted to have people in the community, friends, and even family members "re-present" actions, conversations, and encounters that were part of their daily lives. Burnett's high school friend Charles Bracy played Stan's companion and confidant and also recorded sound. Burnett's own daughter, Angela, played Stan's daughter.

Killer of Sheep engages a palette of emotions that opposes commercial film and television's insistence on an action-driven story with morally legible personalities. Instead of pursuing an upward trajectory toward a familial triumph and a clear feeling of closure, the film unfolds as a series of small events and interactions from approximately Friday afternoon through Sunday morning. Cinema studies scholar Paula Massood notes that the film follows "a cyclical and episodic structure" rather than a streamlined flow of action.[42] *Killer of Sheep* depicts Stan's alienation from his job, his sense of strained compassion for his family, and his ambivalence toward his fellow South Central residents. Burnett would later recall that when making the film, he was thinking about "documenting" the kinds of social phenomena that

FIGURE 27: Still from *Killer of Sheep*, 1977, 16mm; directed, written, produced, and photographed by Charles Burnett; sound by Charles Bracy. 1920 × 1080 ProRes 422 (HQ) transfer from the UCLA Film & Television Archive's restored 35mm interpositive, courtesy of Milestone Films.

occur on a routine basis. Thus, the film captures such activities as Stan Jr. and Angela occasionally bickering and playing outside; Stan working his night shift on the killing floor of the slaughterhouse; Stan and his wife attempting to conjure a feeling of intimacy while slow-dancing; and friends and neighbors drifting in and out of the house.[43]

In *Killer of Sheep*, what is heard is as important as what is seen. Sound had of course been crucial to Burnett's two solo projects. For example, in *Several Friends*, the overlapping voices and impromptu dialogue of the individuals joking with one another in the car and in their homes does not serve a strictly expository purpose; instead, it creates a soundscape of lively camaraderie. Burnett's film *The Horse* makes thoughtful use of recorded music, opening and closing with composer Samuel Barber's 1947 symphony *Knoxville: Summer 1915*. The mournful sounds of violins, bassoons, and clarinets establish a despondent tone for the vignette—foreshadowing the characters' departure from the ranch and the execution of the horse—and also aurally express the child's profound grief. The final freeze-frame image shows the child covering his ears with his hands so as not to hear the sound of the killing.

Killer of Sheep is an auditory archive of African American vernacular music: the hot jazz of Louis Armstrong, the resounding operatic singing of Paul Robeson, the rhythm and blues of Dinah Washington, the ragtime piano of Scott Joplin, and the electric blues guitar of Lowell Fulson. Burnett was surrounded by these sounds growing up in Los Angeles, a city that was a popular migratory destination for Southern blacks and a nexus for African American music. Burnett also encountered this music on family trips back to New Orleans and Vicksburg, Mississippi. In turn, audiences of *Killer of Sheep* are meant to be able to hear resonances and continuities between different musical styles and modes. The film signals that African American music extends to every region of the country, across every genre of popular song, and to every epoch of the recording industry. The film's soundtrack comprises a shared African American culture that orients viewers in the present toward a rich cultural past. Thus, *Killer of Sheep*'s soundscape performs an important social function. As Burnett commented in a 1991 interview: "I think that it is the artist's job to establish links with the past, to give some self-respect to the people, to create the sense of a center. I think that erosion of memory is the design of the establishment. . . . Without history you are nothing. Memory is like coming on an island, something to catch up on and hang onto."[44]

The sound design also constitutes a form of commentary and a vehicle for reflection. Music adds a degree of psychological depth to the characters. For example, music expresses a feeling of frustration when Stan's family and friends embark on what they anticipate will be a pleasant outing to Los Alamitos racetrack. Packed into a car, they head out of Watts with Louis Armstrong's 1928 recording of "West End Blues" playing on the soundtrack ("West End" refers to a summer resort in Orleans Parish, Louisiana). The music and the motion of the car begin in sync, the ignition of the engine coinciding with Armstrong's blistering opening fanfare. Then, the song's slow, plodding melody corresponds to the automobile's steady movement along the road. Soon, however, the solos by Armstrong (trumpet, vocals), Fred Robinson (trombone), and Jimmy Strong (clarinet) begin to express varying degrees of irritation and sorrow. The car gets a flat tire and the group is forced to give up the outing and return home. At the moment the car circles around and begins to ride back on the rim, the song comes to a melancholic close. Here, the thwarted road trip is explicitly symbolic of working-class African Americans being denied access to the California dream of leisure and mobility so often pictured in the postwar age as an automobile gliding along a wide-open freeway.

Music registers the emotions of the characters. In the way that jazz and the blues have historically offered cathartic expression for African American grief without necessarily ensuring simple resolve, the group's misery is articulated through the "West End Blues." An upset Bracy looks at the flat tire and contributes an additional solo to the song:

Shit, man, I *told* you to have a spare tire
got me coming out here to the middle of nowhere
I got to get me to this race out in Los Alamitos,
look here in the ninth race I got me a stag man that I *know* is going to come in

I got me some money man, and you ain't got no spare?
look, look, look, *awwwwwww shit*
I'm out here singing the blues, got my money on a horse that can't lose
and now we're out here with a flat, I always told you to keep a spare, but you
    were a square that's why you can't keep no spare, now how we gonna get
    there, *huh*?

Bracy's rap is a means of coping with disappointment through creative expression. He appears annoyed but also empowered in the moment of the performance. On another level, the presence of the song in the film reflects on Burnett's own self-conception. Armstrong's virtuoso performance of "West End Blues" was *the* piece that announced to the world his arrival as a young trumpeter who could play with discipline and skill with his Hot Five ensemble and also stand out as an unparalleled soloist. So too does Burnett's *Killer of Sheep* constitute his own proclamation of his affiliation with the L.A. Rebellion and his ambitions as an independent artist.[45] Armstrong's journey from the South to some of the country's major media centers, where he found both a stage and a loudspeaker for his talent, is also Burnett's journey.

The struggle for socioeconomic mobility and the challenges set by failing technology are taken up in other parts of the film. In one scene Stan and Eugene purchase a motor and laboriously haul the cumbersome hunk of metal down multiple flights of stairs to the back of their pickup truck. As soon as the car lurches forward, the motor tumbles to the ground, suffering irreparable damage. After they spent so much energy to move the motor, the scene ends with a feeling of stalled motion and suspended time, which in turn relates to Stan's broader frustrations with trying to get ahead.

Another example spotlights children playing in a rubble-filled enclosure, which appears to be the former site of several businesses, a factory, and some homes. Within the dirt and debris-filled enclosure children stack logs, throw stones against the side of a stucco building, climb and jump over an expansive wall, and spin a toy top on the ground. An extreme close-up of a child pounding a concrete cinder block with a wrench gives rise to the booming voice of Paul Robeson singing his 1947 cover of "The House I Live In": "What is America to me? / a name, a map or a flag I see / a certain word, democracy / What is America to me? / the house I live in / a plot of earth, a street / the grocer and the butcher / and the people that I meet / the children in the playground / the faces that I see / all races and religions, that's America to me." Originally written by Abel Meeropol and Earl Robinson in 1942, "The House I Live In" bridged Popular Front and civil rights movements. It was widely sung at May Day rallies and made famous in the short Mervyn LeRoy, Albert Maltz, and Frank Ross film *The House I Live In* (1945), featuring Frank Sinatra. In *Killer of Sheep* the song appears ironic. The disjuncture between the lyrics and the images on-screen suggests that the promise of an

FIGURE 28: Still from *Killer of Sheep*, 1977, 16mm; directed, written, produced, and photographed by Charles Burnett; sound by Charles Bracy. 1920 × 1080 ProRes 422 (HQ) transfer from the UCLA Film & Television Archive's restored 35mm interpositive, courtesy of Milestone Films.

egalitarian America has not been realized. The "plot of earth," "street," "play-ground," "house," and commercial institutions that make up "America" exist in tension with the crippled economy of broken engines, railroad cars rusting in place, and dilapidated buildings.

Burnett wrote in his essay "Inner City Blues," "I think that it is the little personal things that begin to give a hint of the larger picture."[46] The enclosure in *Killer of Sheep* is indeed revealing of the post–Watts Uprising, postindustrial environment of Watts. By the mid- to late 1960s, manufacturing jobs were vacating the central city at an accelerating rate, leaving mainly nonunion, low-paying service and garment industry work. The Chrysler plant closed in 1971, followed by B. F. Goodrich in 1975, Uniroyal in 1978, and US Steel in 1979. Mayor Tom Bradley expanded white-collar opportunities for minorities in the city's public-sector professions, but blue-collar jobs in the central city region shrank considerably. And the west-ward move of aspiring middle-class black families to Leimert Park, Baldwin Hills, and the West Adams district contributed to the widening socio-spatial gap sepa-rating black Angelenos. Urban theorist Edward Soja notes that by 1980, South Central lost forty thousand people and the median family income dropped to $5,900, which was $2,500 below the median for African Americans in the city overall.[47] *Killer of Sheep*'s depiction of the rubble-filled enclosure speaks not only to the situation in Los Angeles, but also to a larger conflict between the lofty beliefs surrounding American narratives of economic mobility and the reality faced by working-class and working-poor minority communities across the country. A decimated mass transit system, inadequate job training, industrial relocation, and underfunded schools hurt the infrastructure of South Central. With the onset of a new decade, the reduction of public funds for community programs, resistance to school busing, pushback against taxes, and an influx of drugs compounded the sense of social fracture in the city.[48]

The scene that immediately follows the children in the enclosure features Stan in the slaughterhouse. The juxtaposition easily lends itself to a metaphorical reading that would imply a grim future for the children (seen as sheep being led to the slaughter, and the older generation of South Central having a hand in the process). Nevertheless, the outdoor scene in the enclosure and the film more generally precludes an interpretation as bleak as that. The children are determined to amuse themselves in a place certainly not intended for this purpose, infusing a feeling of spontaneity and even joy into the experience of the location. They refashion the debris into a playground, refusing to let the weight of the rubble still or silence their imaginations. There is a bricolage-like aesthetic to what they create. The scene itself is aflutter with activity, as all the individuals are in motion, climbing, jumping, throwing, and spinning. They demonstrate the creativity and courage of a community that, as the 1970s progressed into the 1980s, was increasingly ignored by the mainstream media and the civic leaders of the city.

The same year that Burnett finished *Killer of Sheep*, Wolper Productions completed *Roots* (1977). The eight-part docudrama tells the multigenerational slave narrative of the West African villager Kunta Kinte. The series concludes with Kinte's descendants moving from North Carolina to a newly purchased plot of land in Henning, Tennessee. *Roots* and *Killer of Sheep* each focus on the socioeconomic struggles of a black family. However, a gulf separates the two films in their representational approach and reception. Their coexistence speaks to the contentious nature of the historical moment, highlighting the distinct possibilities and severe limitations of minority inclusion. While *Roots* enjoyed the largest television audience to date in the history of the medium, *Killer of Sheep* was at first rarely seen. It was only exhibited at UCLA and then circulated among a limited number of college campuses, churches, and museums.

Roots's docudramatic form conjoined Hollywood period fiction with the truth claims of documentary. The result was a narrative that was swift and sweeping, presenting a strong, character-driven, uplifting story. The miniseries signaled that society was advancing in a progressive direction, toward a more racially integrated polity and increased economic opportunities. The creators of *Roots* took special care in the scripting, casting, and advertising of the project to ensure that a vast cross-section of Americans could identify with the experiences of the characters on-screen. As long as minority lives were packaged for commercial screens as stories of triumph that affirmed American myths of upward mobility, they could be tolerated and even embraced.

By contrast, *Killer of Sheep* constituted a slower, more patient, artisanal cinema, a cinema of detailed looking and listening to everyday rituals and routines. Crafted in a way that resists the tempo, style, and plot arcs of popular cinema, *Killer of Sheep*'s social landscape registers the hardships and pains, both economic and psychological, of life in South Central. But this is not all the film captures. Stan's family and others in the neighborhood appear resilient, determined to confront life's challenges with dignity and resolve. *Killer of Sheep* asserts their humanity as well as protests Hollywood's skewed representation of minority lives and the changing political direction of the metropolis. Burnett's empathetic portrait constituted a new grammar for depicting marginalized communities whose relationship to one another, the city of Los Angeles, and the nation was deeper and more complex than most Americans were ready or willing to realize.

Conclusion

The 1984 Olympics and the
Neoliberalization of Culture

Government is not the solution to our problem; government is the problem.
—PRESIDENT RONALD REAGAN, 1981[1]

TV executives call it "reality programming," like the news. But it isn't exactly news. Some call it "info-tainment," meaning information that is entertaining. Others call it "docu-schlock. Whatever one calls it, shows like this have swept the airwaves."
—JOURNALIST MARSHALL INGWERSON, 1983[2]

The opening ceremony of the 1984 Summer Olympics at the Los Angeles Memorial Coliseum set a new precedent for media-made spectacle. Organized by David Wolper, the July 28 event featured a medley of fast-paced musical vignettes spotlighting scenes from America's past. In "Pioneer Spirit," a fleet of Conestoga wagons and costumed dancers rolled onto the field to the sounds of Aaron Copland's "Rodeo." The dancers then went to work constructing sets that resembled a late eighteenth- or early nineteenth-century town. In "Dixieland Jamboree," an eight-hundred-person marching band formed a riverboat steamship moving along the Mississippi. It opened up into a design resembling a church, as singer Etta James sang the gospel tune "When the Saints Go Marching In." In "Urban Rhapsody," couples in evening gowns and tuxedos transformed segments of the stadium platform into a ballroom as they danced to Irving Berlin's "Cheek to Cheek."

Los Angeles Times arts editor Charles Champlin called the event "history's longest half-time show" where the "American Dream comes wrapped in cellophane out of the Hollywood Dream Factory."[3] Its grandeur was designed to create a memorable experience for all who attended the in-stadium show. Equally important, the event was consciously scaled for television: a spectacle for the small screen. An estimated 2.5 billion people viewed it via satellite and tape delay. On-field shots granted living-room spectators the ability to enjoy the immersive experience of being part of the action. Mobile aerial perspectives allowed them to take in the sweep of human movement at a glance. These shots periodically transformed the performers into abstract compositions of spinning circles and darting lines—so much so that reporters discussed the event as taking Busby Berkeley theatrics in a new direction. At a particularly poignant moment, the stadium's eighty-eight thousand audience members held colored cards in unison so as to form a broad tapestry of flags from around the world.[4]

This opening show resonated with Mayor Tom Bradley's aspiration that the Olympics would cement Los Angeles's status as a "world city." He envisioned Los Angeles as a thriving metropolis, the capital of the Pacific Rim, with the ability to connect Asia, Latin America, and the United States. But the Games also marked the culmination of a gradual transformation to a more conservative political culture. At the dawn of the 1960s, when John F. Kennedy had accepted the presidential nomination of the Democratic Party at the Coliseum, he looked to a New Frontier in which citizens, the liberal state, and the film and television industries would adamantly address the public welfare of the country. The next two decades saw productive uses of, and intense challenges to, liberal institutions and mechanisms of change. As President Ronald Reagan surveyed the inaugural ceremony of the 1984 Olympics from his press box in the top tier of the same stadium, it was clear that much had shifted. This era involved a new conception of individual rights, a retrenchment of big government, and the deregulation of the media industries. An insurgent ethos of privatization fashioned the basis for a new socioeconomic order.

On both a local and a national level, Wolper served as a crucial bridge from the once dominantly liberal to a far more conservative political culture. In addition to planning the opening (and closing) ceremonies, he assumed the role of vice chair of the Los Angeles Olympic Organizing Committee (LAOOC). Wolper was integral to bringing the Olympics to Los Angeles. He also spearheaded public relations, and negotiated rights-related issues for televising the Games. The fact that his company had since early 1977 been operating under the umbrella of Warner Bros. at 4000 Warner Boulevard allowed the producer to devote focused attention to the Olympics. Wolper desired the resources of a large corporation and the chance to work on one project at a time. In planning for the Games, he worked closely with business-minded Peter Ueberroth, the travel executive and head organizer of the Olympics, to ensure that the logistics reduced economic risk and maximized financial gain for the city.

The 1984 Olympics were the first to be funded primarily through private industry. This reflected the Bradley administration's interest in making Los Angeles an alluring place for transnational capital.[5] Also motivating this planning strategy was the growing resistance in California to public spending and high property taxes, which had led to the anti-tax measure Proposition 13 in 1978. The "tax revolt" in California quickly spread to states across the country. The LAOOC paid for the Olympics by way of sponsors, ticket sales, and media coverage. With Wolper at the negotiating table, the LAOOC sold the exclusive right to broadcast the Games to ABC for the gigantic sum of $225 million and then signed with different distributors for the European market. Sixty-four commercial suppliers, thirty-five commercial partners, and sixty-five licensees contributed an additional $157.2 million. To keep the overall hosting costs low, Los Angeles relied on its existing infrastructure for the sports events rather than building elaborate facilities from scratch. The LAOOC made substantial revenue off the Olympics, ending the events with a surplus of around $220 million.[6]

The promotional film *Welcome to Los Angeles: Olympic City, 1984* (1984) advertised the Olympics to corporate participants as well as to domestic and international attendees. The documentary portrayed the city as a high-tech business hub, a mesmerizing tourist destination, and a nexus of cultures from within and beyond the United States. Narrator Stanley Anderson offers an itinerary: people arrive at Bradley International Terminal at the LAX airport, stay in luxurious accommodations such as the Century Plaza and Westin Bonaventure hotels, and watch the sports competitions at arenas all over the region. Anderson makes special mention of the fact that Los Angeles is embracing computer technology to help regulate car traffic and coordinate the circulation of buses and vans for maximum efficiency. When spectators are not frequenting the sports venues, he explains, they can go to the Museum of Contemporary Art, the Olympic Arts Festival, or restaurants "where you can taste the cuisine of every nation in the world."

These activities and exhibitions certainly provided opportunities for Angelenos and visitors to access a vast array of attractions. However, like Wolper's Olympic launch and televised event, these forms of display tended to divorce creative practices from their social origins and to neutralize art's historical and political dimensions. The Los Angeles Olympics promoted the idea of culture as a private asset, a lucrative investment, or a consumable form of pleasant entertainment rather than a public good, a way to criticize the status quo, or a way to advocate for the needs of marginalized groups. In its most extreme form, the opening ceremonies absorbed the tensions and complexities of American culture, transforming them into kitsch.

This is not to say that culture was not *political*. The Games were deeply connected to the Cold War. The Soviet invasion of Afghanistan in 1979 marked the end of détente, prompting president Jimmy Carter's decision to boycott the 1980 Games in Moscow. In the years that followed, President Reagan's "Star Wars" missile defense system, US interventions in Latin America, and the Soviet shooting of the Korean passenger plane KAL007 exacerbated and escalated antagonisms between the two superpowers. The USSR refused to participate in the 1984 Olympics, and Reagan understood the success of the Games as critical to America's position in their adversarial standoff. It was an opportunity to assert the strength of American capitalist democracy to the world and brandish the performances of the country's best athletes.

Reagan embodied the tenets of the New Right and advanced the vision of a cohesive nation predicated on the sanctity of individuals, free enterprise, and Cold War militarism. The Reagan administration shared some similarities with the hawkish foreign policies of the Kennedy and Johnson administrations. But Reagan rejected the perceived liberal government excesses and loosening of social norms. The neoliberal theories of University of Chicago economists such as Milton Friedman were increasingly adopted in mainstream political discourse as a way to ensure postindustrial America's hegemony in a time of global competition.[7] The stories Reagan told about the country and its position in the world found a narrative counterpart in 1980s-era Neoclassical Hollywood, which encompassed the "hard body" action-adventure films of Sylvester Stallone, the family melodramas of Steven Spielberg, and the heroic coming-of-age tales of George Lucas. After all, Reagan was a former B movie actor, now elected to the country's highest office thanks to his uncanny ability to persuasively communicate with audiences in person and especially on the screen. He transformed Hollywood plots into policies and, in turn, inflected the output of the film studios.[8]

As deregulation of the telecommunications industries and the rise of cable television led to a search for profitable shows to fill the airwaves, commercial broadcasting saw great potential in turning documentary and public affairs programming into tabloid entertainment. Notable genres included talk shows (*Geraldo* [1987–96]), courtroom dramas (*The People's Court* [1981–]), crime investigations (*America's Most Wanted* [1988–2012], *Cops* [1989–]), and magazine-style news (*20/20* [1978–], *Entertainment Tonight* [1981–], *A Current Affair* [1986–2005], *Unsolved Mysteries* [1987–2002], *Hard Copy* [1989–99], *Inside Edition* [1988–]). These programs fashioned a Manichean moral lens through which people passed judgment on the world around them. In distinguishing for viewers "unsafe" cities from "secure" suburbs, "perpetrators" from "victims," the "innocent" from the "guilty," television shows tended to stereotype working-class and minority communities, often portraying them as a threat.[9]

Docudrama was also crucial to the political culture of the period. It had emerged as a popular genre of prestige television in the mid-1970s and rose to even greater prominence in the subsequent decade. The financial potential of docudrama incentivized stations and Hollywood producers to capitalize on its wide appeal. Docudramas tended to package the recent and more distant past as something emotionally compelling, centered on the family, and relentlessly affirmative. Wolper remained active during this period, turning out productions like *The Thorn Birds* (1983), *Mystic Warrior* (1984), and *North and South* (1985–86). Docudramas of the decade often constituted "pluck and luck" period narratives in which individuals navigate the vicissitudes of romance, friendship, and family. America, according to the logic of docudrama, is a multiethnic place in which people from different groups, whether they came over on an immigrant boat or a slave ship, suffered, but ultimately overcame obstacles and triumphed. Most of these rags-to-riches narratives centered on white individuals and families struggling to climb the economic ladder. Such stories muted the complexity of how opportunity and oppression, individual achievements and social movements, exclusionary laws and protected freedoms coexisted at the heart of the American experience.

With the onset of a conservative political climate and the shift away from broadcasting imperatives, television stations no longer faced the same responsibility to create a space for underserved communities and hard-hitting public affairs programs. Still, social justice documentarians within Los Angeles and across the country managed to sustain the discourses around the needs of minorities and women as well as the abuses of both state and corporate power. Their flexible models of media production proved critical for engaging with issues of affordable housing in cities, criminalization of drug use, historical amnesia, and American military interventions abroad. Documentarians such as Robert Nakamura and Joe Saltzman gained a foothold within universities and went on to educate a new generation of students from the position of faculty-filmmakers. Festivals in Atlanta, Chicago, Los Angeles, New York, and San Antonio offered a venue for Third World, Asian American, and Chicano cinema. New advocacy groups and publications applied pressure on Hollywood studios and the broadcasting industry to diversify their staffs as well as their output. And low-cost, portable video technologies and local public-access television provided a way for marginalized communities to make their voices heard.

At the same time, the defunding of public institutions such as PBS, the National Endowment for the Humanities, and the National Endowment for the Arts, the suppression of left-leaning social movements, and emerging forms of spectacular melodrama for the small and large screen made producing alternative forms of film and television a significant challenge. The left would have to devise new strategies for political organizing. So too would social justice documentarians now have to devise new strategies to contend with a media environment that was increasingly oversaturated with facile programming and lacking in outlets for the kind of progressive and experimental work that had been critical for the nation's consciousness over the previous two decades.

NOTES

INTRODUCTION

1. Erik Daarstad, *Through the Lens of History: The Life Journey of a Cinematographer* (Hope, ID: Plaudit, 2015), 50–51. My knowledge of Daarstad's life and work also stems from telephone conversations we had on December 21, 2011, and May 5, 2014.

2. Erik Daarstad, *Through the Lens of History*, 46–107.

3. Erik Daarstad letter to Kent Mackenzie, February 1964, in Kent Mackenzie, "A Description And Examination of the Production of *The Exiles*: A Film of the Actual Lives of a Group of Young American Indians" (master's thesis, University of Southern California, 1964), 58–59, 64–65. This thesis and other primary documents related to Mackenzie's projects have been organized into The Mackenzie Files, a collection of documents included on the Milestone DVD rerelease of *The Exiles*, directed by Kent Mackenzie (1961; Harrington Park, NJ: Milestone Film and Video, 2009), DVD.

4. "A City—200 Miles Long? The Story of Los Angeles," *US News and World Report*, September 16, 1955, 47.

5. Laura Pulido, *Black, Brown, Yellow, and Left: Radical Activism in Los Angeles* (Berkeley: University of California Press, 2006), 34–58; James P. Allen and Eugene Turner, *The Ethnic Quilt: Population Diversity in Southern California* (Northridge: California State University, Northridge, 1997), 10–42.

6. Richard Dyer MacCann, *Hollywood in Transition* (Boston: Houghton Mifflin, 1962), 10–19, 116.

7. Stephen Mamber, *Cinema Verite in America: Studies in Uncontrolled Documentary* (Cambridge, MA: MIT Press, 1974); P. J. O'Connell, *Robert Drew and the Development of Cinema Verite in America* (Carbondale: Southern Illinois University Press, 1992); Anna Grimshaw and Amanda Ravetz, *Observational Cinema: Anthropology, Film, and the Exploration of Social Life* (Bloomington: Indiana University Press, 2009), 3–50; Dave Saunders,

Direct Cinema: Observational Documentary and the Politics of the Sixties (London: Wall-flower, 2007); Keith Beattie, *D. A. Pennebaker* (Urbana: University of Illinois Press, 2011); Jonathan B. Vogels, *The Direct Cinema of David and Albert Maysles* (Carbondale: Southern Illinois University Press, 2005). Scott MacDonald's innovative account of Cambridge-area filmmaking looks at "ethnographic" and "personal" documentary in and around Harvard, MIT, museums, archives, the high-tech sector, and public media institutions such as WGBH. Scott MacDonald, *American Ethnographic Film and Personal Documentary: The Cambridge Turn* (Berkeley: University of California Press, 2013).

8. Deirdre Boyle, *Subject to Change: Guerrilla Television Revisited* (New York: Oxford University Press, 1997); Chon A. Noriega, *Shot in America: Television, the State, and the Rise of Chicano Cinema* (Minneapolis: University of Minnesota Press, 2000); Devorah Heitner, *Black Power TV* (Durham, NC: Duke University Press, 2013), 83–122; Phyllis R. Klotman and Janet K. Cutler, *Struggles for Representation: African American Documentary Film and Video* (Bloomington: Indiana University Press, 1999); Bill Nichols, "Newsreel: Film and Revolution," (master's thesis, University of California, Los Angeles, 1972); Michael Renov, *The Subject of Documentary* (Minneapolis: University of Minnesota Press, 2004), 3–20; Cynthia Young, *Soul Power: Culture, Radicalism, and the Making of a U.S. Third World Left* (Durham, NC: Duke University Press, 2006).

9. J. D. Connor, *The Studios after the Studios: Neoclassical Hollywood, 1970–2010* (Stanford, CA: Stanford University Press, 2015); Jeff Menne, *Francis Ford Coppola* (Urbana: University of Illinois Press, 2014); Jerome Christensen, *America's Corporate Art: The Studio Authorship of Hollywood Motion Pictures* (Stanford, CA: Stanford University Press, 2012); Thomas Elsaesser et al., eds., *The Last Great American Picture Show: New Hollywood Cinema in the 1970s* (Amsterdam: Amsterdam University Press, 2004); J. Hoberman, *The Dream Life: Movies, Media, and the Mythology of the Sixties* (New York: New Press, 2003); Lynn Spigel, *TV By Design: Modern Art and the Rise of Network Television* (Chicago: University of Chicago Press, 2008).

10. David James, *The Most Typical Avant-Garde: History and Geography of Minor Cinemas in Los Angeles* (Berkeley: University of California Press, 2005), 13.

11. Ibid., 10.

12. For context see James T. Patterson, *Grand Expectations: The United States, 1945–1974* (New York: Oxford University Press, 1996), 458–709; Sidney M. Milkis, "Lyndon Johnson, the Great Society, and the 'Twilight' of the Modern Presidency," in *The Great Society and the High Tide of Liberalism*, ed. Sidney M. Milkis and Jerome M. Mileur (Amherst: University of Massachusetts Press, 2005), 1–47.

13. The team went on to identify eight divisions for public history, including "research organizations," "media," and "historical preservation." "Editor's Preface," *Public Historian* 1, no. 1 (Fall 1978): 4–7. For more on the early years of the professionalization of "public history" see "Special Issue: Public History: State of the Art, 1980," *Public Historian* 2, no. 1 (Fall 1979); David Glassberg, "Public History and the Study of Memory," *Public Historian* 18, no. 2 (Spring 1996): 7–23.

14. Susan Porter Benson, Steve Brier, Robert Entenmann, Warren Goldstein, and Roy Rosenzweig, "Editors' Introduction," *Radical History Review: Presenting the Past: History and the Public*, no. 25 (October 1981): 3–8. This issue became the basis for Susan Porter Benson, Steve Brier, and Roy Rosenzweig's edited volume *Presenting the Past: Essays on*

History and the Public (Philadelphia: Temple University Press, 1986). For more on shifts in history as an academic discipline in the post–World War II era, see Peter Novick, *That Noble Dream: The "Objectivity Question" and the American Historical Profession* (Cambridge, England: Cambridge University Press, 1998), 415–572.

15. Philip Rosen, *Change Mummified: Cinema, Historicity, Theory* (Minneapolis: University of Minnesota Press, 2001), 240.

16. Jonathan Kahana, *Intelligence Work: The Politics of American Documentary* (New York: Columbia University Press, 2008), 143–266.

17. *Los Angeles Documentary* builds on two approaches to twentieth-century Los Angeles historiography: first, investigations that analyze how business elites, urban boosters, and politicians configured the city to concentrate power into the hands of a white and wealthy few; and second, studies of the city that primarily focus on the forms of expressive culture used by women, minorities, and working-class Angelenos to fight for civil rights and maintain communal ties in the face of oppression. For the former, see for example Mike Davis, *City of Quartz: Excavating the Future in Los Angeles* (New York: Vintage, 1990). For the latter, see Dolores Hayden, *The Power of Place: Urban Landscapes as Public History* (Cambridge, MA: MIT Press, 1997). For a bridge between these two approaches see Norman Klein, *The History of Forgetting: Los Angeles and the Erasure of Memory* (London: Verso, 2008).

CHAPTER 1

1. David Wolper quoted in H. Viggo Andersen, "Golden Years of Hollywood Engross Young TV Producer," *Hartford Courant*, November 26, 1961, 3G. A shorter version of this chapter appeared in Josh Glick, "Wolper's New Frontier: Studio Documentary in the Kennedy Era," *Moving Image* 13, no. 2 (Fall 2013): 22–55.

2. "Mr. Documentary," *Time*, December 7, 1962, 65.

3. "All Those Hats," *Time*, December 7, 1962, 16.

4. Frank Joseph Adinolfi Jr.'s master's thesis on Wolper remains the most comprehensive account of the producer and his studio. It is primarily focused on film form and style rather than the cultural context in which the studio operated. Frank Joseph Adinolfi Jr., "An Analytical Study of David L. Wolper's Approach to Television Documentaries" (master's thesis, University of Southern California, 1974). See also A. William Bluem, *Documentary in American Television: Form, Function, Method* (New York: Hastings House, 1965), 176–79, 181, 183, 190–91.

5. Representations of both real and purely fantastic space-age technology had been a mainstay of American popular culture since the late 1940s. Filmmakers allegorized Soviet invasion (*Invaders from Mars* [1953]), nuclear holocaust (*When Worlds Collide* [1951]), and the showdown between American freedom fighters and fascist or communist villains (*Captain Video and His Video Rangers* [1949–55]) through low-budget and effects-savvy entertainment. Sputnik added a new urgency to American-Soviet competition. See Victoria O'Donnell, "Science Fiction Films and Cold War Anxiety," in *Transforming the Screen 1950–1959*, ed. Charles Harpole (New York: Charles Scribner's Sons, 2003), 169–96; M. Keith Booker, *Monsters, Mushroom Clouds, and the Cold War: American Science Fiction and the Roots of Postmodernism, 1946–1964* (Westport, CT: Greenwood, 2001); Megan Prelinger, *Another Science Fiction: Advertising the Space Race 1957–1962* (New York: Blast, 2010).

6. "H'wood in Sputnik Spurt: Register Satellite Titles in New Space Pic Cycle," *Variety*, October 9, 1957, 2, 60.

7. For more on this topic see Lynn Spigel, *Make Room for TV: Television and the Family Ideal in Postwar America* (Chicago: University of Chicago Press, 1992), 26–72. Around 9 percent of households owned a television in 1950, and close to 90 percent owned one by the end of the decade, according to Cobbett S. Steinberg, *TV Facts* (New York: Facts on File, 1980), 142. See also Gene Wyckoff, *The Image Candidates: American Politics in the Age of Television* (New York: Macmillan, 1968), 13. Programming "in the public interest, convenience, and necessity" stems from the Radio Act of 1927, and was given a more aggressive treatment by the FCC in *Public Service Responsibility of Broadcast Licensees* (Washington, DC: US Government Printing Office, 1946): "Public Interest" programming cohered around "sustaining programs" (shows that did not receive commercial funding or money from advertisers), local live programming, programs devoted to public discussion, and the "elimination of commercial advertising excesses" (12).

8. "Stations Hot for Science Films," *Variety*, November 20, 1957, 30; George Rosen, "TV Beep: 'Come In, Eggheads!,'" *Variety*, December 25, 1957, 1; "Sputnik or Not, Yank Space-Research Films Top USIA Popularity List," *Variety*, January 13, 1960, 1. For context see William Boddy, *Fifties Television: The Industry and Its Critics* (Urbana: University of Illinois, 1990), 187–213.

9. "Film Bartering Is Now Big Business," *Broadcasting*, March 11, 1957, 27–28. Flamingo's catalog included everything from the British travel documentary *Let's Visit the Orkney Islands* (1950) to the *Grand Ole Opry* (1955–56) to *Adventures of Superman* (1952–58).

10. David L. Wolper and David Fisher, *Producer: A Memoir* (New York: Scribner, 2003), 15–24; David Wolper interviewed by Morrie Gelman for the Archive of American Television, Los Angeles, May 12, 1998, parts 1 and 2, accessed September 11, 2014, http://www.emmytvlegends.org/interviews/people/david-wolper.

11. In Wolper's memoir he mentions that the encounter occurred in 1957. In the Archive of American Television interview cited in the previous note, he claims that the interaction took place in 1958. Periodicals as well as other official catalogs and tributes suggest that the meeting happened in early 1958.

12. "Wolper Award Specials: Race for Space," p. 7, box 237, folder 003, David L. Wolper Center, Cinematic Arts Library, University of Southern California (hereafter DWC, CAL, USC); David L. Wolper and David Fisher, *Producer: A Memoir*, 29–33.

13. Mel Stuart, interview by Joshua Glick, August 6, 2010, Los Angeles.

14. Frederick H. Guidry, "Race for Space Spotlighted," *Christian Science Monitor*, April 23, 1960, 6; Larry Wolters, "WGN-TV to Show Missile Film Three Networks Turned Down," *Chicago Daily Tribune*, April 24, 1960, S14; Terry Vernon, "Race for Space WILL Be Seen," *Tele*, April 24, 1960, 1; "Controversial TV Show Set for KTVU Airing," *San Mateo Times*, April 16, 1960, 1; "Wolper's Web Gabs on 'Race for Space,'" *Variety*, March 2, 1960, 50; Jack Gould, "Fourth TV 'Network' Assembled to Show a Film Others Barred," *New York Times*, March 21, 1960, 1.

15. Marie Torre, "Networks' Policy Bans Top-Notch Documentary," *New York Herald Tribune*, February 23, 1960, 40.

16. "Space 'Specials' Will Be Offered Soon on Ch. 3," *Hartford Courant*, March 19, 1961, 13G; "Two Films at Library This Week," *Baltimore Sun*, March 4, 1962, A13; "Area Libraries

to Show Film on Space Race," *Los Angeles Times*, December 27, 1962, H4. *The Race for Space* had a limited theatrical run that allowed it to qualify for the Oscars. Because the documentary was such a high-profile project, critics often discussed it as the first Oscar-nominated television documentary. See for instance "Academy Nominees Listed by Complete Categories: Academy List," *Los Angeles Times*, February 23, 1960, 2; Donald Kirkley, "Look and Listen with Donald Kirkley," *Baltimore Sun*, April 27, 1960, 12. However, in 1956, Disney's *Man in Space* (1955) became the first television documentary to be nominated for an Oscar. See advertisement, *New Journal and Guide*, October 6, 1956, 4; Leonard Maltin, "Introduction for *Man in Space*," in *Tomorrowland: Disney in Space and Beyond* (Burbank, CA: Walt Disney Home Entertainment, dist. Buena Vista Home Entertainment, 2004), DVD.

17. W. H. Pickering to David Wolper, June 21, 1960, in Auriel Sanderson, ed., *The Man with the Dream: A Pictorial Tribute to the Life and 50-Year Career of David L. Wolper* (Hong Kong: Warner Bros. Worldwide Publishing, 1999), 30; John F. Kennedy quoted in Michael Patrick Casey, "Pair of Space Specials Earn Wolper JFK Praise," *Santa Monica Evening Outlook*, December 8–15, 1962, 8A, folder 26, box 167, DWC, CAL, USC. See also Robert Anderson, "'Fourth Network' Airs Space Show," *Chicago Daily Tribune*, April 23, 1960, C10; Cecil Smith, "'Race for Space' Forms 4th Web," *Los Angeles Times*, April 25, 1960, A12; "Rep. Holtzman Raps Nets in Space Show Nix," *Variety*, March 2, 1960, 53.

18. Susan Christopherson and Michael Storper, "The City as Studio, the World as Back Lot: The Impact of Vertical Disintegration on the Location of the Motion Picture Industry," *Environment and Planning D: Society and Space* 4, no. 3 (1986): 305–32. See also Thomas Schatz, *The Genius of the System: Hollywood Filmmaking in the Studio Era* (New York: Metropolitan, 1988), 411–92; Mark Alvey, "The Independents: Rethinking the Television Studio System," in *The Revolution Wasn't Televised: Sixties Television and Social Conflict*, ed. Lynn Spigel and Michael Curtin (New York: Routledge, 1997), 139–58.

19. Susan Christopherson and Michael Storper, "Flexible Specialization and Regional Industrial Agglomerations: The Case of the U.S. Motion Picture Industry," *Annals of the Association of American Geographers* 77, no. 1 (1987): 104–17; Michael Storper, "The Transition to Flexible Specialisation in the U.S. Film Industry: External Economies, the Division of Labour, and the Crossing of Industrial Divides," *Cambridge Journal of Economics* 13, no. 2 (1989): 277–90.

20. Map from Morris J. Gelman, "The Hollywood Story," *Television*, September 1963, 34–35.

21. After a brief stay at 9119 Sunset Boulevard, Wolper Productions' first long-term location in Los Angeles was 8720 Sunset Boulevard, starting in August 1960. This latter studio was technically located on the part of the Strip known as Sunset Plaza. "Wolper Prod. in Major Expansion, with Flock of Telementaries on Tap," *Variety*, August 23, 1961, 23; "Wolper Expands," *Variety*, November 15, 1961, 25; "You've Got to Be a Documentary Lover," *Broadcasting*, November 27, 1961, 76–78. Articles can be found in Wolper Productions et al., General Files—Publicity (clippings: to 1967), folder 008, box 165, DWC, CAL, USC. Also see Auriel Sanderson, ed., *Salute to David L. Wolper on his Fortieth Anniversary in the Entertainment Industry* (Washington, DC: AFI and Warner Bros., 1989), 9–56, Special Collections, DWC, CAL, USC.

22. David L. Wolper, "But Don't Get Me Wrong—I Love New York!," in *A Tribute to David L. Wolper*, ed. Raymond Rohauer (New York: Huntington Hartford Gallery of Modern Art,

1966), 20. See also "Wolper-Sterling's 'H'wood & Movies 400G Telementary," *Variety*, July 27, 1960, 1; "Wolper Orbiting into TV Network Programs; Sets Entertainment Segs," *Variety*, May 10, 1961, 30; "Wolper & Turell's Hot Telementary Tandem," *Variety*, June 7, 1961, 34.

23. "Alan Landsburg: Pick a Genre, He's Produced a Hit in It," *Broadcasting*, December 24, 1979, 65.

24. Arthur L. Grey Jr. "Los Angeles Urban Prototype," *Land Economics* 35, no. 3 (1959): 232–42.

25. Editors, "Intro to the World of Los Angeles," *Holiday*, October, 1957, 49. See also Bill Murphy, *Los Angeles: Wonder City of the West* (San Francisco: Fearon, 1959), 34; Bill Murphy, *Dolphin Guide to Los Angeles and Southern California* (Garden City, NY: Dolphin, 1962); *Los Angeles: Industrial Focal Point of the West* (1959), accessed September 10, 2014, http://catalog.hathitrust.org/Record/009386743; Citizens National Bank, "The New World," *Time*, July 15, 1957, 22.

26. 1960 Democratic National Convention official program, 1–108, box 27B, Theodore H. White Personal Papers *The Making of the President: 1960*, Subject Files: Democratic National Convention, John F. Kennedy Presidential Library (JFKPL), Boston.

27. John F. Kennedy, written with aide Theodore C. Sorensen, acceptance speech, Democratic National Convention, Los Angeles Memorial Coliseum, July 15, 1960, accessed September 12, 2012, http://www.jfklibrary.org/Asset-Viewer/AS08q50YzoSFUZg9uOi4iw.aspx. Also see Arthur Schlesinger Jr., "The New Mood in Politics," in *The Politics of Hope and The Bitter Heritage: American Liberalism in the 1960s*, ed. Sean Wilentz (Princeton, NJ: Princeton University Press, 2008), 105–20.

28. Leslie H. Martinson's 1963 cinematic adaptation of the book *PT 109* depicted Kennedy as a confident and conscientious commander during World War II, performing a lifesaving rescue of his crew. For more on Kennedy's relationship to film and television, see Gene Wyckoff, *The Image Candidates* (New York: Macmillan, 1968), 19–59; Joseph P. Berry Jr., *John F. Kennedy and the Media: The First Television President* (Lanham, MD: University Press of America, 1987); Mary Ann Watson, *The Expanding Vista: American Television in the Kennedy Years* (Durham, NC: Duke University Press, 1994), 3–35; J. Hoberman, *The Dream Life: Movies, Media, and the Mythology of the Sixties* (New York: New Press, 2003), 6–8, 17–44; David M. Lubin, *Shooting Kennedy: JFK and the Culture of Images* (Berkeley: University of California Press, 2003); James N. Giglio, *The Presidency of John F. Kennedy* (Lawrence: University Press of Kansas, 2006), 271–95.

29. John F. Kennedy, "A Force That Has Changed the Political Scene," *TV Guide*, November 14, 1959, 5–7. See also John F. Kennedy, "Address at the 39th Annual Convention of the National Association of Broadcasters," reference box 034, Papers of President Kennedy, President's Office Files, JFKPL; John F. Kennedy, speech to the National Association of Broadcasters, May 8, 1961, accessed February 14, 2017, https://www.youtube.com/watch?v=_2j-PchAVLw. Kennedy saw culture and politics more generally as working together to strengthen a democracy. For example, see John F. Kennedy, "The Arts in America," in *Creative America*, ed. Jerry Mason (New York: Ridge, 1962), 4–8.

30. Newton N. Minow, "Television and the Public Interest," address to the National Association of Broadcasters, May 9, 1961, reprinted as an appendix in Newton N. Minow and Craig L. LaMay, *Abandoned in the Wasteland: Children, Television, and the First Amendment* (New York: Hill and Wang, 1995), 188.

31. Anna McCarthy, *The Citizen Machine: Governing by Television in 1950s America* (New York: New Press, 2010), 1–38, 243–52.

32. Michael Curtin, *Redeeming the Wasteland: Television Documentary and Cold War Politics* (New Brunswick, NJ: Rutgers University Press, 1995), 1–34, 180–96.

33. Cecil Smith, "The Two Hats of Producer Wolper," *Los Angeles Times*, November 11, 1963, D16.

34. Coverage of the program included Courier News Service, "Documentary Film Set on R. Johnson," *Pittsburgh Courier*, May 20, 1961, A18; Calla Scrivner, "Rafer Johnson's Life-Film Slated," *New Journal and Guide*, June 3, 1961, 18; "Rafer Johnson on TV," *New York Amsterdam News*, September 2, 1961, 17; Richard F. Shepard, "Story of a Champion," *New York Times*, September 14, 1961, 63. Johnson went on to serve as an official delegate on Robert Kennedy's presidential ticket in 1968. He was at his side when Kennedy was assassinated outside the Ambassador Hotel in Los Angeles and wrestled the gun away from Sirhan Sirhan. Johnson also had a productive career in Hollywood, appearing in *The Sins of Rachel Cade* (1961), *The Fiercest Heart* (1961), *None but the Brave* (1965), and *Tarzan and the Great River* (1967). For more on his movies see Rafer Johnson and Philip Goldberg, *The Best That I Can Be: An Autobiography* (New York: Doubleday, 1998), 162–68.

35. "'Escape to Freedom' Wolper Entry for USIA," *Variety*, February 13, 1963, 27. See also "You've Got to Be a Documentary Lover," *Broadcasting*, November 27, 1961, 76–78; "USIA Buys Show," *Broadcasting*, December 25, 1961, 49; Wolper Productions et al., General Files—Publicity (Misc.), 165–019, DWC, CAL, USC; Malvin Wald, "Shootout at the Beverly Hills Corral," *Journal of Popular Film and Television* 19, no. 3 (1991): 138–40; Kenneth W. Heger, "Race Relations in the United States and American Cultural and Informational Programs in Ghana, 1957–66," *Prologue* 31, no. 4 (1999): 256–65; Philip K. Scheuer, "Disney Will Revive 'Emil and Detective,'" *Los Angeles Times*, June 24, 1963, D11. At first filmmakers at Wolper Productions shot with 16mm German Arriflex and American Auricon cameras. They soon switched to French Éclair NPR cameras for greater flexibility with shooting sync-sound.

36. Don Page, "Willie Davis Gets His Late Innings," *Los Angeles Times*, September 30, 1961, B5.

37. Bill, "Biography of a Rookie," *Variety*, May 10, 1961, 39. See also "'Biography of a Rookie' to Be Seen," *Van Nuys News*, September 24, 1961, 34-A. James Wong Howe was an esteemed participant on *Biography of a Rookie*, but he was uncomfortable with the fast-paced and streamlined format of commercial television. His assistant, Vilis Lapenieks, adapted well to the environment.

38. A. S. "Doc" Young, "Willie Davis: Television Star," *Los Angeles Sentinel*, September 28, 1961, B11.

39. "Wolper Maps Series of 30-Min. Filmbiogs," *Variety*, October 18, 1961, 29; "'Biography' Segs for So. America," *Variety*, February 14, 1962, 27; "Of-Wolper 'Biog' Hot Syndie Item," *Variety*, April 25, 1962, 24; John C. Waugh, "Wolper Builds on Fact Hunger," *Christian Science Monitor*, May 9, 1962, 6; "Biography Plans Its Second Year," *Broadcasting*, June 4, 1962, 66; Francis Coughlin, "'Biography' Unique: Emphasis Is on Man!," *Chicago Daily Tribune*, January 29, 1963, A4; Val Adams, "Peabody Awards to 18 Announced," *New York Times*, April 25, 1963, 67; Cecil Smith, "Minow Successor Sits for 'Portrait,'" *Los Angeles Times*, June 5, 1963, D18.

40. Advertisement, *Variety*, April 18, 1962, 41.

41. The show was discussed in "Rommel Film," *Los Angeles Times*, March 2, 1962, C14; "D-Day Will Be Relived in TV Film Documentary," *Hartford Courant*, May 20, 1962, 11H; Robert E. Stansfield, "State GOP Convention among Week's Reports," *Hartford Courant*, June 3, 1962, 2G.

42. "Zanuck Calls All D-Day Film 'Fake,'" *Variety*, January 31, 1962, 1. See also Andrew Marton interviewed by Lawrence H. Suid, July 21, 1975, quoted in Lawrence H. Suid, *Guts and Glory: The Making of the American Military Image in Film* (Lexington: University Press of Kentucky, 2002), 169.

43. "Refute Zanuck on D-Day Film," *Variety*, February 7, 1962, 4.

44. Tube, "Tele Review," *Variety*, June 20, 1962, 39; "The Year's Ten Best," *Time*, January 4, 1963, 6. For more on the film and its reception see Bosley Crowther, "Premiere of 'The Longest Day,'" *New York Times*, October 5, 1962, 28; Philip K. Scheuer, "'The Longest Day' Is Also the Biggest," *Los Angeles Times*, October 12, 1962, D13; Donald Kirkley, "Look and Listen with Donald Kirkley," *Baltimore Sun*, June 4, 1962, 6; "D-Day Available," *Broadcasting*, March 11, 1963, 58.

45. Morris J. Gelman, "A Tale of Two Once-Out Companies Spending This Season Very Much In," *Television*, September 1963, 80; George Laine, "Tiny Wolper Firm Pushing Big Networks," *Santa Monica Evening Outlook*, December 8–15, 1962, 3A–9A, folder 26, box 167, DWC, CAL, USC.

46. Cecil Smith, "Educational Television for L.A. on the Way," *Los Angeles Times*, February 17, 1963, L3. See also Ernest Kreiling, "ETV for Los Angeles?," *Los Angeles Magazine*, November 1961, 56.

47. "Will 1962 Be Documentary Year?," *Broadcasting*, December 25, 1961, 19–22. The fact that the networks continued to keep a tight hold over news coverage of foreign policy encouraged Wolper in the direction of cultural history.

48. Robert Drew quoted in P. J. O'Connell, *Robert Drew and the Development of Cinema Verite in America* (Carbondale: Southern Illinois University Press, 1992), 95–97, 100–109. The organization, like Wolper Productions, was primarily comprised of white men. The few women who worked there mainly recorded sound. For more on Drew Associates see Robert Drew, Richard Leacock, and D. A. Pennebaker interviewed by Gideon Bachmann, "The Frontiers of Realist Cinema: the Work of Ricky Leacock" *Film Culture*, nos. 22/23 (Summer 1961): 14–18; Robert Drew, "See It Then: Notes on Television Journalism," *Nieman Reports* 9, no. 2 (April 1955): 2, 34–37. For more on how "direct cinema" was discussed at the time, see Maxine Haleff, "The Maysles Brothers and 'Direct Cinema,'" *Film Comment* 2, no. 2 (1964): 19–23; James Blue, "Thoughts on Cinéma Vérité and a Discussion with the Maysles Brothers," *Film Comment* 2, no. 4 (1965): 22–30; Richard Leacock, interview by James Blue, "One Man's Truth," *Film Comment* 3, no. 2 (1965): 15–22.

49. Drew Associates' film practice at times created moments of ideological instability and provoked network controversy with programs such as *Yanki No!* (1960), which gave voice to Cuban citizens expressing admiration for Fidel Castro and dislike of the United States. Val Adams, "Daly Quits ABC in Policy Battle," *New York Times*, November 17, 1960, 75; Percy Shain, "Night Watch: Anti-Americanism Eyed in Flashy Documentary," *Boston Globe*, December 8, 1960, 46; "Cuban Lashes TV Movie as Pro-Russian," *Chicago Tribune*, December 12, 1960, 27; Herm, "Yanki, No!," *Variety*, December 14, 1960, 27.

50. "The New Life in Old Film," *Broadcasting*, December 9, 1963, 27–30; "Wolper Productions Buys Paramount News," *Broadcasting*, February 11, 1963, 28; "Wolper Par News Buy for $500,000," *Variety*, February 6, 1963, 28.

51. Philip Rosen, *Change Mummified: Cinema, Historicity, Theory* (Minneapolis: University of Minnesota Press, 2001), 225–40.

52. For further analysis of journalists' coverage of Kennedy's assassination and the aftermath, see Barbie Zelizer, *Covering the Body: The Kennedy Assassination, the Media, and the Shaping of Collective Memory* (Chicago: University of Chicago Press, 1992); Christopher Lasch, "The Life of Kennedy's Death: How the Mythology of Kennedy's Assassination Sustains the Mythology of His Career," *Harper's Magazine*, October 1983, 32–36, 38–40; Aniko Bodroghkozy, "Black Weekend: A Reception History of Network Television News and the Assassination of John F. Kennedy," *Television and New Media* 14, no. 6 (2012): 565–78.

53. P. J. O'Connell, *Robert Drew and the Development of Cinema Verite in America*, 62–73, 168–95, 199–201.

54. Norman Mailer, "Superman Comes to the Supermarket," *Esquire*, November 1960, 120.

55. Theodore H. White, *The Making of the President: 1960* (New York: Harper Collins, 1961). For more on White and the Cold War consensus, see Joyce Hoffmann, *Theodore H. White and Journalism as Illusion* (Columbia: University of Missouri Press, 1995).

56. Theodore H. White, *The Making of the President: 1960*, 293. Read more at "'Making of President' Rights Go to Wolper: Two Documentaries Set," *Variety*, February 14, 1962, 42; "Susskind Gives Up Rights to 'Making of President,'" *Los Angeles Times*, February 19, 1962, C13; "'Making of President' as 2 Full-Hr. Specials on Mel Stuart Agenda," *Variety*, March 20, 1963, 30; "Wolper's 470G for a 2-Parter," *Variety*, May 22, 1963, 39; Cecil Smith, "'President, 1960' Film Shaping Up," *Los Angeles Times*, August 19, 1963, C14.

57. Daniel J. Boorstin, *The Image: A Guide to Pseudo-Events in America* (New York: Vintage, 1961), 41–44.

58. Theodore H. White, "Finding Visual Truth in History," *New York Times*, December 29, 1963, 61; William T. Cartwright, interview by Joshua Glick, August 5, 2010, Los Angeles.

59. Theodore H. White, "One Wished for a Cry, a Sob . . . Any Human Sound," *Life*, November 29, 1963, 32E; Theodore H. White (written in consultation with Jacqueline Kennedy), "For President Kennedy: An Epilogue," *Life*, December 6, 1963, 158–59.

60. Cecil Smith, "Kennedy Political Saga Will Unfold," *Los Angeles Times*, December 23, 1963, B10.

61. John Tebbel, "The Making of a President: Politics and Mass Communication in America," in *TV As Art: Some Essays in Criticism*, ed. Patrick D. Hazard (Champaign, IL: National Council of Teachers of English, 1966), 16–17. See also David L. Wolper and David Fisher, *Producer: A Memoir*, 72–77; Jack Gould, "TV: The Campaign of '60: ABC Shows an Absorbing Adaptation of White's 'Making of the President,'" *New York Times*, December 30, 1963, 41.

62. "Assassination Film Premieres Oct. 6," *Philadelphia Tribune*, September 22, 1964, 6.

63. Marlyn E. Aycock, "Film on Assassination of Kennedy Is Dramatic," *Chicago Tribune*, October 8, 1964, D11.

64. "Kennedy Assassination Documentary: Strictly Dignified Promo Strategy," *Variety*, October 7, 1964, 18.

65. Myrow quoted in "'Four Days' Big on Research," *Boston Globe*, October 4, 1964, A61.

66. Advertisement, *Washington Post*, October 9, 1964, B11.

67. Mae Tinee, "Film Depicts Final Hours of Kennedy," *Chicago Tribune*, October 15, 1964, D8; Alex Freeman, "Kim Novak Upsets English Village," *Hartford Courant*, October 14, 1964, 24.

68. Carey McWilliams, "The Making of the Legend," *Book Week*, May 3, 1964, 15.

CHAPTER 2

1. Kent Mackenzie, "A Description and Examination of the Production of *The Exiles*: A Film of the Actual Lives of a Group of Young American Indians" (master's thesis, University of Southern California, 1964), 9. This thesis and other primary documents related to Mackenzie's projects have been organized into The Mackenzie Files, a collection of documents included on the Milestone DVD rerelease of *The Exiles*, directed by Kent Mackenzie (1961; Harrington Park, NJ: Milestone Film and Video, 2009), DVD.

2. *Film Quarterly* 15, no. 3 (Spring 1962): cover.

3. Brian Henderson, introduction to *Film Quarterly: Forty Years—A Selection*, ed. Brian Henderson, Ann Martin, and Lee Amazonas (Berkeley: University of California Press, 1999), 1–8; Eric Smoodin, introduction to *Hollywood Quarterly: Film Culture in Postwar America, 1945–1957*, ed. Eric Smoodin and Ann Martin (Berkeley: University of California Press, 2002), xi–xxiii.

4. Thom Andersen, "This Property Is Condemned," *Film Comment* 44, no. 4 (2008): 39. Thom Andersen directed and wrote *Los Angeles Plays Itself*, and it was edited by Yoo Seung-Hyun (2003; Submarine Entertainment, Cinema Guild, 2014), DVD. Cindy Rowell of Milestone saw Andersen's film and contacted company founders Dennis Doros and Amy Heller about distributing *The Exiles*. The artist Pamela Peters drew heavily on the film for her own documentary project *Legacy of Exiled NDNZ* (2014), which shrewdly explores the impact of urban relocation on the contemporary lives of American Indians in Los Angeles.

5. Kent Mackenzie quoted in "Personal Creation in Hollywood: Can It Be Done?," *Film Quarterly* 15, no. 3 (1962): 33.

6. According to *Variety*, Pressey had "the film factory gates thrown open to him" during a six-month stay. "Dartmouth Pushes Thalberg Course to Prime Students for Film Careers," *Variety*, August 17, 1938, 4.

7. Thomas Fensch, *Films on the Campus* (New York: A. S. Barnes and Company, 1970); Dana Polan, *Scenes of Instruction: The Beginnings of the US Study of Film* (Berkeley: University of California Press, 2007), 175–235.

8. Heather Oriana Petrocelli, "Portland's 'Refugee from Occupied Hollywood': Andries Deinum, His Center for the Moving Image, and Film Education in the United States" (master's thesis, Portland State University, 2012), 18–41; Hans Schoots, *Living Dangerously: A Biography of Joris Ivens* (Amsterdam: Amsterdam University Press, 2000), 159, 167, 172, 179, 182.

9. Andries Deinum, review of Larry Ceplair and Steven Englund, *The Inquisition in Hollywood: Politics in the Film Community: 1930–1960*, *Film Quarterly* 34, no. 2 (1980–81): 60.

10. Andries Deinum, *Speaking for Myself: A Humanist Approach to Adult Education for a Technical Age* (Brookline, MA: Center for the Study of Liberal Education for Adults, 1966),

20. This text was previously published as "The Teaching and Use of Film as Film," and originally as "Memorandum to the Development and Evaluation Committee," G.E.D., November 20, 1962.

11. Kent Mackenzie, "A Description and Examination of the Production of *The Exiles*," 10–14.

12. Andries Deinum quoted in Martin Hall, "Decline of a University," *American Socialist* 3, no. 1 (1956): 22.

13. Jim Karayn, "Cinema Instructor 'Uncooperative' with House Committee," *Daily Trojan*, September 22, 1955, 1; "Mild Red Hearings," *Variety*, July 6, 1955, 2.

14. Martin Hall, "Decline of a University," 22.

15. Filmmaker George Stoney tried to arrange for Deinum to teach at City College of New York, but came up against overwhelming administrative resistance. Lester Beck helped arrange for Mackenzie to teach in the more politically tolerant Pacific Northwest. Erik Daarstad, *Through the Lens of History: The Life Journey of a Cinematographer* (Hope, ID: Plaudit, 2015), 52–53; Andries Deinum, *Speaking for Myself*, 1–7, 19–21, 62–75, 86–94; Heather Oriana Petrocelli, "Portland's 'Refugee from Occupied Hollywood,'" 18–41.

16. Students at USC at this time frequently shot on 16mm Bell and Howell or Mitchell cameras. *A Light for John* (1957) was a noteworthy film made by Mackenzie's peers that also shows Deinum's influence. Warren Brown and Erik Daarstad's documentary focused on a mentally disabled US Air Force veteran living three blocks north of USC with his elderly mother. The film follows John as he sells newspapers near the corner of University Avenue and Jefferson Boulevard, and the parallel experiences of his mother, who sews, shops, and takes care of the family finances.

17. Eric Avila, *Popular Culture in the Age of White Flight: Fear and Fantasy in Suburban Los Angeles* (Berkeley: University of California Press, 2004), 77. See also Jim Dawson, *Los Angeles's Bunker Hill: Pulp Fiction's Mean Streets and Film Noir's Ground Zero!* (Charleston, SC: History Press, 2012); Edward Dimendberg, *Film Noir and the Spaces of Modernity* (Cambridge, MA: Harvard University Press, 2004), 151–65; Mike Davis, *Dead Cities, and Other Tales* (New York: New Press, 2002), 127–41.

18. See for example Robert E. Alexander and Drayton S. Bryant, *Rebuilding a City: A Study of Redevelopment Problems in Los Angeles* (Los Angeles: Haynes Foundation, 1951), 44–45.

19. Wilkinson used the film to rally religious congregations, minority groups, organized labor, and government officials around public housing. *And Ten Thousand More* production files, USC School of Cinematic Arts, Hugh M. Hefner Moving Image Archive. See also Robert Sherrill, *First Amendment Felon: The Story of Frank Wilkinson, His 132,000-Page FBI File, and His Epic Fight for Civil Rights and Liberties* (New York: Nation, 2005), 69–76; "Housing Authority Will Address YMCA Forum," *Los Angeles Sentinel*, December 7, 1950, A3; Don Wheeldin and Jack Young, "Minorities Attacked as Council Reaches Housing Plan Showdown," *Daily People's World*, December 27, 1951, 3.

20. Don Parson, *Making a Better World: Public Housing, the Red Scare and the Direction of Modern Los Angeles* (Minneapolis: University of Minnesota Press, 2005), 137–62.

21. "'Campus Produced' Awards," *Variety*, March 13, 1957, 12; Frances Stevenson, "Two SC Films Win Top National Awards," *Daily Trojan*, March 5, 1957, 1; Marilee Milroy, "Two SC Movies Win 'Look' Award," *Daily Trojan*, March 8, 1957, 1, 6; Edwin Schallert, "Producers Guild Honors Student Film Creators," *Los Angeles Times*, March 5, 1957, 21; letter from Robert

O. Hall to Margaret Herrick, January 2, 1957, 1, *Bunker Hill–1956* production files, USC School of Cinematic Arts, Hugh M. Hefner Moving Image Archive; "*Bunker Hill–1956* Press Advertisement," part of the digital press kit for the documentary in the Mackenzie Files.

22. "Parthenon Pictures—Hollywood," *Business Screen Magazine: Production Review* 18, no. 1 (1957): 32–33; *Business Screen Magazine: Production Review* 19, no. 1 (1958): 153–54. See also Rick Prelinger, *The Field Guide to Sponsored Films* (San Francisco: National Film Preservation Foundation, 2006), vi–xi; Leo C. Beebe, "Industry," in *Sixty Years of 16mm Film* (Des Plaines, IL: Film Council of America, 1954), 88–98; Devin Orgeron, Marsha Orgeron, and Dan Streible, "A History of Learning with the Lights Off," in *Learning with the Lights Off: Educational Film in the United States*, ed. Devin Orgeron, Marsha Orgeron, and Dan Streible (Oxford: Oxford University Press, 2012), 15–66.

23. Dorothy Van de Mark, "The Raid on the Reservations," *Harper's Magazine*, March 1956, 48–53.

24. Sherburne F. Cook, *The Population of the California Indians, 1769–1970* (Berkeley: University of California Press, 1976), 56–57.

25. Ned Blackhawk, "I Can Carry on from Here: The Relocation of American Indians to Los Angeles," *Wicazo Sa Review* 11, no. 2 (1995): 18.

26. By 1970 there were close to twenty-five thousand American Indians living in Los Angeles. Thomas Clarkin, *Federal Indian Policy in the Kennedy and Johnson Administrations, 1961–1969* (Albuquerque: University of New Mexico Press, 2001), 44–80; Nicolas G. Rosenthal, *Reimagining Indian Country: Native American Migration and Identity in Twentieth-Century Los Angeles* (Chapel Hill: University of North Carolina Press, 2012), 49–101; Joan Weibel-Orlando, *Indian Country, L.A.: Maintaining Ethnic Community in Complex Society* (Urbana: University of Illinois Press, 1999), 12–15; Sherburne F. Cook, *The Population of the California Indians, 1769–1970* (Berkeley: University of California Press, 1976), 56–57.

27. Kent Mackenzie, "*The Exiles* Funding Proposal," October 15, 1956, 6, Mackenzie Files.

28. Ibid., 1–11; Kent Mackenzie, "A Description and Examination of the Production of *The Exiles*," 1–33, 137–40.

29. For more on the equipment see *The Exiles* press book, 1–17; and Kent Mackenzie, "A Description and Examination of the Production of *The Exiles*," 57–109, both in the Mackenzie Files.

30. Paul Rotha, *Documentary Film: The Use of the Film Medium to Interpret Creatively and in Social Terms the Life of the People as It Exists in Reality* (New York: Hastings House, 1968), 150–86.

31. Kent Mackenzie, "A Description and Examination of the Production of *The Exiles*," 35.

32. Ibid., 15–19, 128–29, 34–81; *The Exiles* press kit, 9–11, Mackenzie Files; John Morrill, phone interviews by Joshua Glick, January 12, 2012, and May 7, 2014; Erik Daarstad, phone interview by Joshua Glick, May 5, 2014; Burt Prelutsky, "The Film Club Boom," *Los Angeles Magazine*, September 1961, 40–41.

33. Early accounts of *The Exiles* as well as later scholarly articles list the tribal affiliations of each of the main characters. In these, Tommy is sometimes listed as "Mexican" and sometimes as "Mexican and Indian."

34. Kevin Lynch, *The Image of the City* (Cambridge, MA: MIT Press, 1960), 1–13, 32–43.

35. David James, *The Most Typical Avant-Garde: History and Geography of Minor Cinemas in Los Angeles* (Berkeley: University of California Press, 2005), 294–96; Norman Klein, *The*

History of Forgetting: Los Angeles and the Erasure of Memory (London: Verso, 1997), 248; Catherine Russell, "The Restoration of *The Exiles*, the Untimeliness of Archival Cinema," *Screening the Past*, 2012, accessed May 1, 2016, http://www.screeningthepast.com/2012/08/the-restoration-of-the-exiles-the-untimeliness-of-archival-cinema/. For more on urban planning and displacement in the 1950s and 1960s see Don Parson, *Making a Better World*, 137–62.

36. Richard Slotkin, *Gunfighter Nation: The Myth of the Frontier in Twentieth-Century America* (Norman: University of Oklahoma Press, 1998), 472–73, 441–533. This period also saw some more sympathetic films that spoke to civil rights and antiwar debates. However, this latter subset, as Slotkin notes, were "outweighed in number, popularity, and scale by movies that emphasized Indian savagery and the inevitability of wars of extermination" (472). See also Jacquelyn Kilpatrick, *Celluloid Indians: Native Americans and Film* (Lincoln: University of Nebraska Press, 1999), 1–70; Edward Buscombe, *"Injuns!" Native Americans in the Movies* (Cornwall, England: Reaktion, 2006), 23–99.

37. John F. Kennedy, introduction to William Brandon, *The American Heritage Book of Indians*, ed. Alvin M. Josephy Jr. (New York: American Heritage, 1961), 7–8.

38. William Brandon in ibid., 413.

39. Kent Mackenzie, "A Description and Examination of the Production of *The Exiles*," 105–6.

40. Don Parson, *Making a Better World*, 163–86; "TV's Major Role in Dodgers Ballot," *Variety*, June 11, 1958, 38.

41. Mosk, "*The Exiles*," *Variety*, August 30, 1961, 6; "Venice, Vidi, Vice for Newcomers," *Variety*, August 30, 1961, 7. See also "15th Art Festival Opens in Edinburgh," *Baltimore Sun*, August 21, 1961, 13; Penelope Gilliatt, "Resnais on the Lido," *Observer*, September 3, 1961, 22; Robert F. Hawkins, "Postscripts from the Venice Film Festival," *New York Times*, September 10, 1961, X9; Gene Moskowitz, "Avant Garde Indies Defend US Honor in Venice Rundown of Int'l Pic Talents," *Variety*, September 13, 1961, 22.

42. Kent Mackenzie and Erik Daarstad, press kit, 3–17, Mackenzie Files.

43. The William J. Speed quote appears in ibid., 3; Benjamin Jackson, "*The Exiles*," *Film Quarterly* 15, no. 3 (1962): 60–62.

44. Kent Mackenzie, "A Description and Examination of the Production of *The Exiles*," 156–61.

45. Malvin Wald, "Profile of a Filmmaker," *Journal of the University Film Producers Association* 16, no. 2 (1964): 21–22, 26; Bob Thomas, "Newcomer Makes Haunting Picture," *Daily Review*, July 30, 1962, 20. See also Thomas McDonald, "A Cinema Saga of the 'Vanishing American,'" *New York Times*, March 12, 1961, X7; Erwin Bach, "U. of C. Midwest Film Festival Begins," *Chicago Tribune*, April 25, 1963, N12; Matt Weinstock, "Scene Is Always Changing for America's Lost Indians," *Washington Post*, June 24, 1962, G3. A 16mm copy of *The Exiles* did begin to circulate in a limited capacity to film societies and classrooms toward mid-decade, although there is little mention of this in news periodicals, magazines, or the industry trade press.

46. Jonas Mekas, "Cinema of the New Generation," *Film Culture* 21 (1960): 8.

47. Kent Mackenzie quoted in Lois Dickert, "How to Finance a Movie," *Los Angeles Magazine*, June 1962, 60.

48. Ross Lipman, "Kent Mackenzie's *The Exiles*: Reinventing the Real of Cinema," in *Alternative Projections: Experimental Film in Los Angeles, 1945–1980*, ed. David James and Adam Hyman (Bloomington: Indiana University Press, 2015), 163–74.

49. Advertisement, *Variety*, April 18, 1962, 41.

50. Donald Kirkley, "Look and Listen," *Baltimore Sun*, February 12, 1965, 22; Percy Shain, "The Way Out Men Really 'Way Out,'" *Boston Globe*, February 15, 1965, 21; Rick Du Brow, "Documentary Captures Excitement of Research," *Oxnard Press-Courier*, February 15, 1965, 16.

51. Jack Gould, "'Teen-Age Revolution' Shown on ABC," *New York Times*, October 31, 1965, 78; Les, "Teenage Revolution," *Variety*, November 3, 1965, 33.

52. USIA mission statement quoted in Paul P. Kennedy, "Eisenhower Gives Information Plan to Reassure World on U.S. Aims," *New York Times*, October 29, 1953, 1.

53. Edward R. Murrow quoted in "Murrow Hits House Cut in USIA Funds," *Washington Post*, June 20, 1963, A8. See also Richard Dyer MacCann, *The People's Films: A Political History of U.S. Government Motion Pictures* (New York: Hastings House, 1973), 173–200; Wilson P. Dizard Jr., *Inventing Public Diplomacy: The Story of the U.S. Information Agency* (London: Lynne Rienner, 2004), 63–101; Caryl Rivers, "America's New Picture Abroad," *Baltimore Sun*, March 8, 1964, D3.

54. Jean White, "Luster Rubbed Off on USIA," *Washington Post*, March 15, 1964, E1.

55. "Progress Committee Report for 1962," *Journal of the Society of Motion Picture and Television Engineers* 72 (May 1963): 373. Some films produced for commercial purposes were then used by the USIA abroad. For coverage of USIA films in the press, see for example Bosley Crowther, "Films for Democracy," *New York Times*, October 27, 1963, 113; Richard F. Shepard, "Beaming an Image of America to the World," *New York Times*, January 1, 1961, X9; "Murrow Will Seek to Bolster USIA 'On Basis of Truth,'" *New York Times*, January 30, 1961, 1; Francis M. Rackemann Jr., "Getting America's Story Across," *Baltimore Sun*, August 13, 1961, FE1; Dante B. Fascell, Chairman of the Subcommittee, *Winning the Cold War: The U.S. Ideological Offensive: Hearings before the Subcommittee on International Organizations and Movements of the Committee on Foreign Affairs House of Representatives, Eighty-Eighth Congress, First Session*, part 1 (Washington, DC: US Government Printing Office, 1963/64), 16–23; Arthur Schlesinger Jr., "Washington: Fantasy and Reality," *Show*, April 1964, 41.

56. Richard Dyer MacCann, *The People's Films*, 152–72; George Stevens Jr. quoted in Caryl Rivers, "America's New Picture Abroad," *Baltimore Sun*, March 8, 1964, D3.

57. George Stevens Jr. quoted in Murry Schumach, "USIA to Assist Young Directors," *New York Times*, July 13, 1962, 13.

58. Gary Goldsmith, interview by Joshua Glick, June 3, 2014, Los Angeles, and email correspondence, June 21, 2016; Terry Sanders, phone interview by Joshua Glick, January 6, 2017.

59. "Govt. Inagurates [sic] Film Talent Hunt," *Los Angeles Sentinel*, July 23, 1964, B5; Lyndon B. Johnson, address at the centennial commencement of Swarthmore College, June 8, 1964, accessed December 6, 2014, http://www.presidency.ucsb.edu/ws/?pid=26300; "Five Filmmakers Win Government Agency Contract," *Boston Globe*, September 22, 1964, 15; Nicholas J. Cull, "Auteurs of Ideology: USIA Documentary Film Propaganda in the Kennedy Era as Seen in Bruce Herschensohn's *The Five Cities of June* (1963) and James Blue's *The March* (1964)," *Film History* 10, no. 3 (1998): 295–310; Nicholas J. Cull, *The Cold War and the United States Information Agency: American Propaganda and Public Diplomacy, 1945–1989* (Cambridge, England: Cambridge University Press, 2008), 189–254.

60. Gordon Hitchens, "An Interview with George Stevens Jr.," *Film Comment* 1, no. 3 (1962): 5. The 35mm Arriflex camera was commonly used among USIA filmmakers in

the early 1960s. As the decade progressed, the 16mm French Éclair NPR became more favored.

61. Jennifer Horne, "Experiments in Propaganda: Reintroducing James Blue's Colombia Trilogy," *Moving Image* 9, no. 1 (2009): 196.

62. "Visual Arts Lecture Series to Include 4 USIA Films," *New York Times*, February 23, 1965, 40; Jillynn Molina, daughter of Arnold Molina, phone interview by Joshua Glick, June 28, 2016.

63. *The Exiles* got commercial distribution in 1966. "*The Exiles* to Be Released," *New York Times*, January 12, 1966, 28; Kevin Thomas, "Exiles Portrays Indian Life in L.A.," *Los Angeles Times*, June 15, 1967, E12. Mackenzie worked on a number of media projects with varying success before his early death in 1980. His Ford Foundation–backed film about a flamenco guitarist never got off the ground, nor was his 430-page literary manuscript about his time with a wandering California youth ever published or adapted into a film. Mackenzie worked alongside some of his old Wolper Productions colleagues on Saul Bass's *Why Man Creates* (1968). He also made a feature-length, theatrically released observational documentary for Columbia titled *Saturday Morning* (1971) about a group retreat of California teenagers, who over the course of six days talk about their families, friendships, and outlook on the world.

CHAPTER 3

1. I use "uprising" to imply that the unrest in Watts constituted a form of social protest against abusive commercial and political power. This line of interpretation follows how journalists, intellectuals, and scholars use "Uprising" or "Rebellion" to write about the unrest in contrast to the mainstream media's preponderant use of the word "riot" to imply an irrational and violent disturbance. For an in-depth account of the causes, events, and impact surrounding the uprising see Gerald Horne, *Fire This Time: The Watts Uprising and the 1960s* (New York: Da Capo, 1995), 45–167.

2. The Central City Committee had created numerous versions of the Centropolis Plan during the early 1960s. The plan aimed to create a constellation of administrative buildings, tourist sites, high-end apartments, and cultural attractions in the downtown area. Walter J. Braunschweiger, Chair of the Central City Committee, *Centropolis* (Los Angeles: Los Angeles Central City Committee, 1964). Earlier drafts were created in 1960, 1962, and 1963. Mike Davis, *Dead Cities, and Other Tales* (New York: New Press, 2002), 147–54. The Watts Uprising derailed such plans. The uprising resulted in ten million dollars in property damage, more than one thousand injuries, and thirty-four deaths (twenty-eight of whom were black individuals). The uprising covered an area of forty-six square miles, with much of the conflict concentrated in the Watts-Willowbrook neighborhood. Gerald Horne, *Fire This Time*, 3–6.

3. Lyndon B. Johnson, *My Hope for America* (New York: Random House, 1964), 51. Johnson first mentioned the Great Society in a May 7, 1964, speech at Ohio University, followed by a more in-depth elaboration in a May 22, 1964, commencement address at the University of Michigan.

4. John A. McCone, Chair, *Violence in the City—An End or a Beginning? A Report by the Governor's Commission on the Los Angeles Riots* (Los Angeles: Commission on the Los Angeles Riots, 1965).

5. Daniel Patrick Moynihan, *The Negro Family: The Case for National Action* (repr.; Westport, CT: Greenwood, 1981).

6. Stuart Schulberg, "Of All People," *Hollywood Quarterly* 4, no. 2 (Winter 1949): 206–8; Stuart Schulberg, "Making Marshall Plan Movies," *Film News* (September 1951): 10, 19; Tom Mascaro, *Into the Fray: How NBC's Washington Documentary Unit Reinvented the News* (Washington, DC: Potomac, 2012), xvii, 19–61.

7. Daniel Widener, *Black Arts West: Culture and Struggle in Postwar Los Angeles* (Durham, NC: Duke University Press, 2010), 90–114.

8. Budd Schulberg, "One Year Later: Still the Angry Voices (and Tears) of Watts," *New York Times*, August 14, 1966, 105; Hal Humphrey, "Budd Finds Talent Jackpot in Watts," *Los Angeles Times*, August 16, 1966, C14; Stuart Schulberg, "Watts Happening in TV?," *Variety*, January 4, 1967, 83, 104.

9. George Gent, "NBC to Broadcast Writings of Watts Negroes," *New York Times*, June 28, 1966, 91.

10. Percy Shain, "Watts Documentary Hits Hard," *Boston Globe*, August 17, 1966, 14.

11. Poppy Cannon White, "The Poet Voices of Watts," *New York Amsterdam News*, August 27, 1966, 15.

12. Val Adams, "Watts Writers Move Ahead," *New York Times*, October 9, 1966, X21; Walter Burrell, "It Happened in Hollywood," *Chicago Daily Defender*, March 4, 1968, 10.

13. James Thomas Jackson, "Harry Dolan—A Soul on Fire," *Los Angeles Times*, September 27, 1981, M41.

14. "Losers Weepers," *Variety*, February 22, 1967, 42; "Experiment in Television Premieres over NBC," *Los Angeles Times*, February 19, 1967, N39D; Rick Du Brow, "'Losers Weepers' Author Was Janitor a Year Ago," *New Journal and Guide*, March 4, 1967, A4.

15. Stuart Schulberg, "Watts Happening in TV?," 83, 104.

16. Hal Humphrey, "Watts Program Set for March," *Los Angeles Times*, February 1, 1968, C10.

17. Stuart Schulberg, "Watts '68: So Young, So Angry," *New York Times*, March 17, 1968, D23.

18. Ibid.

19. Budd Schulberg, introduction to *From the Ashes* (New York: New American Library, 1967), 14.

20. Joe Saltzman, email messages to Joshua Glick, June 19, 2011, March 5, 2014, and May 29, 2016; Joe Saltzman, interview by Joshua Glick, May 28, 2014, Los Angeles. See also "Valleyites Land 'Trojan' Posts," *Pasadena Independent*, May 13, 1959, 12; Joe Saltzman, "Guest Columnist," *TV Week, Pasadena Independent Star-News*, July 14, 1968, 6, Joe Saltzman Papers, private collection of Joe Saltzman, Palos Verdes Estates, California (hereafter JSP); Joe Saltzman, "An Introduction to *Black on Black*," presented by IJPC and Visions & Voices, USC Annenberg School for Communication and Journalism, October 27, 2008, 3–4.

21. Otto Kerner, Chair, and David Ginsburg, Executive Director, *Report of the National Advisory Commission on Civil Disorders* (New York: Bantam, 1968), 1–29.

22. Ibid., 383–85.

23. Nicholas Johnson, "'White' Media Must Meet Challenge of Negro Antipathy and Disbelief," *Variety*, January 3, 1968, 1, 50. See also Joseph A. Loftus, "News Media Found Lacking in Understanding of the Negro," *New York Times*, March 3, 1968, 71; Whitney Young, "To Be Equal," *Chicago Defender*, May 4, 1968, 11.

24. Allison Perlman, *Public Interests: Media Advocacy and Struggles over U.S. Television* (New Brunswick, NJ: Rutgers University Press, 2016), 46–51. See also "FCC to Deny Licenses in Cases of Bias," *Los Angeles Times*, July 6, 1968, A12; Leonard Zeidenberg, "The Struggle over Broadcast Access," *Broadcasting*, September 20, 1971, 32–43; Leonard Zeidenberg, "The Struggle over Broadcast Access II," *Broadcasting*, September 27, 1971, 24–29.

25. "Black on Black Now Rescheduled," *Los Angeles Sentinel*, June 20, 1968, C11; Joe Saltzman, "Guest Columnist," 6; Helm, "Black on Black," *Variety*, July 24, 1968, 38; Joe Saltzman, "Shooting Notes and Schedule," n.d., JSP; Dan Gingold, phone interview by Joshua Glick, September 30, 2014.

26. Joe Saltzman, interview by Joshua Glick, May 28, 2014, Los Angeles. My account draws on information about the importance of sound in Joe Saltzman, email message to Joshua Glick, June 19, 2011; Joe Saltzman, "An Introduction to Black on Black," 5.

27. Sherman Brodey, "In Local Television the Eye Begins to Open on the Ghetto," *Television*, August 1968, 40; Helm, "Black on Black," 38; "'Black on Black' Special," *Los Angeles Sentinel*, June 9, 1968, B8. See also Robert A. Malone, "Local TV: Public Service with a Capital P," *Broadcasting*, June 22, 1970, 50, 58.

28. "KNXT to Donate 'Black on Black' to L.A. Library," *Los Angeles Sentinel*, March 6, 1969, F4; compiled letters, including those sent from students, 1968–73, JSP; Joe Saltzman, "An Introduction to Black on Black," 6; Joe Saltzman, email messages to Joshua Glick, March 5, 2014, and October 2, 2016.

29. CBS memorandum written by Joe Saltzman to Dan Gingold, August 5, 1968, 1–5, JSP.

30. Jonas Mekas, "On Radical Newsreel," in *Movie Journal: The Rise of the New American Cinema, 1959–1971* (New York: Macmillan, 1972), 305.

31. Michael Renov, *The Subject of Documentary* (Minneapolis: University of Minnesota Press, 2004), 6.

32. Marilyn Buck and Karen Ross, "Newsreel," *Film Quarterly* 22, no. 2 (Winter 1968–69): 44.

33. Robert Kramer, "Newsreel," *Film Quarterly* 22, no. 2 (Winter 1968–69): 47–48.

34. For instance Paul Shinoff interviewed by Paul Eberle, "Our Cameras Are Weapons . . . Our Films Are Tools," *Los Angeles Free Press*, November 22, 1968, 14–15, 20, 27, courtesy of Steve Finger, *Los Angeles Free Press* Archive, Los Angeles.

35. Gene Youngblood, "Guerrilla Newsreels," *Los Angeles Free Press*, March 22, 1968, 31.

36. Laura Pulido, *Black, Brown, Yellow, and Left: Radical Activism in Los Angeles* (Berkeley: University of California Press, 2006), 101.

37. Advertisement, *Los Angeles Free Press*, May 23, 1969, 9; Bill Nichols, "Newsreel: Film and Revolution" (master's thesis, University of California, Los Angeles, 1972), 239–57; advertisement, *Los Angeles Free Press*, May 30, 1969, 11; Dennis Hicks, phone interview by Joshua Glick, May 20, 2016.

38. David James, *The Most Typical Avant-Garde: History and Geography of Minor Cinemas in Los Angeles* (Los Angeles: University of California Press, 2005), 126–33; Dennis Hicks, phone interview by Joshua Glick, May 20, 2016.

39. Cecil Smith, "L.A. Wasteland Gets Shot in Arm," *Los Angeles Times*, September 30, 1964, 14. See also Dick Turpin, "Educational TV to Start Here in Fall," *Los Angeles Times*, December 26, 1963, A1; Cecil Smith, "The ABCs of ETV," *Los Angeles Times*, August 30,

1964, B1. KCET does not have its own independent television archive. To view KCET documentaries and news programs from the 1960s and 1970s, contact the UCLA Film & Television Archive.

40. Sammy Edward Ganimian, "A Descriptive Study of the Development of KCET-TV" (master's thesis, University of California, Los Angeles, 1966), 42–82, 108–14.

41. James L. Baughman, *Television's Guardians: The FCC and the Politics of Programming: 1958–1967* (Knoxville: University of Tennessee Press, 1985), 153–65. For an excellent overview of the origins of public television, see Patricia Aufderheide, "The What and How of Public Broadcasting," in *The Daily Planet: A Critic on the Capitalist Culture Beat* (Minneapolis: University of Minnesota Press, 2000), 85–98; Patricia Aufderheide, "Public Television and the Public Sphere," *Critical Studies in Mass Communication* 8, no. 2 (1991): 168–83.

42. Lyndon B. Johnson, "President Johnson's Remarks on Signing the Public Broadcasting Act, 1967," November 7, 1967, accessed May 3, 2015, https://current.org/2007/11/president-johnsons-remarks-on-signing-the-public-broadcasting-act-1967/.

43. Laurie Ouellette, *Viewers Like You? How Public TV Failed the People* (New York: Columbia University Press, 2002), 23–139.

44. Carnegie Commission on Educational Television, *Public Television: A Program for Action: The Report and Recommendations of the Carnegie Commission on Educational Television* (New York: Harper and Row, 1967), 92.

45. Hal Humphrey, "KCET: They Want to Get Involved," *Los Angeles Times*, July 17, 1967, C24; Walt Dutton, "More Specials for Channel 28," *Los Angeles Times*, September 29, 1967, D18; Hal Humphrey, "Spirits, Finances Higher at KCET," *Los Angeles Times*, January 16, 1968, D12; Cecil Smith, "Los Angeles Coming of Age in Public Affairs TV," *Los Angeles Times*, July 14, 1969, D1; Gerald Astor, *Minorities and the Media* (New York: Ford Foundation, 1974), 24–28; "Canción de la Raza: Song of the People," *KCET Program Guide* 5, no. 10 (October 1968): 2–3.

46. Jesús Salvador Treviño, *Eyewitness: A Filmmaker's Memoir of the Chicano Movement* (Houston: Arte Público, 2001), 1–67; Jesús Salvador Treviño, phone interview by Joshua Glick, April 24, 2015; Laura Pulido, *Black, Brown, Yellow, and Left*, 113–22.

47. "Urie Donation and Instruction," *Back Stage*, April 4, 1969, 6; Jack Jones, "Negro Cameraman Starts Ball Rolling, *Los Angeles Times*, January 27, 1969, B1.

48. Greg McAndrews, ed., *KCET Program Guide* 6, no. 9 (September 1969): 1–10; Ed Moreno quoted in Wayne Warga, "KCET Series Will Attack Cliché Image of U.S. Latin[o]s," *Los Angeles Times*, August 26, 1969, D1, D18. See also Dan Knapp, "Allied Artists Studio Purchased by KCET," *Los Angeles Times*, July 27, 1970, D14.

49. Dan Knapp, "KCET's Show for Chicano Viewers," *Los Angeles Times*, April 3, 1970, F18; Jesús Salvador Treviño, *Eyewitness*, 123–34.

50. Jesús Salvador Treviño, phone interview by Joshua Glick, April 24, 2015.

51. Edward Moreno, "TV Program Ahora Facing Termination," *Los Angeles Times*, April 11, 1970, A4.

52. Chon Noriega, *Shot in America: Television, the State, and the Rise of Chicano Cinema* (Minneapolis: University of Minnesota Press, 2000), 100–164.

53. Diana Loercher, "The Tube: 'Salazar,' 'Company,' and New Lloyd Bridges Series," *Christian Science Monitor*, October 30, 1970, 4.

54. Jesús Salvador Treviño quoted in Jack Jones, "Disputed Mural May Reappear," *Los Angeles Times*, May 23, 1971, B1.

55. Rubén Salazar, "Who Is a Chicano? And What Is It the Chicanos Want?," *Los Angeles Times*, February 6, 1970, B7.

56. Cecil Smith, "'Yo Soy' Captures the Chicano Soul," *Los Angeles Times*, August 17, 1972, F20.

57. Jesús Salvador Treviño quoted in Gregg Kilday, "The Chicano: His Past and Present," *Los Angeles Times*, August 10, 1972, 115. See also Carol Kleiman, "On the Air: WTTW Has Men of Special Talents," *Chicago Tribune*, August 8, 1972, 23; John Carmody, "Politicizing the Chicanos," *Washington Post*, August 12, 1972, E7.

58. "U. of Ill. Coed to Tour USSR," *Chicago Defender*, June 19, 1965, 31; "New TV Series Will Focus on Black Pioneers of West," *Philadelphia Tribune*, August 26, 1969, 13; "Black Cowboys Is [*sic*] Subject on WTTW," *Chicago Daily Defender*, October 17, 1970, 43. In 1985 Booker changed her name to Thandeka, a name given to her by Bishop Desmond Tutu in 1984. The name means "lovable" or "beloved" in Xhosa and Zulu. It is also part of an expression that means "one who is loved by God."

59. Sue Booker, interview by Joshua Glick, March 17, 2015, Boston.

60. Adair was tragically murdered before the film was finished. Cecil Smith, "Voice from Grave on Human Affairs Show," *Los Angeles Times*, September 26, 1970, A2.

61. Sue Booker, interview by Joshua Glick, March 17, 2015, Boston; Jesús Salvador Treviño, *Eyewitness*, 181–90.

62. "KCET Series Begins," *Los Angeles Sentinel*, March 2, 1972, B2A; "Black Prison Experience Depicted on 'Doin It,'" *Los Angeles Sentinel*, July 27, 1972, B2A.

63. Sue Booker quoted in Agnes Sankey McClain, "Essence Woman: Sue Booker," *Essence*, November 1973, 11.

64. Maury Green, "Storefront: News Simply Walks In," *Los Angeles Times*, November 24, 1972, D41.

65. "Tries New Concept," *New York Amsterdam News*, January 27, 1973, C4.

66. For coverage of the series see "'Storefront' News Room Center Opens," *Los Angeles Sentinel*, October 26, 1972, B7; "'Yo People' on Doin' It," *Los Angeles Sentinel*, November 23, 1972, B4A; "Breakfast Choir on KCET Storefront," *Los Angeles Sentinel*, January 11, 1973, B4A; "Black Movie Controversy," *Los Angeles Sentinel*, January 25, 1973, B4A.

67. Kevin Thomas, "Life Comes First, Films Second to Agnes Varda," *Los Angeles Times*, September 7, 1969, Q63; Lynne Littman, interview by Joshua Glick, February 13, 2013, New York.

68. Lynne Littman, interview by Joshua Glick, February 13, 2013, New York.

69. The Woman's Building later moved to a downtown location, 1727 North Spring Street, when the Chouinard building was sold in 1975.

70. Nancy Newhall, "UCLA," in *Fiat Lux: The University of California*, ed. Ansel Adams and Nancy Newhall (New York: McGraw-Hill, 1967), 30.

71. Robert Nakamura interviewed by Adam Hyman and Pauline Stakelon, May 23, 2010, and August 22, 2010, in *Alternative Projections: Experimental Film in Los Angeles, 1945–1980*, pp. 1–29, accessed January 10, 2014, http://alternativeprojections.com/oral-histories/robert-nakamura/.

72. Robert Nakamura, interview by Joshua Glick, May 31, 2014, Los Angeles.

73. Robert Nakamura, interview in *Alternative Projections*, 30–36.

74. John Upshaw, "Exhibit Depicts 'Camps': ASA Display Held," *L.A. Collegian*, November 6, 1970, 3, "Press Clippings," Visual Communications Archive, Little Tokyo, Los Angeles (hereafter VCA).

75. Colin Young, "An American Film Institute: A Proposal," *Film Quarterly* 14, no. 4 (1961): 37–50; John Dempsey, "Wanted: Young Talent For Low-Budget Movies," *Baltimore Sun*, May 5, 1968, F3; "American Film Institute as Culture: Stevens Cites First Year Expansion," *Variety*, July 30, 1969, 39; George Stevens Jr., Michael Webb, and Ernest Callenbach, "About the American Film Institute," *Film Quarterly* 25, no. 2 (1971–72): 36–44; George Stevens Jr., introduction to *Conversations with the Great Moviemakers of Hollywood's Golden Age* (New York: Alfred A. Knopf, 2006), ix–xx; "Seedbed for Ghetto Film," *Variety*, October 9, 1968, 5, 24.

76. Robert Nakamura, interview by Joshua Glick, May 31, 2014, Los Angeles. Nakamura's friend and colleague Kaz Higa came up with the name "Visual Communications." Higa, Ron Hirano, and Nakamura's brother Norman were affiliate members during the beginning of the collective. Karen L. Ishizuka, *Serve the People: Making Asian America in the Long 1960s* (London: Verso, 2016), 159–61.

77. "Visual Communications," *Rafu Shimpo*, December 20, 1972, 36, "Press Clippings," VCA.

78. Stephen Gong, "A History in Progress: Asian American Media Arts Centers, 1970–1990," in *Moving the Image: Independent Asian Pacific American Media Arts*, ed. Russell Leong (Los Angeles: University of California and Visual Communications, 1991), 3.

79. Jesús Salvador Treviño, phone interview by Joshua Glick, April 24, 2015.

80. Kevin Thomas, "Student Films at Royce Hall," *Los Angeles Times*, June 3, 1971, G16.

81. David Ushio, "For the Future: Visual Communications," *Pacific Citizen*, August 6, 1971, 2, "Press Clippings," VCA; "Manzanar Due on TV News," *Rafu Shimpo*, June 5, 1971, n.p., "Press Clippings," VCA. See also letter from Ed Moreno to Bob Nakamura, February 6, 1973, 1, "Issei and Proposal," VCA; Robert Nakamura, interview in *Alternative Projections*, 54.

82. Eddie Wong, Skype interview by Joshua Glick, June 27, 2014.

83. *Asian American People and Places: Ethnic Understanding Series, a Resource Guide* (Los Angeles: Visual Communications / Asian American Studies Central, 1971), 1–2, Special Collections, VCA.

84. Letters are held in "Ethnic Heritage: Correspondence and Guidelines," VCA.

85. For more on the educational media and archival initiatives at VC, see "Archival Project Preserves Our History," *Rafu Shimpo*, December 20, 1972, n.p.; "EUS Series," *Rafu Shimpo*, December 1972, 8–9, "Press Clippings," VCA; "Ethnic Heritage Original Proposal," VCA.

86. Clyde Taylor, "The L.A. Rebellion: New Spirit in American Film," *Black Film Review* 2, no. 2 (Spring 1986): 11.

87. Allyson Nadia Field, Jan-Christopher Horak, and Jacqueline Najuma Stewart, "Emancipating the Image: The L.A. Rebellion of Black Filmmakers," in *L.A. Rebellion: Creating a New Black Cinema* (Berkeley: University of California Press, 2015), 4.

88. Ibid., 19–29.

89. Charles Burnett, interview by Monona Wali, "Life Drawings: Charles Burnett's Realism," in *Charles Burnett: Interviews*, ed. Robert E. Kapsis (Jackson: University of Mississippi Press, 2011), 12–13.

90. Charles Burnett, interview by James Ponsoldt, "This Bitter Earth," in *Charles Burnett: Interviews*, 153–58.

91. Ibid., 157.

92. Allyson Nadia Field, "Rebellious Unlearning: UCLA Project One Films (1967–1978)," in *L.A. Rebellion*, 86.

93. Charles Burnett quoted in Susan Gerhard, "Charles Burnett Celebrates a Milestone," in *Charles Burnett: Interviews*, 177.

CHAPTER 4

1. Ossie Davis quoted in Wayne Warga, "The Issues: Ossie Davis vs. Nat Turner," *Los Angeles Times*, May 12, 1968, D1.

2. Metromedia's headquarters was located at 8544 Sunset Boulevard. Read more about the acquisition at Peter Bart, "TV Film Producer to Broaden Field," *New York Times*, August 31, 1964, 21; Peter Bart, "Metromedia Buys Wolper Concern," *New York Times*, October 23, 1964, 35; Jack Pitman, "Metromedia's Dave Wolper Buyout Underlines Indies' Fiscal Status," *Variety*, October 28, 1964, 26, 42; "Wolper Is Given Metromedia Post," *New York Times*, March 1, 1965, 53; Harold Stern, "Wolper Raps Networks, Outlines Plans," *Hartford Courant*, April 11, 1965, 121.

3. Sammy Edward Ganimian, "A Descriptive Study of the Development of KCET-TV" (master's thesis, University of California, Los Angeles, 1966), 48; Herm Schoenfeld, "Kluge's Aspirations for a 'Thinking Man's Network,'" *Variety*, October 25, 1961, 25. Under the Metromedia tent existed six television stations and five AM-FM radio properties, including the Los Angeles stations KTTV, Metro TV Sales, Metro Radio Sales, the outdoor advertising firm Foster & Kleiser, the Ice Capades, and the merchandising company SuperSpace. John W. Kluge, *The Metromedia Story* (New York: Newcomen Society in North America, 1974).

4. Lyndon B. Johnson, with photographs by Ken Heyman, *This America* (New York: Random House, 1966), 7–8.

5. "'March of Time' as Wolper Syndie Entry," *Variety*, February 17, 1965, 35.

6. G. K. Hodenfield, "Revolution in Three R's Sets Teacher Problems," *Los Angeles Times*, September 6, 1965, 15.

7. William Friedkin, *The Friedkin Connection: A Memoir* (New York: HarperCollins, 2013), 76–77; "Chi's Bill Friedkin Joins David Wolper," *Variety*, August 12, 1964, 30; David L. Wolper and David Fisher, *Producer: A Memoir* (New York: Scribner, 2003), 66–67.

8. Raymond Rohauer, film curator and program director, *A Tribute to David L. Wolper* (New York: Huntington Hartford Gallery of Modern Art, 1966), 3. See also advertisement, Producers Guild of America Award, *Variety*, June 21, 1967, 34; "Mayor Lindsay at the Wolper Film Fest," *Back Stage*, November 11, 1966, 4.

9. The Cousteau programs were known for their innovative technology. The crew used 35mm and 16mm Arriflex cameras, 16mm Éclairs, three Perfectone synchronized sound recorders, waterproof and pressurized housings for underwater recording, and an array of flood lamps for filming near the surface. Walt Dutton, "Study of Cousteau Engrossing," *Los Angeles Times*, April 30, 1966, B3; Clay Gowran, "New Cousteau Role on a Rival Network," *Chicago Tribune*, March 3, 1967, 22; Les Brown, "ABC-TV $3.5-Million for Cousteau Voyage Makes Russian Heads Swim," *Variety*, February 22, 1967, 32, 44; Louise Sweeney, "'Undersea

World of Jacques Cousteau' Tonight on ABC-TV," *Christian Science Monitor*, January 8, 1968, 6; Brad Matsen, *Jacques Cousteau: The Sea King* (New York: Pantheon, 2009), 169–92.

10. Jack Gould, "ABC Gives an Evening to 4 Specials in a Row," *New York Times*, March 7, 1968, 86.

11. "A Primer of Assassination Theories," *Esquire*, December 1966, 205–10, 334–35; Edward Jay Epstein, *Inquest: The Warren Commission and the Establishment of Truth* (New York: Viking, 1966); Richard H. Popkin, *The Second Oswald* (New York: Avon, 1966). See also the contemporaneous Mark Lane, *Rush to Judgment: A Critique of the Warren Commission's Inquiry into the Murders of President John F. Kennedy, Officer J. D. Tippit and Lee Harvey Oswald* (San Francisco: Holt, Rinehart and Winston, 1966); Mark Lane and Emile de Antonio, "'Rush to Judgment,' 'John F. Kennedy': Two Controversial Films," *Film Comment* 2, no. 3 (1967): 2–18.

12. "Wolper Recovers (at a Price) Indie Status: Plans Two Theatricals Yearly," *Variety*, January 15, 1969, 17; "Wolper Productions Inc. Is No More," *Broadcasting*, October 28, 1968, 66; David L. Wolper and David Fisher, *Producer: A Memoir*, 161–62; John F. Lawrence, "Transamerica Merger with Metromedia Set," *Los Angeles Times*, October 11, 1968, E14; "Wolper's Departure Causes Name Change," *Los Angeles Times*, October 23, 1968, G22; advertisement, *Variety*, January 15, 1969, 33.

13. By 1971 the Wolper Organization would be the umbrella organization under which the studio's fiction and nonfiction divisions would operate. The company would locate its headquarters at 8489 West Third Street. For more on studio mergers during the 1960s and 1970s, see Paul Monaco, *The Sixties* (Berkeley: University of California Press, 2003), 30–39; David Cook, *Lost Illusions: American Cinema in the Shadow of Watergate and Vietnam* (Berkeley: University of California Press, 2002), 1–23.

14. Wolper bought the screen rights to Robin Moore's 1965 novel *The Green Berets*; however, he opted out of the adaptation because of pressure from the Pentagon, who considered the project a security risk. "Defense May Help; 'Green Berets' On," *Variety*, September 15, 1965, 22; "Pentagon Fears Fictional Angling; Hence, No Vietnam War Features," *Variety*, May 10, 1967, 7; "Accuse Defense Dept.," *Variety*, November 1, 1967, 22.

15. Vincent Canby, "Screen: World War II from Hollywood," *New York Times*, May 23, 1968, 56.

16. Charles Champlin, "'Devil's Brigade' at Chinese," *Los Angeles Times*, May 22, 1968, C15; George McKinnon, "Brigade—Blood, Brawls," *Boston Globe*, June 17, 1968, 16.

17. Gary Arnold, "Opening: 'The Bridge at Remagen,'" *Washington Post*, July 4, 1969, C6; Clifford Terry, "Bridge at Remagen," *Chicago Tribune*, June 30, 1969, A9. See also "E. Germans: 'Remagen' a CIA Front," *Variety*, August 14, 1968, 14; Ray Loynd, "Czech Crisis: A Piece of Action for Film Troupe," *Los Angeles Times*, September 1, 1968, C1; Hank Werba, "Despite Reds' Czechoslovak Invasion, Wolper Finally Winds His 'Remagen,'" *Variety*, November 27, 1968, 28; advertisement, "The Bridge at Remagen: The Incredible Log of the Motion Picture That Became an International Incident," *Variety*, May 7, 1969, 132–33.

18. Paul C. Johnson, ed., *Los Angeles: Portrait of an Extraordinary City* (Menlo Park, CA: Lane Magazine and Book Company, 1968), 5.

19. Sam Yorty, speech, University of California, Los Angeles, November 21, 1968, online archives of the UCLA Communications Studies Department, accessed January 19, 2017, https://www.youtube.com/watch?v=hz5uAblGC6U. The film premiered at the Samuel

Goldwyn Studio before playing on local television stations. "Council Ok's $50,000 for Film on L.A.," *Los Angeles Times*, April 26, 1967, A3; "Los Angeles' Promotional Pic," *Variety*, January 29, 1969, 6; TV schedule listing, *Oxnard Press Courier*, August 16, 1970, 102; Sam Yorty, *The Yorty Years: The Story of Sam Yorty's Leadership as Mayor of Los Angeles since 1961* (Los Angeles: Friends of Mayor Sam Yorty, 1969).

20. Alphonzo Bell Jr. and aide quoted in Ali Sar, "Bow of Yorty Film Brings Record Downpour, Outcry," *Van Nuys Valley News*, February 9, 1969, 13.

21. Rowland Evans and Robert Novak, "LBJ Film Blackout," *Washington Post*, September 8, 1968, B7.

22. Norman Mailer, *The Armies of the Night: History as a Novel / The Novel as History* (New York: Signet, 1968), 103–4, 109–10, 135.

23. Percy Shain, "The Journey of RFK—Summary of the '60s," *Boston Globe*, February 18, 1970, 74. See also "Journey of Robert F. Kennedy," *Variety*, February 18, 1970, 45; Lawrence Laurent, "Tribute to Kennedy," *Washington Post*, February 18, 1970, B5.

24. Wolper's fiction features during this period met a mixed fate. Critics considered *If It's Tuesday, This Must Be Belgium* (1969) a fresh, offbeat comedy. Other films, such as his screen adaptation of John Updike's *Couples*, never got off the ground due to budgetary difficulties. For a lineup of prospective films, see "If It's '70, It Must Be Wolper," advertisement, *Variety*, December 10, 1969, 80.

25. "Wolper Projects UA Slave Revolt Pic," *Variety*, October 18, 1967, 2; "'Nat Turner' for 20th," *Variety*, January 17, 1968, 3.

26. Christopher Sieving, *Soul Searching: Black-Themed Cinema from the March on Washington to the Rise of Blaxploitation* (Middletown, CT: Wesleyan University Press, 2011), 88.

27. William Styron, *The Confessions of Nat Turner* (New York: Random House, 1966), ix.

28. For articles praising the book, see for example Alden Whitman, "William Styron Examines the Negro Upheaval," *New York Times*, August 5, 1967, 13; John Phillips, "Styron Unlocked," *Vogue*, December 1967, 216–17, 267–71, 278; Eliot Fremont-Smith, "Books of the Times," *New York Times*, October 4, 1967, 45; Edmund Fuller, "Power and Eloquence in New Styron Novel," *Wall Street Journal*, October 4, 1967, 16; Richard Hurt, "Slavery's Quiet Resistance," *Boston Globe*, October 8, 1967, A43; Alfred Kazin, "Instinct for Tragedy: A Message in Black and White," *Chicago Tribune*, October 8, 1967, Q1; Walter J. Hicks, "The Futile Insurrection," *Baltimore Sun*, October 15, 1967, D5.

29. Arthur Schlesinger Jr., "The Confessions of Nat Turner," *Vogue*, October 1, 1967, 143.

30. Raymond A. Sokolov, "Into the Mind of Nat Turner," *Newsweek*, October 16, 1967, 66.

31. James Baldwin quoted in Gene D. Phillips, "Davis Unfair to 'Nat Turner'?," *New York Times*, May 19, 1968, D5.

32. Advertisement, "We Are Proud to Congratulate William Styron," *Variety*, May 15, 1968, 25. See also "No Pulitzer Play Prize; 'Plaza' Was a Contender; Novel Award to 'Turner,'" *Variety*, May 8, 1968, 251.

33. Dick Brooks, national publicity director, "20th-Fox to Release Screen Adaptation of 'The Confessions of Nat Turner,'" March 31, 1969, Nat Turner Clippings Folder, Billy Rose Theatre Division, New York Public Library.

34. Gertrude Wilson, "Styron's Folly," *New York Amsterdam News*, December 30, 1967, 13. The article is a response to and revision of her earlier piece, "Confessions of a Believer," *New York Amsterdam News*, October 21, 1967, 17.

35. Lerone Bennett Jr., "Nat's Last White Man," and Ernest Kaiser, "The Failure of William Styron," in *William Styron's Nat Turner: Ten Black Writers Respond*, ed. John Henrik Clarke (Boston: Beacon, 1968), 5, 65.

36. A. S. "Doc" Young, "The Truth Gap," *Los Angeles Sentinel*, October 26, 1967, D1–D2. See also Eric Foner, ed., *Nat Turner* (Englewood Cliffs, NJ: Prentice-Hall, 1971); Herbert Aptheker, *Nat Turner's Slave Rebellion* (New York: Grove, 1966), 39–56.

37. James Baldwin quoted in Joyce Haber, "A Frank Discussion of 'Nat Turner,'" *Los Angeles Times*, May 29, 1968, C7. See also Norman Jewison, *This Terrible Business Has Been Good to Me: An Autobiography* (Toronto: Key Porter, 2004), 153–55.

38. David Wolper quoted in "Negro Group Sees 'Nat Turner' NSG for Race; Wolper, Jewison: Bum Rap," *Variety*, April 3, 1968, 2.

39. Norman Jewison quoted in Joyce Haber, "A Frank Discussion of 'Nat Turner,'" C7.

40. Norman Jewison quoted in Bill Lane, "Philadelphian's Novel to Be Filmed in This City," *Philadelphia Tribune*, April 20, 1968, 16.

41. "Protest Mounts against Best-Selling Novel 'Confessions of Nat Turner,'" *Philadelphia Tribune*, March 2, 1968, 17; "Furor over Pulitzer [*sic*] Prize Winner as Movie Continues," *New York Amsterdam News*, May 11, 1968, 1.

42. Vantile Whitfield quoted in "Nat Turner Movie Hit: 'Mammoth Movement' Begins," *Los Angeles Sentinel*, March 21, 1968, D3.

43. Ossie Davis quoted in Wayne Warga, "The Issues: Ossie Davis vs. Nat Turner," D1. Davis frequently spoke out about the Turner project and was covered in the local press; for instance see Ossie Davis quoted in Dick Kleiner, "Filming of 'Nat Turner' Draws Negro Opposition," *Bakersfield Californian*, July 4, 1968, 15; Ossie Davis quoted in "Negro Entertainers Air Views on Racial Problems," *Bakersfield Californian*, August 3, 1968, 5.

44. David Wolper quoted in Steven V. Roberts, "Over the 'Nat Turner' Screenplay Subsides," *New York Times*, March 31, 1969, 28.

45. "Peterson to Pen Nat Turner Movie," *Chicago Daily Defender*, June 11, 1968, 11.

46. Louise Meriwether, "BADA Settles 'Nat Turner' Film Dispute," *Los Angeles Sentinel*, February 13, 1969, F2.

47. Maggie Savoy, "NOW—A Good Neighbor Policy for Beverly Hills," *Los Angeles Times*, May 30, 1968, E1, E9.

48. The fundraising advisory board consisted of Wolper, Jewison, and Turman, as well as Oscar-winning film and television producer Harold Mirisch, California democratic political leader Paul Ziffren, and entertainment lawyer J. William Hayes. Sponsors included Alan Bergman, Marvin Mirisch, Robert Mirisch, Greg Morris, Janet Leigh, Kirk Douglas, Henry Mancini, Steve McQueen, Gregory Peck, Andy Williams, Robert Wise, Jeff Hayden, Faye Dunaway, Barbra Streisand, Natalie Wood, Mark Miller, and Gordon Parks. After smaller-scale efforts to provide health care services in the community, the collective endeavors of NOW eventually led to the establishment of the South Central Community Child Care Center. Maggie Savoy, "NOW Gets Rich Start," *Los Angeles Times*, April 16, 1969, H8; Maggie Savoy, "Watts Neighbors: No Time Like NOW for Child Care," *Los Angeles Times*, April 15, 1969, G1; Joyce Haber, "NOW Benefit Is Star-Studded Event," *Los Angeles Times*, April 30, 1969, H16; "Neighbors of Watts Inc. Opens Child Care Center," *Los Angeles Sentinel*, March 11, 1971, A10; "Working Mothers in Watts Get New Child Care Center for Pennies Per Hour," *Los Angeles Sentinel*, April 8, 1971, A1, A10; Betty Liddick, "$60,000 Gift

Buys a Lot of Child Care," *Los Angeles Times*, January 6, 1972, F1; "Watts Auction Party Aids Child-Care Center," *New York Times*, February 21, 1972, 33.

49. "Fox De-fuses Its 'Turner' Pic," *Variety*, February 12, 1969, 5; "Meet Racial Objections Re 'Turner'; Lumet Up as (Unconfirmed) Director," *Variety*, May 7, 1969, 32.

50. Sidney Lumet quoted in "Lumet Ponders Slave Revolt Hazards," *Variety*, September 3, 1969, 6. See also David L. Wolper and David Fisher, *Producer: A Memoir*, 213–15.

51. "Possible Delay of 'Nat Turner' Start," *Variety*, January 14, 1970, 3; "Nat Turner Film Delayed," *Baltimore Afro-American*, January 24, 1970, 10; Bill Lane, "Racial Shockers Cause Viewer Ire," *Los Angeles Sentinel*, April 30, 1970, Section B Supplement, 1.

52. Nat Turner would not surface on the screen until 2003, when the filmmaker Charles Burnett created *Nat Turner: A Troublesome Property*. Through reenactments and interviews, the documentary explored Turner as a historical figure as well as the controversy concerning the various literary and prospective film treatments of his life. Kenneth S. Greenberg, "Epilogue: Nat Turner in Hollywood," in *Nat Turner: A Slave Rebellion in History and Memory*, ed. Kenneth S. Greenberg (Oxford: Oxford University Press, 2003), 243–49.

53. Christopher Sieving, *Soul Searching*, 110–18.

CHAPTER 5

1. Joan Didion, "In Hollywood" (1973), in *The White Album* (New York: Simon and Schuster, 1979), 160.

2. "Mothers Praise 'Wattstax,'" *Chicago Defender*, January 27, 1973, 19.

3. Rob Bowman, *Soulsville, U.S.A.: The Story of Stax Records* (New York: Schirmer, 1997), 268–71, 290–316; Rob Bowman, commentary, *Wattstax: Thirtieth Anniversary Special Edition*, directed by Mel Stuart, 1973 (Burbank, CA: Warner Home Video, 2004), DVD; Robert Gordon, *Respect Yourself: Stax Records and the Soul Explosion* (New York: Bloomsbury, 2013), 289–307.

4. Scott Saul, "'What You See Is What You Get': *Wattstax*, Richard Pryor, and the Secret History of the Black Aesthetic," Post45, August 12, 2014, accessed January 15, 2015, http://post45.research.yale.edu/2014/08/what-you-see-is-what-you-get-wattstax-richard-pryor-and-the-secret-history-of-the-black-aesthetic/.

5. Daniel Widener, "Setting the Seen: Hollywood, South Los Angeles, and the Politics of Film," in *Post-Ghetto: Reimagining South Los Angeles*, ed. Josh Sides (Berkeley: University of California Press, 2012), 180–88; Mike Phillips, "'Rated R Because It's Real': Discourses of Authenticity in *Wattstax*," in *Documenting the Black Experience: Essays on African American History, Culture and Identity in Nonfiction Films*, ed. Novotny Lawrence (Jefferson: McFarland, 2014), 132–52.

6. Bruce M. Tyler, "The Rise and Decline of the Watts Summer Festival, 1965–1986," *American Studies* 31, no. 2 (Fall 1990): 61–64. See also Ray Rogers and Jack McCurdy, "10,000 Turn out for Watts Festival," *Los Angeles Times*, August 14, 1966, C1; Betty Pleasant, "Watts Summer Festival Surpasses Expectations," *Los Angeles Sentinel*, August 18, 1966, A1.

7. "Gunfire in Watts Festival," *Los Angeles Sentinel*, August 8, 1968, A1; Jack Jones, "Watts Violence Takes Toll of 3 Dead, 41 Hurt," *Los Angeles Times*, August 13, 1968, 1.

8. "Panthers Assail Watts Festival, Call Committee Officials Lackeys," *Los Angeles Sentinel*, August 14, 1969, A1.

9. Jim Stewart originally named the company Satellite Records. He and his sister Estelle Axton changed the name to Stax in 1960. Rob Bowman, *Soulsville, U.S.A.*, 70–216.

10. Kwaku Person-Lynn, "Insider Perspectives on the American Afrikan Popular Music Industry and Black Radio," in *California Soul: Music of African Americans in the West*, ed. Jacqueline C. DjeDje and Eddie S. Meadows (Berkeley: University of California Press, 1998), 180–81; Al Bell, interview by Stephen Koch, "Al Bell Takes Us There," *Arkansas Review: A Journal of Delta Studies* 32, no. 1 (April 2001): 49–59; "Says Black Record Firms Must Be Part of Community," *Jet*, September 16, 1971, 30.

11. Brian Ward, *Just My Soul Responding: Rhythm and Blues, Black Consciousness and Race Relations* (London: UCL, 1998), 184.

12. Ibid., 430–50; James D. Kingsley, "Stax's Education Plan for Poor," *Billboard*, May 24, 1969, 1, 78; "'Give a Damn' Extravaganza Held for Needy," *New Journal and Guide*, December 27, 1969, 14; "Carla Thomas, Art Linkletter Back Houston Drug Program," *Atlanta Daily World*, December 29, 1970, 2; "Isaac Hayes Sets Up Foundation to Aid Poor and Elderly Black," *Philadelphia Tribune*, March 30, 1971, 17; "Issac [sic] Hayes Sets Up All-Purpose Foundation," *Chicago Defender*, April 26, 1971, 14; Nat Freedland, "Record Cos. into Public Aid Stance," *Billboard*, March 11, 1972, 31; "Stax Donates to 1st Offender," *Tri-State Defender*, March 25, 1972, 1; "Black Moses in College Benefit Show," *New Journal and Guide*, May 6, 1972, 14; "Hayes Sponsors Housing Project for Poor," *Philadelphia Tribune*, September 16, 1972, 24; "Record Company Formed to Spread Spoken Word," *New Journal and Guide*, May 30, 1970, 14; "Singer, Composer John KaSandra Wages Fight to Be His Own Man," *Philadelphia Tribune*, December 22, 1970, 23.

13. Richard Nixon quoted in Ward Just, "Nixon on Black Capitalism," *Boston Globe*, April 26, 1968, 36.

14. Laura Warren Hill and Julia Rabig, eds., *The Business of Black Power: Community Development, Capitalism, and Corporate Responsibility in Postwar America* (Rochester, NY: University of Rochester, 2012), 25–40; Dean J. Kotlowski, *Nixon's Civil Rights: Politics, Principle, and Policy* (Cambridge, MA: Harvard University Press, 2001), 126–51; Robert E. Weems Jr. and Lewis A. Randolph, "The National Response to Richard M. Nixon's Black Capitalism Initiative: The Success of Domestic Détente," *Journal of Black Studies* 32, no. 1 (September 2001): 66–83.

15. Gerald Posner, *Motown: Music, Money, Sex, and Power* (New York: Random House, 2002), 42–66, 82–84; David Morse, *Motown and the Arrival of Black Music* (New York: Macmillan, 1971), 28–54; Robert Hilburn, "Motown Records Spinning Off into Films, TV," *Los Angeles Times*, April 18, 1971, R1; "Motown Becomes a Monster in the Entertainment World," *Chicago Defender*, January 8, 1972, 19.

16. Michael Aron, "Emperor Gordy," *Los Angeles Magazine*, December, 1972, 39–41, 82–86.

17. Gertrude Gibson, "It's Booker T: The Heat Is On," *Los Angeles Sentinel*, February 13, 1969, F3; Phyl Garland, "Booker T. and the MG's," *Ebony*, April 1969, 97; "Stax Releases Film Soundtrack Single," *New York Amsterdam News*, March 22, 1969, 20; Earl Calloway, "New Disk Release," *Chicago Defender*, June 5, 1969, 17; Richard Green, "Controversial Film Aids Booker T Hit," *New Musical Express*, June 7, 1969, 5; Jell Hell, "Soul Sounds," *New Pittsburgh Courier*, January 18, 1969, 24.

18. Amy Abugo Ongiri, *Spectacular Blackness: The Cultural Politics of the Black Power Movement and the Search for a Black Aesthetic* (Charlottesville: University of Virginia Press, 2010), 154–58.

19. Melvin Van Peebles, *The Making of Sweet Sweetback's Baadasssss Song* (Edinburgh: Payback, 1971), 92–93.

20. Shaw was also the president of the international marketing consulting group Communiplex Inc. He had spearheaded the advertising of Afro-Sheen and Newport Cigarettes to black consumers and had worked with SCLC's Operation Breadbasket in Chicago. Bruce Weber, "Stax Moves in Int'l, Artist, Film Areas," *Billboard*, June 29, 1968, 1, 10; "Peebles Film to Premiere," *New York Amsterdam News*, April 24, 1971, 19; "Chicago Moviemaker's Film Set for Oriental," *Chicago Defender*, April 27, 1971, 12; "Stax Records Music of Van Peebles Film," *Los Angeles Sentinel*, April 29, 1971, B3A; Mike Gross, "Black Tracks Cue New Sales Mart," *Billboard*, July 24, 1971, 1, 10; *Wattstax* [Feature Film] Publicity, 131–010, David L. Wolper Center, Cinematic Arts Library, University of Southern California (hereafter DWC, CAL, USC).

21. "The Black Movie Boom," *Newsweek*, September 6, 1971, 66; Fred Beauford, ed., "The Expanding World of the Black Film," in *Black Creation: The Expanding World of the Black Film* 4, no. 2 (Winter 1973): 25–43. See also B. J. Mason, "Black Cinema Expo '72," *Ebony*, May 1972, 151–60.

22. Junius Griffin quoted in "Junius Griffin Stays," *Variety*, August 30, 1972, 5; "NAACP Blasts 'Super-Nigger' Trend," *Variety*, August 16, 1972, 2; Ed Guerrero, *Framing Blackness: the African American Image in Film* (Philadelphia: Temple University Press, 1993), 69–111.

23. Al Bell quoted in Mike Gross, "Black Tracks Cue New Sales Mart," 1, 10.

24. Lance Williams, "Wattstax: Giving Something Back to Community," *Los Angeles Times*, August 20, 1972, X1; "Wattstax Benefit Show Aided Community Group," *New Journal and Guide*, November 25, 1972, 14.

25. "Motown Entertainment Complex," *Los Angeles Sentinel*, May 20, 1971, G124.

26. Al Bell, commentary, *Wattstax* DVD.

27. Coordinating the production involved communicating across languages, organizing dozens of camera crews, and making a film about an Olympic Games that would be marked by the horrific murder of Israeli athletes. The film evoked a spirit of unity in the face of tragedy, a "united nations" of filmmakers as well as a world united through the shared experience of viewing the documentary. Filmmakers included Miloš Forman, Kon Ichikawa, Claude Lelouch, Yuri Ozerov, Arthur Penn, Michael Pfleghar, John Schlesinger, and Mai Zetterling. "Wolper Resuscitates Dead Olympics Pic for Munich 1972," *Variety*, October 20, 1971, 25; John Goshko, "Film Project of Olympic Proportions," *Washington Post*, September 1, 1972, B1, B3.

28. Keith Beattie, "It's Not Only Rock and Roll: 'Rockumentary,' Direct Cinema, and Performative Display," *Australasian Journal of American Studies* 24, no. 2 (December 2005): 21–41. *Woodstock* producer Bob Maurice stated that his crew went to the festival "to share the joy of that weekend. . . . As a result, the film is quite human and relaxed and simple, but also raw and unpolished." Bob Maurice quoted in Ann Barry, "Woodstock Is Not Over— Film Due Early Next Year," *Baltimore Sun*, December 17, 1969, B4; Michael Wadleigh, *Woodstock: 3 Days of Peace and Music, a Film by Michael Wadleigh* (Philadelphia: Concert Hall

Publications, 1969), 48, Zab W242 +970W, Beinecke Rare Book and Manuscript Library, Yale University, New Haven, Connecticut.

29. See the widely circulated advertisement, *New Journal and Guide*, August 21, 1971, B18.

30. Michael Davenport, "Marathon Soul Festival the First for Ghana," *Los Angeles Times*, April 4, 1971, C16; James Cassell, "Movie Shot at African Festival Links Black Music to Its Roots," *Philadelphia Tribune*, July 27, 1971, 16; Rob Bowman, liner notes, *Soul to Soul* (Burbank, CA: Reelin' in the Years Productions, Rhino Home Video, 2004), DVD; Willie Hamilton, "'Soul to Soul' Not Background Material," *New York Amsterdam News*, August 28, 1971, B9.

31. Mel Stuart, interview by Joshua Glick, August 6, 2010, Los Angeles.

32. "'Wattstax' to Columbia," *Variety*, August 23, 1972, 4; "Wolperized Black-Angled Ballyhoo For 'Wattstax'; Columbia's Angles," *Variety*, February 7, 1973, 5; Bernard F. Dick, *Columbia Pictures: Portrait of a Studio* (Lexington: University Press of Kentucky, 1992), 13–32.

33. "Wattstax '72 Film Shot by 90% Black Crews; 250G Budget for Docu," *Variety*, September 27, 1972, 1, 61; commentary by Mel Stuart, Al Bell, Larry Shaw, Rob Bowman, *Wattstax* DVD; "$73,363 Charities' Wattstax Donation," *Billboard*, September 2, 1972, 66. Most publicity, accounts of production, and reviews of the film noted that local Los Angeles residents provided the testimony. A few actors were interviewed for these conversations, including Ted Lange and Raymond Allen. Mel Stuart, interview by Joshua Glick, August 6, 2010, Los Angeles; Rob Bowman and Al Bell, email correspondence with Joshua Glick, March 7–16, 2015.

34. Contract dated August 14, 1972, "Production of Picture," Sections 2.3–4, p. 4, Special Collections Folder, DWC, CAL, USC.

35. Mel Stuart, interview by Joshua Glick, August 6, 2010, Los Angeles.

36. "Lift Every Voice and Sing" became part of a daily ritual in many schools where there was a black majority of students. Bill Lane, "Evolvement of Black National Anthem," *Los Angeles Times*, March 14, 1971, T30.

37. Commentaries by Isaac Hayes, Mel Stuart, Al Bell, Rob Bowman, and Larry Clark, *Wattstax* DVD.

38. Isaac Hayes, Albert King, Otis Redding, Mavis Staples, Johnnie Taylor, and other Stax artists honed their craft and drew inspiration from performing in church during their early careers.

39. Churches pictured in the film include the Thankful Missionary Baptist Church (8900 South San Pedro Street), the Temple Missionary Baptist Church (8734 South Broadway), the Whole Truth Temple Church of God in Christ (4311 South Avalon Boulevard), and the Church of Divine Inspiration (4777 South Broadway). Jacqueline Cogdell DjeDje, "The California Black Gospel Music Tradition: A Confluence of Musical Styles and Cultures," in *California Soul*, 130–43.

40. Scott Saul, "'What You See Is What You Get,'" 12–13.

41. Larry Shaw quoted in James P. Murray, "Black Movies and Music in Harmony," *Black Creation* 5, no. 1 (Fall 1973): 11.

42. Letter from Larry Shaw to Robert Ferguson, January 5, 1973, *Wattstax* [Feature Film] Correspondence, 201–4852, DWC, CAL, USC. There was an initial complication with the film's release. For seven years Hayes was legally not allowed to perform music from *Shaft*

in productions other than those made by MGM. Thus, Stax was forced to film a soundstage rendition of "Rolling Down the Mountainside" and insert it into the film. "MGM Sues Hayes, Stax, Wolper, et al. on Music Renege," *Variety*, February 7, 1973, 5. The *Wattstax* LP went gold and climbed to number twenty-nine on *Billboard*'s Top LP's and Tapes chart. "Billboard's Top LP's and Tapes," *Billboard*, April 14, 1973, 58.

43. "Wattstax Benefit Show Aided Community Group," *New Journal and Guide*, November 25, 1972, 14.

44. Larry Grant Coleman, "'Wattstax:' Dynamite Film Documentary on Black Creativity,'" *Pittsburgh Courier*, January 27, 1973, 9.

45. Gertrude Gipson, "At Music Center: Wattstax Film Premieres," *Los Angeles Sentinel*, January 25, 1973, section B supplement, 1.

46. "Chicago Mother: *Wattstax* Is a Family Film," *Southeast Independent Bulletin*, February 2, 1973, *Wattstax* [Feature Film] Press Clippings, 201–002, DWC, CAL, USC. Around this time, Stax and Wolper Productions sponsored different kinds of social outreach initiatives related to the film, including a $1,000 college scholarship writing contest, where students submitted essays on "The Black Experience." "'Wattstax' Prod. Set Scholarship," *Cash Box*, February 3, 1973, *Wattstax* [Feature Film] Press Clippings, 131–009, DWC, CAL, USC.

47. Leah Davis, "Wattstax Premiere More Than Glitter," *Soul: America's Most Soulful Newspaper*, March 12, 1973, 2–3.

48. Harry Dolan, "Wattstax in Watts: A Movie of the People Comes to the People," *Wattstax* [Feature Film] Publicity (General)," 201–4852, DWC, CAL, USC.

49. Advertisement, *Los Angeles Sentinel*, March 1, 1973, B4A. See also Richard F. Shepard, "Going Out Guide," *New York Times*, February 15, 1973, 50; "PUSH Host at Premiere for Wattstax," *New York Amsterdam News*, February 10, 1973, A12; "Midwest Disc Jockeys Preview 'Wattstax,'" *Chicago Defender*, February 7, 1973, 13; Reverend Jesse L. Jackson, "Jesse Lauds 'Wattstax,'" *Chicago Defender*, February 17, 1973, 3; "'Wattstax' Opening Has Had Numerous Premieres," *Atlanta Daily World*, March 18, 1973, 12; "Atlanta Premiere of 'Wattstax' Film Boosted by Stars," *Atlanta Daily World*, March 4, 1973, 6; Nancy Giddens, "The Black Political Forum Host [sic] Gala Premiere Showing of Wattstax," *Philadelphia Tribune*, April 10, 1973, 17; "City Social Clubs Participating in SCLC's 'Wattstax' Premiere May 23," *Indianapolis Recorder*, May 12, 1973, *Wattstax* [Feature Film] Press Clippings, 131–009, DWC, CAL, USC.

50. Letter from August Jones to Wolper Pictures LTD, February 7, 1973, *Wattstax* [Feature Film] Publicity, 131–009, DWC, CAL, USC.

51. Vincent Canby, "Film: 'Wattstax,' Record of Watts Festival Concert," *New York Times*, February 16, 1973, 17.

52. Dennis Hunt, "Pryor Highlight of 'Wattstax' Collage," *Los Angeles Times*, February 21, 1973, G10.

53. Joy Gould Boyum, "A Bit More Than Just Music at a Black Concert," *Wall Street Journal*, February 26, 1973, 12.

54. Marian Brayton, "Stax Organization Diversifies Way to Booming Success," *Hollywood Reporter*, January 5, 1973, Box 201–002, 4848, *Wattstax*: Wolper Organization Files (WOF), DWC, CAL, USC.

55. Ron Pennington, "'Wattstax' Added New Scope to Documentaries—Stuart," *Hollywood Reporter*, March 7, 1973, 16, *Wattstax* [Feature Film] Press Clippings, 131–008, DWC, CAL, USC.

56. *Westways*, March 1973, page(s) unknown. *Wattstax* [Feature Film] Press Clippings, 131–009, DWC, CAL, USC

57. "Wattstax Headlines Swiss Festival," *Los Angeles Sentinel*, July 12, 1973, B3A; "Africans Dig 'Wattstax' OAU Envoy Tells Crowd," *Philadelphia Tribune*, May 8, 1973, 12.

58. Mel Stuart quoted in Curtis J. Sitomer, "Films: 'Payday' . . . and a Musical Wander through Watts," *Christian Science Monitor*, March 1, 1973, 14.

59. Advertisement, *New York Times*, February 18, 1973, 174; advertisement, *Wisconsin State Journal*, May 2, 1973; advertisement, *Los Angeles Times*, March 3, 1973, A6; advertisement, *UCLA Daily Bruin*, February 28, 1973, 10. The pertinent *Newsweek* review was Arthur Cooper, "Watts Happening," *Newsweek*, February 26, 1973, 88. *Wattstax* [Feature Films] Press Clippings, 131–008, 131–009, DWC, CAL, USC.

60. *Wattstax* earned a respectable amount: *Variety* reported that the documentary grossed $1,725,207 by the end of 1973. "*Variety* Chart Summary for 1973," *Variety*, May 8, 1974, 68. $73,363 worth of ticket proceeds went to social service institutions. "$73,363 Charities' Wattstax Donation," *Billboard*, September 2, 1972, 66.

61. James P. Murray, "Movie Offerings from Black Moguls," *New York Amsterdam News*, November 30, 1974, D12.

62. "Trina Parks, Superchick, First to Use Karate!," *Baltimore Afro-American*, September 27, 1975, 11; A. H. Weiler, "Strutters," *New York Times*, October 9, 1975, 54.

63. Claude Hall, "Griffin's TV Co. Specials," *Billboard*, November 18, 1972, 1, 48; "Television," *Jet*, April 26, 1973, 66. Stax artists had appeared in similar formats when they visited Los Angeles in the summer of 1965 to appear on *Where the Action Is*, *Hollywood A Go-Go*, and *The Lloyd Thaxton Show*. They also did a live radio broadcast for KGFJ at the Shrine Circus. "Stax and Volt Artists on TV," *Billboard*, August 7, 1965, 4; Robert Gordon, *Respect Yourself*, 110–12.

64. "Stax/Griffin Prod. Form Cohesive Unit," *Billboard*, January 13, 1973, 14.

65. Rob Bowman, *Soulsville, U.S.A.*, 317–71; Nelson George, *The Death of Rhythm and Blues* (New York: E. P. Dutton, 1989), 135–42.

66. David L. Wolper and David Fisher, *Producer: A Memoir* (New York: Scribner, 2003), 183.

CHAPTER 6

1. *Roots* played in Australia, Belgium, Chile, Ecuador, Finland, France, Germany, Israel, Italy, Japan, Singapore, and beyond. David L. Wolper and Quincy Troupe, *The Inside Story of TV's "Roots"* (New York: Warner Books, 1978), 157; Timothy Havens, *Black Television Travels: African American Media around the Globe* (New York: New York University Press, 2013), 29–55.

2. Alex Haley, *Roots: The Saga of an American Family* (Garden City, NY: Doubleday, 1976).

3. Lyndon B. Johnson quoted in Alvin Shuster, "President Signs Bicentennial Bill," *New York Times*, July 9, 1966, 19. See also "Goals Cited for Bicentennial of Revolution," *Los Angeles Times*, April 4, 1968, A7. The original commission consisted of twenty-five members. "Unit Named to Plan 200th Anniversary of U.S. Revolution," *New York Times*, January 19, 1967, 35.

4. Public Law 93–179, enacted December 11, 1973, 697–704, Govtrack.us, accessed February 1, 2017, https://www.govtrack.us/congress/bills/93/hr7446/text.

5. Critics attacked Nixon for staffing the ARBC with members of his 1968 campaign who aimed to use the bicentennial as an advertisement for the Republican Party and for the president's reelection. The ARBC also came under fire for charges that its corporate members were trying to coordinate bicentennial-themed entertainment across the country from which they would directly reap profits. Nan Robertson, "Panel Said to Veto a Single-City Fair for U.S. Birthday," *New York Times*, May 26, 1970, 25; Alfred Stern, "Will There Be a Bicentennial?" *Variety*, January 5, 1972, 122; Robert L. Turner, "Bicentennial World's Fair Rejected," *Washington Post*, May 17, 1972, A22; Alfred Stern, "Big Nothing So Far for 1976 Hurrah," *Variety*, January 3, 1973, 149; Eugene Meyer, "Bicentennial Director Quits; Management Was Criticized," *Washington Post*, August 2, 1972, A8; Donald Bremner, "Picking Up the Bicentennial Pieces," *Los Angeles Times*, July 1, 1973, G4; "'76 Bicentennial Plans Cut Back as Mood Shifts," *New York Times*, July 4, 1973, 1; "Parks Idea Killed," *Los Angeles Times*, May 16, 1973, A5; Peter Carroll, *It Seemed Like Nothing Happened: America in the 1970s* (New Brunswick, NJ: Rutgers University Press, 1990), 185–316; Bruce Schulman, *The Seventies: The Great Shift in American Culture, Society, and Politics* (New York: Free Press, 2001), 121–92; James T. Patterson, *Grand Expectations: The United States, 1945–1974* (New York: Oxford University Press, 1996), 771–90.

6. *The Bicentennial of the United States of America: A Final Report to the People, Volume 1* (Washington, DC: US Government, 1977), 2–9, David Wolper Bicentennial Collection, David L. Wolper Center, Cinematic Arts Library, University of Southern California (hereafter DWC, CAL, USC).

7. Robert Lawlor, *The Bicentennial Book* (New York: Dell, 1975).

8. Kay Cooperman, "L.A. to Open Celebration," *Los Angeles Times*, July 14, 1975, B3.

9. Tom Bradley quoted in J. Gregory Payne and Scott C. Ratzan, *Tom Bradley: The Impossible Dream* (Santa Monica, CA: Roundtable, 1986), 135.

10. Raphael J. Sonenshein, *Politics in Black and White: Race and Power in Los Angeles* (Princeton, NJ: Princeton University Press, 1993), 55–66, 139–90.

11. Daniel Widener, *Black Arts West: Culture and Struggle in Postwar Los Angeles* (Durham, NC: Duke University Press, 2010), 221–25, 234–49.

12. Scott Kurashige, *The Shifting Grounds of Race: Black and Japanese Americans in the Making of Multiethnic Los Angeles* (Princeton, NJ: Princeton University Press, 2008), 280.

13. "Bicentennial Salute Has Foreign Flavor," *Los Angeles Times*, May 24, 1976, D1.

14. Grant Lee, "Bicentennial Bus Tour of Historic L.A.," *Los Angeles Times*, November 24, 1975, D1; Tia Gindick, "Bicentennial Fever—Everybody Else Has It," *Los Angeles Times*, March 4, 1976, E1; "Diverse 'Festival of Faith' to Mark Bicentennial," *Los Angeles Times*, September 18, 1976, 29. For a list of major Los Angeles events, see John W. Warner, administrator, *Comprehensive Calendar of Bicentennial Events West of the Mississippi* (Washington, DC: American Revolution Bicentennial Administration, 1976), 2/20–2/51.

15. Steve Harvey, "Times That Try L.A.'s Soul," *Los Angeles Times*, February 2, 1976, C5.

16. "Open House at Cal State Offers Science Displays," *Los Angeles Times*, January 8, 1976, SG4.

17. Jehane Burns, ed., *The World of Franklin and Jefferson* (Los Angeles: George Rice and Sons, 1976); Josine Ianco-Starrels, "Franklin, Jefferson Opens Tuesday," *Los Angeles Times*, November 7, 1976, L73.

18. Between 1972 and 1982, apparel jobs increased by 13 percent. Around this same period, the service sectors geared toward retail, business, and social utilities grew by 63.5 percent. Roger Keil, *Los Angeles: Globalization, Urbanization and Social Struggles* (New York: John Wiley and Sons, 1998), 95–112. See also Edward Soja, *Postmodern Geographies: The Reassertion of Space in Critical Social Theory* (London: Verso, 1989), 191–208.

19. Robert Herzbrun, "The Bonaventure: The Most Astonishing New Hotel of All," *Los Angeles Magazine*, July 1976, 74. See also J. Gregory Payne and Scott C. Ratzan, *Tom Bradley*, 137–51.

20. Laurie Gottlieb, "In the Spirit of '76," *Los Angeles Times*, March 21, 1976, R20; Kathy Burke and Deborah Cipolla, "100,000 Line Route to See 'World's Longest Parade,'" *Los Angeles Times*, July 5, 1976, 1, 3, 14; Cilla Brown, "2 Disney Parks to Present Shows for Bicentennial," *Los Angeles Times*, February 19, 1975, E1, E8; Mary Murphy, "Filmex to Celebrate Bicentennial," *Los Angeles Times*, January 5, 1976, E10; Jody Jacobs, "Glorious Night for Filmex Opening," *Los Angeles Times*, March 23, 1976, E2.

21. Joyce Haber, "Telly Draws Ace," *Los Angeles Times*, February 27, 1975, F8.

22. David Wolper, "An Overwhelming Experience," in *The Bicentennial of the United States of America*, vol. 1, p. 3, DWC, CAL, USC.

23. Tammy S. Gordon, *The Spirit of 1976: Commerce, Community, and the Politics of Commemoration* (Amherst: University of Massachusetts Press, 2013), 47.

24. Ibid., 47–67.

25. Charles Hillinger, "Bicentennial Spirit—U.S. Steaming at Full Throttle," *Los Angeles Times*, June 26, 1975, B1, B31; George Moneyhun, "All Aboard the Freedom Train!," *Christian Science Monitor*, March 31, 1975, 3; Edward Yalowitz, *"All Aboard, America"—The American Freedom Train: 1975–1976: Commemorative Program* (Chicago: American Freedom Train Foundation, 1975), 27–30.

26. Daniel Boorstin quoted in "America at the Movies," ed. John W. Warner, administrator, American Revolution Bicentennial Administration, folder 8140, ARBA box 340, DWC, CAL, USC.

27. George Stevens Jr. quoted in Marlene Cimons, "Washington on View: Hollywood's Gift to Bicentennial," *Los Angeles Times*, June 30, 1976, G17.

28. Tom Shales, "A Silver Screening," *Washington Post*, June 28, 1976, B1; Grant Lee, "That's 'Movies' for Bicentennial," *Los Angeles Times*, August 2, 1976, E1.

29. "Bicentennial Film Production Agreement and Budget between the American Film Institute and the American Revolution Bicentennial Administration," February 6, 1975 (revised February 21, 1975), p. 2, folder 8140, ARBA box 340, DWC, CAL, USC.

30. *The Glorious Fourth* included on-location reporting from hospitals, firehouses, and parks around the country, a special edition of *Meet the Press*, and a Texaco-sponsored variety show titled "Bob Hope's Bicentennial Star-Spangled Spectacular." *In Celebration of US* covered local parades, fireworks, craft festivals, and a roundtable with Henry Aaron, Daniel Boorstin, and Margaret Mead reflecting on American history. *The Great American Birthday Party* consisted of President Ford's speech at Philadelphia's Independence Hall, live reporting from the Washington Monument in Washington, DC, and the Gateway Arch in St. Louis, and sweeping views of ships entering New York Harbor. Leonard Traube, "The American Bicentennial," *Variety*, January 9, 1974, 104; "Networks Detail Efforts for the Bicentennial," *Broadcasting*, March 3, 1975, 34–35; "Bicentennial Eyes and Ears," *Broadcasting*,

July 12, 1976, 19–20. For more on network programming, including ABC's bicentennial edition of *Schoolhouse Rock!* (1975–76) and CBS's *Bicentennial Minutes* (1974–76), see John W. Warner, administrator, *Comprehensive Calendar of Bicentennial Events*, John W. Warner, administrator (Washington, DC: American Revolution Bicentennial Administration, 1976), 1/7–1/10.

31. Henri Langlois quoted in *The Man with the Dream: A Pictorial Tribute to the Life and 50-Year Career of David L. Wolper*, ed. Auriel Sanderson (Hong Kong: Warner Bros. Worldwide, 1999), 2. See also "Langlois Schedules Wolper Film Retro," *Variety*, October 2, 1974, 2.

32. Marshall Berges, "Home Q&A: David Wolper," *Los Angeles Times*, April 28, 1974, M42.

33. Tom Bradley, proclamation, City of Los Angeles, plaque, DWC, CAL, USC; "Walk of Fame Star for Wolper," *Los Angeles Times*, March 15, 1976, E17.

34. William Paley quoted in Gerald Fraser, "Museum of Broadcasting Opens with Paley Gift," *New York Times*, November 10, 1976, 80. See also "50 Years of History on Instant Replay," *Los Angeles Times*, November 10, 1976, E9.

35. "Library of Congress Names Division Head," *Hartford Courant*, May 29, 1978, 4.

36. Thomas W. Hoffer and Richard Alan Nelson, "Evolution of Docudrama on American Television Networks: A Content Analysis, 1966–1978," *Southern Speech Communication Journal* 45 (1980): 150–52. See also Thomas W. Hoffer and Richard Alan Nelson, "Docudrama on American Television," *Journal of the University Film Association* 30, no. 2 (1978): 21–27; William A. Bluem, *Documentary in American Television: Form, Function, Method* (New York: Hastings House, 1965), 17–92, 180–204. For an international case studies approach to docudramas, see Alan Rosenthal, ed., *Why Docudrama? Fact-Fiction on Film and TV* (Carbondale: Southern Illinois University Press, 1999); Robert B. Musburger, "Setting the Stage for the Television Docudrama," *Journal of Popular Film and Television* 13, no. 2 (1985): 92–101; Derek Paget, *No Other Way to Tell It: Docudrama on Film and Television* (Manchester: Manchester University Press, 2011), 171–230.

37. While the term "documentary drama" had been used sporadically since the 1930s to describe humanistic forms of documentary in radio, film, and television, the term "docudrama" began to appear with increasing frequency around the late 1960s and early 1970s. Examples include Cecil Smith, "Hope Gets Away with TV Murder," *Los Angeles Times*, February 25, 1970, C15; Percy Shain, "John and Sam Adams, Samuel Quincy Star in Massacre," *Boston Globe*, May 14, 1971, 52; Cecil Smith, "Burgess Meredith as Franklin in Congress '76 Docu-drama," *Los Angeles Times*, June 20, 1971, R31B; George McKinnon, "'No Go' Docudrama of IRA," *Boston Globe*, August 2, 1973, 54.

38. Frank Swertlow quoted in Academy of Television Arts and Sciences Docu-drama Symposium, 1979, ed. Lee Margulies, *Emmy Magazine*, Summer 1979, D11, DWC, CAL, USC.

39. David Lowenthal, "The Bicentennial Landscape: A Mirror Held Up to the Past," *Geographical Review* 67, no. 3 (1977): 257.

40. "History of America Topic of New Series," *Los Angeles Times*, July 17, 1973, C14.

41. Robert Guenette quoted in Mimi Mead, "The Undebunkable George Washington," *Christian Science Monitor*, November 23, 1973, 22.

42. John J. O'Connor, "TV: ABC Pursues the Real George Washington," *New York Times*, November 27, 1973, 82; Mimi Mead, "Patriotism, Even for Cynics," *Baltimore Sun*,

December 30, 1973, TV16; Howard Thompson, "TV Review: 'Lincoln: Trial by Fire' on ABC Tomorrow," *New York Times*, January 19, 1974, 63; John J. O'Connor, "TV: 'Yanks Are Coming,'" *New York Times*, April 22, 1974, 70.

43. Lawrence Laurent, "'Last Days' Concludes 'Sandburg's Lincoln,'" *Washington Post*, April 11, 1976, 4.

44. Van Wyck Brooks, "Carl Sandburg's Lincoln," *Forum* 75, no. 4 (1926): 632; James Hurt, "Sandburg's Lincoln within History," *Journal of the Abraham Lincoln Association* 20, no. 1 (1999): 55–65.

45. Merrill D. Peterson, *Lincoln in American Memory* (New York: Oxford University Press, 1994), 271–310.

46. Hal Holbrook quoted in Jerry Buck, "Now Holbrook Is Abe Lincoln," *Hartford Courant*, September 8, 1974, 1F.

47. Cecil Smith, "Man Behind the Face of Lincoln," *Los Angeles Times*, August 5, 1974, E14.

48. Henry Mitchell, "And a Gathering to Dwell on History," *Washington Post*, September 6, 1974, B1; Earl Calloway, "Hal Holbrook Is Great as Abe Lincoln," *Chicago Defender*, February 12, 1975, 22; Percy Shain, "Holbrook Excels as Lincoln the Prairie Lawyer," *Boston Globe*, April 7, 1975, 35; John Carmody, "Sandburg's 'Lincoln': Fine Fare," *Washington Post*, April 7, 1975, B1; John Carmody, "Hail to Hal Holbrook's 'Unwilling Warrior': TV's Bicentennial Best," *Washington Post*, September 3, 1975, C11; "Hal Holbrook Stars as Abe Lincoln," *Chicago Defender*, December 9, 1975, 20; John Carmody, "A Moving Portrait of the Lincolns," *Washington Post*, September 6, 1974, B1; "Lincoln Portrayal Poignant," *Boston Globe*, September 6, 1974, 55.

49. Wolper Productions also created other films and programs in the early to mid-1970s that focused on minority subjects. The film and short-lived spinoff series *Get Christie Love!* (1974) starred black actress Teresa Graves as an LAPD detective whose hip irreverence and martial arts mastery enable her to take on criminals. The comedy series *Chico and the Man* (1974–78) featured a curmudgeonly WASP, Ed (Jack Albertson), who spends his days in his car repair garage in East Los Angeles battling his quick-witted Chicano employee Chico (Freddie Prinze). In *Welcome Back, Kotter* (1975–79), Gabe Kotter returns to his old Bensonhurst, Brooklyn, high school to teach the low-performing class known as the "Sweathogs." The classroom is an arena for daily jousting between its African American, Jewish, Italian, and Puerto Rican students.

50. Shirley Rose Higgins, "Mexico: Good Stand-in for U.S. West," *Chicago Tribune*, April 13, 1975, C6.

51. *I Will Fight No More Forever* won awards at the Chicago International Film Festival and the Columbus Film Festival, and was honored with a certificate of merit from the Southern California Motion Picture Council. John Carmody, "Native American Tragedy," *Washington Post*, April 14, 1975, B7; "Struggle of Nez Perce Recalled," *Hartford Courant*, April 14, 1975, 20; "Ratings Surprises," *Washington Post*, April 25, 1975, B8; Bill Carter, "In the First Week of 1976, TV Begins in Earnest to Milk the Bicentennial," *Baltimore Sun*, January 7, 1976, B4; "Public Occurrences," *Washington Post*, November 4, 1976, VA15; Lee Margulies, "Top Shows as Teaching Tools," *Los Angeles Times*, January 4, 1977, F9; "Roaring Brook to Have Film, Folk Music," *Hartford Courant*, April 25, 1977, 33A; "Ethnic Event to Feature Indian Films," *Hartford Courant*, December 26, 1977, 37D.

52. Terrence O'Flaherty, "Using Television's Power for Human Kindness," *Baltimore Sun*, May 25, 1975, TW34.

53. "Watts Parade Slated Saturday," *Los Angeles Sentinel*, December 9, 1976, A1; advertisement, *Los Angeles Times*, April 24, 1975, SG4.

54. Linda Williams, *Playing the Race Card: Melodramas of Black and White from Uncle Tom to O. J. Simpson* (Princeton, NJ: Princeton University Press, 2001), 220–51. See also Leslie A. Fiedler, *The Inadvertent Epic: From Uncle Tom's Cabin to Roots* (Ontario: Canadian Broadcasting Corporation, 1979), 71–85.

55. Ossie Davis and Ruby Dee, *With Ossie and Ruby: In This Life Together* (New York: William Morrow and Company, 1998), 338–40, 366–68; David L. Wolper and Quincy Troupe, *The Inside Story of TV's "Roots,"* 34–48; "Haley on TV Tells How He Traced Family to Africa," *New York Amsterdam News*, April 22, 1972, C5.

56. Alex Haley, "Dedication," in *Roots: The Saga of an American Family* (Garden City, NY: Doubleday, 1976), v.

57. "ABC to Develop 'Roots,' 'U.S.A.' as TV Novels," *Los Angeles Times*, January 24, 1975, G26.

58. Les Brown, "ABC-TV Plans to Stress Serializations of Novels," *New York Times*, December 14, 1974, 59; "TV Networks See Future for Mini-Series," *Hartford Courant*, January 19, 1975, 11F; Cecil Smith, "The 'TV Novel' Comes of Age," *Los Angeles Times*, April 22, 1975, H17.

59. See for example Kay Gardella, "Adaptation of Roots Is Another Epic Idea for ABC," *Chicago Tribune*, October 2, 1976, SD6.

60. Harry F. Waters and Vern E. Smith, "One Man's Family," *Newsweek*, June 21, 1976, 73.

61. Advertisement, *Variety*, January 26, 1977, 48–49.

62. "The Effects of 'Roots' Will Be with TV for a Long Time," *Broadcasting*, February 7, 1977, 52, 56.

63. Vernon Jarrett, "An Epic TV Tale of Our Heritage," *Chicago Tribune*, January 30, 1977, A6; *Broadcasting*, July 18, 1977, cover; Sander Vanocur, "Roots: A New Reality," *Washington Post*, January 19, 1977, B1, B8; Donald K. Richmond, "TV's 'Roots': A Real Eye-Opener," *New Journal and Guide*, February 5, 1977, 15.

64. Tom Bradley, proclamation, City of Los Angeles, plaque, DWC, CAL, USC.

65. Brandon Stoddard quoted in Stephen Zito, "Out of Africa," *American Film*, October 1976, 13.

66. "'Roots' Takes Hold in America," *Newsweek*, February 7, 1977, 26.

67. Alex Haley quoted in William Marmon, "Why 'Roots' Hit Home," *Time*, February 14, 1977, 72.

68. William Marmon, "Why 'Roots' Hit Home," 69–75.

69. Horace Newcomb, "Lincoln Episode, Although Enjoyable, Marred by Outdated Technique," *Baltimore Sun*, January 21, 1974, B3; Horace Newcomb, "A Questionable Use of Time and Money—'The Yanks Are Coming,'" *Baltimore Sun*, April 23, 1974, B5. See also Cecil Smith, "Opening Salvo of U.S. Heritage Series," *Los Angeles Times*, November 27, 1973, C14.

70. Martin Duberman, "How Honest Was Abe? How Noble Was Walt?," *New York Times*, January 11, 1976, D1.

71. John J. O'Connor, "Historical Dramas—Fact or Fancy?," *New York Times*, May 25, 1975, 127; Michael J. Arlen, "The Air," *New Yorker*, May 19, 1975, 82–89.

72. John E. Cooney, "Kunta Kinte Reduced to Soap Opera," *Wall Street Journal*, January 24, 1977, 16. For more background on the process of adapting the book to the miniseries as well as historical inaccuracies in the project, see Leslie Fishbein, "*Roots*: Docudrama and the Interpretation of History," in *Why Docudrama?*, 271–95.

73. Bill Carter, "'Roots' Is Better TV Than Most, but Not What It Should Be," *Baltimore Sun*, January 24, 1977, B1; Dorothy Gilliam, "The Series: History Off Balance," *Washington Post*, January 28, 1977, B1; Carlos E. Russell, "Say Roots Bypassed Some Key Elements of Black History," *New York Amsterdam News*, February 12, 1977, D9; Jessica Davis, "Too Many Modifications Mar 'Roots' Production," *New Pittsburgh Courier*, February 19, 1977, 11; William A. Henry III, "Docu-dramas—Is TV Tampering with History?," *Boston Globe*, February 20, 1977, E1; Robert L. Allen, ed., "Forum: A Symposium on Roots," *Black Scholar* 8, no. 7 (1977): 36–42. Essays in that last ("Forum") include "Roots: Melodrama of the Black Experience" by sociologist Robert Staples; "Roots: A Modern Minstrel Show" by poet and critic Clyde Taylor; "Roots: Urban Renewal of the American Dream" by poet and critic Chinweizu; "Roots: An Electronic Orgy in White Guilt" by columnist Chuck Stone; and "Roots: Rebirth of the Slave Mentality" by *Black Scholar* publisher Robert Chrisman.

74. Matthew Frye Jacobson, *Roots Too: White Ethnic Revival in Post–Civil Rights America* (Cambridge, MA: Harvard University Press, 2006), 11–71.

75. John J. Stewart, "Journey to Your Past," in Jeane Eddy Westin, *Finding Your Roots: How Every American Can Trace His Ancestors—At Home and Abroad* (Los Angeles: J. P. Tarcher, 1977), 5. See also F. Wilbur Helmbold, *Tracing Your Ancestry: A Step-by-Step Guide to Researching Your Family History* (Birmingham, AL: Oxmoor House, 1976).

CHAPTER 7

1. Robert Nakamura interviewed by Adam Hyman and Pauline Stakelon, May 23, 2010, and August 22, 2010, in *Alternative Projections: Experimental Film in Los Angeles, 1945–1980*, pp. A66, accessed February 10, 2015, http://alternativeprojections.com/oral-histories/robert-nakamura/.

2. The Peoples Bicentennial Commission (PBC) was based in Washington, DC, and Boston. Started in 1971, the PBC's aim was to connect the political and economic oppression of the late 1700s to the injustices of the present moment perpetrated by "corporate tyranny" and a complicit government. Ted Howard, *The P.B.C.: A History* (Washington, DC: Peoples Bicentennial Commission, 1976).

3. J. Hoberman, "One Big Real Place: BBS from *Head* to *Hearts*," Criterion Collection Website, November 28, 2010, https://www.criterion.com/current/posts/1671-one-big-real-place-bbs-from-head-to-hearts. For more on the origins and development of BBS see the collection of essays that accompanies the Criterion Collection release *America Lost and Found: The BBS Story* (New York: Criterion Collection, 2010), DVD.

4. Bert Schneider and Peter Davis quoted in Gene Robertson, "Outstanding Documentary," *Sun Reporter*, March 1, 1975, 40. For articles about Davis's CBS documentaries see Jack Gould, "Hunger Is Not for Quibbling," *New York Times*, June 23, 1968, D19; Rick Brow, "Sensitivity Sessions: Experiment with Racial Groups New Dimension," *New Journal and Guide*, January 10, 1970, 14; Jack Gould, "TV: CBS: Explores Pentagon Propaganda Costs," *New York Times*, February 24, 1971, 83; William C. Woods, "The Selling of the Pentagon,"

Washington Post, February 26, 1971, B1; William C. Woods, "The Awarding of 'The Selling,'" *Washington Post*, April 21, 1971, B14. For more on the production history and reception of *Hearts and Minds* see the collection of short essays included on the Criterion Collection release *Hearts and Minds*, directed by Peter Davis (1974; New York: Criterion Collection, 2002), DVD; David Grosser, "'We Aren't on the Wrong Side, We Are the Wrong Side': Peter Davis Targets (American) Hearts and Minds," in *From Hanoi to Hollywood: The Vietnam War in American Film*, ed. Linda Dittmar and Gene Michaud (New Brunswick, NJ: Rutgers University Press, 1990), 269–82.

5. Rex Reed quoted in Bob Thomas, "Hearts and Minds: Vietnam Documentary," *Washington Post*, October 23, 1974, C7.

6. Gregg Kilday, "The Skirmishing over 'Hearts,'" *Los Angeles Times*, November 15, 1974, G1, G18–19.

7. Stephanie Harrington, "First an Undeclared War Now an Unseen Film," *New York Times*, November 17, 1974, 153; Kevin Thomas, "'Hearts, Minds' Opens to Qualify for Oscars," *Los Angeles Times*, December 20, 1974, H22–23; Gary Arnold, "'Hearts and Minds': A Scrapbook of Sorrow," *Washington Post*, January 31, 1975, B1.

8. Vincent Canby, "'Hearts and Minds,' a Study of Power," *New York Times*, March 24, 1975, 38. Also see Martin Knelman, "Hearts and Minds," *Globe and Mail*, April 12, 1975, 17.

9. William J. McGill, Chairman, *A Public Trust: The Report of the Carnegie Commission on the Future of Public Broadcasting* (New York: Bantam, 1979), 9–20. For an account of Treviño's career during this time see Jesús Salvador Treviño, *Eyewitness: A Filmmaker's Memoir of the Chicano Movement* (Houston: Arte Público, 2001), 259–337.

10. John J. O'Connor, "Should Public Television Be Playing It Safe?," *New York Times*, March 23, 1980, D35. See also John Carmody, "PBS New Season: Money Worries and Compromise but Hanging in There," *Washington Post*, September 29, 1974, H1; Dick Adler, "Public Airwaves: The Public Has Plenty to Say," *Los Angeles Times*, February 17, 1976, E1; John J. O'Connor, "New Play Series Long on Talent, Short on Funds," *New York Times*, October 17, 1976, 99; Patricia Aufderheide, "Public Television and the Public Sphere," *Critical Studies in Mass Communication* 8, no. 2 (1991): 168–83; James Ledbetter, *Made Possible by . . . : The Death of Public Broadcasting in the United States* (London: Verso, 1997), 89–114, 160–93; David M. Stone, *Nixon and the Politics of Public Television* (London: Garland, 1985), 317–41.

11. Treviño was scheduled to complete television projects on the themes of "Chicano love" and "growing up Chicano" for McGraw-Hill, but the films were never completed. The company took issue with Treviño's leftist politics. Additionally, El Teatro Campesino was unwilling to support Treviño in his creative and editorial choices.

12. Jesús Salvador Treviño interviewed by Jim Miller, "Chicano Cinema," *Cineaste* 8, no. 3 (1978): 38–41. See also Jesús Salvador Treviño interviewed by Stephanie Sapienza, May 29, 2010, in *Alternative Projections: Experimental Film in Los Angeles, 1945–1980*, 30–36, accessed January 15, 2016, https://alternativeprojections.com/assets/Uploads/Jesus-Trevino-Oral-History-Transcript.pdf.

13. Jesús Salvador Treviño quoted in Ying Ying Wu, "A Chicano View at the Border," *Los Angeles Times*, June 3, 1979, L29.

14. Jason Johansen, "Landmark Chicano Film Premiere," *Los Angeles Times*, May 29, 1979, F7; Cart, "Raíces de Sangre," *Variety*, June 20, 1979, 19. See also "Valley Variety," *Los Angeles Times*, July 10, 1975, SF3; "Mexican Heritage Films Scheduled," *Los Angeles Times*,

April 15, 1976, WS10; "Chicano Film Festival to Open Tonight at 7 at the E.L.A. Library," *Los Angeles Times*, October 5, 1976, F10; "Calendar," *Washington Post*, May 6, 1977, D11.

15. "KNBC's Bicentennial Series, 'The Rebels,'" *Los Angeles Sentinel*, April 22, 1976, B.

16. Sue Booker, "Unique Collection: Black History in a Back-Lot Store," *Los Angeles Times*, December 4, 1973, C1; Sue Booker, "The Old and the Young: One on One in the Classroom," *Los Angeles Times*, March 11, 1976, E1; Sue Booker, "George Washington Carver: Nature Spoke to Him," *Los Angeles Sentinel*, February 14, 1974, A1.

17. Lynne Littman quoted in Mary Murphy and Cheryl Bentsen, "Coming to Grips with the Issue of Power," *Los Angeles Times*, August 16, 1973, E1, E8–20.

18. Mary Murphy, "AFI Women: A Camera Is Not Enough," *Los Angeles Times*, October 27, 1974, O1, O92; Grant Lee, "Where Are the Women Directors?," *Los Angeles Times*, June 20, 1980, G1; Susan Smith, "The AFI's Workshops for Women: An Assessment," *Los Angeles Times*, September 13, 1979, F27; Louise Sweeney, "Lights! Camera! Affirmative Action!," *Christian Science Monitor*, August 14, 1979, B12, B16.

19. "KCET to Air Programs by, for, about Women," *Los Angeles Times*, October 17, 1975, H26.

20. Linda Gross, "'Till Death Do Us Part' in Women's Film Series," *Los Angeles Times*, May 7, 1977, B11. See also "Outstanding Programs: KCET, KOCE Win CPB Honors," *Los Angeles Times*, February 13, 1976, F30; Cecil Smith, "Public Look at Women's Lives," *Los Angeles Times*, July 25, 1977, F12; Joan Levine, "Women's Film Series at the Royal, *Los Angeles Times*, April 15, 1977, G23.

21. Andrew Deener, *Venice: A Contested Bohemia in Los Angeles* (Chicago: University of Chicago Press, 2012), 40–43, 145–53. See also Horst Schmidt-Brümmer, *Venice California: An Urban Fantasy* (New York: Grossman, 1973), 7–30.

22. Susan Squire, "A Walking Tour of the New Venice," *Los Angeles Magazine*, October 1974, 64. See also Ginger Harmon, "Don't Look Now, but Venice Is Coming Back!" *Los Angeles Magazine*, October 1974, 58–63.

23. Dial Torgerson, "Venice: Everything Is Changing, Especially the People," *Los Angeles Times*, November 18, 1973, C1. See also Milton Takei, "Evictions of Elderly," *Free Venice Beachhead*, March 1973, 4, "Venice Community," box 108, Barbara Myerhoff Papers, University of Southern California; Skip Ferderber, "Outsized Rents Put Elderly to Flight," *Los Angeles Times*, March 23, 1975, WS1; Patricia Adler, *A History of the Venice Area: A Part of the Venice Community Plan Study* (Los Angeles: Department of City Planning, 1969).

24. Barbara Myerhoff, *Number Our Days: A Triumph of Continuity and Culture among Jewish Old People in an Urban Ghetto* (New York: Simon and Schuster, 1978), 1–40; Amy Hill Shevitz, "Jewish Space and Place in Venice," in *California Jews*, ed. Ava. F. Kahn and Marc Dollinger (Lebanon, NH: University Press of New England, 2003), 65–76.

25. Marc Kaminsky, "Introduction," in Barbara Myerhoff, *Remembered Lives: The Work of Ritual, Storytelling, and Growing Older* (Ann Arbor: University of Michigan Press, 1992), 20. See also Eleanor Hoover, "Old Jews of Venice: Culture Is Survival-Oriented," *Los Angeles Times*, September 26, 1976, C1, C3.

26. Cecil Smith, "28 Tonight: A New Approach to the News," *Los Angeles Times*, August 1, 1976, M2.

27. Lee Margulies, "Venice Jews in TV Documentary," *Los Angeles Times*, October 4, 1976, E13. See also John J. O'Connor, "TV: Moving Study of the Elderly," *New York Times*, May 10, 1977, 46.

28. Gary Arnold, "Foreign Romance and Summer Repertory: Film Notes," *Washington Post*, June 1, 1977, D10.

29. Barbara Myerhoff, *Remembered Lives*, 277–304.

30. Lynne Littman quoted in Cecil Smith, "Lynne Littman: Flight from PBS," *Los Angeles Times*, May 9, 1980, G1.

31. Ibid. After *Number Our Days*, Littman did make the documentaries *Once a Daughter* (1979), about the intimate conflicts between four different pairs of mothers and daughters, and *In Her Own Time* (1985), about Myerhoff's fieldwork and battle with cancer. Littman then directed the antiwar realist fiction film *Testament* (1983), which focused on a mother coping with her dying family and local community after a nuclear bomb explosion. Beverly Beyette, "A Mother-Daughter Day of Dialogue," *Los Angeles Times*, May 15, 1979, F1; Sheila Benson, "'Testament' Testifies on Behalf of Humanity," *Los Angeles Times*, November 3, 1983, I1; Howard Rosenberg, "Television Feels Its Way toward Issue Movies," *Los Angeles Times*, November 10, 1983, K1; Sheila Benson, "Time Offers Look into Hasidic Life: Myerhoff," *Los Angeles Times*, December 7, 1985, E1.

32. Frank Chin ed., *Aiiieeeee!: An Anthology of Asian-American Writers* (Washington, DC: Howard University Press, 1974).

33. Kats Kunitsugo, "On Margin: Communicating Visually," *Pacific Citizen*, February 28, 1975, 4, "Press Clippings," Visual Communications Archive, Little Tokyo, Los Angeles (hereafter VCA); "West L.A. Library Lists July Events," *Los Angeles Times*, June 27, 1976, WS4; "Akira Kurosawa Films to Be Shown at East L.A. College," *Los Angeles Times*, December 3, 1976, G34; Linda Gross, "Students' Best in 'UCLA in Focus,'" *Los Angeles Times*, June 3, 1977, G17.

34. Advertisement, "Press Clippings," VCA.

35. Linda Gross, "Asian-American Points of View," *Los Angeles Times*, May 14, 1976, F17.

36. Franklin Odo, "Preface," in *ROOTS: An Asian American Reader* (Los Angeles: Visual Communications / UCLA Asian American Studies Center, 1971), vii.

37. Franklin Odo, ed., *In Movement: A Pictorial History of Asian America* (Los Angeles: Triangle Lithograph, 1977), 6–7, 146–47.

38. "Groups in Little Tokyo Demand Evictions Delay," *Los Angeles Times*, August 5, 1976, E6; Ray Hebert, "Halt in Evictions at Hotel in Little Tokyo Sought," *Los Angeles Times*, January 18, 1977, D1; Lynn Simross, "Redevelopment in Little Tokyo Stirs Conflict among Citizens," *Los Angeles Times*, February 27, 1977, J1, J7; Nancy Yoshihara, "Otani: High Rise, Low Profile," *Los Angeles Times*, February 27, 1977, F1, F3; Ray Hebert, "Three Evicted; Razing Begins in Little Tokyo," *Los Angeles Times*, July 7, 1977, C3; "Little Tokyo Apartments Underway," *Los Angeles Times*, June 10, 1979, H10.

39. Jan-Christopher Horak, "Tough Enough: Blaxploitation and the L.A. Rebellion," in *L.A. Rebellion: Creating a New Black Cinema*, ed. Allyson Nadia Field, Jan-Christopher Horak, and Jacqueline Najuma Stewart (Berkeley: University of California Press, 2015), 120–21, 124.

40. For more details on particular L.A. Rebellion films and filmmakers, see UCLA Film & Television Archive's extensive online resource https://www.cinema.ucla.edu/la-rebellion

/story-la-rebellion. Looking for meaningful professional opportunities, L.A. Rebellion filmmakers worked on a variety of jobs during and after their time at UCLA. Larry Clark taught a film workshop at the Performing Arts Society of Los Angeles. Jamaa Fanaka and Thomas Penick labored in the fringe sectors of Hollywood. The AFI-educated director Oscar Williams and Burnett's frequent collaborator Roderick Young worked together on one of New World Pictures' first major films on black militancy, *The Final Comedown* (1972). Young also continued to work as a photographer. For more on the work of L.A. Rebellion filmmakers in various sectors of the media industries, see "Performing Arts Society Reorganized," *Los Angeles Sentinel*, September 13, 1973, B2A; "Festival of Performing Arts Starts," *Los Angeles Sentinel*, February 26, 1970, A5; "Photography Exhibit Due," *Los Angeles Sentinel*, May 14, 1970, A5; Roberta Ostroff, "Up against the Wall," *Los Angeles Times*, January 31, 1971, U22; St. Clair Bourne, "'Final Comedown' Sends an Unclear Message," *New York Amsterdam News*, June 17, 1972, C8; John Rhodes, "'Final Comedown' Is Rejection of Ghetto," *Philadelphia Tribune*, June 17, 1972, 23; George Gent, "Black Films Are In, So Are Profits," *New York Times*, July 18, 1972, 22.

41. Victor Vazquez, "Press Book," 2007 Milestone Restoration and Re-release of *Killer of Sheep*, accessed September 4, 2013, http://www.killerofsheep.com/images/KOSfinalPK.pdf; Charles Burnett commentary, *Killer of Sheep*, directed by Charles Burnett (2014; New York: Milestone Film and Video, 1977), DVD.

42. Paula Massood, "An Aesthetic Appropriate to Conditions: *Killer of Sheep*, (Neo) Realism, and the Documentary Impulse," *Wide Angle* 21, no. 4 (1999): 28.

43. Charles Burnett, interview by Joshua Glick, May 6, 2016, Los Angeles.

44. Charles Burnett interviewed by Aida A. Hozic, "The House I Live In," *Callaloo* 17, no. 2 (Spring 1994): 475.

45. Terry Teachout, *Pops: A Life of Louis Armstrong* (Boston: Houghton Mifflin Harcourt, 2009), 112–17; John Burnett, "West End Blues," NPR, April 6, 2000, accessed June 23, 2013, http://www.npr.org/2000/08/06/1080400/west-end-blues.

46. Charles Burnett, "Inner City Blues," in *Questions of Third Cinema*, ed. Jim Pines and Paul Willemen (London: BFI, 1989), 226.

47. Edward Soja, *Postmodern Geographies: The Reassertion of Space in Critical Social Theory* (London: Verso, 1989), 197–215.

48. Josh Sides, *L.A. City Limits: African American Los Angeles from the Great Depression to the Present* (Berkeley: University of California Press, 2003), 172–97.

CONCLUSION

1. Ronald Reagan, first inaugural address, January 20, 1981, American Presidency Project, accessed March 5, 2017, http://www.presidency.ucsb.edu/ws/?pid=43130.

2. Marshall Ingwerson, "Call It 'Info-tainment' or 'Docu-schlock,' This Is Popular TV," *Christian Science Monitor*, December 14, 1983, 1.

3. Charles Champlin, "Under Olympic Spirit Beats a Heart of Gold," *Los Angeles Times*, August 2, 1984, F1.

4. Kenneth Reich, "Wolper Will Produce Olympic Ceremonies," *Los Angeles Times*, August 19, 1983, D1; Kenneth Reich, "Goose Bumps Promised for Olympic Ceremonies," *Los Angeles Times*, May 2, 1984, C1; Tony Kornheiser, "Grand Opening," *Washington Post*, July

29, 1984, F1; Dan Sullivan, "Hollywood Just Showing Off a Bit," *Los Angeles Times*, July 29, 1984, H3; Peter May, "Olympics Open with Splendor of Hollywood," *Hartford Courant*, July 29, 1984, A1. Wolper definitely aimed for extravagance; see for instance David Wolper quoted in "Coming Soon: A Colossal Curtain Raiser, Fabulous Finale," *United: The Magazine of the Friendly Skies*, December 1983, 59.

5. Kenneth Reich, "Bradley Entrusts Olympics Hopes to Private Panel," *Los Angeles Times*, June 4, 1978, A1.

6. Ken Reich, "Private Enterprise Captures the Gold," *Los Angeles Times*, December 30, 1984, D1; Wayne Wilson, "Sports Infrastructure, Legacy and Paradox of the 1984 Olympic Games," in *The 1984 Los Angeles Olympic Games: Assessing the 30-Year Legacy*, ed. Matthew P. Llewellyn et al. (London: Routledge, 2015), 144–48; Barry A. Sanders, *The Los Angeles 1984 Olympic Games* (Charleston, SC: Arcadia, 2013), 7–39.

7. David Harvey, *A Brief History of Neoliberalism* (Oxford: Oxford University Press, 2005), 5–86; Bruce Schulman, *The Seventies: The Great Shift in American Culture, Society, and Politics* (New York: Free Press, 2001), 193–252; Peter Carroll, *It Seemed Like Nothing Happened: America in the 1970s* (New Brunswick, NJ: Rutgers University Press, 1990), 317–50.

8. Stephen Prince, *A New Pot of Gold: Hollywood under the Electronic Rainbow, 1980–1989* (Berkeley: University of California Press, 2000), 1–141; Susan Jeffords, *Hard Bodies: Hollywood Masculinity in the Reagan Era* (New Brunswick, NJ: Rutgers University Press, 1994), 1–23; Michael Rogin, *Ronald Reagan, The Movie and Other Episodes of Political Demonology* (Berkeley: University of California Press, 1987), 1–43.

9. Kevin Glynn, *Tabloid Culture: Trash Taste, Popular Power, and the Transformation of American Television* (Durham, NC: Duke University Press, 2000), 1–45.

SELECTED BIBLIOGRAPHY

Adinolfi, Frank Joseph. "An Analytical Study of David L. Wolper's Approach to Television Documentaries." Master's thesis, University of Southern California, 1974.

Andersen, Thom. "This Property Is Condemned." *Film Comment* 44, no. 4 (2008): 38–39.

Anderson, Christopher. *Hollywood TV: The Studio System in the Fifties*. Austin: University of Texas Press, 1994.

Astor, Gerald. *Minorities and the Media*. New York: Ford Foundation, 1974.

Aufderheide, Patricia. *The Daily Planet: A Critic on the Capitalist Culture Beat*. Minneapolis: University of Minnesota Press, 2000.

———. "Public Television and the Public Sphere." *Critical Studies in Mass Communication* 8, no. 2 (1991): 168–83.

Avila, Eric. *Popular Culture in the Age of White Flight: Fear and Fantasy in Suburban Los Angeles*. Los Angeles: University of California Press, 2004.

Banham, Reyner. *Los Angeles: The Architecture of Four Ecologies*. Berkeley: University of California Press, 1971.

Baughman, James L. *Television's Guardians: The FCC and the Politics of Programming, 1958–1967*. Knoxville: University of Tennessee Press, 1985.

Benson, Susan Porter, Stephen Brier, and Roy Rosenzweig. Introduction to *Presenting the Past: Essays on History and the Public*, xv–xxiv. Philadelphia: Temple University Press, 1986.

Blackhawk, Ned. "I Can Carry on from Here: The Relocation of American Indians to Los Angeles." *Wicazo Sa Review* 11, no. 2 (1985): 16–30.

Bluem, William A. *Documentary in American Television: Form, Function, Method*. New York: Hastings House, 1965.

Boddy, William. *Fifties Television: The Industry and Its Critics*. Urbana: University of Illinois Press, 1990.

Boorstin, Daniel J. *The Image: A Guide to Pseudo-Events in America*. New York: Vintage, 1961.

Bowman, Rob. *Soulsville, U.S.A.: The Story of Stax Records*. New York: Schirmer, 1997.

Boyle, Deirdre. *Subject to Change: Guerilla Television Revisited*. New York: Oxford University Press, 1997.

Carnegie Commission on Educational Television. *Public Television: A Program for Action: The Report and Recommendations of the Carnegie Commission on Educational Television*. New York: Harper and Row, 1967.

Carroll, Peter. *It Seemed Like Nothing Happened: America in the 1970s*. New Brunswick, NJ: Rutgers University Press, 1990.

Christensen, Jerome. *America's Corporate Art: The Studio Authorship of Hollywood Motion Pictures*. Stanford, CA: Stanford University Press, 2012.

Clarkin, Thomas. *Federal Indian Policy in the Kennedy and Johnson Administrations, 1961–1969*. Albuquerque: University of New Mexico Press, 2001.

Cook, David A. *Lost Illusions: American Cinema in the Shadow of Watergate and Vietnam 1970–1979*. New York: Charles Scribner's Sons, 2000.

Cull, Nicholas J. *The Cold War and the United States Information Agency: American Propaganda and Public Diplomacy, 1945–1989*. Cambridge, England: Cambridge University Press, 2008.

Curtin, Michael. *Redeeming the Wasteland: Television Documentary and Cold War Politics*. New Brunswick, NJ: Rutgers University Press, 1995.

Daarstad, Erik. *Through the Lens of History: The Life Journey of a Cinematographer*. Hope, ID: Plaudit, 2015.

Davis, Mike. *Dead Cities, and Other Tales*. New York: New Press, 2002.

Deener, Andrew. *Venice: A Contested Bohemia in Los Angeles*. Chicago: University of Chicago Press, 2012.

Deinum, Andries. *Speaking for Myself: A Humanist Approach to Adult Education for a Technical Age*. Brookline, MA: Center for the Study of Liberal Education for Adults, 1966.

Didion, Joan. *The White Album*. New York: Simon and Schuster, 1979.

Einstein, Daniel. *Special Edition: A Guide to Network Television Documentary Series and Special News Reports, 1955–1979*. Metuchen, NJ: Scarecrow, 1987.

Fensch, Thomas. *Films on the Campus*. New York: A. S. Barnes and Company, 1970.

Field, Allyson Nadia, Jan-Christopher Horak, and Jacqueline Najuma Stewart. "Emancipating the Image—The L.A. Rebellion of Black Filmmakers." In *L.A. Rebellion: Creating a New Black Cinema*, edited by Allyson Nadia Field, Jan-Christopher Horak, and Jacqueline Najuma Stewart, 1–53. Berkeley: University of California Press, 2015.

Friedkin, William. *The Friedkin Connection: A Memoir*. New York: HarperCollins, 2013.

Gomery, Douglas. *Hollywood Studio System: A History*. London: BFI, 2005.

Gong, Stephen. "A History in Progress: Asian American Media Arts Centers, 1970–1990." In *Moving the Image: Independent Asian Pacific American Media Arts*, edited by Russell Leong, 1–9. Los Angeles: University of California, Los Angeles, and Visual Communications, 1991.

Gordon, Robert. *Respect Yourself: Stax Records and the Soul Explosion*. New York: Bloomsbury, 2013.

Gordon, Tammy S. *The Spirit of 1976: Commerce, Community, and the Politics of Commemoration*. Amherst: University of Massachusetts Press, 2013.

Grimshaw, Anna, and Amanda Ravetz. *Observational Cinema: Anthropology, Film, and the Exploration of Social Life*. Bloomington: Indiana University Press, 2009.

Haley, Alex. *Roots: The Saga of an American Family*. Garden City, NY: Doubleday, 1976.

Harvey, David. *A Brief History of Neoliberalism*. Oxford: Oxford University Press, 2005.

Havens, Timothy. *Black Television Travels: African American Media around the Globe*. New York: New York University Press, 2013.

Hayden, Dolores. *The Power of Place: Urban Landscapes as Public History*. Cambridge, MA: MIT Press, 1995.

Heitner, Devorah. *Black Power TV*. Durham, NC: Duke University Press, 2013.

Henderson, Brian. Introduction to *Film Quarterly: Forty Years—A Selection*, edited by Brian Henderson, Ann Martin, and Lee Amazonas, 1–8. Berkeley: University of California Press, 1999.

Hoberman, J. *The Dream Life: Movies, Media and the Mythology of the Sixties*. London: New Press, 2003.

Hoffer, Thomas W., and Richard A. Nelson. "Evolution of Docudrama on American Television Networks: A Content Analysis, 1966–1978." *Southern Speech Communication Journal* 45 (1980): 149–63.

Horne, Gerald. *Fire This Time: The Watts Uprising and the 1960s*. Charlottesville: University Press of Virginia, 1995.

Howard, Ted. *The P.B.C.: A History*. Washington, DC: Peoples Bicentennial Commission, 1976.

Ishizuka, Karen. *Serve the People: Making Asian America in the Long 1960s*. London: Verso, 2016.

Jacobson, Matthew Frye. *Roots Too: White Ethnic Revival in Post–Civil Rights America*. Cambridge, MA: Harvard University Press, 2006.

James, David. *The Most Typical Avant-Garde: History and Geography of Minor Cinemas in Los Angeles*. Los Angeles: University of California Press, 2005.

Johnson, Lyndon B. *My Hope for America*. New York: Random House, 1964.

Kahana, Jonathan. *Intelligence Work: The Politics of American Documentary*. New York: Columbia University Press, 2008.

Kapsis, Robert E., ed. *Charles Burnett: Interviews*. Jackson: University of Mississippi Press, 2011.

Keil, Roger. *Los Angeles: Globalization, Urbanization and Social Struggles*. New York: John Wiley and Sons, 1998.

Kennedy, John F. Introduction to *The American Heritage Book of Indians*, edited by Alvin M. Josephy Jr., 7–8. New York: American Heritage, 1961.

Kerner, Otto, Chair, and David Ginsburg, Executive Director. *Report of the National Advisory Commission on Civil Disorders*. New York: Bantam, 1968.

Klein, Norman M. *The History of Forgetting: Los Angeles and the Erasure of Memory*. London: Verso, 1997.

Kotlowski, Dean J. *Nixon's Civil Rights: Politics, Principle, and Policy*. Cambridge, MA: Harvard University Press, 2001.

Kurashige, Scott. *The Shifting Grounds of Race: Black and Japanese Americans in the Making of Multiethnic Los Angeles*. Princeton, NJ: Princeton University Press, 2008.

Lipman, Ross. "Kent Mackenzie's *The Exiles*: Reinventing the Real of Cinema." In *Alternative Projections: Experimental Film in Los Angeles, 1945–1980*, edited by David James and Adam Hyman, 163–74. Bloomington: Indiana University Press, 2015.

Lowenthal, David. "The Bicentennial Landscape: A Mirror Held Up to the Past." *Geographical Review* 67, no. 3 (1977): 253–67.

Lynch, Kevin. *The Image of the City*. Cambridge, MA: MIT Press, 1960.

MacCann, Richard Dyer. *The People's Films: A Political History of U.S. Government Motion Pictures*. New York: Hastings House, 1973.

MacDonald, Scott. *American Ethnographic Film and Personal Documentary: The Cambridge Turn*. Berkeley: University of California Press, 2013.

Mailer, Norman. *The Armies of the Night: History as a Novel / The Novel as History*. New York: Signet, 1968.

Mamber, Stephen. *Cinema Verite in America: Studies in Uncontrolled Documentary*. Cambridge, MA: MIT Press, 1974.

Mascaro, Tom. *Into the Fray: How NBC's Washington Documentary Unit Reinvented the News*. Washington, DC: Potomac Books, 2012.

Massood, Paula. "An Aesthetics Appropriate to Conditions: *Killer of Sheep*, (Neo)realism, and the Documentary Impulse." *Wide Angle* 21, no. 4 (1999): 20–41.

McCarthy, Anna. *The Citizen Machine: Governing by Television in 1950s America*. New York: New Press, 2010.

McCone, John A. *Violence in the City—An End or a Beginning? A Report by the Governor's Commission on the Los Angeles Riots*. Los Angeles: Commission on the Los Angeles Riots, 1965.

Minow, Newton N., and Craig L. LaMay. *Abandoned in the Wasteland: Children, Television, and the First Amendment*. New York: Hall and Wang, 1995.

Monaco, Paul. *The Sixties: 1960–1969*. New York: Charles Scribner's Sons, 2001.

Morse, David. *Motown and the Arrival of Black Music*. New York: MacMillan, 1971.

Musburger, Robert B. "Setting the Stage for the Television Docudrama." *Journal of Popular Film and Television* 13, no. 2 (1985): 92–101.

Myerhoff, Barbara. *Number Our Days: A Triumph of Continuity and Culture among Jewish Old People in an Urban Ghetto*. New York: Simon and Schuster, 1978.

Myerhoff, Barbara, and Marc Kaminsky. *Remembered Lives: The Work of Ritual, Storytelling, and Growing Older*. Ann Arbor: University of Michigan Press, 1992.

Newhall, Nancy, and Ansel Adams. *Fiat Lux: The University of California*. New York: McGraw-Hill, 1967.

Nichols, Bill. "Newsreel: Film and Revolution." Master's thesis, University of California, Los Angeles, 1972.

Noriega, Chon. *Shot in America: Television, the State, and the Rise of Chicano Cinema*. Minneapolis: University of Minnesota Press, 2000.

O'Connell, P. J. *Robert Drew and the Development of Cinema Verite in America*. Carbondale: Southern Illinois University Press, 1992.

Odo, Franklin Shoichiro. *In Movement: A Pictorial History of Asian America*. Los Angeles: Triangle Lithograph, 1977.

Ongiri, Abugo Amy. *Spectacular Blackness: The Cultural Politics of the Black Power Movement and the Search for a Black Aesthetic*. Charlottesville: University of Virginia Press, 2010.

Ouellette, Laurie. *Viewers Like You? How Public TV Failed the People*. New York: Columbia University Press, 2002.

Paget, Derek. *No Other Way to Tell It: Docudrama on Film and Television*. Manchester: Manchester University Press, 2011.

Parson, Don. *Making a Better World: Public Housing, the Red Scare and the Direction of Modern Los Angeles*. Minneapolis: University of Minnesota Press, 2005.

Patterson, James T. *Grand Expectations: The United States, 1945–1974*. New York: Oxford University Press, 1996.

Perlman, Allison. *Public Interests: Media Advocacy and Struggles over U.S. Television*. New Brunswick, NJ: Rutgers University Press, 2016.

Peterson, Merrill D. *Lincoln in American Memory*. New York: Oxford University Press, 1994.

Polan, Dana. *Scenes of Instruction: The Beginnings of the U.S. Study of Film*. Berkeley: University of California Press, 2007.

Posner, Gerald. *Motown: Music, Money, Sex, and Power*. New York: Random House, 2002.

Prince, Stephen. *A New Pot of Gold: Hollywood under the Electronic Rainbow, 1980–1989*. Berkeley: University of California Press, 2000.

Pulido, Laura. *Black, Brown, Yellow, and Left: Radical Activism in Los Angeles*. Berkeley: University of California Press, 2006.

Renov, Michael. *The Subject of Documentary*. Minneapolis: University of Minnesota Press, 2004.

Rogin, Michael. *Ronald Reagan, the Movie and Other Episodes of Political Demonology*. Berkeley: University of California Press, 1987.

Rohauer, Raymond, ed. *A Tribute to David L. Wolper*. New York: Huntington Hartford Gallery of Modern Art, 1966.

Rosen, Phillip. *Change Mummified: Cinema, Historicity, Theory*. Minneapolis: University of Minnesota Press, 2001.

Rosenthal, Alan, ed. *Why Docudrama? Fact-Fiction on Film and TV*. Carbondale: Southern Illinois University Press, 1999.

Rosenthal, Nicolas G. *Reimagining Indian Country: Native American Migration and Identity in Twentieth-Century Los Angeles*. Chapel Hill: University of North Carolina Press, 2012.

Rotha, Paul. *Documentary Film: The Use of the Film Medium to Interpret Creatively and in Social Terms the Life of the People as It Exists in Reality*. New York: Hastings House, 1968.

Sanderson, Auriel, ed. *The Man with the Dream: A Pictorial Tribute to the Life and 50-Year Career of David L. Wolper*. Hong Kong: Warner Bros. Worldwide, 1999.

Saul, Scott. "'What You See Is What You Get': *Wattstax*, Richard Pryor, and the Secret History of the Black Aesthetic." Post45, August 12, 2014. Accessed January 15, 2015. http://post45.research.yale.edu/2014/08/what-you-see-is-what-you-get-wattstax-richard-pryor-and-the-secret-history-of-the-black-aesthetic/.

Saunders, David. *Direct Cinema: Observational Documentary and the Politics of the 1960s*. London: Wallflower, 2007.

Schoots, Hans. *Living Dangerously: A Biography of Joris Ivens*. Amsterdam: Amsterdam University Press, 2000.

Schulberg, Budd. Introduction to *From the Ashes: Voices of Watts*, edited by Budd Schulberg, 1–24. New York: New American Library, 1967.

Sieving, Christopher. *Soul Searching: Black-Themed Cinema from the March on Washington to the Rise of Blaxploitation*. Middletown, CT: Wesleyan University Press, 2011.

Slotkin, Richard. *Gunfighter Nation: The Myth of the Frontier in Twentieth-Century America.* Norman: University of Oklahoma Press, 1998.

Smoodin, Eric. Introduction to *Hollywood Quarterly: Film Culture in Postwar America, 1945–1957,* edited by Eric Smoodin and Ann Martin, xi–xxiii. Berkeley: University of California Press, 2002.

Soja, Edward. *Postmodern Geographies: The Reassertion of Space in Critical Social Theory.* London: Verso, 1989.

Sonenshein, Raphael. *Politics in Black and White: Race and Power in Los Angeles.* Princeton, NJ: Princeton University Press, 1993.

Spigel, Lynn. *Make Room for TV: Television and the Family Ideal in Postwar America.* Chicago: University of Chicago Press, 1992.

Stevens Jr., George. Introduction to *Conversations with the Great Moviemakers of Hollywood's Golden Age at the American Film Institute,* edited by George Stevens Jr., ix–xx. New York: Alfred A. Knopf, 2006.

Stone, David M. *Nixon and the Politics of Public Television.* London: Garland, 1985.

Storper, Michael, and Susan Christopherson. "Flexible Specialization and Regional Industrial Agglomerations: The Case of the U.S. Motion Picture Industry." *Annals of the Association of American Geographers* 77, no. 1 (1987): 104–17.

Suid, Lawrence H. *Guts and Glory: The Making of the American Military Image in Film.* Lexington: University Press of Kentucky, 2002.

Treviño, Jesús Salvador. *Eyewitness: A Filmmaker's Memoir of the Chicano Movement.* Houston: Arte Público, 2001.

Van Deburg, William L. *New Day in Babylon: The Black Power Movement and American Culture, 1965–1975.* Chicago: University of Chicago Press, 1992.

Watson, Mary Ann. *The Expanding Vista: American Television in the Kennedy Years.* New York: Oxford University Press, 1990.

White, Theodore H. *The Making of the President: 1960.* New York: Harper Collins, 1961.

Widener, Daniel. *Black Arts West: Culture and Struggle in Postwar Los Angeles.* Durham, NC: Duke University Press, 2010.

Williams, Linda. *Playing the Race Card: Melodramas of Black and White from Uncle Tom to O. J. Simpson.* Princeton, NJ: Princeton University Press, 2001.

Williams, Raymond. *Television: Technology and Cultural Form.* London: Routledge, 1974.

Wolper, David L., and David Fisher. *Producer: A Memoir.* New York: Scribner, 2003.

Young, Cynthia. *Soul Power: Cultural Radicalism and the Formation of a U.S. Third World Left.* Durham, NC: Duke University, 2006.

Zelizer, Barbie. *Covering the Body: The Kennedy Assassination, the Media, and the Shaping of Collective Memory.* Chicago: University of Chicago Press, 1992.

INDEX

The term "Hollywood" refers generically to the Los Angeles-based commercial film and television industries. "Los Angeles" and "L.A." designate the city at large.

Depending on the discussion in the text, names in glosses may be those of production companies, producers, directors, cinematographers, writers, or other production crew members.

ABC (American Broadcasting Company): *ABC's Bell and Howell Close-Up!*, 25; *Brian's Song*, 168; and Cousteau documentaries, 113; *The Great American Birthday Party*, 159, 238–39n30; and the L.A. Olympics, 154, 204, 238–39n30; Littman at, 187–88; and *The Race for Space*, 19; *Rich Man, Poor Man*, 167–68. See also *I Will Fight No More Forever; Roots*

Abrams, Ron, 80

Acción Chicano (Treviño/Marquez TV series), 88–89

Adair, Cleophus, 89, 225n60

Adinolfi, Frank Joseph, Jr., 209n4

AFI (American Film Institute), 97–98, 159–60, 183, 245–46n40

African Americans: in Bradley coalition, 155–56; and the church, 77, 91, 129, 140–41, 146, 202, 234nn38–39; discrimination against, 73, 76–77, 101–2, 141; as filmmakers, 101–6, 126, 130–31, 182. First African Film Festival, 103; and the Kerner Commission Report, 75–76; liberation movement, 95; as portrayed on television, 27, 76–77. See also *Biography of a Rookie*; black cinema; Booker, Sue; Burnett,

Charles; *The Confessions of Nat Turner;* L.A. Rebellion; racism/racial discrimination; *Roots;* South Central L.A.; Stax Records; *The Rafer Johnson Story;* Watts; *Wattstax;* Watts Uprising

The Age of Kennedy (NBC documentary film), 39

¡Ahora! (Treviño/Moreno TV Series), 84–85

Aiiieeeee! (Chin, Chan, Inada, Wong, editors), 191

Airwoman (Littman/KCET documentary), 92

Alan Landsburg Productions (film production company), 161

Alea, Tomás Gutiérez, 97

Alien Land Law (California) (1913), 189

Allen, Charles, 84, 89

Allen, Steve, 73

Alliance for Progress (Kennedy administration program), 63

Alonzo, John, 115, 135, 148

Alvarez, Luis Echeverría, 180

America (Newsreel documentary), 79

America at the Movies (AFI/ARBA bicentennial documentary), 159

The American (Frankenheimer TV film), 55

255

KGFJ (L.A. radio station), 91

Kidd, Paul, Jr., 91

Killer of Sheep (Burnett feature): cast and characters of, 195; and civil rights, 198–99; and crew members of, 135; distribution of, 200; documentary style of, 195–96; financing of, 195; and Louis Armstrong, 196–98; and *Roots*, 200–201; social issues as topics in, 195–96, 198–200; soundscape of, 196–98; as South Central portrait, 195–96, 199–201; stills from, 196fig27, 199fig28; structure of, 195–96; and Watts, post-Uprising, 199–200

"Kin and Communities" symposium, 186

King, Albert, 127, 139

King, Martin Luther, Jr., 75, 114, 129, 130–31, 137, 171

Kinloch, John, 43

Kites and Other Tales (Ohashi/VC documentary), 191

The Klansman (Stax/Columbia feature), 147

Klein, Norman, 53

Kluge, John, 107

KNBC (L.A. TV station), 182

Knoxville: Summer 1915 (Barber symphony), 196

KNX (L.A. radio station), 76

KNXT (L.A. TV station), 75–78

Korean Americans, 101, 193

Korean War, 22, 64, 69, 119

Korea: The 38th Parallel (Wolper TV documentary), 112

Kramer, Robert, 79

Krim, Arthur, 36–37

KTLA (L.A. TV station), 69

KTTV (L.A. TV station), 19, 55, 107, 227n3

Kubo, Duane, 98, 189–91

Kunta Kinte (Haley ancestor; *Roots* protagonist), 153, 168, 173, 200

Kuramoto, June, 189–90

Kurashige, Scott, 156

labor issues, 26, 84, 88, 93, 180–81, 217n19

L.A. Collective (KCET nonfiction division), 85–86

Lady Sings the Blues (Paramount/Berry Gordy feature), 136, 167

Landsburg, Alan, 10, 22, 22fig2, 24fig3, 58, 108, 111, 160–61

Lang, Fritz, 43

Langlois, Henri, 160

Lapenieks, Vilis: as *Biography of a Rookie* cinematographer, 28, 59, 213n37; in Deinum's seminars, 44; on *Fallguy* production crew,

59; as *Four Days* cinematographer, 38; as *Hollywood* series cinematographer, 27; as *Little Shop of Horrors* cameraman, 59; and Mackenzie, 50; as *Night Tide* cameraman, 59; as *Seven Days* cinematographer, 109–10; as Wolper Productions cinematographer, 22, 24fig3, 59

La Raza History (Treviño/Torres TV documentary vignettes), 85

La Raza Unida Party, 88–89, 179

L.A. Rebellion (African American filmmakers group): and blaxploitation films, 194; Burnett in, 102–3, 194, 198; and Ethno-Communications, 101; film styles and characteristics of, 101–3; industry jobs of filmmakers in, 245–46n40; social issues as topics of, 174; and UCLA, 135, 194

Last Days (*Sandburg's Lincoln* episode), 164

The Last Picture Show (BBS Productions feature), 176

"L.A. Thirteen" (Treviño newsreel), 84

Latin America, 63, 82, 96–97, 187, 194, 204

Lawlor, Robert, 155

Leacock, Richard, 4, 32

The Learning Tree (Parks, Sr. feature), 167

leftist community and filmmaking, 8, 78, 82, 97, 103, 122–23, 243n11. *See also* New Left

Legacy of Exiled NDNZ (Peters documentary), 216n4

The Legend of Marilyn Monroe (Wolper documentary), 33

The Legend of Nigger Charley (Paramount feature), 132

Leigh, Janet, 230–31n48

LeRoy, Mervyn, 198

liberalism: at AFI, 98; and *Black on Black*, 78; Black Power movement vs., 134; in Bradley coalition, 155; and *The Confessions of Nat Turner*, 119, 122; in crisis, 108–9; in *I Will Fight No More Forever*, 172; of Mackenzie, 40, 66; and neoliberalism, 202–6; and the New Frontier program, 203; Newsreel vs., 82; in *Roots*, 171; of Saltzman, 74; and Stax Records, 130, 133–34; of Styron, 119; of Wolper Productions, 6, 16, 27, 33, 63, 106, 115–19, 149, 160–61. *See also* Cold War

Library of Congress, 18, 24fig3, 42, 160

"Life Not Death in Venice" (multimedia event series), 186

A Light for John (Daarstad thesis documentary), 1, 217n16

Lincoln, Abraham, 162–63, 171

racism/racial discrimination: and American
mass media, 75–76; in blaxploitation films,
194; Bradley vs., 156; in commercial television, 102; and *Darktown Strutters*, 148; and
economic exploitation, 81; in the entertainment industry, 76–77, 101–3, 119; Ethno-
Communications vs., 102; in Hollywood, 65,
101–2, 194; independent documentaries on,
71; and *The Klansman*, 147; at KNXT, 75; in
L.A., 117; and Proposition 14, 71; and *Soledad*,
89; at WLBT, 75–76; and Wolper Produc-
tions, 9, 27–28. *See also* African Americans;
Asian Americans; Mexican Americans
Radford, J. Allen, 184
Radical History Review (journal), 7
Rado, Jim, 92
Rafelson, Bob, 175–76
The Rafer Johnson Story (Wolper TV documen-
tary), 2, 27–29, 59, 118–19, 133
Ragni, Jerry, 92
Raíces de Sangre (*Roots of Blood*) (Treviño
feature), 180–82
Rainbow Pictures (film production company), 178
Raksin, Ruby, 29
Ralph Story's Los Angeles (KNXT TV series), 75
Raybert Productions (film production com-
pany), 176
La Raza Nueva (Treviño documentary), 84
Reagan, Ronald, 7, 12, 118, 202–4
The Rebels (KNBC series), 182
Redding, Otis, 234n38
Red Power movement, 164
Reed, Rex, 178
Reir, John, 101
religion, 77, 91, 140–41, 169, 198, 217n19
Renoir, Jean, 44, 102
Renov, Michael, 79
Repression (Hicks/Murphy documentary), 81–82
Revolution in the Three R's (Wolper TV docu-
mentary), 111
Reynolds, Tommy, 51
Richardson, Donald K., 169
Rich Man, Poor Man (Irwin Shaw novel; ABC
docudrama), 167–68
"La Rielera" (Mexican Revolution song), 88
The Rise and Fall of the Third Reich (Wolper
documentary), 112
Robertson, Cliff, 115
Rocha, Glauber, 194
Rockefeller, Nelson, 82, 118
"Rodeo" (Copeland composition), 202
Rogosin, Lionel, 56–57

Rohauer, Raymond, 113
Romero, Ned, 164–65
Romney, George, 118
Roosevelt, Franklin D., 31
Roots (Haley novel; Wolper/ABC docudrama):
overview, 153–74; and the American bicentennial, 149, 153–54, 167, 173–74; in American
melodrama tradition, 165; book vs. docudrama titles of, 170; cast and characters of,
168, 171–72; on the cover of *Time* magazine,
critics' reviews of, 169, 171–74; and the debates on the bicentennial, 149; as docudrama
innovator, 153; as Emmy award winner, 169;
and ethnic white revival, 173; and *Killer of
Sheep*, 200–201; as media event, 165–74; and
minorities in America, 200–201; origins of,
165–67; plot of, 153, 168, 171; premier of, 153;
production crew of, 167–68; publicity for, 169,
200; ratings/share of, 169; and slavery, 154,
168–69, 171–73, 200; stills from, 172fig22; tar-
get audience for, 200–201; as *Time* magazine
cover story, 170–71, 170fig21; women in, 168
Rose, Barbara, 80
Rosen, Morrie, 185–86
Rosen, Philip, 7–8, 33
Rostow, Walt, 177–78
Roundtree, Richard, 131, 168
Ruby, Jack, 37–39
Rush to Judgment (Lane book), 114
Rusk, Dean, 110
Russell, Catherine, 53
Ryan, Cornelius, 30
Ryden, Hope, 32

Sad Figure Laughing (*Sandburg's Lincoln* epi-
sode), 163
Saga of Western Man (TV docudrama series), 161
Salazar, Rubén, 86–87
Salmon, Herman "Fish," 30, 59
Salt of the Earth (Biberman feature), 80
Saltzman, Joe, 71, 74–76, 78, 206. See also *Black
on Black*
Sandburg, Carl, 11, 163–64, 171
Sandburg's Lincoln (Wolper/NBC TV docudra-
ma), 11, 163–64, 171
"The Sand-Clock Day" (Dolan autobiographical
essay), 73
Sanders, Terry, 42
San Francisco Broadcasting Industry Award, 86
Sanjinés, Jorge, 194
Saul, Scott, 142
The Savage Eye (Meyers feature), 56